W9-AVB-102

THE GREAT
DIVIDE

Power, Conflict, and Democracy:
American Politics Into the Twenty-first Century

Power, Conflict, and Democracy:
American Politics Into the Twenty-first Century

Robert Y. Shapiro, Editor

This series focuses on how the will of the people and the public interest are promoted, encouraged, or thwarted. It aims to question not only the direction American politics will take as it enters the twenty-first century but also the direction American politics has already taken.

The series addresses the role of interest groups and social and political movements; openness in American politics; important developments in institutions such as the executive, legislative, and judicial branches at all levels of government as well as the bureaucracies thus created; the changing behavior of politicians and political parties; the role of public opinion; and the functioning of mass media. Because problems drive politics, the series also examines important policy issues in both domestic and foreign affairs.

The series welcomes all theoretical perspectives, methodologies, and types of evidence that answer important questions about trends in American politics.

THE
GREAT
DIVIDE

*Religious and Cultural Conflict
in American Party Politics*

Geoffrey Layman

Columbia University Press
New York

Columbia University Press
Publishers Since 1893
New York   Chichester   West Sussex

Copyright © 2001 Columbia University Press
All rights reserved
(∞)
Library of Congress Cataloging-in-Publication Data

Layman, Geoffrey
    The great divide : religious and cultural conflict in American party politics / Geoffrey
Layman.
        p. cm. — (Power, conflict, and democracy)
    Includes bibliographical references and index.
    ISBN 0-231-12058-3 (alk. paper) – ISBN 0-231-12059-1 (alk. paper)
    1. Religion and politics–United States–History. 2. Political parties–United
States–History. 3. United States–Religion. I. Title . II. Series.

    BL2525 .L39 2001
    306.2'6'0973–dc21
                                                                                          00-047547

        Casebound editions of Columbia University Press books are printed
                    on permanent and durable acid-free paper.
                    Printed in the United States of America
                        c 10 9 8 7 6 5 4 3 2 1
                        p 10 9 8 7 6 5 4 3 2 1

To Amy, with love

CONTENTS

PREFACE

THE 2000 PRESIDENTIAL ELECTION was supposed to be the election in which the Republican party (GOP) distanced itself from the Christian Right, the coalition of political organizations made up principally of committed evangelical Protestants with highly conservative views on moral and cultural issues such as abortion, homosexual rights, and prayer in the public schools. Governor George W. Bush of Texas—one of the "pragmatic" Republican governors who place far more emphasis on issues such as education, tax cuts, welfare reform, and health care than on moral and cultural matters—was supposed to waltz to the nomination. In doing so, he was to move the GOP away from its highly conservative stands on abortion and other social issues and generally rescue the party from the grip of the religious and cultural right.

By early February of 2000, it was very clear that that was not going to happen. Bush, embroiled in a tight nomination contest with Senator John McCain of Arizona, had made an appearance at Bob Jones University, a hard-line fundamentalist college in South Carolina; had proposed that the party platform retain its traditional support for a constitutional amendment banning abortion; and had said that he was unlikely to appoint any openly gay individuals to his cabinet. Meanwhile, not only had the Christian Right not been pushed to the background of the Republican campaign, it had become the major issue. Christian Right leaders such as Pat Robertson, the founder of the powerful Christian Coalition, and Jerry Falwell, the founder of the once-powerful Moral Majority, offered strong and highly public support for Bush, and evangelical Protestants voted overwhelmingly for the governor in Republican primaries. McCain lashed out at the nearly unanimous support Bush received from the Republican "establishment," and when he and the media talked about the GOP establishment, the Christian Right was clearly one of the groups they had in mind. Later in the month, McCain labeled Falwell and Robertson "the forces of evil" and traveled to their home state of Virginia to publicly denounce them.

How did the Republican party, a party that just more than 20 years earlier had been made up primarily of upper-income economic conservatives with ties to moderate and liberal mainline Protestant churches, arrive at this position? How did it get into a situation in which, to secure the party's presidential nomination, its front-runner would have to rely on an evangelical constituency that included more Democrats than Republicans as late as 1988. How did the leaders of this traditionally Democratic, and for that matter traditionally apolitical, constituency become part of the Republican "establishment"? This transformation was one of the most dramatic in American party politics in this century. Overwhelmingly Democratic in the late 1970s, devout evangelical Protestants became markedly more Republican over the course of the 1980s and 1990s. By 2000, they represented the most reliable and most active part of the Republican electoral coalition.

George W. Bush made appeals to this constituency because he had to. With McCain winning significant support from independents and Democrats who voted in Republican primaries, Bush needed a very strong showing among the base of the Republican party. That base is no longer mainline Protestant country-club members. It is politically active religious and cultural conservatives, particularly those who belong to evangelical churches.

Another story told in this book is less well publicized. As the GOP has become a party of religious conservatives with traditional moral and cultural values, the Democratic party has moved in just the opposite direction. It has witnessed an influx of religious liberals and secularists, or the nonreligious, and their liberal views on moral and cultural matters have become deeply entrenched in Democratic politics. Perhaps the religious and cultural left's influence within the Democratic party did not become an issue in the 2000 nomination campaign because the Democratic presidential candidates knew better than to cross culturally liberal groups. Vice President Al Gore and former senator Bill Bradley each took pains to establish himself as the candidate most committed to the pro-choice position on abortion. Both made vigorous appeals to feminists and homosexual rights advocates.

The American political parties, in short, are fully engaged in a new form of religious and cultural political conflict. The old political divisions among Protestants, Catholics, and Jews are still around, but they have greatly weakened. Surpassing their importance is now a new party cleavage. It places not only evangelical Protestants, but also religious conservatives from a range of faith traditions, on the Republican side. On the

Democratic side are secularists and religious liberals from a range of faith traditions.

This book attempts to provide an understanding of how this religious cleavage developed. Scholars must do two things if they are to understand this process. First, they must examine this religious divide from the perspective of party politics. Religion may be unique in the way that it influences politics, but we may learn a lot about religious change in the party system from the viewpoint of a general account of the party change process. Understanding the institutional structure of the political parties and the political incentives of their members may help us to comprehend why partisan religious change developed as it did. Second, they must examine the religious cleavage over a substantial period of time to discover the extent to which it has grown, how it has grown, and whether it will continue to grow. These are the two main things I try to do in this book. I draw on the major theoretical and empirical models of the partisan change process to develop an account of religious change in party politics. I then test that model using data on party leaders, officeholders, activists, and voters from the 1960s through the 1990s.

The large majority of what follows has not previously appeared in print. Some parts of chapters 3 and 4 are reported in my article "Culture Wars in the American Party System: Religious and Cultural Change among Partisan Activists since 1972" (*American Politics Quarterly* 27 [1999]: 89–121; reprinted by permission of Sage Publications). However, some parts of the analysis from that article were revised for those chapters, and a substantial amount of new material was added. Some parts of the analysis in chapter 5 are similar to the analysis in my article "Religion and Political Behavior in the United States: The Impact of Beliefs, Affiliations, and Commitment from 1980 to 1994," *Public Opinion Quarterly* 61 (1997): 228–316. However, all these analyses have been revised substantially.

This book began as my doctoral dissertation at Indiana University. I thank my dissertation committee there—Ted Carmines, Margie Hershey, Bob Huckfeldt, Irving Katz, and Jerry Wright—for their help and support in laying the initial foundations of the project. Ted deserves special thanks both for the guidance he provided as my main adviser on the dissertation and for reading and offering helpful comments on more recent versions of the manuscript.

Fortunately for the reader, this final product bears scant resemblance to the dissertation. The overarching question is the same. However, the theoretical sections have been modified and expanded greatly. I have completely changed my conceptual and operational definitions of religion. I have greatly expanded the range of data used. And all the empirical analyses not only are completely new but also address a range of new substantive questions.

The political science department at Vanderbilt University provided a supportive environment for the task of transforming the dissertation into a book. My colleagues John Geer and Bruce Oppenheimer deserve particular thanks for reading and rereading various parts of the manuscript and offering useful comments and criticisms. I also appreciate the fact that they occasionally stopped talking about campaigns, Congress, and Commodore basketball long enough to listen to an idea or two about religion and party politics. Also, Vanderbilt provided me with a sabbatical, part of which was used to complete this book, and financial support during that sabbatical. My colleagues Brad Palmquist and Richard Tucker provided useful methodological advice.

Numerous colleagues in the field of religion and politics have offered criticisms and suggestions, both in the guise of anonymous reviewers and in their roles as conference participants, that have made this a much better book. John Green and Bud Kellstedt deserve particular thanks for reading and commenting on parts of the manuscript. I am especially grateful to John for patiently responding to long and rambling e-mail messages about the conceptualization and measurement of religion and various and sundry other topics.

My friend, graduate school colleague, and sometimes coauthor, Tom Carsey, has borne the particular burden of putting up with me since I first formed the idea for this project many years ago. Tom read various parts of the book and offered helpful advice at all stages of the project's development. His support and friendship are much appreciated.

The bulk of the data used here came from the Inter-University Consortium for Political and Social Research at the University of Michigan. This project would not have been possible without the wealth of publicly available data archived at the consortium. Some of the data, however, came from other sources. I thank Tod Baker for providing me with data from a 1984 study of state convention delegates that he and his colleagues conducted. Particular thanks are due to Rick Herrera for providing me with some of the survey data on national convention delegates used in chapters 3 and 4 and for offering helpful advice on how to actually use it.

Columbia University Press, its editorial staff, and anonymous reviewers provided valuable suggestions that made this into a considerably better book than it otherwise would have been.

My parents, Rod and Tinky Layman, deserve special credit for leading me to the topic of this book. They were heavily involved in Republican politics in Virginia in the late 1970s and early 1980s, a time when the Christian Right was first forming and was making significant inroads into the Virginia GOP. Their participation on the moderate-Republican side of intraparty battles with the Christian Right, and their dragging me to the conventions and caucuses where these battles took place, were what sparked my initial interest in religion and party politics. Beyond that, their love and support has been invaluable.

Finally, this book is dedicated to my wife, Amy. She has never known me when I was not working on this project in some form. Yet, through all that, she agreed to marry me and has not yet divorced me. For that, she deserves my undying devotion and possibly consideration for sainthood. Her love, understanding, and encouragement have made writing this book, and life in general, a much more pleasant and joyful experience.

THE GREAT
DIVIDE

Cultural Conflict in American Society and Politics

> There is a religious war going on in this country, a cultural war as critical to the kind of nation we shall be as the Cold War itself, for this is a war for the soul of America.
>
> PATRICK J. BUCHANAN,
> at the 1992 Republican national convention

THE CULTURAL CALL to arms issued by Pat Buchanan in a nationally televised speech was not atypical of the proceedings at the Republican party's 1992 national convention in Houston. The GOP's nominee, incumbent president George Bush, was an Episcopalian who had supported a woman's right to choose an abortion as late as 1980 and was still viewed with considerable suspicion by politically active evangelical Christians. However, the characteristics of the delegates, the stances taken in the platform, and the statements made by prime-time speakers—in sum, the image of the GOP presented to citizens watching or reading about the happenings in Houston—all suggested a convention and a party dominated by religious and cultural traditionalism.

Over 22 percent of the convention delegates were fundamentalist Christians, over 66 percent attended worship services regularly, and 52 percent were either members of or were sympathetic to the political movement known as the Christian Right.[1] On the issue of abortion, the party platform argued that "the unborn child has a fundamental individual right to life which cannot be infringed" and called for a constitutional amendment to ban the procedure. The platform also offered strong opposition to the extension of civil rights protections to homosexuals and to same-sex marriages, while stating the Republicans' vigorous support for voluntary prayer in the public schools and for "traditional family values."

In addition to the statements by Pat Buchanan, prime-time viewers were treated to a speech by televangelist and Christian Right leader Pat Robertson, who stated, "When [Democratic presidential nominee] Bill Clinton talks about family values, he is not talking about either families or values. He is talking about a radical plan to destroy the traditional family and transfer its functions to the federal government." Vice President Dan Quayle told the convention that "the gap between us and our opponents is a cultural divide," while his wife, Marilyn, admonished the women's liberation movement, asserting that "most women do not want to be liberated from their essential nature as women."

The Republican gathering in Houston was not the only national party convention in 1992 to stake out definitive ground on cultural and moral matters. Just as George Bush was an unlikely standard-bearer for moral traditionalism, Democratic nominee Bill Clinton, a Southern Baptist from Arkansas who often campaigned in churches, who often infused his speeches with religious language, and who had been at the forefront of the centrist "New Democrat" movement within his party, was not closely identified with cultural liberalism. And the Democratic party, desperate to capture the White House for the first time since 1976, made a concerted effort to present an image as moderate as its candidate. However, one need not have dug much below the surface of the Democratic convention in New York to find a stark contrast to the GOP's religious and cultural conservatism. Nearly 19 percent of the convention's delegates were atheists, agnostics, or individuals not affiliated with any religion, and over 55 percent of the delegates indicated that they rarely attended worship services. The party's platform asserted the fundamental "right of every woman to choose" an abortion, stated the party's intention to protect the civil rights of homosexuals, and criticized discrimination against gays and lesbians by the armed services. Cultural liberalism was also evident in the words spoken from the podium, particularly those regarding the abortion issue. The first words spoken by the convention's chairperson were, "My name is Ann Richards. And I am pro-choice and I vote." Six pro-choice Republican women, speaking at the Democratic convention, offered severe criticisms of their party's abortion stands, with one speaker accusing President Bush of forming "an unholy political alliance with the most extreme antichoice interest groups in America."[2] The presidential nominee contrasted his own abortion position with the incumbent's, stating that "he won't guarantee a woman's right to choose. I will."

This snapshot of the 1992 national conventions suggests that the two major political parties in the United States have become participants in a new form of religious and cultural conflict that scholars, journalists, activists, and politicians have labeled America's "culture war" (Hunter 1991; Gitlin 1995; Dionne 1991). The most visible components of this struggle are the divisive, highly emotional battles over cultural issues such as abortion, women's rights, homosexual rights, and the role of religion in public education. However, just as the debate over the Kansas–Nebraska bill in 1854, the controversy over the coinage of silver in the 1890s, the Montgomery bus boycott of 1955, and the dispute over the legalization of marijuana in the 1960s were all symptomatic of larger struggles for the soul of America, the battles over these particular political issues are manifestations of a broader struggle to shape and define the fundamental assumptions of American public and private culture. As sociologist James Davison Hunter notes in his highly influential and aptly titled book *Culture Wars,* "America is in the midst of a culture war that has had and will continue to have reverberations not only with public policy, but within the lives of ordinary Americans everywhere" (1991: 34).

At the heart of the culture wars are deep-seated religious and moral divisions. On one side of the contemporary cultural divide are individuals with orthodox religious beliefs and affiliations and with high levels of religious commitment. These religious traditionalists tend to have a "commitment . . . [to] an external, definable, and transcendent" source of moral authority (Hunter 1991: 44). Thus, they believe in certain nonnegotiable moral "truths" and see these truths as the backbone of American society. At the other end of the cultural continuum are individuals who have progressive religious beliefs and lower levels of religious commitment, together with individuals who have abandoned organized religion altogether. The vision of moral authority held by these secularists and religious "liberals" tends to be a relativist one. They reject the moral truths of the orthodox camp and instead see moral authority as changing with the boundaries of human knowledge and the circumstances of human experience (Wuthnow 1988, 1989; Hunter 1991). As traditional-values champion William Bennett has described the contemporary cultural conflict, "America is divided between people who believe there's moral decline and people who say, 'What do you mean by moral decline?'"[3]

The proponents of the culture wars thesis argue that, like previous cultural conflicts, it has important implications for American political behavior and party politics (Wuthnow 1989; Hunter 1991). They contend that the political parties should become divided along orthodox–progressive lines, with religious and moral traditionalists moving into the Republican party and with the Democratic party becoming the home of moral and cultural progressivists. Other researchers add a caveat, arguing that partisan gaps between the orthodox and progressive elements of the major faith traditions have emerged, but political differences among Protestants, Catholics, and Jews remain (Green et al. 1996; Kellstedt et al. 1997; Layman and Green 1998).

This book, like other work in political science, tries to see if these scholars are right. However, to a greater extent than previous research on religion and politics, this book offers a comprehensive account of the relationship between the new religious and cultural divide and the American political party system. Drawing on the leading theories of partisan change, it develops a model of religious and cultural change in party politics and then tests this model using an extensive pool of data on the religious, cultural, and political orientations of the parties' elites and activists and of ordinary citizens, from 1960 through 1996.

THE EMERGENCE OF THE CONTEMPORARY CULTURAL CONFLICT

The roots of today's cultural conflict can be traced to the development of a new cleavage in American religion in the late nineteenth and early twentieth centuries. This cleavage would be confined within the boundaries of churches and religious institutions for several decades. However, it would be translated eventually into a societal division with important implications for American culture and politics. That translation was spurred by the growth in the numbers and influence of individuals who rejected traditional religious and cultural values in the 1960s and early 1970s, and by the backlash of religious and cultural traditionalists against this new morality in the late 1970s and the 1980s.

The early years of the American polity were distinguished by the relative absence of cultural and religious conflicts. Through the first half of the nineteenth century, American society was an overwhelmingly Protestant one, and the predominant views were those of evangelicalism: the inerrancy of the Bible, the divinity of Christ, the necessity of "born-again" adult conversion experiences for salvation, and a commitment to evangelizing or "spreading the Word" (Smith 1998; Hunter 1983; Oldfield 1996; Green et al. 1996). This evangelical Protestant hegemony characterized not only the religious orientations of ordinary citizens, but also the moral visions that informed the major institutions of public life (Smith

1998; Marsden 1980; Hunter 1983, 1991). As religious historian George Marsden notes, "Evangelicalism . . . had much to do with shaping American culture in the nineteenth century. Most major reform movements, such as antislavery or temperance, had a strong evangelical component. Evangelicals had a major voice in American schools and colleges, public as well as private, and had much to do with setting dominant American moral standards" (1991: 2). Describing the evangelical dominance of American public culture more succinctly, sociologist Christian Smith contends that "they were *the* establishment" (1998: 2, emphasis in the original).

The exalted cultural position of orthodox Protestantism, however, did not go unchallenged for long. The second half of the nineteenth century brought with it a massive influx of Catholic and Jewish immigrants from Ireland, Italy, and eastern Europe and, as a result, an end to the cultural consensus in American society. Catholics, Jews, and Protestants differed sharply in doctrinal beliefs and in styles of religious practice. Moreover, the tensions caused by religious differences among the three faith traditions were exacerbated by differences in ethnicity, language, social class, and culture (McCormick 1986; Green and Guth 1991; Hunter 1991). The relationships among these "ethnoreligious" groups were often hostile, and the hostilities had clear political ramifications. As late as the 1960s, nonsouthern Protestants could generally be counted on to support Republican candidates, while Catholic and Jewish constituencies usually represented Democratic strongholds (Erikson, Lancaster, and Romero 1989; Axelrod 1972; Sundquist 1983).[4]

Despite their religious differences, there was a fundamental agreement among the three major faith traditions. Protestants, Catholics, and Jews all shared a commitment to a transcendent source of moral authority—in fact, to the same transcendent source of moral authority—and agreed that American public culture should be shaped by biblical tenets. As Rabbi Solomon Schecter announced at the opening of the Jewish Theological Seminary of America in 1903, "This country is, as everybody knows, a creation of the Bible, particularly of the Old Testament" (quoted in Hunter 1991: 71). The nineteenth-century tensions among Catholics and Protestants and Christians and Jews thus gave way in the twentieth century to a consensus that Judeo-Christian beliefs and teachings should be upheld as the backbone of American society (Wuthnow 1988; Oldfield 1996). This conviction was evident in the Supreme Court's decision in *Zorach v. Clauson* (1952), when the Court noted that "we are a religious people whose institutions presuppose a Supreme Being."

The reduction in animosity among Catholics, Protestants, and Jews in this century did not result in the end of religion-based cultural conflict in the United States. Instead, there emerged a new form of cultural conflict, one based less on membership in a faith tradition and more on religious commitment and the orthodoxy of religious belief. The social and political impact of this new cleavage would not be felt strongly until the 1960s and 1970s. However, the catalyst for its development was the emergence of modern, industrial life in the late nineteenth and early twentieth centuries (Green and Guth 1991; Hunter 1991; Smith 1998).

The idea that modernization has deleterious effects on traditional religious faith is a widely accepted one among social scientists (cf. Lechner 1991; Tschannen 1991; Chaves 1994). Along with modernity comes a host of societal developments that change the place of religion in society, lessen the credibility of its tenets, and ultimately reduce the commitment of individuals to it. Modern science tends to undermine the credibility of religious faith by offering rationalistic explanations for phenomena attributed by religion to supernatural, divine forces. The rapid urbanization of industrialized societies takes individuals out of religiously and culturally homogeneous small towns and rural areas and puts them in close proximity to other individuals from very different religious and cultural traditions. Thus, the reenforcement of religious belief that results from cultural homogeneity is replaced by the weakening of religious faith that results from daily contact with contradictory beliefs and cultural norms. The development of modern communication ensures that even those who remain in small towns and rural areas are exposed to new, conflicting ideas and information. Finally, modern society brings with it a division of life into public and private spheres. Religion tends to be relegated to the realm of private devotionalism and thus loses much of its influence on the larger culture (Wilson 1966; Inkeles 1983; Wallis and Bruce 1992).

Despite very high levels of economic and technological development and a great deal of social and geographic mobility, religion—whether defined as affiliation, belief, or participation—has been remarkably persistent in the United States, more so here than in almost any other advanced industrial society (Wald 1997; Sherkat and Ellison 1999). However, in recent decades, modernity has taken a toll on religious commitment in some segments of American society, particularly the more affluent, better-educated, and urbanized ones (Wallis and Bruce 1992; Wald 1997; Hunter 1983, 1991). Before that, it threatened the dominant role of orthodox beliefs in Protestant, Catholic, and Jewish theology. The rise of modern, industrial life and the discoveries of modern science in the late nineteenth century led some religious leaders to rethink traditional creeds, to rationalize religious doctrines to conform to modern beliefs (Smith 1998; Marty 1986; Wuthnow 1986, 1988; Hunter 1991).

Within Protestantism, proponents of the "New Theology" attempted to reconcile traditional theology with the discoveries of modern scientific inquiry, deemphasizing the supernatural and miraculous aspects of biblical writings and focusing largely on the ethical aspects. Meanwhile, advocates of the "social gospel" called for less emphasis on individual conversion and more emphasis on societal betterment. Within Catholicism, certain bishops began to focus more on social reform, and the Americanist movement sought to deemphasize Roman traditions and integrate the Catholic Church into the mainstream of modern American society. Within Judaism, the Reform movement sought to move the Jewish faith away from a focus on traditional beliefs and ritualistic observances and toward an emphasis on ethical idealism.

These concessions to modernism did not, however, go unchallenged by the defenders of traditional religiosity. Portions of all three faith traditions rose up to reaffirm orthodox beliefs and practices (Hunter 1983, 1991; Smith 1998; Chandler 1984; Oldfield 1996). Among Protestants, for example, the "Fundamentalist" movement emerged to militantly oppose modernist theology and particularly to reassert biblical inerrancy (the view that the Bible is the Word of God and is authoritative in all matters) (Marsden 1987; Smith 1998). Fundamentalists fought to reestablish orthodox control of the major Protestant denominations and to restore the place of traditional religious values in the schools, focusing particularly on keeping Darwinian evolutionism out of the curriculum.

The battles between traditionalists and modernists created significant divisions within the major faith traditions in the early twentieth century. However, until the last few decades of the twentieth century, the conflict was largely between religious leaders and did not erupt into a broader cleavage in American society and politics. The reason clearly was that, even though progressive leaders had gained strength within religion, particularly within the mainline Protestant denominations (Smith 1998; Oldfield 1996), most Americans tended toward the traditionalist side of the cultural divide. Even by 1950, the large majority of the mass public remained committed to the traditional morality of the nineteenth century (Hunter 1983).

In fact, the decade of the 1950s represented a high point in American religiosity and in the role of religion and traditional morality in

American culture. The number of Americans belonging to churches increased from 64.5 million (50 percent of the population) in 1940 to 114.5 million (63 percent of the population) by the end of the 1950s (Dionne 1991), and this increase in religious devotion spurred Congress to adopt new forms of religious recognition. The words "under God" were inserted into the pledge of allegiance, and the phrase "In God We Trust" was placed on the currency. Even the new medium of television, with its shows focusing on traditional family structures and earnest moral lessons, reflected the grip that conservative cultural norms had on the country. As journalist E. J. Dionne Jr. argues, "In the 1950s, television adhered to a strict (and in the eyes of its critics, stultifying) moral code. Programs such as 'The Adventures of Ozzie and Harriet' and 'Leave it to Beaver' celebrated domesticity and 1950s 'traditional values.' . . . [They] were thoroughly consistent with the preachings of the conservative churches" (1991: 223).

Even while taking pains to avoid favoring a particular faith tradition, President Eisenhower summed up the role of religion in American public life in the 1950s, declaring that "our government makes no sense unless it is founded on a deeply felt religious belief—and I don't care what it is" (quoted in Dionne 1991: 218).

The role of traditional morality and religion in American society, however, met a stern challenge in the 1960s. And, once again, the catalyst for the challenge was growing modernity, particularly the dramatic increase in higher education after World War II. The young, highly educated "baby boomers" who came of age politically in 1960s antiestablishment causes such as the civil rights movement, the anti–Vietnam War movement, and the women's rights movement rebelled against traditional values such as achievement, authority, and patriotism, and they were particularly hostile to traditional morality and religion (Kaufman 1970; Stewart 1974; Gitlin 1987; Dionne 1991). These largely secular young people adopted the stance of a counterculture, characterized by a "distrust of established authority and a rejection of conventional definitions of religion, morality, and patriotism" (Miller and Levitin 1984: 6), and brought with them a "New Politics" that pushed moral and cultural matters to the political forefront. The "New Left" attacked the values of the "Old Left" establishment and sought a freer lifestyle on a whole host of issues: abortion, drugs, relations between the sexes, and the treatment of homosexuals. As symbolized by the counterculture's catchphrase "If it feels good, do it," the young, politically active secularists of the 1960s sought to instill a new permissiveness and moral tolerance into American public culture.

And, in retrospect, they were quite successful. Many contemporary observers suggested that attempts to push the United States toward moral liberalism would crumble under the weight of a morally traditional majority. Richard Nixon spoke of a "silent majority" standing in opposition to the New Politics. Although writing from different partisan perspectives, Kevin Phillips in *The Emerging Republican Majority* (1969) and Richard Scammon and Benjamin Wattenberg in *The Real Majority* (1970) agreed that social and cultural liberalism potentially represented the undoing of the Democratic party's majority status. However, the 1960s and 1970s witnessed a growing influence of secularists and of moral liberalism in American public life. The percentage of secularists in the citizenry quadrupled over the 1960s and 1970s (Hunter 1991) and young, culturally progressive secularists gained disproportionate influence within institutions such as the federal bureaucracy, the national news media, and the entertainment industry (Lichter and Rothman 1983; Rothman and Lichter 1983).

Just as 1950s television reflected the moral traditionalism of that decade, television and movies in the 1960s and 1970s increasingly came to reflect the permissiveness of the counterculture, challenging traditional sexual morality and focusing on nontraditional family structures. In the 1950s, even the married couples on television slept in separate beds. In the 1970s, the lead character on television's *Maude* made the decision to have an abortion. As conservative historian James Hitchcock notes, "Those who controlled the media realized that there was a substantial audience which had broken with traditional moral values and wanted entertainment which ventured into forbidden territory in hitherto forbidden ways. . . . Traditional moral values were ridiculed, assaulted, and ground into dust" (1982: 81–82).

The impact of cultural liberalism was also felt in the political arena. Although the New Left attacked "establishment liberalism" and the Democratic party, it did not desert the Democrats, instead fostering challenges to liberal orthodoxy within the party. In 1968, the antiwar presidential nominating campaigns of Robert Kennedy and Eugene McCarthy first brought elements of the New Left into the Democratic party. In 1972, the nomination of George McGovern confirmed the influence of a variety of left-oriented protest movements. Groups representing homosexuals, feminists, and the young demanded—and received—a seat at the

Democratic table. As suggested by its Republican-coined label as the party of "acid, amnesty, and abortion," the Democratic party of McGovern became closely identified with the New Left and cultural liberalism. And, despite McGovern's monumental defeat in 1972, political scientists Warren Miller and Teresa Levitin (1984) suggest that that was not such a bad position for a party. Miller and Levitin take issue with the notion that the themes of the New Politics were losing themes and argue that McGovern's failures were caused more by his personal shortcomings than by the unpopularity of his issue agenda. They label Nixon's "silent majority" the "silent minority" and show that support for the New Politics agenda grew substantially during the early part of the 1970s, with outright supporters coming to greatly outnumber outright opponents.

The growing numbers of secularists and cultural liberals and their growing influence in American public life were crucial to the eruption of the cultural conflict not only because they generated significant cultural differences in American society but also because they triggered the political reawakening of those at the opposite end of the cultural continuum. Because the focus of their faith was on individual piety rather than social betterment, and because of their distaste for a larger society that ridiculed their fights against alcohol and evolutionism in the 1910s and 1920s as backward and morally oppressive, evangelical Protestants had stayed away from politics for nearly a half century (Oldfield 1996; Guth 1983; Smith 1998; Hunter 1983). The evangelical disdain for politics was summed up well by future Christian Right leader Jerry Falwell in 1965, when he argued that "we have few ties to this earth. . . . Believing in the Bible as I do, I would find it impossible to stop preaching the pure saving Gospel of Jesus Christ and begin doing anything else, including fighting communism or participating in civil rights reforms. . . . Preachers are not called upon to be politicians but to be soul winners. Nowhere are we commissioned to reform the externals" (Falwell 1987: 290).

However, the growing social and political influence of secularism, the desertion of traditional morality by the entertainment industry, and Supreme Court decisions removing religion from the public schools, banning state restrictions on abortion rights, encompassing pornography under freedom of speech, and threatening government aid to religious schools "struck at the core of traditionalist values and the institutions in which they were embodied" (Guth et al. 1988: 363). These developments were repugnant to religious conservatives not only because they threatened the place of traditional moral values in the larger society, but also because, in the eyes of evangelicals, they threatened their ability to preserve their own subculture and pass their values on to their children (Oldfield 1996; Neuhaus 1987; Reichley 1987; Glazer 1987). Falwell expressed these sentiments in 1980, when he argued, "We're not trying to jam our moral philosophy down the throats of others. We're simply trying to keep others from jamming their amoral philosophies down our throats."[5] Family Research Council leader and future Republican presidential candidate Gary Bauer echoed them in 1989, arguing, "Our opponents will often picture us attempting to exert our values on the rest of society. I think the people we work with see it as they were willing to go about their lives with a sort of separate but equal existence and that it's the culture that keeps pushing more into their homes and their schools and so forth. So they see what has happened in the last ten years as being more of a reaction of self defense than as an effort to violate American pluralism" (quoted in Oldfield 1996: 55).

In response, conservative Protestants abandoned their apolitical moorings in the late 1970s and early 1980s. With encouragement and assistance from organizations such as the Moral Majority, the Religious Roundtable, the Christian Voice, and later the Christian Coalition and the Family Research Council, religious conservatives became actively involved in battles over cultural issues such as abortion, the place of religion in the public schools, pornography, gender equality, and homosexual rights, and they infiltrated the ranks of the Republican party to fight these battles (Guth 1983; Oldfield 1996). In contrast to his testimony to political agnosticism in 1965, Jerry Falwell argued in 1980 that "the day of the silent church is passed. . . . We're here to stay. . . . Preachers, you need as never before to preach on the issues, no matter what they say or what they write about you. Get involved, registered, informed, and voting."[6]

The cultural progressivism of the 1960s and 1970s and the orthodox response of the 1970s and 1980s drew the lines for a new form of American cultural conflict. Divisions between religious traditions now have given way to divisions both between and within traditions. Together with secularists, religious liberals within all of the major faith traditions battle with their religiously conservative counterparts not only for the soul of their religions, but also for the soul of American culture (Wuthnow 1988, 1989; Hunter 1991). Some scholars argue that these new cultural tensions may be even more deep-seated than the old ones. The basic agreement on moral authority shared by Catholics, Jews, and Protestants has been replaced by a conflict centering on the acceptance or disavowal of transcendent sources of moral authority (Hunter 1983, 1991; Wuthnow 1988, 1989; Heinz 1983; Marsden, 1987). Thus, when abortion rights advocates call for a fundamental right to personal privacy and abortion opponents point to the fundamental right to life of the fetus; when homosexual rights advocates speak of the right of individuals to freely express their sexuality and their opponents point to biblical teachings on the proper family structure and proper sexual relations; when religious school, school choice, and school prayer proponents talk about restoring the role of religion and traditional moral values in education and their opponents point to the need for diversity and free-thinking in the public schools, they are not pursuing different means to a common moral end. They are working from fundamentally different assumptions about moral authority and whether or not there should even be a common source of morality guiding American public and private life. In sum, cultural conflict today "no longer revolve[s] around specific doctrinal issues or styles of religious practice and organization but around our most fundamental and cherished assumptions about how to order our lives—our own lives and our lives together in this society" (Hunter 1991: 42).

RELIGIOUS CONFLICT AND THE POLITICAL PARTIES

The religious and cultural conflict in contemporary American society has important implications for a wide range of public and private institutions. This book focuses on their implications for what are perhaps the paramount institutions in American politics. It is a book about the American political parties, how they have responded to the cultural conflict, how they have been affected by it, and also how they have shaped it.

The culture wars theorists argue that, just as past cultural clashes affected party politics in important ways, the current conflict should reshape contemporary party politics, making the Republican party into a coalition of religious and cultural traditionalists from a variety of faith traditions, and the Democratic party into the political home of religious and moral liberals (Wuthnow 1989; Hunter 1991). Other scholars disagree and contend that a traditionalist–modernist religious cleavage has not emerged in contemporary party politics (Manza and Brooks 1997; Sims 1996). A third group of researchers falls somewhere in the middle. They agree that there are significant political differences between the orthodox and modernist elements of the major faith traditions. But they take issue with Hunter's claim that the contemporary cultural cleavage makes "the distinctions that long divided Americans—those between Protestants, Catholics, and Jews—virtually irrelevant" (1991: 43), arguing that even when religious orthodoxy is taken into account, important political divisions remain between individuals who belong to different faith traditions (Leege and Kellstedt 1993b; Green et al. 1996; Kellstedt et al. 1997; Jelen 1997).

This book supports the latter view. There is some constancy in religious politics: Catholics are still more Democratic than Protestants, and Jews remain more Democratic than Christians. Recent decades, however, have witnessed substantial change. The most orthodox elements of the major faith traditions have become increasingly Republican relative to their modernist counterparts. Such a change in the character of party politics has important consequences for the future of the Democratic and Republican parties and for the future of the cultural conflict in the United States.

Implications for American Politics

The most obvious repercussions are for the parties' bases of support and possibilities for electoral success. At the close of World War II, American politics revolved around the social welfare issues associated with the New Deal that Franklin Roosevelt offered in response to the Great Depression. Following FDR's lead, Democrats were committed to the idea of an activist role for government in managing the economy and providing for the general welfare; Republicans stood in opposition. Not surprisingly, the Democratic party received its strongest support from the groups that had been most adversely affected by the depression: lower-income individuals, unskilled workers, northern blacks, and ethnic and religious minorities. This coalition, along with the party's nearly unanimous support from white southerners, helped to ensconce the Democrats as the majority party in American politics until at least the 1970s. The Republicans, meanwhile, were relegated to minority status as the party of upper-status white Protestants from outside the South.

These coalitions began to change in the 1960s as Democratic support for federal intervention into southern racial matters led to an exodus of southern whites and other racial conservatives from their historic partisan home. White southerners did not immediately gravitate toward the Republican party, but they did provide an important base of support for the GOP in presidential elections, as well as hope for a future national Republican majority (Phillips 1969). The strong support of northern blacks for the Democratic party became nearly unanimous and was now accompanied by the overwhelming support of the newly enfranchised

African-Americans in the South (Carmines and Stimson 1989; Black and Black 1987, 1992).

The cultural conflict has the potential to create even more substantial changes in the parties' New Deal coalitions as well as in the electoral balance between them. Cultural traditionalism may enable the Republican party to reach beyond its traditional base of upper-status white Protestants from mainline denominations such as Episcopalian, Presbyterian, and United Methodist and to attract support from traditionally religious and traditionally Democratic groups such as evangelical Protestants, southern whites, conservative Catholics, and African-Americans.

A coalition of religious traditionalists from most of the major Christian traditions also would put the GOP in a far better electoral position than it held in the four decades following the Great Depression, particularly given the growth in the membership of conservative Protestant churches since World War II (Kelley 1972; Bibby and Brinkerhoff 1983; Perrin, Kennedy, and Miller 1997). On the other hand, conservative cultural stances may lessen the GOP's appeal to its traditional supporters as better-educated, more affluent individuals tend to be less traditionally religious and more culturally liberal than lower-status citizens (Sherkat 1991, 1998; Johnson 1997). Moreover, with the steady increase in the number of nonreligious individuals (Sherkat and Ellison 1999) and with the growing moral permissiveness of the larger culture, cultural conservatism may ultimately prove to be a losing position for the Republicans.

Cultural liberalism may enable the Democratic party to attract the growing numbers of secularists in the American electorate and to appeal to disaffected upper-status Republicans. However, it also has the potential to alienate some black Protestants and working-class Catholics—the traditional core of the Democratic coalition—and to further estrange white southerners from the Democratic party.[7] In the end, the cultural conflict carries risks, but it also creates opportunities for both political parties.

Partisan polarization along religious and cultural lines also may affect Americans' levels of support for the two-party system in general. Despite the polarized nature of the rhetoric on cultural issues, most Americans have somewhat ambivalent, generally moderate attitudes toward them (Hunter 1994). Moreover, polls consistently show that a substantial majority of citizens find other types of political concerns to be more pressing (Abramson, Aldrich, and Rohde 1999). However, if the parties' activists and electoral coalitions are becoming more polarized along religious and cultural lines, it is likely that their candidates and their platforms will take increasingly strong, uncompromising stands on these issues. This may contribute to weakened party attachments and a general disenchantment with politics among a citizenry that grows tired of polarized cultural rhetoric and wants the nation's political leaders and institutions to move on to more salient matters.

In fact, E. J. Dionne, in his critically acclaimed book *Why Americans Hate Politics* (1991), argues that the reason for the political malaise that characterizes contemporary American society—declining participation in politics, declining trust in leaders and governmental institutions, and a declining sense of political efficacy—can be traced to the continued division between the major ideological camps and political parties on the social and cultural issues that emerged in the 1960s and 1970s and to their inability to find agreeable solutions to these problems. He contends that "we are suffering from a false polarization in our politics, in which liberals and conservatives keep arguing about the same things when the country wants to move on. The cause of this false polarization is the cultural civil war that broke out in the 1960s" (1991: 11). Dionne suggests that the endurance of cultural divisions between the Democrats and Republicans may lead Americans to search for a political alternative to the two major parties, in particular to a centrist third party that offers consensus solutions to the cultural issues and focuses its attention on the more pressing economic and foreign policy concerns of the twenty-first century. To an extent, Dionne's predictions came true soon after he made them, as independent candidate Ross Perot won nearly 20 percent of the vote in the 1992 presidential election—the largest percentage of the presidential vote won by a third-party candidate since Theodore Roosevelt's Bull Moose campaign in 1912—and led the Democratic and Republican candidates in the polls in the early summer with a centrist campaign that avoided strong stands on the divisive cultural issues and focused on matters such as trade policy, government reform, and balancing the federal budget.

Finally, partisan religious polarization may affect the ability of the parties to foster a peaceable end to the contemporary cultural conflict. Although his claims are seen as far too dire by some scholars (Kellstedt et al. 1994; Horton 1994; Wald 1997; Williams 1997), Hunter (1994) argues that the culture war poses a fundamental threat to American democracy. Not only are the two sides unwilling to compromise with each other, but, since each side presupposes the illegitimacy of the other, there is virtually no communication between them. Thus, the possibility of reaching a consensus solution through democratic institutions is quite small.

Given the important role that political parties play in translating public preferences into electoral outcomes and in coordinating the actions of elected officials (Schattschneider 1942; Key 1964; Aldrich 1995), any democratic resolution to the cultural conflict necessarily will involve the two parties. And, since their primary goal is to win elections, parties would seem to be prime candidates to nurture a cultural consensus. To maintain the support of the electorate, parties need to appeal to the "median voter"—to the center of the electorate—and they need to reach solutions to pressing policy problems. However, if there are growing religious and cultural differences between party activists and supporters, the parties may not be able to play such a role and instead may contribute to the highly polarized nature of the cultural debate. Hunter argues that the parties already have fallen into this trap as "neither party offers anything more than the slogans of solidarity for the already committed" (1994: 218). If this is the course the parties continue to take, they not only may fail to be part of the solution to the cultural conflict, but also may be part of the problem. Since the stances of political leaders often influence the views of ordinary citizens (cf. Zaller 1992; Page and Jones 1979), polarized cultural stances by the political parties, their candidates, and their leaders may contribute to further cultural polarization in the mass public.

The Next Steps in the Research Agenda

Since the Christian Right emerged on the national political stage in 1980, there has been a good deal of research on religion and the political parties. Its basic conclusion has been that the contemporary religious cleavage does affect American party politics. Religious conservatives from most of the major Christian traditions, but particularly among evangelical Protestants, tend to support the Republican party, while the Democratic party draws its support disproportionately from the ranks of religious liberals in the major faith traditions and secularists. Although these partisan religious differences tend to be most evident among political activists (Green et al. 1996; Green, Guth, and Fraser 1991; Guth and Green 1986, 1987, 1989; Baker, Steed, and Moreland 1991; Baker and Steed 1992; Rozell and Wilcox 1995; Hertzke 1993), there is evidence of similar differences in the parties' mass coalitions (Green et al. 1996; Miller and Shanks 1996; Kellstedt, Smidt, and Kellstedt 1991; Jelen 1991; Kellstedt 1989; Wilcox 1992; Lopatto 1985). In short, this scholarship has been very effective in demonstrating the importance of religion in contemporary American politics.

However, from the perspective of understanding the link between religion and *party* politics, important questions remain unanswered. Most fundamentally, political scientists, to a large degree, do not know how long the religious and cultural divisions in the party system have existed and whether or not they have grown over time. Without such crucial information, we lack not only the context to judge the extent to which partisan change has occurred, but also the ability to make sound predictions about the future size of the religious and cultural cleavage between the parties. Researchers also have yet to satisfactorily address important questions about how the cleavage has become manifest in the party system: How closely has the religious polarization of the parties been tied to polarization on particular types of policy issues? Which of the two parties was affected first by the contemporary religious cleavage and why? Have particular candidates played a significant role in bringing this religious division into party politics?

To reach answers to these crucial questions, the literature on religion and party politics needs to take two very important steps. First, it must develop a strong theory explaining why the contemporary religious cleavage has become manifest in party politics and the process through which it has done so. There are cogent theoretical accounts of how and why religion affects political attitudes and behavior and of the political reemergence of conservative Christians (cf. Jelen 1991; Wilcox 1992; Leege and Kellstedt 1993b; Green et al. 1996; Oldfield 1996), but not yet of the role of the parties in bringing the contemporary religious cleavage to the forefront of American politics. Just as the emergence of the slavery issue in American politics in the 1850s and of racial issues in the mid-1960s was fostered by the strategic incentives and behaviors of party leaders and activists (Riker 1982; Carmines and Stimson 1989), the political manifestation of cultural conflict in the 1980s and 1990s cannot be understood apart from the incentives and actions of actors within the political party system, nor, as John Aldrich (1995, 1999) argues, can any period of fundamental political change.

To understand why the issues surrounding the cultural conflict became partisan issues in the first place, why one political party was affected by the cultural cleavage before the other, and the role of particular candidates in bringing the religious cleavage into party politics, one must understand the relationship between the cultural conflict on the one hand and the strategic incentives of leaders within both parties and the rules and structures of both parties on the other hand. To understand the growing partisan importance of the contemporary religious divide, one must understand the relationship between political change among party elites, changing patterns of participation among party activists, and changes in the perceptions and loyalties of ordinary citizens. In short, to understand the impact of religion on contemporary American politics, we need a theory of party politics that explains its relationship to religious and cultural divisions in society.

Second, research needs to examine the relationship between religion and party politics over a series of elections. Most research on religion and politics relies on data collected at one point in time or over a rather small number of years. It provides a snapshot of the relationship between religion and political behavior. However, all the previous periods of partisan change, even the cataclysmic change associated with the Great Depression and Franklin D. Roosevelt's New Deal, have taken shape over a series of elections, generally spanning more than one decade (Sundquist 1983). Thus, by not examining the ebbs and flows of the relationship between religion and political behavior over a substantial period, the literature on religion and politics does not provide a comprehensive account of the development of religious and cultural cleavages in American party politics. To reach answers to questions about how long the religious division in the party system has existed, the extent to which it has grown over time, the extent to which it has been tied to particular political issues, and the degree to which particular candidacies have encouraged its development, research on religion and politics needs to take a considerably more long-term perspective than it has to this point.

THE PLAN OF ATTACK

This book attempts to take these necessary next two steps in our understanding of the religious and cultural division of party politics. Drawing on the major theoretical accounts of the realignment and partisan change process, I develop a model of religious and cultural change in the political party system. I then employ a sizeable collection of data on party elites, activists, and identifiers from the early 1960s through the late 1990s to test the propositions of the model and to examine the nature of the religious divisions between the political parties and the process through which they have developed.

Chapter 1 begins the journey by presenting the model of partisan religious change. Chapter 2 sets the groundwork for subsequent empirical analyses by discussing various ways of conceptualizing the religious cleavage. Using data from a nationwide survey of public opinion and electoral behavior, I show that the contemporary divide is defined adequately by neither the culture wars model, which envisions a struggle between theological conservatives and liberals across the boundaries of faith traditions, nor the "ethnoreligious" model, which envisions a conflict between members of the various faith traditions, but rather by a combination of religious affiliations, beliefs, and behaviors.

In chapters 3 and 4, I discuss the consequences of the religious and cultural cleavage for the most important actors in the partisan change process: the parties' activists. Chapter 3 employs data on the delegates to the parties' national nominating conventions from 1972 to 1996 to examine the growth in religious differences between Democratic and Republican activists and to describe the process through which that growth has occurred. It shows that the proportion of committed evangelical Protestants in the Republican party and of secularists in the Democratic party has grown over time, as has the overall level of religious polarization between the parties' activists. The growth of this religious cleavage has been associated with an increase in the differences between the attitudes of Democratic and Republican activists on cultural issues as well as between the cultural stands taken in the parties' quadrennial platforms. Chapter 4 uses those same data to analyze the consequences of the religious polarization of party activists for political and ideological conflict both between and within the parties. I conclude that there are ideological, stylistic, and motivational differences between activists from different religious groups in the same parties. However, over time, those differences have become less significant in comparison to the cultural differences between activists from the same religious groups but in different parties.

Chapter 5 examines changes in the religious composition of the parties' mass coalitions. Using data from national public opinion surveys from 1960 through 1996, I show that there has been a clear reshaping of the party affiliations of committed evangelical Protestants, from Democratic to strongly Republican, as well as a substantial increase in the overall level of religious and cultural polarization between the two party coalitions. Chapter 6 focuses on the connection between religious and cultural change at the elite and activist levels of party politics and religious and cultural changes in the parties' mass coalitions. I show that change in the religious and cultural orientations of party elites, specifically Democratic and Republican members of Congress, and activists has led to an increase in the proportion of citizens seeing the parties as polarized on religious, moral, and cultural matters as well as a change in the affect of particular religious groups for the two parties. These developments have, in turn, produced an increase in the religious differences between the Republican and Democratic electoral coalitions.

Chapter 7 seeks answers to two very important questions about the impact of religion on contemporary American electoral behavior: How does it matter? And, when (or for whom) does it matter? I show that the effect of traditionalist–modernist religious orientations is exerted primarily through their influence on moral values and cultural attitudes and is greatest for those individuals who are concerned about cultural matters, who attend churches where politics is a topic of discussion from the pulpit and among parishioners, and who live in states where party elites and activists are most divided along religious lines.

Chapter 8 concludes the book by discussing the broader, and future, implications of the religious and cultural division of the American party system, both for party politics and for democratic politics more generally. I argue that, despite protestations from political observers that cultural issues are not relevant to most Americans, and despite pleas from both Democrats and Republicans for their parties to ignore their religiously and culturally extreme wings, the religious and cultural differences between the two parties are not likely to disappear in the near future, and, in fact, may increase. I also contend, however, that these divisions do not represent a fundamental threat to the two major parties or, more importantly, to American democracy.

Notes

1. All the statistical information on the religious characteristics of Republican and Democratic convention delegates in 1992 comes from the 1992 Convention Delegate Study conducted by Warren E. Miller and Richard Herrera.

2. Quoted in "'92 Democratic Convention," *The Los Angeles Times*, Southland Edition, July 15, 1992, p. A8.

3. Quoted in Fred Barnes, "Family Feud: The Religious Right vs. Republicans," *The New Republic*, April 17, 1995, p. 13.

4. Although weakened somewhat, the basic pattern of Protestants being the most Republican of the three major faith traditions, Jews being the

most Democratic, and Catholics lying somewhere between holds even today (Wald 1997).

5. Quoted in William Greider, "Would Jesus Join the Moral Majority?" *The Washington Post,* Final Edition, October 13, 1980, p. D1.

6. Quoted in Doug Willis, "Pastor Says God Opposes ERA," The Associated Press, October 30, 1980. [Internet, WWW]. *Available:* LEXIS-NEXIS Academic Universe; ADDRESS: *http://web.lexis-nexis.com/universe.*

7. The fact that the South is the most religious and morally conservative region of the country is well documented (Reed 1972; Stark and Bainbridge 1985; Shibley 1996; Smith, Shikkink, and Bailey 1998).

CHAPTER I

Explaining Religious and Cultural Change in the Party System

A NEW SET OF divisions has emerged in American religion. Those divisions have been translated into an often intense conflict over the proper definition of moral authority and the proper role of that authority in American public culture. What does that mean for party politics in the United States? Do all major social conflicts become partisan conflicts? More particularly, does the highly emotional and polarized nature of the contemporary cultural debate mean that the parties' electoral coalitions inevitably will become divided along religious and cultural lines? The answer is no: Societal divisions do not necessarily become partisan divisions. For social conflicts—whether they are religious, cultural, racial, economic, or sectional in nature—to produce a significant change in the party coalitions, they must give rise to powerful new political issues that cut across the existing lines of partisan division, appeal to the strategic calculations of political actors within the parties, arouse a response among the most politically active segments of the electorate, and ultimately lead to changes in the mass public's perceptions of and feelings toward the two major parties.

In this chapter, I present a framework, outlined in figure 1.1, for understanding partisan change along religious and cultural lines. I suggest that the reason that the traditionalist–modernist religious cleavage (step 1 in the figure) has emerged in party politics is precisely because it is associated with a powerful, highly emotional set of political issues (step 2) that cut across the previous lines of partisan division and appealed to the strategic calculations of party politicians (step 3) and the passions of political activists (step 4). The initial appearance of a cultural gap between the parties (step 5) led ultimately to a restructuring of the Democratic and Republican coalitions because the parties' distinct stands on these

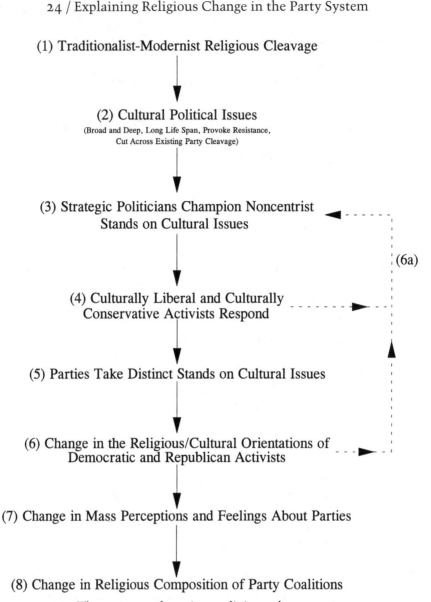

(1) Traditionalist-Modernist Religious Cleavage

(2) Cultural Political Issues
(Broad and Deep, Long Life Span, Provoke Resistance,
Cut Across Existing Party Cleavage)

(3) Strategic Politicians Champion Noncentrist
Stands on Cultural Issues

(6a)

(4) Culturally Liberal and Culturally
Conservative Activists Respond

(5) Parties Take Distinct Stands on Cultural Issues

(6) Change in the Religious/Cultural Orientations of
Democratic and Republican Activists

(7) Change in Mass Perceptions and Feelings About Parties

(8) Change in Religious Composition of Party Coalitions

FIGURE 1.1. The process of partisan religious change

political issues triggered a change in the religious and cultural orientations of their activist bases (step 6). These activist-level changes encouraged party candidates and leaders to take even more extreme positions on cultural issues (step 6a) and also contributed to a change in the way the mass public views the two parties and the way religious traditionalists and modernists feel about the parties (step 7). This change in the public's perceptions of and affect toward the parties evolved into a change in the religious and cultural composition of the parties' electoral coalitions (step 8).[1]

Before proceeding to the discussion of the relationship between the cultural conflict and the political parties, one caveat is in order. Those readers familiar with the political science literature on electoral change may wonder whether the religious and cultural change in party politics constitutes a partisan realignment. The answer is, it depends on how realignment is defined. If realign means "to reorganize or make new groupings of," as it does in the tenth edition of the *Merriam-Webster's Collegiate Dictionary*, then I certainly am describing a process of party realignment. The contemporary religious cleavage has fostered new political issues that cut across the preexisting lines of partisan division and stimulate the passions of large numbers of citizens. The distinct stands that the parties have taken on these issues have led to a reorganization of the party coalitions along religious lines.

The scholarly definition of realignment, however, is not as simple as *Merriam-Webster's*. Since V. O. Key introduced the term into the lexicon of political science with his theory of critical elections (1955) and his discussion of "secular realignment" (1959), realignment has come to mean something more than a durable reorganization of the party coalitions. It has become imbued with the notion of a "critical election," an election dominated by discussions of a new political issue, in which the large majority of voters choose partisan sides based on their views on the new issue, and which produces a rapid and dramatic change in the party system (Sundquist 1983). Realignment also has become associated with "conflict displacement," the idea that one dominant line of partisan cleavage is replaced by another, or that a new set of issues surpasses the previously dominant issues in importance (Schattschneider 1960; Sundquist 1983). Other work describes a realignment as a wholesale change in the partisan balance of power, with one party replacing the other as the majority party in American politics (Campbell et al. 1960; Burnham 1970).

The religious and cultural transformation of party politics has produced none of these things to their full measure. Although some elections have been more important than others in placing the parties on opposite sides of the cultural divide, there has not been a single "critical election" in which the religious differences between the parties have grown from negligible to substantial levels. Also, the issues associated with the contemporary cultural conflict have not displaced older issues on the political stage. These new issues exist alongside the still-important social welfare issues that emerged with the Great Depression and the New Deal in the 1930s and the racial issues that emerged with the civil rights movement in the 1960s, and there is no evidence of a decline in party differences on the older issues (Carmines and Layman 1997). Finally, although partisan religious change has had important consequences for the balance of power between the two parties, it has not produced a new majority party. The Republican party is in a far more competitive position now than it was when the issues surrounding the cultural conflict emerged. However, there are still more Democratic identifiers than Republican identifiers in the electorate, and the GOP has not yet been able to gain control of both Congress and the White House at the same time.

So the partisan religious and cultural change does not meet the criteria of some scholarly definitions of realignment. However, it has produced a substantial and important transformation in party politics, analogous to the long-term, issue-driven partisan transformations described by the theoretical models of James Sundquist (1983), Edward Carmines and James Stimson (1989), and Stuart Elaine MacDonald and George Rabinowitz (1987). In this chapter, I draw on the work of these and other scholars to map theoretically the religious and cultural change that has occurred in party politics over the last thirty years.

The chapter takes shape in three steps. First, I describe the relationship between social cleavages, such as the contemporary religious cleavage, and political issues and the qualities necessary for those issues to produce significant partisan change. Second, I discuss the necessary role of strategic politicians within the parties in creating partisan differences on powerful new political issues such as abortion, school prayer, and homosexual rights. Finally, I describe the process through which party differences on the new issues grow and are translated into a division of the parties' electoral coalitions along the lines of the social cleavage giving rise to those issues.

THE ROLE OF POLITICAL ISSUES IN THE PARTISAN CHANGE PROCESS

Most of the literature on party systems and partisan change considers changes in the social group composition of the parties (Key 1955, 1959; Lipset and Rokkan 1967; Burnham 1970; Ladd with Hadley 1975; Petrocik 1981, 1998; Sundquist 1983). In other words, it examines changes associated with what Allardt and Pesonen (1967) term "structural" cleavages—cleavages such as religion, ethnicity, geography, and language that differentiate social groups on something other than purely political grounds—as opposed to strictly political or ideological, "nonstructural" divisions. This study also focuses on the division of the political parties along the lines of a structural cleavage. It examines the partisan consequences not just of attitudes toward particular political issues, but of real differences in religious affiliation, belief, and commitment.

As figure 1.1 shows, for a structural cleavage to create change in the party system, it must be associated with a genuine *political* issue or set of issues (step 2). Since the purpose of a political party is to organize individuals and interests in order to gain control of the government (Downs 1957), structural cleavages must give rise to grievances that people look to the government to redress. A cleavage may produce a very intense conflict between those on its two sides, but if the participants seek a non-political solution to the conflict—whether it be a private solution, a solution driven by changes in culture or morality, or a solution driven by the economic market—it should not affect the political parties.

The literature on partisan change identifies four major transformations of American party politics prior to the 1970s: the upheavals of the 1850s and 1860s through which the Republican party replaced the Whig party as one of the two major parties; the period of the 1890s during which the Democratic party established itself as the party of farmers and laborers in the South and West, the Republican party became the party of industrial interests in the Northeast and Midwest, and the Republicans built a national majority; the elections of the 1930s, in which the Democratic party built a majority coalition of lower-status whites and racial, ethnic, and religious minorities, leaving the Republicans with a coalition of upper-status, nonsouthern white Protestants; and the decade of the 1960s, during which African-Americans became almost unanimously Democratic and white southerners began to leave their historic Democratic party home.

All four of these periods were associated with important structural cleavages in American society: the first with a sectional cleavage, the second with a sectional cleavage combined with an occupational and class cleavage, the third with an economic and class cleavage, and the fourth with a racial cleavage. However, the changes in party politics during these eras did not occur simply because of the depth of the societal fissures that were present. They occurred because the structural cleavages gave rise to powerful new political issues, issues that involved a clear question about what the government should do. In the 1850s, the question was, What should the government do about slavery? In the 1890s, What should the government do about the economic hardships faced by farmers and about the grievances raised by them through the Populist movement? In the 1930s, What should government do about the Great Depression, and more generally the problem of poverty? And in the 1960s, What should government do to ensure civil rights for the black residents of the South? (Sundquist 1983; Carmines and Stimson 1989).

Necessary Characteristics

Of course, even if a social cleavage is associated with a set of political issues, it will not necessarily lead citizens to reshape their political behavior and partisan ties. To produce a transformation of party politics, the issues must meet four key requirements: the conflict over the issues has to be both broad and deep, the issues must be on the political agenda for a relatively long time, the issues have to have the capacity to provoke resistance, and the new conflict must cut across the existing lines of party cleavage (Schattschneider 1960; Sundquist 1983; Carmines and Stimson 1989; Carmines 1991).

Breadth and Depth

For an issue to produce significant change in party politics, the conflict over it must be both broad and deep; a large number of people must feel strongly about it (Sundquist 1983; Schattschneider 1960). Unless individuals feel somewhat passionately about the issue—unless they have not only intellectual orientations but also emotional orientations toward it—they will not rethink their party loyalties on the basis of their positions on it, nor will they rethink their decisions on whether or not to be active in a political party and which party to be active in because of it.

What types of issues are likely to arouse such intense feelings in a large number of citizens? Carmines and Stimson's (1980, 1989) answer is "easy" issues: highly emotional issues that can be responded to at a "gut" level without a base of factual knowledge or contextual understanding. Given the low levels of political information and attentiveness of most Americans, it is only easy issues that will capture enough attention and produce enough strong attitudes to produce a large-scale mass response. "Hard" issues—issues such as federal communications policy, environmental regulations, or monetary policy that require political so-phistication and technical knowledge for decision making—are not likely to capture the attention of enough of the mass public for a long enough period of time to lead to any measure of partisan change. Sundquist (1983) concurs by arguing that the issues most likely to produce partisan trans-formations are issues that have a strong moral component: issues that are viewed by citizens in good-versus-evil terms.

There is no doubt that some issues are inherently "easier" than oth-ers. Abortion and affirmative action are easier to understand and arouse stronger emotions than interstate commerce laws. However, it is entirely possible that politicians can turn hard issues into easy issues by framing them in highly simplistic, emotional terms. For example, the primary is-sue in the 1896 election—the question of whether silver should be used as currency and the ratio at which it should be valued relative to gold—could hardly be described as inherently easy. However, when the leaders of the Populist party and the two major parties used this issue as an emo-tional symbol of a larger battle between East and West and financiers and farmers, it became an easy issue and led to what political scientists con-sider to be one of the major partisan realignments in American history (Durden 1965; Sundquist 1983). Thus, the question is not just whether the issue is inherently easy, but also whether it is infused with moral over-tones and framed in a simple manner by political elites.

Life Span

Many issues that capture the attention of and arouse passionate feelings in large portions of the electorate arise during the course of a given po-litical campaign but do not create durable partisan change. The Water-gate crisis and Gerald Ford's pardon of Richard Nixon in 1974, the Iran hostage crisis in 1980, the pledge of allegiance issue and Massachusetts's furlough program in 1988, Bill Clinton's draft record in 1992, and his impeachment over an affair with a White House intern in 1998 are re-cent examples. These issues may lead voters to defect from their partisan ties, and they may influence election outcomes. However, because they are linked to particular candidates and leaders or are quickly resolved, they are not salient for a long enough period to lead individuals to re-shape their long-term party identifications and decisions on party ac-tivism. To produce a significant change in party politics, an issue must not only arouse strong feelings among a large number of people but also do so over a series of several elections (Carmines and Stimson 1989; Car-mines 1991; Sundquist 1983).

Capacity to Provoke Resistance

Many issues that are easily understood and framed in highly emotional terms do not effect any noticeable change in the party system because they are not the basis of partisan conflicts; the parties do not take distinct stands on them. A necessary, though not sufficient, precondition for the parties' taking distinct stands on an issue is that the issue represent a real conflict, that there be large numbers of people on both sides of the issue (Sundquist 1983; Schattschneider 1960). Issues such as prohibiting flag burning, requiring children to say the pledge of allegiance, fighting drug use, and reducing crime rates arouse intense emotions in large numbers of Americans. However, they do not lead to change in the party system because the vast majority of citizens are in favor of such proposals. The parties and their candidates thus have no incentives to take different positions on the issues, and citizens then have no reason to rethink their partisan attachments.

It is true that political elites—government officials, political candidates, party leaders—play an important role in shaping public opinion and thus in creating polarization in the mass public. As John Zaller (1992) demonstrates, when elites from different parties or from different ideological camps take clearly different stands on an issue, the result is often a "polarization effect," in which the opinions of individuals—particularly the most politically attentive individuals—who share the partisan or ideological predispositions of one group of elites move toward its position, while the individuals who share the predispositions of the other group of elites move toward *its* position. So there is the possibility that political elites might create polarization on an issue on which most citizens agree. However, if public sentiment is strongly on one side of an issue, it is very likely that most political candidates and leaders will be on that side as well. In this case, the elite consensus should create what Zaller terms a "mainstream effect," in which public opinion moves toward the elites' shared position, and the effect of elite position-taking is to move the public toward even greater support for the majority position.

Cuts Across Existing Lines of Partisan Cleavage

There are many conflicts that arouse strong feelings among a large number of people but do not create a substantial change in the party system. They do not foster partisan change because they reinforce the existing party coalitions; they divide the electorate along the same lines as the issues that produced the current partisan alignment. In recent years, for example, new issues such as reform of the welfare system and government provision of health care have captured the attention of the American public and have been the source of highly emotional political debates. These issues may well have had a noticeable effect on voting behavior and led to some alteration in individuals' party ties. However, they have not led to a fundamental restructuring of the philosophical and social bases of the party coalitions because they involve the same basic question as the New Deal issues that emerged in the 1930s—the proper role of government in providing for the welfare of its citizens—and divide the electorate along basically the same class-based lines. To produce a significant change in the social composition of the parties' coalitions, an issue must cut across the existing lines of partisan cleavage, dividing voters along social and ideological lines that are different from those of the current alignment (Schattschneider 1960; Sundquist 1983; MacDonald and Rabinowitz 1987; Carmines and Stimson 1989; Carmines 1991).

THE RELIGIOUS–CULTURAL CLEAVAGE AND ITS RELATED ISSUES

The contemporary cultural conflict is a powerful and highly emotional struggle. However, that alone does not explain why it has produced a division in party politics, leading secularists and religious modernists into the Democratic party and religious traditionalists into the Republican party. A large part of the explanation is that the cultural cleavage has given rise to powerful new issues, all involving questions about proper government action. Decisions by the Supreme Court and changes in the culture and the media in the 1960s and the 1970s produced issues such as the legality of abortion, whether constitutional provisions should be extended to protect the rights of homosexuals and the distribution of pornography, whether prayer should be allowed in the public schools, and whether the Constitution should be amended to guarantee the equality of women. These are political issues that large numbers of citizens feel strongly about, that have been on the political agenda for a fairly long time, that have aroused the passions of individuals with both traditionalist and modernist perspectives, and that cut across the preexisting lines of party cleavage.

Breadth, Depth, and Life Span

Because they tap deep-seated moral and religious values, issues such as abortion, homosexual rights, women's rights, and school prayer tend to produce highly emotional responses and to be viewed in terms of good versus evil. They clearly fit the mold of Carmines and Stimson's "easy" issues. Then, they are made even easier by the dualistic, highly emotional, and symbol-laden way in which political activists and elites present them to the public (Hunter 1994). The fact that abortion, a fairly complex issue about which many people have rather ambivalent feelings, is nearly always presented as a pro-life versus pro-choice dichotomy is just one illustration. Hunter (1994: 50–60) presents numerous other examples of such distorting, overly impassioned rhetoric. For instance, pro-choice activists have used slogans like "keep your rosaries off our ovaries," while pro-life proponents rally around slogans such as "abortion is murder." The pro-choice side has labeled the pro-life side as "antifemale bigots of the religious right," while pro-lifers have labeled pro-choicers as "radical feminists of the proabortion lobby." The pro-choice forces argue that "antichoice extremists want to silence discussion and take away all of our choices, one by one," while pro-lifers contend that "when pro-choice organizations talk about 'unwanted' children, they presume that they have a right to dispose of unwanted people any way they wish."

This overheated rhetoric and the moral and religious underpinnings of the issues have produced intense feelings in a large number of individuals. As evidence, consider the fact that attitudes on moral and cultural issues are considerably more stable over time (in panel surveys) than attitudes toward social welfare and foreign policy issues and are almost as stable as long-term ideological and partisan identifications (Converse and Markus 1979). More anecdotally, actions such as the shooting of doctors who perform abortions, the bombing of abortion clinics, and the recent slayings of admitted homosexuals are indications of the intense emotions these issues arouse. To be sure, these actions are quite rare, but the fact that a few people are willing to take the lives of others and risk significant jail time, or even their own lives, because of their views on cultural issues suggests just how strongly many people feel about them. And the willingness to take considerable risks on behalf of one's stands is not restricted to the cultural right. Individuals who protest the public expression of religious faith in the schools and public places in their communities and individuals who identify themselves as homosexuals and speak out in favor of homosexual rights risk social ostracization and perhaps violent action against themselves.

Moreover, these issues have been an important part of the political scene for nearly three decades in the case of abortion and even longer in the case of women's rights and prayer in the public schools. Over that

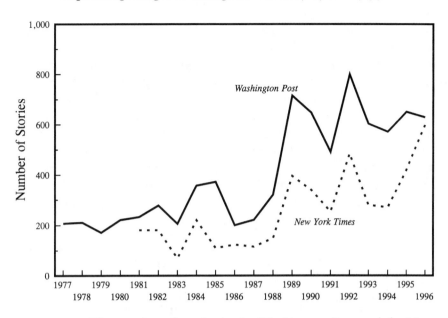

FIGURE 1.2. The number of stories in the *Washington Post* and the *New York Times* concerning cultural issues, 1977–1996
Note: The number is the total number of stories on abortion, homosexual rights, and school prayer.
Source: LEXIS-NEXIS Academic Universe

period, the salience of moral and cultural matters appears to have increased. In chapter 6 of this book, I use public opinion surveys to show that the importance of these issues in the mass electorate has increased. Meanwhile, as figure 1.2 shows, the attention given to cultural issues by two major national newspapers—the *New York Times* and the *Washington Post*—has increased considerably. The focus of these two newspapers on the issues of abortion, homosexual rights, and school prayer was much greater in the 1990s than it was in the late 1970s and 1980s.[2]

Capacity to Provoke Resistance

Part of the reason why the traditionalist–modernist cleavage that emerged in American religion at the beginning of the twentieth century did not have an effect on partisan politics until much later is that, for fifty or sixty years afterward, most citizens remained on one side of the divide: the traditionalist side. However, the growing numbers and cultural influence of secularists and religious liberals in the 1960s and 1970s not only meant that there were significant numbers of people on both sides of the cultural cleavage, but also forced those on the conservative side, in particular evangelical Protestants, to come out of political hiding and mobilize themselves for cultural and political battle. The potential for the contemporary religious cleavage to reshape party politics may have increased even further as a result of polarizing trends in American religion, in particular the growth in secularism and conservative Protestantism together with the declining membership of moderate and liberal Protestant churches (Sherkat and Ellison 1999). These religious developments may well be increasing the number of troops for battle in the contemporary cultural conflict, thereby enhancing its potential impact on the party system.

Cuts Across Existing Lines of Partisan Cleavage

The issues associated with the traditionalist–modernist religious cleavage cut directly across the class-based cleavage that has shaped party politics for more than sixty years. As table 1.1 shows, higher-income individuals are much more conservative than lower-income individuals on a classic social welfare issue—government's responsibility to provide citizens with jobs and a good standard of living—and it is these attitudes that traditionally have aligned upper-status voters with the Republican party and lower-status voters with the Democratic party. However, just the opposite is true for cultural and theological issues. Lower-income citizens are much more likely than their more affluent counterparts to believe that the Bible is literally true, while individuals in the higher-income brackets are considerably more likely than individuals of lesser means to support unrestricted abortion rights. The table also shows that there is virtually no relationship between one's attitude on government's social welfare role and one's view of the Bible or abortion attitude. Conservative cultural stands by the Republican party and liberal cultural stands by the Democratic party clearly have the potential to create significant changes in their activist bases and electoral coalitions.

STRATEGIC POLITICIANS AS CATALYSTS FOR PARTY POLARIZATION

Even if a set of political issues meets these four requirements, it will not lead to a restructuring of the parties' electoral coalitions along the lines

TABLE 1.1

The relationship between income and social welfare attitude, view
of the Bible, and abortion attitude, and the relationship between social
welfare attitude and view of the Bible and abortion attitude

Variable	Income			Social Welfare Attitude[a]		
	Low	Middle	High	Liberal	Moderate	Conservative
Government responsibility to provide jobs/standard of living						
Government's responsibility	36.2	25.0	18.2			
Neutral	23.6	21.7	19.5			
Individual responsibility	40.3	53.3	62.4			
View of the Bible						
Not the Word of God	13.0	13.8	18.0	18.7	14.8	13.5
Word of God, but not literal	41.1	49.2	57.9	41.7	56.5	51.0
Literally true	45.9	37.0	24.2	39.7	28.7	35.5
Abortion						
Never allow	15.6	12.7	8.6	13.0	7.9	11.6
Allow when rape/ incest/danger to life	32.7	29.2	24.6	24.5	26.4	32.7
Allow when clear need	16.0	13.9	18.4	15.5	18.5	15.8
Always allow	35.6	44.2	48.5	47.0	47.3	39.9

Source: 1996 National Election Study.

[a]Social welfare attitude is response to the question on government responsibility to provide jobs.
Liberals are respondents who said it is government's responsibility, moderates are respondents who
were neutral, and conservatives are respondents who said it was the responsibility of the individual.

Data are given in percentages.

of the social cleavage from which it arose if the parties do not take distinct stands on it. If the two parties both straddle the issues, staking out centrist positions, or if they both take noncentrist but similar positions, there will be no reason for citizens to rethink their party loyalties.

However, if the new issues reflect a genuine societal conflict and arouse strong emotions in large numbers of people, as the cultural issues do, is it not inevitable that the parties will take polarized stands on them? I, and some other students of partisan change, believe the answer is no. Unless a new set of issues appeals to the strategic incentives of political actors within the party system (step 3 in figure 1.1)—in other words, unless party leaders, candidates, or other politicians see a potential for the new issues to enhance their strategic political positions—the parties will not take distinct stands on the issues and the issues will not effect partisan change (Schattschneider 1960; Riker 1982; Carmines and Stimson 1989).

Of course, as James Sundquist argues, the American political parties are far too large and loosely organized to be "beings with calculating minds" (1983: 328) who take extreme stands on new issues only if this is rational or in their best strategic interests. That might be true of highly centralized, closed parties in which party decisions such as nominations and the content of party platforms are made by a small number of leaders with no public participation. And the American parties of the nineteenth century, while very decentralized because of the federal structure of government, did not involve the general public in their internal decisions. Presidential candidates were selected by congressional party caucuses in the early years of the republic. After the 1830s, they were chosen in national party conventions by delegates who were handpicked by state and local party leaders and thus were obliged to carry out the wishes of those party "bosses."

However, the contemporary American parties are far from closed. The Progressive reforms of the early twentieth century brought with them the direct primary, which gave ordinary party identifiers a role in the selection of party candidates and thus in the definition of party policy. The McGovern-Fraser reforms of the Democratic party's nomination process in the early 1970s, and the Republican party's subsequent adherence to the same general principles, went a step further and took candidate selection almost entirely out of the hands of party leaders and gave it to the politically active citizens who participate in party primaries and caucuses. Thus, the parties today are "extraordinarily open to participation by any group that seeks to use a party for its purposes" (Sundquist 1983: 328).

Maybe strategic party politicians who champion extreme stands on new issues are not necessary for the parties to take polarized positions on them. The parties may take distinct stands on the new issues simply because large, impassioned groups develop on opposite sides of the issues (step 2 in figure 1.1), and those groups enter and gain influence within the parties by taking advantage of the opportunities for ordinary citizens to participate in their internal decision making—in primaries, caucuses, and conventions. In short, if the group on one side of the issues becomes involved in the primaries, caucuses, and conventions of one party, and the group on the other side of the issues becomes involved in the primaries, caucuses, and conventions of the other party (step 4), then the groups, if they are big enough and active enough, simply can force the parties to take polarized stands on the issues (step 5). As Sundquist asserts, "When a society polarizes, so do the parties" (1983: 328).

However, there are two reasons to expect that the emergence of partisan cleavages on new issues does depend on party politicians having strategic incentives to espouse noncentrist views on them. First, strategic political leaders often play an important role in developing new issues (Riker 1982), and attention to new issues by politicians generally increases the salience of those issues in the mass public (Schattschneider 1960; Carmines and Stimson 1989). Moreover, polarized stands by political leaders may contribute to the polarization of public opinion on an issue (Zaller 1992).

Second, the fact that the parties are open to new groups does not necessarily mean that the groups will come into the parties. These groups have a range of options besides involvement in one of the two major parties for the political expression of their views. They might get involved in interest group politics, raising money from people who hold similar views and using that money and their numerical strength to put pressure on elected officials to support their positions. Or, rather than trying to fight the established leaders of one of the two major parties, whose incentives are generally to downplay and take a moderate course on powerful, new issues (Sundquist 1983; Carmines 1991), insurgent groups may find the option of forming a new party focused specifically on the new issues to be more appealing.[3]

Thus, for a group with extreme positions on a new set of issues to choose one of the two major parties as their political vehicle, the group must have some reason to believe either that one of the parties currently represents its views, or that one of the parties may come to represent these views.[4] That reason generally takes the form of a candidate or some other politician within the party appealing to the group's ideological sensibilities. So, even in a very permeable party system, societal polarization does not inevitably produce party polarization. Instead, the large groups that have formed on the contrasting sides of a new issue (step 2 in figure 1.1) must be attracted into the opposing parties by party politicians who, for strategic and other reasons, promote the new issues and take noncentrist stands on them (step 3). Once they become active in the parties (step 4), the polarized groups can then push the parties toward distinct stands on the issues (step 5).

Who Will Promote the New Issues?

The types of issues just described—issues that are salient to large numbers of people, arouse strong emotions, relate to a real conflict in society, and cut across the existing lines of partisan cleavage—should be intriguing to strategic politicians. As Schattschneider contends, "The effort in all political struggle is to exploit cracks in the opposition while attempting to consolidate one's own side" (1960: 67). Since these issues may well accomplish the first goal, they have great potential to change the political balance of power or perhaps to strengthen further the position of those currently in power.

Of course, the issues also carry substantial risks. If they have the potential to split your opponent's coalition, then they also may shatter your own. Who is willing to take that risk? The logical answer is political "losers." Existing political alignments are based on a particular set of issues, and these issues invariably favor some political groups over others. It is the political actors who are disadvantaged by the current alignment (the political losers) who have incentives to promote new issues in an attempt to shift the political balance of power (Schattschneider 1960; Riker 1982; Carmines and Stimson 1989).

Research on partisan change generally denotes members of the minority party as political losers and members of the majority party as political winners. The majority party's coalition is held together by the issues of the current alignment, so that party wishes to maintain the preeminence of those issues and tries to deemphasize the new issues. The minority party has less to lose and more to gain from powerful new issues. These issues may split the majority coalition and propel the current minority to majority status. At worst, they also may split the minority party coalition and force it to retain its current minority status. It is, thus, minority party politicians who champion new sets of issues that cut across existing lines of partisan cleavage. For example, Riker (1982) credits Whig party politicians, attempting to divide the northern and southern wings of the majority Democratic party, with pushing the slavery issue to a dominant position on the political agenda of the 1840s and 1850s. Carmines and Stimson (1989) assert that the minority Republican party abandoned its traditional support for civil rights and adopted a stance of racial conservatism in 1964 for partly strategic reasons. Conservative racial stands would allow the GOP to distinguish itself from the Democrats on civil rights, thus splitting the Democrats' majority coalition of African-Americans, southern whites, and working-class northern whites. The notion that minority parties are more likely than majority parties to champion divisive new issues is an appealing one. After all, a large part of the reason that people are involved in party politics is to win. Winning brings not only the opportunity to advance one's ideological agenda, but also material opportunities, such as patronage and closer government contacts, and social opportunities, such as attending inaugurals and fraternizing with people in power.[5] If one's party is already winning, why would one wish to call attention to powerful new issues that may jeopardize those opportunities?

On the other hand, just because an individual politician's party is winning politically does not necessarily mean that he or she is winning politically. We can equate the successes and failures of a party with those of its members if we assume that the parties are relatively unified "teams" of political actors who share a common set of political goals. Then, it is clearly in the interest of all of the members of the winning team, the majority party, to maintain the focus on the agenda of the current alignment and in the interest of all of the members of the losing team, the minority party, to shift the agenda to a new set of issues. Such an assumption, however, may be valid only in a closed party system and, again, the contemporary American parties are extraordinarily open. Thus, they are not unified teams but collections of groups and individuals competing for control. To again quote Sundquist, "An American party should be thought of not as a rational organism with some kind of collective brain making coherent strategic judgements, but as a terrain to be fought over" (1983: 328).

As with any competition, the struggle for control of a political party produces winners and losers. That means that *political losers exist not only between but also within the parties.* Within either party, there may be losing factions: groups who prefer candidates other than the ones whom the party nominates, and policy options other than the ones the party advocates. Although being a member of a losing faction within the majority may entail more material and professional benefits than being a member of any faction of the minority party, it may bring few ideological benefits. In fact, the policies imposed by the controlling faction of the majority party may be almost as repugnant to a losing faction within that party as they are to members of the minority party. Therefore, it may be in the interest not only of the minority party but also of losing factions in both parties to interject into party politics new issues that have the potential to disrupt the existing political balance.

The participatory nominating process in contemporary American politics gives rise to a third group of strategic politicians with incentives to exploit powerful new issues: candidate entrepreneurs seeking a personal base of support. The primary-centered nominating process, together with the decline of mass-based party machines, increases in the sophistication of campaign technologies, changes in campaign finance, and the pervasive political role of television, has led to a new era of candidate-centered politics (Wattenberg 1991). In this era, candidates no longer can stand simply on the parties' traditional policy positions and rely on the support of traditional party followings. Rather, they must develop their own ideological identities and independent bases of support.

In most contemporary nomination campaigns, particularly when the incumbent president is from the other party or is not seeking reelection, there are multiple candidates seeking to become a party's standard-bearer. Most of these candidates have very similar stands on the issues that traditionally have separated the two parties, and all are competing for the support of the voters and activists who traditionally have supported their party. In this situation, an effective strategy, particularly for candidates who are less known or less popular with the traditional party following, may be to raise new issues that attract new constituencies into the nominating process. Here, the distinctions between the minority party and the majority party as potential champions of new issues become much less relevant. Candidates from both parties want their party to win elections and would like their party to be in a long-term majority position. Far more proximate, however, is the goal of defeating their fellow partisans for the party's nomination. If a powerful new issue will help them do that, candidates from either party will raise it.

In sum, there are three types of political actors within the contemporary American parties who may have strategic incentives to emphasize and espouse strong positions on new issues: members of the minority party, members of losing factions within both parties, and candidates seeking a support base within an open nominating process. If any of these strategic politicians do champion an extreme position on the new issues, they may attract new activists who share that position into the party system, thus pushing the parties toward distinct stands on the issues.

STRATEGIC POLITICIANS AND THE RELIGIOUS–CULTURAL CONFLICT

This expanded notion of the incentives of strategic politicians helps to explain the emergence of the contemporary cultural issues into partisan politics because it was the majority party that first took noncentrist stands on these matters. Prior to the late 1960s, there was something of a cultural consensus in the party system. Both parties were dominated by members of mainline religions, Catholics and Jews in the Democratic party and mainline Protestants in the GOP (Axelrod 1972; Carmines and Layman 1997). Neither party contained a large number of secularists (Carmines and Layman 1997) nor showed many signs of cultural or moral progressivism. As Alan Wolfe argues, even the Democrats' liberal redistributive programs were imbued with a sense of moral traditionalism: "New Deal programs often assumed a two-parent family and a family wage" (1994: 105). Although the parties generally were committed to traditional values, religious orthodoxy did not play a large role in either party, as evangelical Protestants remained largely apolitical (Oldfield 1996).

It was the majority Democrats, not the minority Republicans, who were the first party to disrupt this cultural harmony, and the break came in 1972. It was in 1972 that the Democratic party nominated George McGovern, a liberal senator from South Dakota who was a staunch opponent of the Vietnam War, supported amnesty for draft evaders, favored reduced penalties for marijuana use, and opposed calls for a national ban on abortion (White 1973). McGovern's embracing of New Politics themes won him the overwhelming support of the young cultural liberals, particularly on college campuses, who had become active in the antiwar movement, and that support won the New Left a conspicuous and influential role at the party's 1972 national convention. Describing the prominent place at the convention of abortion rights and homosexual rights activists in *The Making of the President 1972*, political journalist Theodore White writes, "One could . . . watch the parade of women across the podium. The women were forcing into politics matters never before publicly discussed at a national convention—for example, the laws of sex. . . . These women at the podium, in the presence of the nation, now insisted they be allowed to control the fruit of their bodies. . . . Then came homosexuals to the microphone and camera, men openly demanding before the nation that the coupling of males be accepted not furtively, but as a natural and legal right" (1973: 180).

In addition to these symbolic gestures, the secularists and cultural liberals had considerable influence on the stands taken in the 1972 Democratic platform (Kirkpatrick 1976). It asserted the party's strong support for the Equal Rights Amendment and tolerance for alternative lifestyles and, in a subsection entitled "The Right to be Different," held that

"Americans should be free to make their own choice of lifestyles and private habits without being subject to discrimination or prosecution." Although ultimately not included in the platform, there was strong support at the convention for a pro-abortion plank proposed by feminist organizations. So, although recent accounts of cultural politics have focused principally on the Republican party, the Democratic party made a clear move to the cultural left several years before the Christian Right first became associated with the GOP.

Why would the Democratic party, a majority party whose coalition was based on New Deal–era social welfare issues and included culturally conservative groups such as Catholics and southern whites, take the lead in advancing highly liberal stands on the moral and social issues? Well, first of all, the established leadership of the Democratic party clearly did not decide to champion cultural liberalism. In fact, it resented the influence of the culturally liberal New Left within the party, a sentiment conveyed in 1972 by Al Barkan, director of the Committee on Political Education (COPE), the political arm of the American Federation of Labor and Congress of Industrial Organizations (AFL/CIO), when he said, "We aren't going to let these Harvard-Berkeley Camelots take over our party" (quoted in White 1973: 38).

Instead, it was individual presidential candidates such as Eugene McCarthy and especially George McGovern who decided to take liberal stands on the New Politics issues, thereby mobilizing large numbers of cultural liberals into their presidential campaigns and thus into the party. There is no doubt that ideological conviction played a key role in these decisions, but one also can make a compelling case that these candidates, although in the majority party, were political losers and thus had strategic incentives to advance liberal cultural views.

For example, McGovern, unlike Edmund Muskie and, particularly, Hubert Humphrey—his two principal opponents for the 1972 Democratic nomination—did not have, as a senator from South Dakota and someone clearly associated with the pro-reform elements in the party, the support of the dominant faction of the party: its urban, blue-collar, labor-union wing. So to win the nomination he had to appeal to a constituency other than the traditional Democratic base, and the antiwar campus radicals and New Left activists were an attractive possibility. These groups had become very active politically and, although they had largely avoided party politics, they had demonstrated a sympathy for outsider candidacies with their support for McCarthy and Robert Kennedy in the 1968 Democratic campaign.

Moreover, these young activists would play a much more important role in the Democratic nomination process in 1972 than they had in 1968 because of the reforms that McGovern himself played the lead role in authoring. The McGovern-Fraser reforms not only made the nominating process more open and much less dominated by party leaders, but also mandated that women, blacks, and young people be represented proportionately to their numerical strength in states, thus ensuring greater representation of New Left, women's rights, and civil rights advocates.

McGovern's strong antiwar record and well-publicized battles with the Democratic establishment certainly had the potential to attract New Left support, but to fully realize that potential, the candidate and his advisers realized that he would have to appeal also to the New Left's liberal sensibilities on cultural issues (Anson 1972; White 1973; Miller and Levitin 1984). As White notes,

> The attack on the establishment . . . was the central cultural concept of the McGovern campaign. It came, however, with a corona of less important but more vivid cultural issues that made him one of the most luminous figures in the orthodoxy of the [New Left] Movement. In part, the vivid quality of his lesser issues was forced on him by his enemies, in part by his own strategy. He had had to recruit his army and its troops from the most extreme of the peace groups and the young of the campus—and if their cultural values were not majority cultural values, nonetheless tactic demanded he pursue them. . . . He was for amnesty—and on the campus, students shrilled with delight. He felt, and specifically stated, that abortion was a matter best left to state governments—but he left no doubt that he, personally, was for it. . . . He was for civilizing the extravagant penalties exacted in many states for the use of marijuana. (1973: 115)

The influence of secularism and cultural liberalism within the Democratic party in the 1970s certainly made the Republican party a more attractive political option for religious conservatives, particularly the traditionally Democratic evangelical Protestants. However, the mobilization of evangelicals into the Republican party was far from inevitable. The presidential nomination of born-again Christian Jimmy Carter in 1976 allowed the Democrats to move back toward the cultural center and attracted considerable support from conservative Protestants (Oldfield 1996). Moreover, evangelicals had long had strong apolitical tendencies, and the initial efforts of organizations such as the Moral Majority and the Religious Roundtable to mobilize conservative Christians into politics were met with suspicion and distaste by a large proportion of the evangelical clergy and laity (Guth 1983; Shupe and Stacey 1983; Guth et al. 1997). It was only through painstaking organizational efforts and large commitments of financial resources that the Christian Right was able to attract a large number of conservative Protestants into Republican party politics.

The formation of the early organizations of the Christian Right was not a venture undertaken independently by evangelical clergy. Rather, conservative religious leaders such as Jerry Falwell, Pat Robertson, and Ed McAteer were strongly encouraged and actively assisted in the formation of evangelical political groups by the leaders and operatives of the highly conservative secular political movement known as the New Right. New Right leaders such as Richard Viguerie, Paul Weyrich, and Howard Phillips played a critical role in convincing evangelical religious leaders to become involved in politics (Himmelstein 1983; Reichley 1987; Oldfield 1996). As Viguerie notes, "[Weyrich] and Howard Phillips spent countless hours with electronic ministers like Jerry Falwell, James Robison, and Pat Robertson, urging them to get involved in conservative politics" (1980: 56). Moreover, the eventual mobilization of religious conservatives into the Republican party was greatly assisted by Ronald Reagan's highly conservative rhetoric on cultural issues such as abortion, school prayer, and the Equal Rights Amendment in his 1980 campaign and during his eight-year presidency (Miller and Wattenberg 1984; Oldfield 1996).

Why would conservative Republican politicians enthusiastically court evangelical activists and voters through a culturally conservative issue agenda? Again, political principle surely played a role, but strategic considerations should not be discounted. The GOP was clearly the minority party in the late 1970s. It had reason for optimism in the 1960s and early 1970s with two presidential victories and the apparent break in the Democratic party's stranglehold on the South (cf. Phillips 1969). Even then, however, the Republicans were still a distinct minority in Congress, far more voters identified with the Democrats than with the Republicans, and the Democrats maintained a strong advantage in subpresidential elections in the former Confederacy (Sundquist 1983; Lamis 1988). By the late 1970s, the political winds seemed to have shifted away from the GOP. Watergate brought the party's national-level ascent to a screeching halt and contributed to an overwhelming congressional victory for the Democrats in 1974. Jimmy Carter's election in 1976 and particularly his strong showing in the southern states gave the Democrats hope for a return of the solid South, a return that undoubtedly would destroy the presidential majority the Republicans had built in 1968 and 1972. In sum, Republican leaders had reason to try anything that might restructure the political situation of the late 1970s. As one party official stated in the early 1980s, "When you are as distinct a minority as we are, you welcome anything short of the National Order of Child Molesters" (quoted in Guth 1983: 36).

Cultural conservatism had the potential to be that disruptive force. It appealed to evangelical Christians, a large and growing bloc of voters who had traditional ties to the Democratic party but, because of their apolitical tendencies, fit more into the mold of unattached voters. And since the late 1960s, observers had noted the potential of social issues to divide the Democratic coalition (Scammon and Wattenberg 1970; Phillips 1969). When compared to the Democrats' largely liberal positions, conservative stands on issues such as abortion, women's rights, and homosexual rights might appeal to morally traditional groups such as working-class whites, Catholics, and even African-Americans that represented the core of the Democratic electoral coalition. Cultural conservatism also would reenforce the appeal that the GOP's conservative stands on racial issues had for southern whites disillusioned with the Democratic party. Of course, these stands also had the potential to alienate the party's upper-status core of support. However, as the long-term minority party, the Republicans may have been willing to take that risk.

In addition to the Republicans' disadvantage in interparty competition, the conservative wing of the GOP had been, to a large extent, a loser in intraparty competition. The Republicans' moderate-liberal wing had been dominant for most of the years from 1940 to the mid-1970s (Rae 1989). The party had nominated presidential candidates from this faction in all the election years of the 1940s and 1950s. The conservative wing gained control in 1964 in securing the nomination of Barry Goldwater, and Richard Nixon made overtures to conservatives in the 1968 and 1972 campaigns. However, many of Nixon's policies won praise from the liberal-Republican Ripon Society, and his successor, Gerald Ford, was clearly a moderate (Rae 1989). To gain firm control of the party, conservatives needed to bring a new constituency into Republican politics that would provide consistent support for conservative candidates and policies. Evangelical Christians were a large, unattached constituency, and cultural conservatism provided a way to draw them into the GOP. The strategic attraction of social and moral issues for conservative Republicans was evidenced by Paul Weyrich's statement in 1980: "The New

Right is looking for issues that people care about and social issues, at least for the present, fit the bill" (quoted in Reichley 1987: 79). In short, the issues associated with the contemporary religious cleavage held a strong strategic attraction to the minority party as well as to losing factions and politicians within both political parties.

FROM ELITE CHANGE TO MASS CHANGE: THE RELIGIOUS POLARIZATION OF THE PARTIES' COALITIONS

By the 1980 election, the parties had taken one of the crucial steps in the partisan change process: They had taken distinct stands on the highly emotional, cross-cutting issues of the contemporary religious and cultural cleavage. Strategic politicians such as George McGovern in the Democratic party, and Ronald Reagan and the political leaders of the New Right in the Republican party, had championed clearly liberal and conservative stands, respectively, on the cultural issues. These positions attracted new groups of activists into Democratic and Republican party politics, and the success of the McGovern and Reagan campaigns permitted those activists a considerable amount of influence within the two parties. As culturally liberal as the 1972 Democratic platform had been, the 1980 Republican platform was nearly as, if not more, culturally conservative. It called for constitutional amendments to ban abortion and to "restore the right of individuals to participate in voluntary, nondenominational prayer in schools." Although President Carter was less culturally liberal than McGovern, the influence of cultural liberalism in the Democratic party in 1980 remained strong enough that the platform affirmed the Democrats' strong support for the Equal Rights Amendment, "recognize[d] reproductive freedom as a fundamental human right," and noted their opposition to restricting federal funding of abortions for poor women.

Thus, the question faced by the political party system in 1980 was, would this gap in the parties' cultural stands lead to a substantial change in the nature of the parties' coalitions in the mass electorate? Most models of issue-driven partisan change do view polarization on a new set of issues at the elite levels of party politics—for example, in the stands of party nominees, in the voting records of the parties' members of Congress, or in the positions taken in party platforms—as the catalyst for the polarization of the mass-party coalitions along the same lines (Carmines and Stimson 1989; Carmines 1991; MacDonald and Rabinowitz 1987;

Sundquist 1983). However, the emergence of elite-level differences on an issue does not lead inevitably to mass-level polarization. The parties' elites take distinct stands on a large number of issues, but most of these issues "most of the time lie dormant, stirring interest only in those especially informed and affected. They lend no weight to the color, tone, and meaning of partisan debate. They neither define party systems nor undergird party alignments" (Carmines and Stimson 1989: 159). It is the very rare issue that produces a long-term transformation in the parties' mass coalitions.

So what is required for elite-level party polarization on new issues (step 5 in figure 1.1) to produce lasting change in the parties' mass coalitions (step 8)? As step 7 in figure 1.1 points out, two things are necessary. First, the electorate's image of the parties has to change. Before they will reshape their party loyalties on the basis of the new issues, citizens must become aware that the parties have clear stands on the issues and that there is a difference between those stands (Carmines and Stimson 1989). Second, the new issues must alter citizens' feelings about the parties. As Carmines and Stimson put it, the "public must not only perceive a difference in party issue stands, but it must also care about this difference" (1989: 161). Those individuals with polarized positions toward the issues should come to feel more positively toward the party whose stands on them are closer to their own and more negatively toward the other party.

If the new issues are easily understood and highly emotional, as the cultural issues are, then the second requirement follows naturally from the first. If citizens become aware of changing, and polarizing, party positions toward such issues, then, almost by definition, their feelings about the parties should change. However, since ordinary citizens are notoriously uninterested in, inattentive to, and uninformed about politics—a particularly relevant example is the fact that only 21 percent of citizens in 1980 recognized that the Republican party supported a pro-life amendment to the Constitution (Delli Carpini and Keeter 1996)—then how do they become aware of such changes? As step 6 in the figure points out, the answer lies, to a large extent, in the political behavior of party activists: individuals who work on behalf of the parties and their candidates but are not professional politicians themselves.

For most party activists, political participation is occasional (Nexon 1971; Carmines and Stimson 1989). They participate when they are stimulated by a policy position or a political candidate; they are not active when they are less inspired. Thus, when a party's elites take a noncentrist stand on a new issue, activists should respond rapidly. Individuals who are not active in the party but have a proclivity for political activity may become involved in the party if they are sympathetic to that stance. Current party activists who are less enthusiastic about the extreme positions on those issues may disengage from party activity. To be specific, if Democratic candidates, officeholders, and platforms move to more liberal stands on cultural issues while their Republican counterparts move to more conservative stands, then the Democratic activist base should become more culturally liberal while the GOP activist base becomes more culturally conservative.

This rapid response of political activists to changes in the issue positions of party elites and platforms plays a large role in facilitating the mass response to those changes (Carmines and Stimson 1989). Berelson, Lazarsfeld, and McPhee (1954) argue that there is a two-step flow of communication in American politics. A small number of citizens are politically active and attentive. They know the policy positions of political candidates and leaders and structure their political behavior accordingly. Far more citizens do not pay attention to politics and thus do not have firsthand knowledge of the positions of political leaders. However, they can respond to those positions by taking political cues from their friends, family members, and coworkers who do pay attention to politics and have some knowledge of political developments.

Thus, even if they are initially unaware of changes in the parties' policy positions, politically inattentive citizens can infer that those changes have occurred by observing the behavior of political activists in their communities or social circles. For example, if individuals notice that some of their friends, neighbors, and coworkers who are devout Christians and have traditional moral values and cultural beliefs are becoming increasingly active in the Republican party while other people they know who are not religious and have more modern moral and cultural values have become active in the Democratic party, they may deduce that the GOP is becoming the party of moral and cultural conservatism while the Democratic party is becoming the home of moral and cultural liberalism.

That two-step flow of communication may be particularly important on the right-hand side of the cultural divide, particularly among evangelical Protestants. One of the early strategies of the organizations of the Christian Right was to convince ordinary evangelicals to vote Republican and to become active in the Republican party by first persuading the ministers of their churches to become active in conservative and Republican politics (Guth 1983; Hertzke 1993; Oldfield 1996). As a result of the strong role that evangelical clergy play in shaping the behavior of their parishioners (Beatty and Walter 1989; Guth et al. 1997), the hope of Christian Right leaders was that if they could talk evangelical ministers into becoming active in culturally conservative politics and espousing conservative views on cultural–political issues from the pulpit, evangelical congregations would follow suit. Another reason that evangelical churches are a strong source of political cues is because the congregation is the primary source of friendships and social interaction for many, if not most, of its members (Ammerman 1987; Wald, Owen, and Hill 1988, 1990). Individuals pick up political cues not just from messages delivered from the pulpit, but also from interactions with politically active fellow parishioners. At the same time, nonevangelical churches also provide political cues to their members (Huckfeldt, Plutzer, and Sprague 1993; Verba, Schlozman, and Brady 1995) and culturally liberal political groups have, in recent years, begun to focus on liberal Protestant churches as bases for mobilizing individuals into Democratic party politics (Green 1997).

The importance of party activists lies not only in translating changes in the issue positions of party elites into changes in the mass images of the parties, but also in effecting those changes in elite positions (step 6a in the figure). The influence of activists over the outcomes of nomination campaigns is well documented, and it is their support for candidates who take extreme positions on new issues that gives those positions their initial strength within a party. Moreover, their role is not limited to a choice within a preexisting pool of candidates who have fixed policy positions. They affect the nature of the pool and the stances of the candidates within it. The decisions of candidates on whether or not to seek a party's nomination are affected by how well their political principles and positions conform to the ideological tendencies of party activists, and the candidates who do run often alter their issue positions to conform to the views of party activists (Brams 1978; Chappell and Keech 1986; Aldrich 1995).[6] Activists' influence also is not restricted to nomination politics. Their decisions on whether or not to lend their time and energy to a candidate can have a substantial impact on general election outcomes.

Through their influence on campaign outcomes, party activists have a profound influence on the nature of the policy positions associated with the parties. Why do Republican presidential candidates, and the platforms adopted by their nominating conventions, consistently take highly conservative positions on cultural issues when the conventional wisdom among journalists and other political observers is that such positions are losing ones in national elections? Why do Democratic candidates and their platforms take highly liberal cultural stands when such stands have the potential to alienate many black, Catholic, and lower-status voters? The answer to both questions is, for the most part, that the candidates have taken these positions because they had to to gain the support of their parties' activists, support that was necessary to win nominations and general elections.

My argument, in short, is that the connection between the initial introduction of cultural liberalism and cultural conservatism into the Democratic and Republican parties by strategic politicians such as McGovern, Reagan, Weyrich, and Viguerie and the transformation in the religious composition of the parties' mass coalitions have been greatly facilitated by party activists. It was the party activity of culturally liberal and culturally conservative individuals that first established the strength of these positions within the parties and that encouraged subsequent Democratic and Republican candidates to take polarized cultural stands. It was also the party activity of cultural liberals and conservatives that helped cultural change at the elite levels of party politics to register with the mass electorate and led ultimately to long-term change in the religious composition of the parties' mass coalitions.

The remainder of this book provides an empirical sketch of that path, from the introduction of cultural issues into party politics to long-term changes in the religious and cultural orientations of the parties' electoral coalitions. Following a discussion in chapter 2 of the proper conceptual and empirical definition of the contemporary religious cleavage, I examine the growing division of Democratic and Republican activists along the lines of that cleavage. Next, I trace the emergence of a religious divide in the parties' mass coalitions from the 1960s through the 1990s and examine the links between religious and cultural change at the elite, activist, and mass levels of partisan politics. I then delve more deeply into the questions of how and when this religious cleavage matters for contemporary political behavior.

NOTES

1. It is, of course, true that the degree of partisan polarization along the lines of a new conflict does not continue to grow at a constant rate over time. Even in the absence of attempts by party leaders to move their parties back toward the political center on an issue, the growth of party polarization in-

evitably stops at some point (Carsey and Layman 1999). However, the focus of this book is not on what stops the growth of or starts the decline in partisan religious polarization. The concluding chapter does address this, but the focus here is on why partisan religious polarization has increased over the last three decades.

2. The computation of the number of stories on these issues was performed through a search under the "government and political news" heading in the LEXIS-NEXIS Academic Universe [Internet, WWW], using the keywords "abortion," "homosexual OR gay AND rights OR discrimination," and "school AND prayer." The reason for the starting points of 1977 for the *Washington Post* and 1981 for the *New York Times* is that these were the first full years in which stories from these newspapers were archived in the LEXIS-NEXIS Academic Universe.

3. In previous periods of partisan change, a number of groups with extreme positions on new issues have found neither party particularly receptive to their views and decided to go the third-party route. Examples include the antislavery activists who formed the Liberty party, the Free-Soil party, and eventually the Republican party in the 1840s and 1850s, and the agrarian forces that formed the Greenback party in the 1870s and the People's (or Populist) party in the 1890s.

4. This conclusion is supported by formal-theoretical accounts of party activism that demonstrate that the greater the ideological distance between an individual's policy positions and those of the party whose views are closest to his or hers, the less likely it is that the individual will be active in or support either of the two parties (Aldrich 1983a; Brams 1978).

5. A considerable body of literature suggests that political activists have become more "purposive," more concerned with ideological goals and less concerned with material goals, social goals, and partisan victory (Wilson 1962; Conway and Feigert 1968; Roback 1980). However, activists still place a good deal of importance on partisan and social goals (Miller and Jennings 1986), and even people who initially are focused on purposive goals become more concerned with partisan victory the longer they are active in the party (Abramowitz, McGlennon, and Rapoport 1986).

6. Recent Republican politics contains several examples of the effects of activists on candidates' policy positions and decisions on whether or not to seek the party's nomination. Neither George Bush nor Bob Dole was strongly associated with cultural conservatism earlier in his political career. However, in their successful campaigns in 1988, 1992, and 1996 to be nominated by a Republican party whose activists were quite culturally conservative, both candidates took very conservative stands on cultural issues such as abortion. The same phenomenon is evident in the case of Steve Forbes, who opposed a constitutional ban on abortion in his 1996 campaign for the Republican nomination but took very conservative stands on cultural issues

in his campaign for the 2000 nomination. Pat Robertson's 1988 presidential campaign is credited with mobilizing a large number of previously inactive evangelicals, particularly those from the Pentecostal and charismatic wings of evangelicalism, into Republican politics (Hertzke 1993; Oldfield 1996). However, Robertson might never have sought the Republican nomination if he had not counted on significant support from the evangelicals who already were active in the Republican party. The presence of culturally conservative candidates such as Dan Quayle, Pat Buchanan, Alan Keyes, and Gary Bauer in the early field for the GOP's nomination in 2000 also may indicate the effect of the strong presence of cultural conservatism among Republican activists on the political decisions of potential candidates.

CHAPTER 2

Conceptualizing Religion and Religion-Based Political Conflict

THE CENTRAL THESIS of this book, like that of an array of recent research on religion and politics, is that the religious differences between the activist bases and electoral coalitions of the Democratic and Republican parties are growing. Of course, for as long as there have been mass political parties in the United States, there have been differences in the religious characteristics of their coalitions (Benson 1961; Lipset 1964; Formisano 1971). In fact, even the earliest studies of American voting behavior viewed religion as a politically significant characteristic (Lazarsfeld, Berelson, and Gaudet 1948; Berelson, Lazarsfeld, and McPhee 1954; Campbell and Cooper 1956). So the relevant question for this study is not simply, "Does religion matter for American party politics and political behavior?" Of course it does; it always has. The question is, "Has the nature of the religion and politics connection changed and how much has it changed?" In other words, when I say that the parties' activists and mass coalitions are becoming increasingly divided along religious lines, what do I mean by religion? What definition of religion provides the best characterization of the relationship between religion and contemporary American party politics? And is that relationship fundamentally different from that which has traditionally existed between religion and partisan political behavior?

There are many different ways to conceptualize religion. Religion may mean an affiliation with a particular church, denomination, or religious movement. It may mean beliefs about the nature of God, humankind's relationship to God, and the sources of moral authority. It may mean a style of religious practice or a set of religious activities, and those activities may be public or private in nature. Religion, of course, encompasses all of these things, but the question is, "Which of these aspects of religious experience is most relevant for and most closely connected to politics?" Traditionally, political scientists and historians examining the religious bases of partisan politics have emphasized religious affiliation. From this perspective, the most politically important religious factor was association with a family of religious denominations and organizations— a religious "tradition"—and the key political differences were between Protestants, who outside of the South tended to identify with the Republican party, and Catholics and Jews, who were largely affiliated with the Democratic party (cf. Berelson, Lazarsfeld, and McPhee 1954). Other analysts have added more religious traditions to this short list, but with the same underlying assumption: that religious affiliation drives political behavior.

Those scholars who see a religiously motivated "culture war" in American society and politics employ a very different conceptualization of religion. The cultural conflict is not between members of different denominational families, but between individuals with fundamentally different religious beliefs and moral worldviews. Thus, the important political differences are not between Protestants, Catholics, and Jews, but between the members of those groups who have conservative, or traditional, religious beliefs and their counterparts who have liberal, or modern, beliefs and moral outlooks. Religious conservatives tend to identify with the Republican party, while religious liberals tend to be Democrats (Wuthnow 1988; Hunter 1991). Other researchers contend that differences in religious activities and styles of religious practice work to reenforce the theologically based cultural and political divisions within faith traditions. Individuals who engage in traditional religious practices—attending worship services, reading the Bible, engaging in daily prayer—tend to have more conservative cultural attitudes and political outlooks and tend to support the Republican party and its candidates, while less devout individuals tend to be more culturally liberal and supportive of the Democratic party (Wald, Kellstedt, and Leege 1993; Guth and Green 1993; Layman 1997; Petersen and Donnenwerth 1997).

Of course, while religious beliefs and practices may have become more politically important, creating cultural, ideological, and partisan cleavages within faith traditions, there is considerable evidence that affiliation with a tradition still matters politically. Catholics, Jews, and black Protestants remain more Democratic than white Protestants. The two major traditions within white Protestantism—evangelical Protestants and mainline Protestants—may be growing more politically distinct as the members of the more orthodox evangelical denominations grow more loyal to the Republican party than are their counterparts in the less traditional, mainline denominations. And seculars, those individuals who are not part of a religious tradition, have become a bigger component of the Democratic coalition (Green et al. 1996; Miller and Shanks 1997; Layman 1997). Thus, it appears that the proper conceptualization of religion for contemporary American politics is one that encompasses all three of the major aspects of religion: religious belonging (or affiliation), religious believing (or theology), and religious behaving (or practices).

That is the very argument that I make in this chapter. I discuss various ways of conceptualizing religion and its connection to political attitudes and behavior. I concentrate on an "ethnoreligious" model of religion and politics that focuses on religious belonging, seeing political differences arising primarily between individuals with different religious affiliations, and the "culture wars" model, which envisions political cleavages, both within and across faith traditions, based on religious beliefs and behaviors. I then offer a model of religion and political behavior that combines belonging, believing, and behaving and test it using a very recent national survey of the American electorate. I conclude by discussing the various strategies I use in this book for measuring religious orientations when I am confronted with different data sources and when I have different objectives for the empirical analyses.

CONCEPTUALIZING RELIGION

Scholars have long understood religion to be a multidimensional phenomenon (Stark and Glock 1968; Wilcox 1990b; Kellstedt et al. 1997). Not only are there many religious communities in the United States, there are many different ways to be religious within the context of these communities. Thus, the starting point for determining how religion affects political behavior is to identify the major dimensions of American religion. The literature identifies three major components of religion that are potentially important for politics: believing, behaving, and belonging.

Religious beliefs are at the center of descriptions of the contemporary cultural conflict (Hunter 1991; Wuthnow 1988). They also are at the core of religion itself. As Lyman Kellstedt and his colleagues argue, "At its core, religion is a set of beliefs about the divine, humankind's relationship to it, and the consequences of that relationship" (1996: 175; see also Stark and Bainbridge 1985; Leege and Kellstedt 1993a). Believing provides the substantive content of religion, capturing the basic worldview and values of religious people, and thus serves as the central motivation for religious belonging and behaving.

Belief is also the element of religion that has the clearest link to political attitudes, particularly when it comes to the issues surrounding the cultural conflict. It is, of course, true that attitudes on abortion, women's rights, and homosexual rights are influenced by one's style and frequency of religious behaviors, as well as by the religious groups to which one belongs, but at their core, the religious effects on these attitudes are the effects of religious beliefs regarding the sanctity of human life, the point at which life begins, the proper purposes of the sex act, and the appropriate ordering of familial relationships. Thus, despite the fact that religious affiliation—specifically classification as Protestant, Catholic, or Jewish—traditionally has been the only religious variable included in studies of political behavior, religious beliefs play an important role in American politics, and several scholars have identified beliefs as the central variable for understanding contemporary political behavior and partisan religious alignments (cf. Miller and Wattenberg 1984; Rothenberg and Newport 1984; Hunter 1991; Jelen 1991).

Although it certainly does not capture the whole range of relevant religious beliefs, a common conceptualization of believing employed in studies of religion and politics is doctrinal orthodoxy: the combination of beliefs traditionally regarded as central to the acceptance of faith. Considerable research has shown doctrine to be a potent source of political values and attitudes (cf. Wilcox 1990b; Jelen 1991; Kellstedt and Smidt 1993), and doctrinal orthodoxy is typically defined as some combination of beliefs about the sources of religious authority—such as the authority of Scripture—and the appropriate relationship of individuals to the divine—such as the necessity of adult conversion experiences.

Religious behaving refers to the actual practice of religious faith and thus is related closely to believing. Scholars distinguish between two types of religious behaviors: ritual activity, such as attending worship services, and private devotionalism, such as personal prayer (Stark and Glock 1968; Leege, Wald, and Kellstedt 1993). Many scholars also include the subjective salience of religion, or the perceived importance of religion to an individual, under behaving (cf. Guth and Green 1993). Although religious salience is an attitudinal variable, it provides a good indication of an individual's commitment to religion and thus his or her propensity to participate in religious activities.

In studies of political behavior, religious behaving is often viewed as a conditional variable, affecting the impact that religious beliefs and affiliations have on political attitudes and decisions. Individuals who are more active in the church are more likely to pick up political cues from clergy and fellow parishioners, thus providing a closer link between religious belonging and beliefs on the one hand and political behavior on the other hand (Wald, Owen, and Hill 1988, 1990; Welch et al. 1993; Wald, Kellstedt, and Leege 1993). Individuals who find religion to be a more salient factor in their lives are more likely to use their religious beliefs and affiliations as guides for political behavior (Kellstedt, Smidt, and Kellstedt 1991; Guth and Green 1993).

However, numerous studies also show that religious behavior has a direct impact on political orientations, with more religious individuals being more likely than their less religious counterparts to take conservative attitudes on political issues, particularly cultural ones, and to support the Republican party and its candidates (Green, Guth, and Fraser 1991; Cook, Jelen, and Wilcox 1992; Guth and Green 1993; Layman 1997; Sherkat and Ellison 1997). Furthermore, research on political participation shows that religious involvement is an important source of political activity, providing important skills and organizational resources for political mobilization (Peterson 1990; Rosenstone and Hansen 1993; Verba, Schlozman, and Brady 1995).

A typical and useful way to conceptualize religious behaving is religious commitment: the combination of behaviors traditionally regarded as normative for the practice of faith (e.g., church attendance, attending confessions, and praying the rosary for Catholics; church attendance, personal prayer, and Bible reading for Baptists). Commitment is typically operationalized by combining the frequency of worship attendance, personal prayer, and religious salience (Kellstedt et al. 1996).

Religious belonging refers to an individual's affiliation with a religious community. Scholars at times employ distinctive sets of religious beliefs and practices to define these communities. For example, evangelical and fundamentalist Christians have been defined by beliefs such as biblical inerrancy and the necessity of "born-again" conversion experiences (cf. Miller and Wattenberg 1984; Rothenberg and Newport 1984; Wilcox 1990b; Kellstedt and Smidt 1996). Charismatic Christians have been defined by practices such as speaking in tongues (Smidt et al. 1996). In contrast, affiliation with a religious community involves not only possessing certain beliefs and carrying out certain behaviors, but also conscious recognition of membership in a social group. To be sure, religious groups are defined primarily by distinctive beliefs and behaviors, but that does not preclude the belonging aspect of religion from playing an important role in shaping cultural and political orientations.

First, it is within these social groups that religious beliefs and behaviors arise. For example, the beliefs that are considered orthodox or traditional vary across religious groups. Doctrinal orthodoxy for Baptists may mean viewing the Bible as literally true and believing in a literal hell, while a belief in the infallibility of the pope may be more central to Catholic orthodoxy. Furthermore, certain groups are more likely than others to espouse and encourage orthodox beliefs; Protestant orthodoxy is more likely to be found in Pentecostal churches than it is in Episcopalian churches. Appropriate or expected religious behaviors also are determined by religious group memberships. For example, religious commitment may mean attending confession weekly for Catholics, but daily Bible reading for Baptists or performing charitable acts within the community for Jews. Moreover, membership in some groups may lead to greater religious commitment than membership in other groups does. The Assemblies of God may expect a greater dedication of time, energy, and resources from its members than the United Methodist Church expects from its congregants.

Second, religious group memberships may play a vital role in linking religious beliefs to political attitudes and behavior. For example, all individuals who have fundamentalist Protestant beliefs—for example, the beliefs that the Bible is literally true, that the only way to salvation is through Jesus Christ, and that the Devil really exists—should have conservative attitudes on cultural issues such as abortion, school prayer, and homosexual rights, and should tend to support the party and candidates that are most conservative on those issues. However, how strong the link between doctrinal fundamentalism and cultural and political conservatism is may depend on whether the individual actually attends a fundamentalist church. The connection should be more robust for those doctrinal fundamentalists who belong to evangelical or fundamentalist churches where orthodox beliefs predominate than for those doctrinal fundamentalists who belong to churches where more liberal religious beliefs are in the majority. The former should be more likely than the latter to have conservative attitudes on cultural issues and to support culturally conservative political candidates.

At least two aspects of religious group membership may act to facilitate the link between religious beliefs and political attitudes and behavior. The first is the influence of religious leaders. Messages delivered from the pulpit often have a profound effect not only on the religious outlooks of church members, but also on their political attitudes and actions (Beatty and Walter 1989; Welch et al. 1993; Guth et al. 1997). Furthermore, even if clerical discussions of politics and clerical political activism do not directly shape political orientations, they may play an important role in making faith relevant for political decisions (Welch et al. 1993; Guth et al. 1996). Religious leaders also play a significant part in encouraging individuals of like religious beliefs to become involved in the political process (Beatty and Walter 1989; Verba, Schlozman, and Brady 1995). In fact, one of the principle strategies of the organizations of the Christian Right has been to enlist the help of evangelical Protestant clergy in mobilizing their parishioners into Republican party politics (Guth 1983; Oldfield 1996).

The second is the general importance of social context and group memberships in filtering the flow of political information to individuals and in shaping individual political attitudes (cf. Berelson, Lazarsfeld, and McPhee 1954; Putnam 1966; Huckfeldt and Sprague 1987; Huckfeldt and Kohfeld 1989). For many individuals, congregations and other religious group memberships are a major source of primary group friendships and social interactions (Ammerman 1987; Wald, Owen, and Hill 1988, 1990; Huckfeldt, Plutzer, and Sprague 1993). Through this interaction and the resulting perceptions of shared interest, religious as well as political and social beliefs are shaped and reenforced (Wald, Owen, and Hill 1988, 1990; Huckfeldt, Plutzer, and Sprague 1993).

So to return to the example of individuals who have fundamentalist Protestant beliefs, those doctrinal fundamentalists who belong to churches or other religious organizations where those beliefs predominate will be more likely than those doctrinal fundamentalists who do not to receive social and clerical reenforcement of not only their conservative religious beliefs, but also their tendencies toward political conservatism. Thus, the link between orthodox religious beliefs and support for conservative political positions and candidates should be stronger for the former than for the latter. In fact, Wald, Owen, and Hill (1988) show that the theological conservatism of one's congregation has a significant influence on one's moral and political conservatism even when personal theology is controlled. Because of the importance of religious belonging in shaping religious beliefs and behaviors and in connecting these other religious orientations to politics, studies of religion and politics continue to demonstrate the political importance of religious affiliation (Wilcox 1990b; Kellstedt, Smidt, and Kellstedt 1991; Green, Guth, and Fraser

1991; Kellstedt and Green 1993; Kellstedt et al. 1996, 1997; Miller and Shanks 1996).

For some individuals, religious belonging means affiliation with a denomination, which is "a set of religious institutions . . . that are formally linked to one another, and which share common beliefs, practices, and commitments" (Kellstedt and Green 1993: 54–55), and examples of which are the United Methodist Church, the Presbyterian Church in the U.S.A., and the Southern Baptist Convention. For others, belonging means affiliation with a religious movement that cuts across denominational boundaries. Religious movements are "conscious efforts to alter existing denominations" (Kellstedt and Green 1993: 57), and examples include fundamentalism and the charismatic movement. A useful and increasingly popular conceptualization of belonging is religious tradition: a group of denominations, movements, and other related institutions that share common beliefs, behaviors, and origins (Kellstedt and Green 1993; Kellstedt et al. 1996).

The literature shows religious tradition to be an important predictor of political attitudes and behavior (Kellstedt and Green 1993; Kellstedt et al. 1996, 1997; Wald 1997; Layman and Green 1998) and identifies six major religious traditions in the United States: evangelical Protestants, mainline Protestants, black Protestants, Roman Catholics, Jews, and the nonreligious or seculars. The evangelical Protestant tradition includes white Protestants affiliating with denominations such as the Southern Baptist Convention and other Baptist churches, the Assemblies of God, the Wisconsin and Missouri Synod Lutherans, and Church of Christ that emphasize traditional beliefs regarding the authority of Scripture (e.g., the Bible is the authoritative Word of God), the belief that Jesus Christ is the only way to salvation, religious conversion or a born-again experience as a necessity for salvation, and evangelizing or "spreading the Word" (Hunter 1983; Dayton and Johnston 1991; Kellstedt et al. 1996). Mainline Protestant refers to those white Protestants affiliating with denominations such as the Episcopal Church, the United Methodist Church, the Evangelical Lutheran Church in America, and the Presbyterian Church in the U.S.A. that tend to favor greater harmony between religion and modernity, are less likely to emphasize biblical infallibility and born-again conversion experiences, and tend to focus more on social reform than on converting nonbelievers (Kellstedt, Smidt, and Kellstedt 1991). The black Protestant tradition is composed of African-Americans who belong to churches primarily within the Baptist and Methodist denominational families. These churches espouse much of the same doctrine as the white evangelical churches, but historically they have remained separate from white churches and have been much more likely to emphasize a "liberation theology," stressing the place of deliverance for the oppressed in Christian faith (Lincoln and Mamiya 1991; Fowler, Hertzke, and Olson 1999).

MEASURING RELIGIOUS TRADITION, DOCTRINAL ORTHODOXY, AND RELIGIOUS COMMITMENT

The analysis in this book employs data from a wide variety of sources. However, the source that offers the richest data both on individual political behavior and mass partisan alignments and on the religious orientations of individual citizens and how they have affected political behavior over time is the American National Election Studies (NES), the major academic study of the American electorate conducted during every federal election year by the Center for Political Studies at the University of Michigan.[1] In all but one of its election-year surveys from 1980 through 1996—the one exception being 1982—the NES has included questions that make it possible to construct reliable measures of respondents' religious traditions, levels of doctrinal orthodoxy, and degrees of religious commitment.

This has been particularly true of the NES surveys conducted in the 1990s. Between 1988 and 1990, NES significantly expanded the list of religious denominations with which respondents might identify. It also increased the number of questions with which to measure doctrinal orthodoxy and religious commitment (Leege and Kellstedt 1993b). The NES surveys from 1990 through 1996 thus provide the most sophisticated measures of religion that have been available in this long-running series, or, for that matter, of any studies of political behavior that have been conducted over significant periods of time. Here, I illustrate my general strategy for measuring religious tradition, doctrinal orthodoxy, and religious commitment by discussing the measurement of these variables in the most recent presidential-year NES survey, the one conducted in 1996.

Using the questions on denominational affiliation and other religious orientations in the 1996 NES and following recent work on religious traditions (Kellstedt and Green 1993; Kellstedt et al. 1996), I identify ten different categories of religious belonging. These include the five major American traditions—evangelical Protestants, mainline Protestants, black

Protestants, Catholics, and Jews—and seculars. They also include the Eastern Orthodox tradition and two categories of smaller Protestant traditions aggregated into "conservative nontraditional" and "liberal nontraditional" categories because of their small numbers. The former category includes groups that adhere to certain parts of traditional Protestant doctrine but "add a special revelation to Christian orthodoxy" (Kellstedt et al. 1996: 179), such as the Church of Jesus Christ of the Latter-day Saints (Mormons) and Jehovah's Witnesses. The latter group includes religions that have "explicitly abandoned key elements of Christian orthodoxy" (Kellstedt et al. 1996: 179), such as the Unitarian-Universalists. My final category is "other religions" and consists of the very small number of Muslims, Buddhists, and members of other non-Judeo-Christian religions.

A more thorough discussion of the steps in assigning respondents to these various traditions and the various denominations and religious movement identifications included in each religious tradition is presented in appendix A1.[2] In general, however, this assignment followed three steps. First, the respondents who identified themselves as members of specific denominations (e.g., United Methodist, Southern Baptist, Presbyterian Church in the U.S.A.) were assigned to the appropriate traditions. Second, following Kellstedt et al. (1996), respondents stating ambiguous affiliations such as "Protestant" or "Christian" or identification with a denominational family such as Methodist or Lutheran, rather than a specific denomination, were assigned to traditions based on religious practices and identifications as well as race. For example, those general "Methodists" who are not black, display a minimal level of religious commitment, and identify themselves (in a question separate from religious affiliation) as evangelical, fundamentalist, or charismatic Christians are assigned to the evangelical Protestant tradition. Those who are not black, display a minimal level of religious commitment, and identify themselves as "liberal to moderate" Christians are assigned to the mainline Protestant tradition. Those who are black and display a minimal level of religious commitment are assigned to the black Protestant tradition. Those who do not display a minimal level of religious commitment are assigned to the secular category.

Third, I construct a "low commitment" variable based on questions about frequency of prayer, worship attendance, and religious guidance or salience. Those respondents who almost never attend church, pray very infrequently, and receive no guidance from religion in their lives are placed in the secular category, even if they do identify with a specific denomination or religious movement. These individuals are members of a religious tradition in name only and are likely to receive virtually no political or spiritual cues from the tradition's religious leaders or other members.

The NES includes one item that is clearly a measure of religious belief: respondent's view of the Bible. Although literal (i.e., the Bible is the authoritative Word of God, and all of it is literally true) and inerrant (i.e., the Bible is the Word of God, and, although all of it may not be literally true, it is authoritative in all matters of faith) views of the Bible are more central to theological orthodoxy in the evangelical tradition than in other traditions (Kellstedt et al. 1997), authoritative views of the Bible do distinguish the more theologically conservative members of most traditions from their more liberal counterparts (Kellstedt and Smidt 1993). Research also shows that conservative biblical views are more likely to lead to political conservatism and support for the Republican party among those individuals who read the Bible frequently than among infrequent readers. Thus, I expand the three-category Bible scale in the NES into four categories by dividing respondents who have literal views of the Bible into frequent and infrequent Bible readers.[3]

Another question in the 1996 NES that may serve as a measure of beliefs is one asking respondents whether or not they consider themselves to be born-again Christians. Although the born-again item is often regarded as a measure of religious identification, it also indicates a belief in the necessity of adult conversion experiences for salvation (Wilcox 1990b; Kellstedt, Smidt, and Kellstedt 1991),[4] and it may help to distinguish the most theologically conservative members of the whole range of Christian traditions (Jelen, Smidt, and Wilcox 1993). Thus, I measure doctrinal orthodoxy by summing respondents' scores on the expanded Bible measure and the born-again indicator.

The NES includes two measures of religious behavior—frequency of church or synagogue attendance and frequency of prayer—as well as religious salience, or the amount of guidance individuals receive in their lives from religion. These three measures are combined to form an index of religious commitment.[5]

LINKING RELIGION TO POLITICS

Over the past two decades, considerable evidence has accumulated regarding the political relevance of religious tradition, religious commitment, and doctrinal orthodoxy (see Wald 1997; Fowler, Hertzke, and Olson 1999 for reviews of this voluminous literature). All three aspects of religion are related to vote choice (cf. Wilcox 1992; Green et al. 1996), partisanship and party coalitions (cf. Green et al. 1996; Kellstedt et al. 1997; Layman 1999), and a variety of issue positions (Guth et al. 1993; Layman and Carmines 1997; Guth et al. 1996). It is also clear that, although conceptually distinct, belonging, behaving, and believing are closely related to one another. Religious traditions are defined in part by distinctive beliefs and practices; religious commitment and doctrinal orthodoxy are defined within the context of particular religious traditions. So if these aspects of religion are related to politics and to each other, the question is, "How do they matter politically?" Do they act independently of each other, or do they act in conjunction? Does one of the factors capture the effects of the other, or do they all have important influences on political behavior?

The literature offers two primary models of the relationship between belonging, believing, and behaving on the one hand, and political behavior and partisan coalitions on the other hand. The first of these is the "ethnocultural" or "ethnoreligious" model. Developed primarily by historians (McCormick 1986; Kleppner 1970, 1987; Swierenga 1990), but implicit in the work of some political scientists (cf. Campbell and Cooper 1956; Lipset 1964), this model emphasizes religious belonging. Religion is thought of primarily as a social group phenomenon, with membership in a religious tradition being closely linked to other aspects of culture, such as ethnicity, race, and region. Here, religious behaving and believing reenforce belonging to produce distinctive group identifications and distinctive cultural and political values.

So the focus of the ethnoreligious perspective is on political differences between, and not within, religious traditions, and most analyses of political behavior based on it focus on the effects of religious tradition and not on the effects of beliefs or behaviors. However, religious commitment and doctrinal orthodoxy do matter in this model. They matter in the sense that the most committed and orthodox members of a tradition are the most attuned to the dominant values of the tradition. So they are more likely than the less committed and orthodox members of the tradition to possess the political perspectives characteristic of the tradition (Kleppner 1979), and their political outlooks should be most different from those of members of other traditions with different worldviews and values.

For example, the communitarianism of the Jewish faith and the liberation themes prevalent in the African-American church should mean that the most orthodox and committed members of those traditions are the most likely to take liberal positions on social welfare issues and issues of civil rights and liberties and thus the most likely to identify with and vote for the Democratic party. Meanwhile, the individualist "Protestant ethic" should mean that the most orthodox and committed white Protestants are the most likely to have conservative attitudes on economic and social welfare issues and, accordingly, to support the Republican party (cf. Parenti 1967).

The ethnoreligious model appears to fit well with much of American political history, considering the sharp political differences that have existed between Protestants, Catholics, and Jews and the early work on political behavior that identified religious group affiliation as a major factor driving voting decisions (Lazarsfeld, Berelson, and Gaudet 1948; Berelson, Lazarsfeld, and McPhee 1954). Even today, scholars recognize that white Protestants are more Republican and conservative than Catholics, black Protestants, Jews, and seculars (Guth and Green 1991; Green et al. 1996; Miller and Shanks 1996).

In fact, the most publicized recent development in religion and politics, the strong and growing attachments of evangelical Protestants to the Republican party (Kellstedt 1989), can be explained by the ethnoreligious model. The dominant moral and cultural values in evangelicalism are quite conservative. So it is not surprising, from an ethnoreligious standpoint, that evangelicals have aligned themselves with a party that has taken very conservative stands on moral and cultural matters. It is also not surprising that Republican loyalties are strongest among the most committed evangelicals (Miller and Shanks 1996), who should be most attuned to the dominant values of the tradition.

At the same time, the high degree of social integration within and social isolation between religious traditions that was the basis for ethnoreligious politics (Kleppner 1979) has greatly subsided, particularly outside the evangelical camp, and thus so have the tensions and political differences between ethnoreligious groups such as mainline Protestants, Catholics, and Jews. Moreover, other recent findings in the literature on religion and politics do not square with the ethnoreligious model. For example, Catholic and mainline Protestant clergy and institutions have tended to be committed in recent years to principles such as economic and social justice, racial equality, and nonmilitary solutions to international conflicts. From an ethnoreligious perspective, we would expect the most committed members of those traditions to share those perspectives and thus be more likely than their less devout counterparts to support the Democratic party and its candidates. However, recent research shows that the most committed Catholics and mainline Protestants are, in fact, the members of their traditions who are least likely to have liberal political attitudes and to identify with and vote for the Democratic party (Kellstedt et al. 1996, 1997).

For these and other reasons, the ethnoreligious model has appeared to some scholars to be an outdated account of religious influence on politics. Thus, a second model has emerged, and that is, of course, the "culture wars" model discussed in the introduction. Developed primarily by sociologists (Hunter 1991; Wuthnow 1988), but implicit in the work of some political scientists (Lopatto 1985; Layman and Carmines 1997), this model sees the relevant political divisions as being within, rather than between, religious traditions. Instead of reenforcing religious belonging, doctrinal orthodoxy and religious commitment cut across the lines of traditions to create the same kinds of distinctive values among adherents in all religious traditions. Thus, the key political differences are no longer between members of different traditions, but between religious "traditionalists," or individuals with high levels of orthodoxy and commitment, and religious "modernists," or individuals with low levels of orthodoxy and commitment, across the whole range of religious traditions.

In other words, the political effects of believing and behaving are not tradition specific but are consistent across faith traditions. For example, the most orthodox and committed members of all traditions should be the most likely to partake of traditionalist values and thus to take conservative positions on cultural issues such as abortion, homosexuality, and pornography and to support the Republican party. The least orthodox and committed members of those traditions should be the most likely to partake of modernist values and thus to have liberal cultural views and Democratic partisan loyalties. If the culture wars model is correct, then commitment and doctrine should have independent effects apart from religious tradition, perhaps even to the extent that religious tradition is no longer relevant politically.

In contemporary religion and politics, it is likely that the ethnoreligious and culture wars models are ideal types and the reality lies somewhere between. Even if the relationship between religion and party politics is being restructured along the lines suggested by the culture wars thesis, it is entirely possible that we are currently in a transitional period (Kellstedt et al. 1997). In other words, doctrinal orthodoxy and religious commitment may be becoming more politically important, and their effects may be growing increasingly independent of religious tradition. But until the reshaping of political alignments along theological and behavioral lines is complete, the political impact of religious tradition will still linger. Of course, it is also possible that because of the persistence of theological, cultural, and socioeconomic differences between religious traditions, religious belonging will always be important, even if doctrine and commitment also emerge as politically important factors. Thus, the political similarities between orthodox Jews, conservative Catholics, and fundamentalist Protestants on the one hand and their more progressive counterparts on the other hand may be growing, and traditionalist–modernist political divisions within traditions may be expanding. But there may remain differences between even the most orthodox elements of the various religious traditions as well as between their more progressive components.

There are two more-specific reasons to believe that the reality of contemporary religion and politics lies somewhere between the ethnoreligious and culture wars models. First, some of the recent developments in the political influence of religion seem to, in some ways, fit with both perspectives. As I noted previously, the strong attachments of committed evangelical Protestants to the Republican party do not run counter to the ethnoreligious viewpoint. However, those attachments also are highlighted in the work of culture wars proponents who see the support of the most orthodox Protestants for the conservative party as evidence of the strong connection between theological conservatism and political conservatism (Wuthnow 1989; Hunter 1991). In reality, evangelical Republicanism is probably indicative of both ethnoreligious and theological influences on politics. It certainly is a case of traditionalist religious beliefs translating into conservative political attitudes and attachments, just as the culture wars model suggests. But research showing that traditionalist evangelicals are more conservative and Republican than mainline Protestants and Catholics with similar religious beliefs (Kellstedt et al. 1997) suggests that the connection between doctrine and political behavior is fostered and reenforced within the context of a religious tradition, much as the ethnoreligious model suggests. At the same time, the evidence that modernist evangelicals are more liberal and Democratic than religious traditionalists in the mainline and Catholic communities (Kellstedt et al. 1997) suggests that beliefs and behaviors do create liberal–conservative political alliances across the boundaries of religious traditions.

Second, the way that religion is connected to politics may depend on the nature of the political issue agenda, or, more specifically, on the salience of particular issues to individuals or within the context of a campaign. Cultural issues such as abortion and homosexual rights are central to the culture wars thesis. The most orthodox members of all traditions tend to have conservative attitudes toward them, while the most progressive members of all traditions tend to have liberal views on them (Layman and Green 1998). Thus, these issues facilitate a consistent link between theological and political conservatism across a range of religious communities, and when they are salient, culture wars patterns should hold. However, on other issues, say, economic and social welfare issues, the connection between theological orthodoxy and conservative attitudes is not as clear, and the positions of religious people may depend more on the distinctive values and worldviews of their religious traditions—for example, evangelical Protestant individualism versus Jewish communitarianism—in addition to their socioeconomic, ethnic, and racial attributes. So when these issues are most salient, religious tradition may have more political impact than doctrinal orthodoxy and religious commitment (Layman and Green 1998).

It appears that the most appropriate model of contemporary religion and political behavior is one that incorporates elements of both ethnoreligious and culture wars politics. The model should account for the possibility that religious commitment and doctrinal orthodoxy have effects on political attitudes and partisan ties independent of religious tradition, just as the culture wars thesis suggests. However, it also should account for political differences between religious traditions and the possibility that the effects of beliefs and behaviors are dependent on tradition, just as the ethnoreligious viewpoint contends. In the next section, I develop such a model and test it by using the 1996 NES survey.

AN EMPIRICAL MODEL AND ANALYSIS OF THE POLITICAL IMPACT OF RELIGION

To test both the ethnoreligious and culture wars models simultaneously and to capture the possibility that contemporary American politics contains elements of both frameworks, I use the following statistical model:

$$Y = b_0 + b_1(\text{religious tradition}) + b_2(\text{doctrinal orthodoxy}) + \quad (2.1)$$
$$b_3(\text{religious commitment}) + b_4(\text{tradition} \times \text{orthodoxy}) +$$
$$b_5(\text{tradition} \times \text{commitment}) + b_6(\text{controls}),$$

where Y is the political attitude or behavior to be explained and the controls are a set of sociodemographic variables.[6] Following the ethnoreligious perspective, this model allows religious tradition to exert an independent influence on political behavior by including dummy variables for mainline Protestants, Catholics, black Protestants, Jews, and seculars, using evangelical Protestants as the comparison category.[7] As suggested by the culture wars thesis, the model allows doctrinal orthodoxy and religious commitment to have effects on political attitudes and behavior independent of the influence of religious tradition. However, following the ethnoreligious assertion that the effects of orthodoxy and commitment are tradition specific, working to reenforce the dominant values within religious traditions, the model allows their effects to vary by tradition. It does so by including a set of interactions between the variables for religious tradition and orthodoxy and between the tradition variables and commitment. These interaction terms capture differences across religious traditions in the political impact of doctrine and commitment.

I test this model using six different dependent variables: moral traditionalism (the degree to which an individual is committed to traditional moral values and is intolerant of those with different moral outlooks), attitudes toward cultural issues such as abortion and homosexual rights, attitudes toward the groups such as fundamentalist Christians and feminists that are involved in the cultural conflict, political ideology, party identification, and the 1996 two-party presidential vote.[8] The first three dependent variables are central to the theory of culture wars. Hunter (1991) argues that differences in moral values, or specifically different notions of moral authority, are at the heart of the differences between the orthodox and progressive camps. Moreover, issues such as abortion, prayer in the public schools, women's rights, and homosexual discrimination provide the framework for the specific battles of the culture war, and groups such as fundamentalist Christians, homosexuals, and feminists provide the troops for these battles. Thus, if the culture wars thesis is correct, there should be a clear connection between doctrinal orthodoxy and religious commitment on the one hand and moral traditionalism and conservative attitudes toward cultural issues and groups on the other. The last three dependent variables are indicators of general political orientations and should provide insight into whether the contemporary relationship between religion and politics reflects the culture wars model, the ethnoreligious model, or elements of both.

To keep the analyses in this book interesting and intelligible to all readers, I present most of the statistical estimates in appendices and focus in the text on the predicted values (or probabilities) of the dependent variables that come from those estimates. A complete understanding of my argument can be garnered simply by reading the text and ignoring the statistical appendices. However, for the reader interested in such things, all the details of the statistical analyses are contained in the appendices.

Appendix B1 presents the estimates of equation 2.1 for the six dependent variables. Table 2.1 shows three sets of predicted values or probabilities for each dependent variable and for each of the six major religious traditions.[9] The first row for each dependent variable shows the predicted values of the variable at various levels of religious commitment when doctrinal orthodoxy is held constant at its mean for each particular tradition.[10] The second row for each variable shows its predicted values at various levels of doctrinal orthodoxy when religious commitment is held constant at its mean for each tradition. The third row shows the combined effects of orthodoxy and commitment, or the predicted values when both doctrine and commitment are allowed to vary within religious traditions.

The predictions appear to be strongly supportive of the culture wars model. Among evangelicals, mainline Protestants, and Catholics, the three largest traditions in American religion, both commitment and doctrinal orthodoxy create differences not only in the moral values and cultural issues and groups that are central to the cultural conflict, but also in the general political orientations of ideological identification, party identification, and the presidential vote. In all three of these traditions, more committed and doctrinally orthodox individuals are more morally traditional, more culturally conservative, more likely to identify themselves as political conservatives, and more supportive of the GOP and its candidates than are less committed and more doctrinally liberal individuals.

Also important is the fact that it is the combination of doctrinal and behavioral differences that produces the clearest divisions within traditions. In none of these traditions do commitment and doctrinal orthodoxy work at cross-purposes, and there are only a few instances where the effect of either commitment or doctrine is conspicuously smaller than the effect of the other. It appears that the relationship between religion and politics in the United States is by no means defined solely by differences between religious traditions, as research on political behavior typically has assumed. Instead, religious beliefs and behaviors work together to create important cultural and political cleavages within traditions, and the ideological nature of those cleavages is fairly consistent across the three largest traditions.

However, before jumping to the conclusion that the culture wars model provides a complete explanation of the political influence of religion while the ethnoreligious model provides an outdated account, two things should be noted. First, although religious traditions are far from culturally or politically unified, they still matter a great deal. On moral and cultural matters, the most committed and orthodox evangelicals are more conservative than the most committed and orthodox mainline Protestants, Catholics, and black Protestants. Seculars and Jews are more morally and culturally liberal than even the least committed and orthodox members of any of the four major Christian traditions. With regard to general political orientations, the most committed and orthodox evangelicals are more Republican than their counterparts in mainline churches, who are more conservative and Republican than the most committed and orthodox Catholics. Jews, and to a lesser extent seculars, are more liberal and Democratic than almost any Catholics or white Protestants. Black Protestants are far more Democratic than any tradition besides Jews.

Second, the size and direction of the effects of doctrinal orthodoxy and religious commitment vary across religious traditions. The patterns for black Protestants are very different from those for Catholics and white Protestants. Greater commitment and doctrinal conservatism do seem to lead to greater moral traditionalism, cultural conservatism, and even general political conservatism among black Protestants. However, the effects of these variables are less consistent and less substantial for black Protestants than for members of the three predominantly white Christian traditions. The differences are even more stark with regard to party identification and presidential voting behavior. Rather than leading to stronger support for the Republican party, greater religious commitment among black Protestants leads to stronger Democratic loyalties. Just as the ethnoreligious model suggests, those who are most deeply ingrained within the black Protestant tradition are those most likely to adopt its traditionally liberal and pro-Democratic values. Of course, black Protestants at all levels of commitment and doctrine were nearly unanimous in their support of Clinton.

There are also variations in the influence of orthodoxy and commitment across the predominantly white Christian traditions. The effect of commitment is generally greatest among evangelical Protestants, a result that is not surprising given the strong religious and cultural conservatism

TABLE 2.1

Predicted values and probabilities of various dependent variables by religious tradition and levels of religious commitment and doctrinal orthodoxy

	Religious Tradition and Level of Doctrine/Commitment[a]													
	Evangelical Protestant			Mainline Protestant			Catholic			Black Protestant			Jewish	Secular
Dependent Variable	Low	Mid.	High	Low	Mid.	High	Low	Mid.	High	Low	Mid.	High		
Moral values														
Commitment[b]	.63	.69	.74	.53	.57	.62	.50	.54	.58	.51	.54	.58	.44	.47
Doctrine[c]	.64	.69	.73	.53	.57	.62	.51	.54	.57	.55	.54	.54		
Commit. & doc.[d]	.58	.69	.79	.49	.57	.66	.47	.54	.61	.52	.54	.57		
Cultural issues														
Commitment[b]	.41	.47	.54	.34	.35	.37	.34	.37	.39	.35	.37	.39	.19	.29
Doctrine[c]	.43	.47	.51	.31	.35	.39	.33	.37	.40	.34	.37	.40		
Commit. & doc.[d]	.36	.47	.58	.29	.35	.41	.31	.37	.43	.32	.37	.42		
Cultural groups														
Commitment[b]	.54	.59	.64	.49	.51	.53	.47	.49	.51	.53	.54	.56	.36	.43
Doctrine[c]	.55	.59	.63	.46	.51	.56	.44	.49	.54	.51	.54	.57		
Commit. & doc.[d]	.50	.59	.68	.44	.51	.58	.43	.49	.55	.50	.54	.59		
Ideology														
Commitment[b]	.55	.62	.69	.53	.55	.57	.49	.51	.53	.51	.52	.53	.43	.47
Doctrine[c]	.60	.62	.64	.54	.55	.56	.48	.51	.54	.51	.52	.53		
Commit. & Doc.[d]	.53	.62	.71	.51	.55	.59	.46	.51	.56	.50	.52	.54		

Party identification														
Commitment[b]	.46	.55	.55	.64	.53	.54	.55	.38	.41	.44	.27	.24	.21	.23
Doctrine[c]	.53	.55	.57	.50	.54	.58	.38	.41	.44	.22	.24	.26		
Commit. & doc.[d]	.44	.55	.66	.49	.54	.59	.35	.41	.47	.26	.24	.22		.42
Presidential vote														
Commitment[b]	.40	.57	.72	.39	.43	.47	.29	.32	.37	.02	.02	.03	—[e]	
Doctrine[c]	.51	.57	.63	.39	.43	.47	.27	.32	.39	.05	.02	.02		
Commit. & doc.[d]	.34	.57	.77	.35	.43	.51	.24	.32	.43	.04	.02	.02		.25

Source: 1996 American National Election Study.

Presidential vote is coded 1 for Republican and 0 for Democratic. All other variables range from 0 (most liberal/Democratic) to 1 (most conservative/Republican).

[a] The "middle" level of doctrine and commitment is the mean value for the particular religious tradition. "Low" doctrine/commitment is one standard deviation below the tradition mean. "High" doctrine/commitment is one standard deviation above the tradition mean. The values for Jews and seculars were computed with both doctrine and commitment held at their means for those two groups.

[b] Commitment varies from low to high and doctrine is held constant at its mean value for the religious tradition.

[c] Doctrine varies from low to high and commitment is held constant at its mean value for the religious tradition.

[d] Both doctrine and commitment vary from low to high.

[e] All the Jewish respondents in the sample voted for Bill Clinton, so they were dropped from the analysis, and a predicted probability cannot be estimated for Jews.

of evangelicalism and its recently developed strong ties to political conservatism and the Republican party. In fact, the effect of commitment is consistently larger than the effect of doctrinal orthodoxy for evangelicals. Among mainline Protestants, by contrast, the effect of orthodoxy tends to be greater than the effect of commitment, and this is particularly true for cultural attitudes and party identification. This finding may result from the fact that mainline clergy tend to be more theologically and politically liberal than evangelical clergy, they tend to place less emphasis on cultural issues in their messages (Guth et al. 1997), and mainline congregations are less uniformly conservative than those in evangelical churches. So, while there is a consistent link between doctrinal orthodoxy and political conservatism and Republicanism across both white Protestant traditions, just as the culture wars model predicts, the political impact of commitment is very dependent on whether one is affiliated with an evangelical or mainline church, just as the ethnoreligious model contends.

The evidence suggests that the reality of contemporary religion and politics lies somewhere between the culture wars and ethnoreligious models. Theological and behavioral orthodoxy do lead to cultural and political conservatism across the three largest religious traditions. However, the size and direction of the effects of religious beliefs and behaviors vary across traditions, and there remain clear differences in political attitudes and behavior among traditions.

Moreover, while there is clearly a traditionalist–modernist religious cleavage in current American politics, it is based not just on theological conservatism, but also on religious affiliation. In other words, there are not only ideological and partisan differences between traditionalists and modernists within the major religious traditions, there are also ideological and partisan differences between the religious tradition most committed to Protestant orthodoxy, namely, the strongly Republican evangelical tradition, and the individuals with the least orthodox religious affiliations, namely, seculars, those individuals with no ties to a church or religious community.

The focus of the chapters that follow this one is on the extent to which the traditionalist–modernist division in American party politics has grown over time. In examining this, I focus on the traditionalist–modernist cleavage in both of its forms. I ask whether the political gap within traditions between the most orthodox and committed members and the least orthodox and committed members has grown over time. And I ask whether the Republican ties of committed evangelical Protestants and the Democratic ties of seculars have increased over time.

Data and the Measurement of Religion in the Remaining Chapters

All the analyses of religion and party politics in this book include measures of religious belonging, believing, and behaving, and most of them follow the scheme laid out in equation 2.1. However, because some of the data sources that I use are not as thorough in their coverage of religious orientations as are the NES surveys, and because some of the analyses call for ways of incorporating the religious measures that are different from that in the equation, it is at times necessary to modify—for the most part only slightly—the general scheme of measuring religion and modeling its political impact. To maintain the continuity of the discussion in chapters 3 through 7, I outline here the various data sources used in the analyses in those chapters and the measures of religion fashioned for those data.

The Religious Orientations of National Convention Delegates

To examine religious and cultural change among partisan activists, chapters 3 and 4 focus on the delegates to the Democratic and Republican national nominating conventions. Chapter 3 examines changes from 1972 to 1996 in the religious orientations of Democratic and Republican delegates. Chapter 4 explores the relationship between those orientations and delegates' attitudes on issues, candidate preferences, and political motivations. Most of the data for these analyses come from the Convention Delegate Studies (CDS) conducted by Warren E. Miller and others from 1972 to 1992.[11] These surveys represent far and away the longest and most comprehensive longitudinal series on the political attitudes and behavior of party activists. They provide an excellent means for assessing not only aggregate change in the composition of the parties' convention delegations, but also change over time in the attitudes and orientations of individual activists. The 1980, 1984, and 1988 CDS surveys each contained panel components, reinterviewing respondents to previous studies whether or not they were delegates to the conventions in those years.[12] While I rely primarily on the cross-sectional components of the CDS,[13] I do at times employ these panel components to assess the degree to which aggregate shifts resulted from individual-level change.

The CDS is also the only national-level longitudinal study of party activists to consistently contain indicators of religious orientations. Although the CDS contains fewer religious items than the NES surveys, it contains enough religious items to form valid measures of religious orientations and to accurately assess religious trends among the parties' delegates. Each of the five studies contained questions about denominational affiliation and frequency of church or synagogue attendance. Each CDS from 1980 to 1992 included a question concerning religious salience, or the amount of guidance provided by religion. The 1988 and 1992 CDS asked respondents if they considered themselves to be fundamentalist Christians.

The focus of the analysis in chapter 3 is on religious traditions and church attendance. This is true not only because they are the only items included in all of the CDS surveys, but also because they have been at the core of most research on partisan religious trends (Green et al. 1996; Miller and Shanks 1996; Manza and Brooks 1997) and, as noted above, because the traditionalist–modernist political cleavage takes shape not just within religious traditions, but also between traditions. I combine the various denominations in the CDS into eight religious traditions— mainline Protestant, evangelical Protestant, black Protestant, Catholic, Jewish, Mormon, Eastern Orthodox, and secular[14]— and divide some of the religious traditions into "regular" attenders (those individuals who attend church almost every week or more) and "nonregular" attenders (those who attend less often than almost every week).

One difficulty with the CDS data is that their denominational codings include only a very small number of evangelical denominations (see appendix A1). Thus, many evangelical Protestants are probably hidden in the CDS' "other Protestant" category and, since the CDS coding includes most of the mainline Protestant denominations, it is likely that most "other Protestants" are evangelicals. Therefore, I examine the growth of evangelical Protestantism in the GOP in two ways. First, I use all the CDS surveys to examine change in the percentage of Republican delegates affiliated with particular evangelical denominations. Second, using the 1988 and 1992 CDS, I broaden the evangelical category to include not only those delegates affiliated with the evangelical denominations contained in the CDS coding, but also those "other Protestants" who identify themselves as fundamentalist Christians (cf. Green et al. 1996). I then use these two studies to examine differences in the percentage of various cohorts of Republican delegates included in this broader, and probably more accurate, category of evangelical Protestants.[15]

In addition to changes in the types of religious traditions with which Republican and Democratic activists are affiliated, chapter 3 examines changes in the church attendance and religious salience of the two parties' delegates. Since there was no CDS survey conducted in 1996, I employ surveys of 1996 Republican and Democratic national convention delegates conducted by the *New York Times* and CBS News to examine the religious and cultural orientations of delegates in 1996.[16]

Most of the analyses in chapter 4 use only the 1988 and 1992 CDS, surveys that contained both the church attendance and religious salience measures. Thus, those analyses examine the independent and interdependent impact of religious tradition and religious commitment on delegates' political orientations.

Religious Change in the Parties' Mass Coalitions

In chapter 5, I examine the changes in the party loyalties and voting patterns of religious groups in the mass electorate and in the religious composition of the parties' electoral coalitions from 1960 through 1996. The bulk of the chapter focuses on the partisan orientations of particular religious traditions and of regular and nonregular worship attenders within those traditions. The reason for this focus is partly methodological: The only religious questions in the NES surveys prior to 1980 (with the exception of the 1964 and 1968 surveys, which contained a question about the Bible) were about religious affiliation and church attendance. But, as noted previously, it is also partly substantive.

The coding of religious affiliations is not as detailed in the NES surveys prior to 1990 as it is in those from 1990 through 1996. However, it is still possible to assign respondents to one of the five major religious traditions (evangelical, mainline, and black Protestants; Catholics; and Jews) or to the secular, conservative nontraditional, liberal nontraditional, Eastern Orthodox, or "other religion" categories. The construction of these traditions and the definition of regular and nonregular church attenders are discussed in appendix A1.

The last section of chapter 5 examines changes in the political impact of doctrinal orthodoxy and religious commitment within religious traditions from 1980 through 1996. The NES surveys prior to 1988 did not ask respondents how often they prayed or read the Bible, so the measure of religious commitment used in this analysis is simply the sum of worship attendance and religious salience. The measure of doctrinal orthodoxy is simply the sum of respondents' answers to the questions about their views of the Bible and whether or not they are born-again Christians. These measures also are employed in chapter 7 in path analyses of the political impact of religion from 1980 through 1996.

Developing an Index of Religious Traditionalism

The preceding discussion and analysis indicate that religion is a multi-dimensional concept and should be operationalized through multiple, independent indicators such as religious tradition, doctrinal orthodoxy, and religious commitment. The large majority of the analysis in this book employs multiple religious measures and examines the political orientations of various religious traditions and the political impact of religious beliefs and behaviors within those traditions, similarly to equation 2.1. However, there are certain parts of the analysis for which a multidimensional measurement strategy may prove cumbersome to analyst and reader alike, and for which a single measure of the traditionalist–modernist religious cleavage may be more straightforward and analytically powerful.

For example, one of the key propositions in chapter 1 is that religious change in the parties' mass electoral coalitions follows from change in the stands of Democratic and Republican leaders, candidates, and officeholders on cultural issues. To test that proposition, it is necessary to conduct an analysis of the link over time between the alignment of party elites on cultural issues and the religious composition of the parties' mass coalitions, an analysis I present in chapter 6. If I were to maintain the multidimensional measurement scheme in this analysis, I would examine the connections over time between the cultural alignment of party elites and the party affiliations of evangelical Protestants with high levels of doctrinal orthodoxy and commitment, between the elite alignment and the party affiliations of evangelicals with low levels of orthodoxy and commitment, between the elite alignment and the party affiliations of mainline Protestants with high levels of orthodoxy and commitment, between the elite alignment and the party affiliations of mainliners with low levels of orthodoxy and commitment, and so on. In short, I would present ten or twelve analyses of the linkage between the aggregate positions of party elites on cultural issues and the party identifications of religious groups in the mass electorate. Such an account might capture the full complexity of changes in the relationship between religion and partisanship, but it would make for a very long chapter, and it might prove very difficult for the reader to determine what all the analyses, in the end, mean for the division of the parties' coalitions along traditionalist–modernist religious lines.

By contrast, an analysis of the relationship over time between the cultural-issue alignment of Democratic and Republican elites and the alignment of the Democratic and Republican mass coalitions on a single indicator of religious traditionalism would not capture the full complexity of the changes in religion and mass politics. However, it would provide a much more straightforward account of the effect of changes in the cultural stands of party elites on changes in the traditionalist–modernist gap between the parties' mass coalitions, and it might lead to more powerful and more interpretable insights about the links between elite and mass partisan change.[17] Other analyses of the connection over time between elite and mass alignments on single ideological dimensions, such as the work of Adams (1997) on the abortion issue and particularly the work of Carmines and Stimson (1989) on issues of racial desegregation, have yielded important insights about not only the process of party polarization on particular issues, but also the partisan change process in general.

It is generally a mistake to sacrifice accuracy for empirical simplicity. Accordingly, I use the more complex multidimensional measure of religion whenever possible, at times even in conjunction with the single indicator of religious traditionalism. But for certain portions of chapters 3, 5, 6, and 7, a unidimensional measure of the traditionalist–modernist cleavage should provide a much more elegant, powerful, and interpretable analysis.

So the question is, "Is it possible to construct a single measure that is a reliable indicator of traditionalist–modernist religious orientations?" Of course, such an indicator should incorporate religious belonging, believing, and behaving since all three are related to political behavior and since the traditionalist–modernist religious cleavage is defined not just by doctrinal orthodoxy and religious commitment, but also by religious tradition. In fact, past research has incorporated belonging, believing, and behaving into a single measure of religious traditionalism by combining measures of doctrinal orthodoxy, religious commitment, and an ordinal measure of the traditionalism or orthodoxy of religious affiliations (Green, Guth, and Fraser 1991; Guth and Green 1996; Layman and Carmines 1997). Such a measure has proven to be a powerful predictor of the political affiliations of activists and ordinary voters, in fact demonstrating a more substantial political impact than other leading indicators of cultural traditionalism–modernism (Layman and Carmines 1997).

Combining doctrinal orthodoxy and religious commitment into a single measure of religious traditionalism is relatively uncontroversial. The two are closely related,[18] they are both associated with moral traditionalism and cultural conservatism, and, as I showed in table 2.1, it is the combination of orthodoxy and commitment that produce the clearest cultural, moral, and political divisions within religious traditions. Lyman Kellstedt and his colleagues (1997) contend that religious orthodoxy within traditions is defined by both beliefs and behaviors, and they combine the two into measures of religious traditionalism within faith traditions. I follow the same practice in forming a measure of "doctrinal–behavioral traditionalism," which I use in chapter 7 to examine the relationship between religious traditionalism–modernism and voting behavior within religious traditions.[19]

Attempts to rank religious traditions according to orthodoxy, however, have proven to be more disputable. Critics argue that orthodoxy is tradition specific. For example, orthodox beliefs among Catholics are entirely different from those among Baptists. Thus, one can not say with any degree of certainty that Baptists are any more or less orthodox than Catholics (Grant, Mockabee, and Monson 1997).

However, there are two things that point to the possibility that one may be able to rank-order religious affiliations according to religious traditionalism or orthodoxy. The first is the empirical evidence that there are clear differences in the acceptance of traditionalist moral values by different traditions. As table 2.1 shows, even when variations in doctrinal orthodoxy and religious commitment are taken into account, there remain differences in the moral traditionalism of various religious traditions. Evangelical Protestants at all levels of orthodoxy and commitment have noticeably more traditional moral values than mainline Protestants, black Protestants, and Catholics at similar levels of orthodoxy and commitment. Jews and seculars have clearly more progressive moral values than members of any of the other religious traditions. Of course, the fact that Catholics have less traditional moral values than evangelical Protestants does not necessarily mean that they are less traditionally religious or orthodox, but the results are suggestive.

Second, several scholars have ranked religious denominations along the lines of orthodoxy or conservatism, and such scales have served as proxies for the degree to which individuals are committed to traditional religious values such as belief in God and an afterlife (Stark and Glock 1968; Beatty and Walter 1984; Roof and McKinney 1987; Green and Guth 1991; Guth and Green 1996). Accordingly, there is clear evidence that the predominant beliefs and practices of clergy and parishioners in some denominations or religious movements are more traditional than those of their counterparts in other denominations or movements. For example, religious leaders and parishioners in the Assemblies of God are clearly more committed to orthodox Protestant beliefs and values than their counterparts in the United Church of Christ. In fact, the mainline–evangelical divide in American Protestantism is based inherently on commitment to Protestant orthodoxy. The denominations included in the mainline tradition are those that have abandoned many aspects of Protestant orthodoxy in an attempt to reconcile their faith with modern life. The denominations in the evangelical tradition are those that have embraced modernity with much less zeal and have sought to preserve traditional Protestant beliefs and practices (Hunter 1983; Kellstedt et al. 1996; Smith 1998).

Some scholars make even finer distinctions among Protestant denominations on the basis of adherence to traditional Protestant orthodoxy and accommodation to modernity. Roof and McKinney (1987), for example, identify three groups of Protestants: liberals, moderates, and conservatives. The liberal wing, which includes denominations such as Episcopalians and the United Church of Christ, "sought to accommodate modernity by redefining religious truth in ways that minimized conflict with science and biblical higher criticism and by developing Social Gospel ministries in response to new needs arising from urbanization and industrialization" (Roof and McKinney 1987: 79).[20] The conservative wing, the wing that "insisted upon the inerrancy of the Scriptures, the primacy of religion over science, and concern with individual salvation" (Roof and McKinney 1987: 79), includes most of the denominations and movements in the evangelical Protestant tradition. The moderate wing falls between the liberals and conservatives in its commitment to orthodoxy and acceptance of modernity and includes mainline Protestant denominations such as the United Methodists, Disciples of Christ, and Evangelical Lutherans. Stark and Glock (1968) form measures of the adherence of denominations to general Christian orthodoxy—belief in such core Christian principles as the existence of God, the divinity of Jesus Christ, and the authenticity of biblical miracles—and find similar liberal, moderate, and conservative groupings among Protestant denominations.

Within the evangelical tradition, distinctions often are made between fundamentalist Protestants, who interpret the Bible literally and favor a strict separation from the secular society, and less orthodox "neoevangelical" Protestants, who see the Bible as authoritative but do not interpret it literally, and who are less suspicions of integration into the larger society (Hunter 1983; Kellstedt and Smidt 1996; Oldfield 1996). Although they tend to be less separatist and their religious practices are far different from those of fundamentalists, charismatic Protestant groups such as the Assemblies of God and the Pentecostal Holiness church do share the strict adherence to orthodox Protestant beliefs of fundamentalists (Stark and Glock 1968; Guth and Green 1996). Thus, at least among white Protestants, the literature does point to an ordinal ranking of religious affiliations: liberal Protestants, moderate Protestants, neo-evangelicals, and fundamentalists and charismatics, from least to most orthodox.

Outside the mainline and evangelical camps, the traditions that are easiest to assign to a position on the denominational orthodoxy scale are black Protestants, the smaller nontraditional Protestant groups, and seculars. The black Protestant and conservative nontraditional groups certainly have unique religious histories and some beliefs that fall outside orthodox Protestantism, but they also share many of the same beliefs as white evangelical Protestants. They may be placed appropriately between the moderate Protestant and neoevangelical categories.[21] The liberal nontraditional groups have abandoned some orthodox beliefs in favor of fuller integration within modern society and may be grouped appropriately with the liberal Protestants (cf. Green and Guth 1991). Since seculars generally have abandoned religion and its associated practices and beliefs altogether, they clearly should fall at the low end of any measure of the traditionalism of religious affiliations (cf. Guth and Green 1996).

Since the beliefs and styles of religious practice that are accepted among Catholics and Jews are far different from the traditional doctrine and practices of Protestantism, placing these traditions on the ordinal scale is a more difficult task. Past research, however, does provide some guidance. Stark and Glock (1970) find that Catholics are very similar to the moderate Protestant denominations in terms of commitment to orthodox Christian beliefs. However, in the time since Stark and Glock's research, commitment to orthodox Catholic beliefs has declined among Catholic parishioners, and Catholics have fallen slightly behind moderate Protestants in their adherence to general Christian orthodoxy (Roof and McKinney 1987). It may be appropriate to place Catholics between liberal and moderate Protestants (cf. Green and Guth 1991).[22] Although there is considerable variation within Judaism, most Jews have low levels of religious commitment and do not hold common religious beliefs such as the belief in life after death (Harrison and Lazerwitz 1982; Roof and McKinney 1987). The fact that Jews identify with a religious tradition may display a level of religious commitment greater than that of seculars. However, the appropriate place for Jews on this scale of religious orthodoxy seems to be below that of liberal Protestants (cf. Green and Guth 1991).

Based on these assessments of the religious traditionalism of various groups, my denominational orthodoxy scale and the values assigned to each category of the scale are as follows:

Seculars = 0
Jews = 1
Liberal Protestants and liberal nontraditional = 2
Catholics = 3
Moderate Protestants = 4
Black Protestants and conservative nontraditional = 5
Neoevangelicals = 6
Fundamentalists and charismatics = 7.

Not surprisingly, this scale is very similar to past efforts to array religious affiliations according to Christian orthodoxy (Stark and Glock 1968; Roof and McKinney 1987; Green and Guth 1991; Guth and Green 1996). Moreover, the scale is strongly related to all the measures of doctrinal orthodoxy and religious commitment, and it has a monotonic relationship with the doctrinal–behavioral traditionalism measure.[23] For certain analyses in chapter 7—namely, path analyses of the direct and indirect effects of religious orientations on partisanship and voting behavior, and analyses of the conditions under which traditionalist–modernist religious orientations are more or less strongly related to voting behavior—I combine the denominational orthodoxy scale with measures of doctrinal orthodoxy and religious commitment, to form a "religious traditionalism" index.[24]

Unfortunately, the analysis in chapter 6 of the connections over time between religious and cultural change at the elite, activist, and mass levels of party politics cannot make use of a religious traditionalism index that incorporates doctrinal orthodoxy and a full measure of religious commitment. The NES surveys prior to 1980 contain measures of only religious affiliation and church attendance, and to begin in 1980 would ignore the potentially important developments that occurred in or before that year—for example, the cultural liberalism of the McGovern candidacy in 1972, the formation of the Christian Right in the late 1970s, and the cultural conservatism of the Reagan campaign in 1980—and would make it impossible to tell whether or not important trends in the religious composition of the party coalitions began in or before 1980.

So is it possible to form a valid indicator of the traditionalist–modernist religious cleavage with only measures of religious affiliation and worship attendance? Clearly, a measure that includes no independent indicator of religious beliefs and only one gauge of religious commitment is less than ideal. However, it is true that religious belonging forms and shapes religious beliefs, that religious affiliation has been used in past research as a proxy for beliefs (Kellstedt 1989; Guth and Green 1996), and that my denominational orthodoxy scale is strongly and monotonically related to doctrinal orthodoxy. Moreover, since the members of a religious tradition who are frequent attenders of worship services tend to be more committed than less frequent attenders to the orthodox beliefs and practices of the tradition as well as to religious values that are common to all traditions (cf. Roof and McKinney 1987), it may be possible to form a measure of religious traditionalism that is more finely grained and more accurate than the denominational orthodoxy scale by combining that scale with frequency of church attendance.

One way to combine denominational orthodoxy and worship attendance simply would be to add one point to the denominational orthodoxy scale for frequent attenders and subtract one point for infrequent attenders. However, that assumes that the difference in the traditionalism or orthodoxy of regular and nonregular attenders is equal across the denominational categories. In reality, that difference is likely to grow as denominational orthodoxy increases.

The more orthodox denominations should provide parishioners with a more homogeneous, uniformly traditionalist religious context than do the less orthodox denominations. Members of fundamentalist and charismatic churches should receive consistently orthodox religious messages from their pastors and, in their interaction with other parishioners, should encounter individuals with uniformly traditionalist religious outlooks. Frequent attenders of these churches thus should be significantly more orthodox in their religious beliefs and styles of religious practice than are infrequent attenders. The religious context in less orthodox denominations should be more heterogenous and, of course, less traditionalist. Members of mainline Protestant and Catholic churches should receive a widely varied set of religious cues through their religious participation. Some of the messages delivered by clergy will have orthodox themes, but many will have a liberal or progressive theme. Some parishioners will have highly conservative religious beliefs, while others will be much more liberal (Wald, Owen, and Hill 1990; Wald 1997; Guth et al. 1997). Thus, the difference in the religious orthodoxy of regular and nonregular church attenders should be less in these traditions than in evangelical and fundamentalist denominations.

To test the hypothesis that the difference in religious traditionalism between regular and nonregular worship attenders grows larger as denominational orthodoxy increases, I conducted a regression analysis, using the NES surveys from 1980 through 1996, in which doctrinal–behavioral traditionalism was the dependent variable and denominational orthodoxy, the dichotomous church attendance variable (nonregular/regular), and their interaction were the independent variables.[25] The results were as follows:

$$\text{Traditionalism} = .33 + .05(\text{denominational orthodoxy}) + .09(\text{church attendance}) + .02(\text{denominational orthodoxy} \times \text{church attendance}),$$

with all coefficients reaching high levels of statistical significance ($p < .001$).[26] This indicates that the difference in religious traditionalism between regular and nonregular worship attenders does increase as denominational orthodoxy increases. The difference is .11 for Jews (1 on the denomination scale), .13 for liberal Protestants (2), .15 for Catholics (3), and so on.

What is the proper way, then, to incorporate the larger effect of church attendance on religious traditionalism for more orthodox denominations than for less orthodox groups? Well, the regression results indicate that the slope of religious traditionalism on denominational orthodoxy is approximately 1.4 times greater $(.05 + .02)/.05$ for regular church attenders than for nonregular church attenders. Thus, if I arbitrarily set the difference in scale points between nonregular attenders in various denominational categories at 1 (the same difference between categories in the denominational orthodoxy scale), then the difference in scale points between regularly attending members of the denominational categories should be 1.4. The resulting measure of religious traditionalism, which I call the religious orthodoxy scale, is as follows:[27]

	Nonregular Attenders	Regular Attenders
Seculars	0	—
Jews	0	2
Liberal Protestants	1	3.4
Catholics	2	4.8
Moderate Protestants	3	6.2
Blacks/Conservative nontraditional	4	7.6
Neoevangelicals	5	9
Fundamentalists and charismatics	6	10.4

TABLE 2.2
Predicted moral values and cultural attitudes by
denominational orthodoxy and church attendance

Denominational Orthodoxy and Church Attendance	Moral Traditionalism	Cultural Issues	Cultural Groups
Seculars	.52	.21	.44
Jews			
Nonregular	.52	.21	.44
Regular	.57	.26	.49
Liberal Protestants			
Nonregular	.54	.23	.47
Regular	.61	.29	.52
Catholics			
Nonregular	.57	.26	.49
Regular	.65	.33	.56
Moderate Protestants			
Nonregular	.60	.28	.52
Regular	.68	.36	.59
Black Protestants/conservative nontraditional			
Nonregular	.63	.31	.54
Regular	.72	.40	.63
Neoevangelicals			
Nonregular	.65	.33	.56
Regular	.76	.43	.66
Fundamentalists and charismatics			
Nonregular	.68	.36	.58
Regular	.80	.47	.69

Source: 1996 National Election Study.

The entries are the predicted values from regressions of moral traditionalism, cultural issue attitudes, and cultural group evaluations on the religious orthodoxy scale and several demographic variables. All the demographic variables were held constant at their means to compute the predictions. All the dependent variables range from 0 (most liberal) to 1 (most conservative).

The religious orthodoxy scale not only captures theoretical differences between various religious denominations and between frequent and infrequent worship attenders within those denominations, but also appears to be quite empirically valid. Its correlation with doctrinal–behavioral traditionalism (created with all indicators of doctrinal orthodoxy and religious commitment except church attendance with the NES surveys from 1980 through 1996) is a very robust .61. Moreover, table 2.2 presents the predicted values from regression analyses in which moral traditionalism, attitudes toward cultural issues, and evaluations of the groups involved in the cultural conflict are the dependent variables, and the religious orthodoxy scale and several demographic variables are the independent variables. The differences in the moral values and cultural attitudes of different denominational groups and of frequent and infrequent church attenders within those groups are comparable to the differences between religious traditions and between the most and least orthodox and committed members of those traditions shown in table 2.1. Seculars and Jews have less traditional moral values and more liberal cultural attitudes than do members of Christian denominations. Evangelical and fundamentalist Protestants are more morally traditional and culturally conservative than mainline Protestants and Catholics. The most committed members of all denominational groups have more conservative moral and cultural views than their less committed counterparts. Finally, the gap between individuals with high and low levels of religious commitment is greater in the evangelical and fundamentalist denominations than it is in less orthodox denominations.

In sum, this religious orthodoxy scale does not substitute for independent measures of religious beliefs and behaviors. However, it does provide a fair representation of the moral and cultural differences across and within religious traditions. Thus, it, like the religious traditionalism index—which combines denominational orthodoxy, doctrinal orthodoxy, and religious commitment—and the index of doctrinal–behavioral traditionalism—which combines doctrinal orthodoxy and religious commitment—should be useful for examining the traditionalist–modernist cleavage between the two parties in certain parts of the analysis.

NOTES

1. In this book, I use data from the NES surveys from 1960 through 1996. The surveys from 1960 through 1968 were conducted by the Survey Research Center at the University of Michigan. The surveys from 1970 through 1996 were conducted by the Center for Political Studies at the University of Michigan. All these data were made available by the Inter-University Consortium for Political and Social Research. Most of the data from 1960

through 1992 come from the 1952–1992 NES cumulative data file (Miller and the National Election Studies 1994). The data for 1994 come from the 1994 NES postelection survey (Rosenstone et al. 1995) and the data for 1996 come from the 1996 NES pre- and postelection surveys (Rosenstone et al. 1997). Neither the original collectors of the data nor the consortium bear any responsibility for the analyses or interpretations presented here.

2. Appendix A1 presents a detailed discussion of all the religious measures used in this and subsequent chapters.

3. There is a monotonic relationship between this four-category Bible scale and the indicators of moral and cultural traditionalism used later in the chapter. Respondents who believe that the Bible is not the Word of God are more morally and culturally liberal than those who believe that the Bible is the Word of God but should not be taken literally. The latter are more liberal than respondents who believe that the Bible is literally true but are infrequent readers, who, in turn, are more liberal than Biblical literalists who are frequent readers. There is also a monotonic relationship between the Bible item and measures of religious commitment as well as identification as a born-again Christian.

4. Of course, saying that one is a born-again Christian does not necessarily indicate a belief that one must have an adult conversion experience to be saved. However, there is likely to be a very high correlation between being willing to identify one's self as a born-again Christian and believing in the necessity of conversion.

5. As noted earlier, the religious beliefs and practices that are considered appropriate and important vary across religious traditions. So, ideally, one would like to have different measures of doctrinal orthodoxy and religious commitment for different traditions. Unfortunately, there are not enough religious items in the NES or any other study that examines political behavior over a series of elections to do this. However, the results presented here are consistent with those of analyses using data that do have enough religious indicators to form tradition-specific measures of orthodoxy and commitment (Kellstedt et al. 1997).

6. The demographic controls are education, income, southern residence, gender, age, and union membership. I do not include a control for race because I include a dummy variable for black Protestants, almost all of whom are black.

7. Members of smaller non-Protestant religions, Eastern Orthodox religions, and non-Judeo-Christian religions are dropped from the analysis.

8. The measurement of all issue attitudes, group attitudes, and values involved in the analyses is discussed in appendix A2. The first three dependent variables are all indices ranging from most liberal to most conservative. Ideology is a seven-point scale ranging from extremely liberal to extremely

conservative. Party identification is a seven-point scale ranging from strong Democrat to strong Republican. For this analysis, all these variables are coded to range from 0 (most liberal/Democratic) to 1 (most conservative/ Republican). The vote is coded 0 for Clinton voters and 1 for Dole voters.

9. For all of the variables except the presidential vote, the entries in the table are the predicted values from a regression model. For the vote, the entries are the probabilities of voting for Dole predicted from a logit model.

10. The effects of doctrine and commitment are presented by showing the predictions for low, middle, and high values on the two variables for each tradition. The middle value is simply the mean for the tradition. The low value is one standard deviation below the mean, and the high value is one standard deviation above the mean. All the control variables are held constant at their means for the entire sample. The predictions for Jews and seculars are for their mean values on both doctrine and commitment. The dummy variables for both those groups were, for statistical purposes, interacted with doctrine and commitment. However, because of the very small number of Jews in the sample and because seculars do not really constitute a religious tradition, providing a context for the effects of doctrine and commitment, I show only the predictions for the mean values.

11. Miller was joined by Elizabeth Douvan, William J. Crotty, and Jeane Kirkpatrick for the 1972 study; M. Kent Jennings and Barbara G. Farah for the 1980 study; Jennings for the 1984 and 1988 studies; and Richard Herrera for the 1992 study. The 1992 CDS surveyed 1,858 Democratic delegates and 995 Republican delegates to the 1992 national conventions. See Miller and Jennings (1986) and Herrera (1992) for the number of observations in and response rates to the 1972–1988 CDS. Since there was no CDS conducted in 1976, measures of the attitudes and characteristics of 1976 delegates are taken from the 2,035 respondents to the 1980 CDS who were delegates in 1976. The 1980 CDS was designed specifically to study both 1980 delegates and 1976 delegates (Miller and Jennings 1986). It surveyed all the delegates to both the 1976 and 1980 conventions and included roughly the same number of delegates from both years. The 1972 and 1980 CDS surveys were made available by the Inter-University Consortium for Political and Social Research. The 1984 through 1992 surveys were obtained directly from Richard Herrera. Neither the consortium, nor Professor Herrera, nor the original collectors of the data bear any responsibility for the analyses or interpretations presented here.

12. The 1980 CDS surveyed 1,373 delegates to the 1972 conventions who responded to the 1972 survey. The 1984 CDS surveyed 654 delegates to the 1972 conventions who responded to the 1972 survey, 1,018 delegates from 1976 who responded to the 1980 survey, and 1,262 delegates from 1980 who responded to the 1980 survey. The 1988 CDS surveyed 767 delegates

from 1976 who responded to the 1980 survey, 921 delegates from 1980 who responded to the 1980 survey, and 1,392 delegates from 1984 who responded to the 1984 survey.

13. Since some of the CDS surveys have interviewed respondents to past studies even if they were not delegates in that particular year, they contain a broader sample of activists than simply the delegates to the parties' conventions in particular years. Specifically, they contain samples of individuals who were active in the parties' presidential campaigns in a particular year whether or not they were convention delegates in that year. Past research has focused on these presidential campaign activists (cf. Miller and Jennings 1986; Layman and Carsey 1998). However, it is only current convention delegates that have a hand in drafting the parties' platforms, and only current delegations reflect the outcomes of the nomination process in that year. For these reasons, I focus primarily on delegates only. However, the religious and cultural trends for the broader sample of presidential campaign activists in the CDS are very similar to, although slightly less pronounced than, those presented for convention delegates.

14. Mormons generally are included in the larger family of "conservative nontraditional" religions, but they are the only one of these groups included in the denominational codings of the CDS. With the exception of the 1972 CDS, the only Eastern Orthodox religion included in the denominational codings was Greek Orthodox. The 1972 CDS included a coding for Eastern Orthodox but not a separate one for Greek Orthodox. A final religious group that is used for statistical purposes includes those respondents who identified their affiliation as "other Protestant" or "other religion." Since the only other religious variable besides denomination included in the 1972 CDS was church attendance, there is not enough information to assign individuals with these ambiguous responses to one of the traditions. Some of the analyses in chapter 4 employ only the 1988 or 1992 CDS and are able to assign some of these respondents to one of the traditions.

15. Respondents are assigned to cohorts based on the year in which they were first delegates. Data on the 1992 cohort come from the 1992 CDS, and data from the 1972–1988 cohorts come from the 1988 CDS. Since the 1988 CDS contained a panel component, it surveyed a large number of individuals who were delegates to the conventions from 1972 to 1984 even if they were not delegates in 1988. It included 461 respondents in the 1972 cohort, 673 in the 1976 cohort, 833 in the 1980 cohort, and 1,093 in the 1984 cohort. The analyses in chapter 4 use only this second measure of the evangelical tradition.

16. These surveys interviewed 509 Democratic delegates and 1,310 Republican delegates. Since the wording of most of the religious and cultural questions in these surveys differs from that in the CDS, they do not allow a direct comparison between 1996 delegates and delegates to earlier conven-

tions (except on the issue of abortion, on which the polls used four-point scales similar to those in the CDS). However, they do contain enough data on the religious and cultural orientations of party activists in 1996 to provide a general sense of whether the religious and cultural trends observed among activists from 1972 to 1992 continued through 1996.

17. Another part of the analysis for which a single indicator of religious traditionalism is useful, and perhaps necessary, is the examination in chapter 7 of the circumstances under which traditionalist–modernist religious orientations matter for political behavior. The question there is, do factors such as cultural-issue salience, political awareness, and political discussion in religious settings lead to a stronger connection between traditionalist–modernist orientations and electoral choice? To answer it, I conduct logit analyses of the vote that include multiplicative interaction terms between a factor such as cultural salience and an individual's degree of religious traditionalism. If I were to use multiple measures of the traditionalist–modernist cleavage, for example, doctrinal orthodoxy, religious commitment, and religious tradition, I would have multiple, closely related interaction terms in the statistical models. That might create problems for statistical estimation as well as for interpretation. In contrast, a single interaction term between a factor such as cultural salience and a single indicator of religious traditionalism would provide for much more straightforward estimation and interpretation.

18. The correlation between doctrinal orthodoxy and religious commitment in the 1996 NES is .61.

19. I call this measure doctrinal–behavioral traditionalism to distinguish it from a "religious traditionalism" index that combines doctrinal orthodoxy, religious commitment, and the orthodoxy of religious belonging. The doctrinal–behavioral traditionalism measure in the 1996 NES is formed by summing respondents' scores on the Bible item, the born-again indicator, frequency of prayer, frequency of worship attendance, and religious salience. Its reliability coefficient (alpha) is .84 for all respondents, .80 for evangelicals, .75 for mainline Protestants, and .61 for Catholics. The measure ranges from 0 (most modernist) to 1 (most traditionalist).

20. Roof and McKinney also include Presbyterians (or specifically the Presbyterian Church in the USA) in the liberal Protestant category. However, in terms of general Christian orthodoxy, measured through belief in God, the divinity of Jesus Christ, the authenticity of biblical miracles, and the existence of the Devil, Stark and Glock (1968) show that Presbyterians are closer to "moderate" denominations such as United Methodist and Disciples of Christ than they are to "liberal" denominations such as Episcopalians and Congregationalists. Similarly, Green and Guth (1991) place Presbyterians with the moderate mainline denominations in their denominational orthodoxy scale.

21. There may be some argument for placing black Protestant and

conservative nontraditional denominations at the same scale position as neo-evangelicals since these groups share many of the same beliefs. However, other scholars have placed black Protestants at one scale position below the neoevangelical denominations (Green and Guth 1991), and neoevangelicals have levels of doctrinal orthodoxy in the 1996 NES that are significantly higher than those of black Protestants ($p < .05$) and conservative nontraditionals ($p < .005$).

22. Since there are strong arguments for including Catholics and moderate Protestants in the same category of any scale of religious orthodoxy, I also performed all the analyses in which I used this denominational scale with Catholics and moderate Protestants grouped together. The decision to place Catholics in the category just below moderate Protestants has almost no consequence for the findings presented in this book.

23. In the 1996 NES, the correlation coefficients for the relationship between denominational orthodoxy and other religious indicators are as follows: .45 for the Bible measure, .52 for the born-again indicator, .44 for frequency of prayer, .44 for frequency of church attendance, .43 for religious salience, and .58 for doctrinal–behavioral traditionalism. The mean value of doctrinal–behavioral traditionalism is .17 for seculars, .29 for Jews, .35 for liberal Protestants, .45 for Catholics, .49 for moderate Protestants, .64 for black Protestants and conservative nontraditionals, .66 for neoevangelicals, and .73 for fundamentalists and charismatics.

24. These analyses are performed in addition to, not in place of, analyses examining the political impact of religious traditionalism within the context of faith traditions. In the analyses using just the 1996 NES, the religious traditionalism index is formed by summing respondents' standardized scores on the denominational orthodoxy scale, the expanded Bible measure, the born-again indicator, frequency of worship attendance, frequency of prayer, and religious salience. In a principal components analysis of these items, all six load strongly (.70 or greater) on a single component, which explains 58 percent of the total variance in the six items. The reliability coefficient (alpha) of the index is .85. In the analyses using the NES surveys from 1980 through 1996, the religious traditionalism index combines denominational orthodoxy, view of the Bible, the born-again indicator, frequency of worship attendance, and religious salience. The reliability coefficient of the index is .74 in 1980, .75 in 1984, .78 in 1988, .80 in 1992, and .80 in 1996.

25. Since church attendance is one of the independent variables, the doctrinal–behavioral traditionalism measure used here was constructed without church attendance.

26. The r-squared for this regression is .43. Since the equation was estimated with data pooled from all the NES surveys from 1980 through 1996, I also included dummy variables for each survey year other than 1980 as independent variables.

27. I also made some partly arbitrary decisions to set the starting values for the scale. Since there are virtually no seculars who attend church regularly, all seculars are assumed to be nonregular attenders and given the baseline score of 0. So the starting values for the scale are really those for Jews. To set those values, I followed the original decision rule of subtracting one point from the denominational scale for nonregular attenders—thus a score of 0 for Jews who do not attend regularly—and adding one point for regular attenders—thus a score of two for Jews who do attend regularly. The rest of the scale values are based on the assumption that the difference between nonregular attenders in the denominational categories is 1 and the difference between regular attenders is 1.4.

CHAPTER 3

Religious and Cultural Change Among Party Activists

As noted in chapter 1, party activists play a critical role in the partisan change process. If activists do not respond when a candidate, party leader, or other political entrepreneur champions a new political issue, the issue may have little effect on the party system. It is likely to be what Carmines and Stimson (1989) term an "unsuccessful adaptation." If activists do respond to the issue innovation (i.e., individuals aroused by the issue become active on behalf of it and the political leaders who advance it), the issue may have a long-lasting impact on party politics.

Activists have such an effect on the partisan impact of new issues and cleavages for two reasons. First, in a nation where political apathy is abundant, politically attentive and active citizens can have a considerable influence on the political opinions and behavior of their friends, families, and coworkers. Thus, change among party activists often leads to changes in the mass public's perceptions of the parties' stands on particular issues and, at times, to a reshaping of the parties' mass coalitions (Carmines and Stimson 1989). Second, the importance of activists is not limited to translating changes among party elites into changes in mass political behavior. Activists also play a role in bringing about that elite-level change. If a significant number of activists are aroused by a new issue position advocated by a particular candidate, then other candidates may be encouraged to take that position, the party's platforms may champion that stance, and eventually the party's elected officials may attempt to translate that position into public policy.

In this chapter, I focus on religious and cultural change among a particularly important group of activists: the delegates to the parties' quadrennial national conventions. In a sense, convention delegates are much like other activists. Of course, the GOP always has reserved a certain number of delegate slots for its party and elected officials, and the Democrats ensured that a certain proportion of their delegates would be party and elected leaders by creating "superdelegates" in the early 1980s. However, the majority of delegates are not professional politicians but simply citizens who happen to be very active in party politics (Miller and Jennings 1986). Thus, like other activists, convention delegates may serve as opinion leaders in their local communities and provide an important link between elite change and mass change. In fact, since they are among the most active activists, change among delegates may have a particularly large impact on mass images of the parties' policy stands.

There are also a number of ways in which convention delegates are not like other activists and may play an even more important role in the partisan change process. One of those is the influence that delegates may have on the political behavior of other activists. Aldrich (1983a, 1983b) argues that the entry into or exit from a party by any activist affects the political behavior of other activists by shifting the party's mean ideological position. Delegates, however, may have more impact than ordinary activists on the participation decisions of other individuals. Delegates have a hand in shaping the parties' platform, the only official statement of a party's policy positions.[1] Few citizens are aware of what is in these platforms, but politically attentive and active individuals may view the platform as an important signal of the political directions in which the party is moving. Delegates also may affect the behavior of other activists through their positions in the party. Although most are not elected officials or national-level party officials, a majority of delegates hold or have held official positions in their state or local parties.[2] These positions may enhance not only their ability to shape local perceptions about the party's policy stances but also their influence on the decisions of other politically attentive individuals on whether or not to become active in the party. For example, Republican activity by a member of the local Church of God may encourage other Church of God members in the community to become active in the GOP. However, a Church of God member being elected county Republican chairman is likely to draw far more Church of God members into local Republican politics.

Delegates also may have more influence than ordinary activists on the issue positions that the parties' candidates and elected officials take. The parties' platforms constrain not only the positions of presidential candidates, but also the priorities and positions of incumbent presidents (Pomper and Lederman 1980; Budge and Hofferbert 1990). Moreover, the important role that most convention delegates play in state or local party politics may mean that political candidates at all levels have strong incentives to appeal to them.

The parties' national conventions provide an appropriate place to begin the search for religious and cultural change, not only because of what their potential effects on elite and mass political behavior are, but also because of the political process that they reflect. Nominating politics is the most likely arena for the introduction of new partisan issues and cleavages. Candidates for a party's nomination have incentives to emphasize new issues to mobilize new activists behind their campaigns, and the entry of these new activists into nominating politics has been greatly eased by the parties' nomination reforms. Nominating politics is also the primary battleground in the factional struggle for party control. The ultimate goal of the various groups in a party is to determine what types of candidates the party nominates and what types of policy stands those candidates take. Since the composition of the parties' convention delegations reflects the outcomes of the nomination process, the emergence of new cleavages in party politics and changes in the balance of power within the parties should be evident in the characteristics of convention delegates.

In her study of the 1972 party conventions, Kirkpatrick (1976) argues that that election year represented a marked increase in the cultural differences between the two parties. Although the religious composition of the parties had long been distinct, with Republicans being an overwhelmingly Protestant party and with Catholics and Jews representing a large portion of the Democratic coalition and activist base, the members of both parties generally had been committed to traditional Judeo-Christian values and to traditional American values regarding authority, work, and family. The partisan differences that emerged in 1972 were caused not by any sudden increase in the religious and cultural traditionalism of Republican activists but instead by the pervasive secularism and cultural liberalism of the Democratic supporters of George McGovern.

Unfortunately, there are few data on party activists prior to 1972,[3] and what does exist does not provide an adequate examination of activists' religious and cultural orientations. So it is difficult to assess the accuracy of Kirkpatrick's portrayal of 1972 as a critical juncture in the cultural polarization of the parties.[4] However, it is quite possible to address another important question: What has happened among party activists since 1972? Have the religious differences between the two parties grown? Or has the partisan religious polarization that political scientists and other observers have taken notice of only recently really existed since the early 1970s and either not increased noticeably or even decreased since then?

ACTIVISTS, CANDIDATES, AND PARTISAN RELIGIOUS CHANGE

Any change in the aggregate religious orientations of party activists should result largely from religious replacement: secularists and religious liberals disengaging from Republican party activity and being replaced by newly active religious conservatives, religious conservatives disengaging from Democratic party activity and being replaced by newly active religious liberals and secularists.[5] Thus, to understand why and how partisan religious change has occurred, it is necessary to understand why individuals with various religious orientations become active in, remain active in, or cease to be active in party politics.

In a prominent account of party activism, John H. Aldrich (1983a, 1983b, 1995) modifies the Downsian (1957) spatial model of voting behavior to explain the decisions of individuals to engage in or refrain from party activity. Aldrich argues that an individual is more likely to become active in or remain active in a party as the distance between the policy positions of that party and the individual's own positions grows smaller relative to the distance between the individual's positions and those of the other party.[6] Because the issues most closely associated with the contemporary religious cleavage are the cultural issues, change in the aggregate religious characteristics of party activists should be closely related to change in the parties' stands on issues such as abortion, homosexual rights, and school prayer. According to Aldrich's logic, a move by the Republican party to the right on cultural issues should increase the likelihood of Republican activity by religious conservatives, and of Democratic activity by religious liberals and secularists. A shift by the Democratic party to the cultural left should have a similar effect on the participation decisions of individuals in these religious groups.

If individuals' decisions about whether to participate in party activity are driven by their perceptions of the parties' positions on certain issues, then how do potential activists form these perceptions?[7] One possibility is that individuals evaluate the parties' positions on an issue through the mean positions of current activists (Aldrich 1983a). This implies that there should have been a steady growth after 1972 in the religious cleavage between Republican and Democratic activists. The mobilization of secular activists into the Democratic party in 1972 shifted the mean position of Democratic activists on cultural issues to the left. This should have increased the attraction of Democratic party activity for other secularists and religious liberals and made Republican party activity more appealing to religious conservatives. This change in the religious composition of the parties should have resulted in further polarization of the parties' mean cultural positions, which in turn should have attracted even more religious traditionalists into the GOP and even more religious modernists and secularists into the Democratic party.

Empirical evidence supports the assumption that the positions of current party activists shape individuals' perceptions of the parties' policy stances (cf. Carmines and Stimson 1989). However, it is likely that the participation decisions of current and potential activists are shaped also by the stands of the parties' leading candidates. First of all, candidates are a party's most visible activists, and survey data show that support for particular candidates is the most prevalent motivation for party activity (Miller and Jennings 1986). The parties' nominees should have the greatest impact on potential activists' perceptions of the parties' positions. However, candidates who lose nomination campaigns also may affect these perceptions, since they often exert a substantial impact on the positions taken in the parties' platforms. Moreover, even if potential activists do not see the positions of a candidate for the nomination as the party's positions, they may be attracted to party activity by a desire for the party to adopt that candidate's stands.

Second, if potential activists' perceptions of the parties' stands are shaped only by the positions of the parties' current activists, then there is no mechanism to begin a process of partisan change. Activist-level change requires an influx into one of the parties of new activists whose positions on an issue differ enough from the mean position of current activists on the issue that their entry into the party creates a noticeable shift in that mean. However, if potential activists determine where the party stands on an issue only through the current activist mean, then there should not be an incentive to become active for individuals whose positions on the issue differ significantly from that mean. Thus, there must be some factor other than the positions of current activists to motivate party activity by these individuals. That factor may be the positions of party candidates. Candidates for a party's nomination, particularly those who lack the support of party leaders or the traditional activist base of the party, may have incentives to take issue positions that differ from the activist mean so that they can attract new and different types of support.

These stands may draw in new activists whose views lead to a shift in the party's mean position on an issue.

Such a description of the participation decisions of potential activists provides a good explanation for the influx of culturally liberal secularists into the Democratic party in 1972. If the participation decisions of these secular individuals had been based only on the mean cultural position of current Democratic activists, their incentives to become active in the Democratic party would have been small, since Democratic activists had rather traditional cultural attitudes prior to 1972 (Kirkpatrick 1976). However, the attempts by George McGovern to appeal to the cultural liberalism and anti–Vietnam War sentiments of these young voters drew them into Democratic activity and thus shifted the party's mean position on cultural matters to the left.

Because the policy stands of party candidates often diverge from the mean position of current activists, the growth of religious polarization between Democratic and Republican activists should not occur at a constant rate. Instead, the rate of religious change should be accelerated or decelerated in particular years by the cultural-issue positions of the parties' leading candidates. When leading Republican and Democratic candidates take cultural positions that are more centrist than the mean position of activists in their respective parties, the growth of partisan religious polarization should be less—and in fact the extent of polarization may decline from previous levels—than it would be if candidates were located at the activist mean. When Democratic and Republican candidates take cultural positions that are more polarized than are the activist means in their respective parties, the growth of partisan religious polarization should be greater than it would be if candidates were located at the activist mean.

Thus, one might expect the degree of religious polarization between the parties' delegates to decrease between 1972 and 1976. Although the secularism of the 1972 Democratic convention may have encouraged other secularists and religious modernists to become active in Democratic politics after 1972, the nomination of Jimmy Carter, a born-again Christian from Georgia with far less liberal cultural stands than George McGovern, may have decreased the attraction of Democratic activity for these individuals and renewed the enthusiasm of religious conservatives for the Democratic party. In the 1980s, however, partisan religious polarization should have increased as the organizations of the Christian Right became involved in the GOP; Ronald Reagan, the party's nominee in 1980 and 1984, took very conservative stands on cultural and moral issues; and the Democrats nominated candidates such as Walter Mondale and Michael Dukakis with more liberal cultural sensibilities than Carter.

Partisan religious differences may have increased even more sharply in the 1990s as the Christian Right became even more influential within the Republican party (Oldfield 1996; Rozell and Wilcox 1995, 1997), and Republican candidates such as Pat Robertson in 1988 and Pat Buchanan in 1992 and 1996 took extremely conservative cultural stands. These developments should have attracted even more religious traditionalists to Republican activity and perhaps led to a countermobilization of secularists and religious liberals into the Democratic party.

In this chapter, I assess the accuracy of these expectations by first examining change from 1972 to 1996 in the religious orientations of Republican and Democratic national convention delegates. Next, I explore the link between that religious change and changes in the attitudes of party activists on cultural issues such as abortion and women's rights and in the cultural and moral stands taken in the parties' platforms.

The Changing Religious Face of Party Activists

The two religious groups that are at the forefront of the cultural conflict are committed evangelical Protestants, with their very traditional religious and moral views, high levels of religious commitment, and very conservative attitudes on cultural issues; and secularists, who tend to reject traditional moral values and have very liberal views on cultural matters. If the parties are being polarized along religious and cultural lines, it should be most apparent among these two groups. An increasing proportion of Republican activists should be evangelicals, particularly committed evangelicals who attend church regularly. An increasing proportion of Democratic delegates should be secularists.

Part A of figure 3.1 shows the percentage of regularly attending evangelical Protestants among Republican delegates from 1972 to 1992, and part C shows the percentage of seculars among Democratic delegates over this period. They show this for both all delegates and first-time delegates, a group of particular interest since shifts in the parties' positions on cultural issues should lead to the mobilization of new party activists. In part B, evangelical Protestants are defined as all members of evangelical denominations and all "other Protestants" who are self-identified fundamentalists. It shows the percentages of Republican cohorts from 1972 to

1992 who are regularly attending evangelical Protestants according to this broader definition.

Parts A and B of the figure clearly demonstrate the steady ascendance of committed evangelicals within the Republican party after 1976, and this increase is particularly marked among first-time delegates.[8] The consistent nature of this pattern could be explained in large part by a model of partisan change that did not consider the effects of candidates: the increase in evangelicalism among Republican activists between 1976 and 1980 made Republican activity more attractive for other evangelicals, and their entry into the party increased the appeal of GOP participation for even more conservative Protestants.

However, the effect of Republican presidential candidates on this pattern of partisan change should not be discounted. It is, of course, true that the noticeable increase in the proportion of regularly attending evangelicals between 1976 and 1984 coincided with large-scale efforts by the newly formed organizations of the Christian Right to mobilize evangelical Protestants into Republican politics. It is unlikely, however, that their efforts would have been as successful as they were without the assistance of Ronald Reagan. In contrast to the 1976 Republican nominee, Gerald Ford, who ran a centrist campaign and devoted little attention to social and moral issues, Reagan embraced both the principles of the new evangelical political movement and the movement itself. Both Reagan and the Republican platform in 1980 emphasized traditional morality and took highly conservative stands on issues such as abortion, the Equal Rights Amendment (ERA), prayer in the public schools, and homosexual rights.

Reagan also reached out more directly to evangelicals, attending rallies and other events sponsored by Christian Right organizations and declaring at one, "I know you can't [endorse] me, but I want you to know that I endorse you and what you are doing" (quoted in Oldfield 1996: 117). Although many Christian Right leaders criticized the Reagan administration for not fulfilling its promises on cultural issues, Reagan continued his efforts to appeal to evangelicals while in office. The administration provided support for antiabortion and pro–school prayer amendments, and, although unsuccessful in those efforts, it was able to gain further restrictions on federal funding for abortion and greater opportunities for religious expression in the public schools. Reagan also appointed a handful of Christian Right figures to positions within the administration (Guth 1983; Oldfield 1996). Clearly, Ronald Reagan's two presidential campaigns and his presidency signaled to potential activists that the GOP was moving to the religious and cultural right.

A. Percentage of Evangelical Republicans

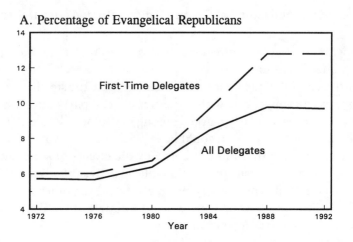

B. Percentage of Evangelical Republicans (Including Fundamentalist "Other Protestants") in Various Cohorts

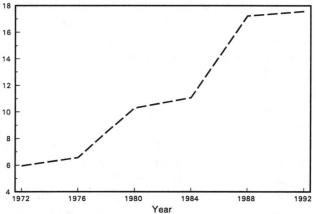

C. Percentage of Secular Democrats

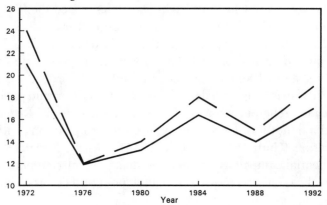

FIGURE 3.1. The percentage of regularly attending evangelicals among Republican delegates and the percentage of secularists among Democratic delegates from 1972 to 1992

Note: The number of observations ranges from 631 to 955 for all delegates and from 484 to 784 for first-timers in part A; it ranges from 168 to 519 in part B; and it ranges from 839 to 1,425 for all delegates and from 815 to 1,351 for first-timers in part C. *Source:* Parts A, C: 1972–1992 Convention Delegate Studies; part B: 1988–1992 Convention Delegate Studies

The unusually high percentage of committed evangelicals at the GOP's 1988 convention also may be explained by candidate-related factors. Pat Robertson, a prominent televangelist and Christian Right leader, sought the Republican nomination in 1988. Although he did not come close to winning, Robertson's campaign attracted a number of previously inactive evangelicals into Republican politics. Perhaps most significant about the Robertson campaign was its appeal to the charismatic and Pentecostal wings of the evangelical movement. The first wave of Christian Right mobilization in the early 1980s had been centered largely among neoevangelicals and fundamentalists, while charismatics and Pentecostals remained largely inactive (Oldfield 1996). Robertson's campaign played a large role in broadening the appeal of Christian Right and Republican activity to all parts of the evangelical constituency (Hertzke 1993).

The pattern of secularism among Democratic delegates is considerably different. Just as Kirkpatrick (1976) showed, secularists were a strong presence at the 1972 Democratic convention, comprising 21 percent of all delegates and 24 percent of first-time delegates.[9] Clearly, McGovern's culturally liberal campaign provided a strong impetus for secular activism in 1972 (and probably discouraged activism by more traditionally religious individuals), as an overwhelming majority of these delegates preferred McGovern as the party's nominee.[10]

Particular candidacies also may provide some insight into the inconsistency of the Democratic pattern after 1972. The conservative religious orientations, more moderate cultural stands, and ties to the culturally traditional South of Jimmy Carter, the party's nominee in 1976 and 1980, undoubtedly contributed to the sharp drop in secularism among Democratic delegates after 1972. In fact, some scholars denote the born-again Carter's candidacy as an important catalyst for the political reawakening of evangelical Christians in the late 1970s (Miller and Wattenberg 1984; Oldfield 1996).

There was a clear growth in Democratic secularism between 1976 and 1992, but it took shape in fits and starts. Reflecting the nomination of a more culturally liberal candidate, Walter Mondale, in 1984 and the growth of religious traditionalism in the Republican party, the proportion of secular Democratic delegates increased noticeably between 1976 and 1984. However, that proportion declined again between 1984 and 1988, and the explanation again may lie in certain presidential candidacies. Although the party nominated Michael Dukakis, the "first truly secular" presidential candidate in American history (Wills 1990: 60), in 1988, the campaigns of two of Dukakis's chief rivals, Jesse Jackson and Al Gore, may have attracted a more religious set of activists to Democratic activity. Jackson's 1988 campaign relied heavily on African-American churches to mobilize support and therefore attracted unusually large numbers of black Protestants to Democratic activity (Hertzke 1993).[11] Gore's campaign focused its efforts on winning the support of moderate and conservative voters, especially in his native South (Hadley and Stanley 1996). As a result, it mobilized an unusually large number of committed mainline Protestants into Democratic politics.[12]

The percentage of secular Democrats again rose noticeably between 1988 and 1992. This increase may simply reflect the resumption of the trend of ascending secularism from 1976 to 1984. There were also two factors unique to the 1988–1992 period that may have increased the benefits of Democratic activity for secularists. First, although the 1992 Democratic nominee, Bill Clinton, made appeals to cultural conservatives in the South, his two chief rivals for the nomination, Paul Tsongas and Jerry Brown, took quite liberal cultural stands and received considerable support from seculars.[13]

Second, the Republican party was moving farther away from the cultural views of secularists as the influence of religious conservatives in both national and state Republican politics was growing (Rozell and Wilcox 1995, 1997). In particular, the combination of two developments affecting state politics may have provided strong motivation for seculars to become active in the Democratic party. Supreme Court decisions such as *Webster v. Reproductive Health Services* in 1989 and *Hodgson v. Minnesota* in 1990 gave the states more freedom to restrict abortion rights. This potential threat to the cultural values and policy preferences of secularists may have become more real as the Christian Right began to focus on and have success in state-level Republican politics after Pat Robertson's failed presidential bid in 1988 (Rozell and Wilcox 1995, 1997; Oldfield 1996). In fact, the success of the Christian Right in mobilizing its activists into local and state politics in the 1990s already has produced a significant countermobilization effort by religiously liberal groups such as the Call for Renewal and the Interfaith Alliance. The organization of the latter parallels that of Robertson's Christian Coalition. It has developed strong grassroots chapters and has been quite successful at mobilizing liberal Protestants, traditional supporters of the GOP, in support of the Democratic opponents of Christian Right–backed candidates (Green 1997).

These trends among secular Democrats and evangelical Republicans should have consequences for the presence of other religious groups in the two parties. The ascent of committed evangelicals in the GOP should decrease the appeal of Republican activity for secularists and the less devout members of other traditions. In contrast, the more committed members of other religious traditions—for instance, mainline Protestants, and particularly Catholics—share some aspects of the moral traditionalism and cultural conservatism of evangelicals. Their percentages should not decline much as those of evangelicals rise. The post-1976 growth of secularism in the Democratic party should decrease the benefits of Democratic activity for evangelicals and highly committed members of other traditions. However, it should not lead to a decline in the proportion of the nominally religious Democratic activists who affiliate with a religious tradition but are not active in that religion.

Table 3.1 shows the percentage of first-time Republican and Democratic delegates to national conventions from 1972 to 1992 in each of the eight religious traditions. The three largest traditions—mainline Protestant, evangelical Protestant, and Catholic—are divided into regular and nonregular attenders. Despite the trends among evangelical and secular activists, it is apparent that the parties are not close to being full

TABLE 3.1
Religious tradition and participation of first-time Democratic and
Republican convention delegates, 1972–1992

Religious Tradition and Attendance Level	Year					
	1972	1976	1980	1984	1988	1992
Democrats						
Secular	24.13%	11.90%	13.94%	17.35%	14.99%	18.93%
Black Protestant	6.88	4.29	5.89	6.96	7.88	7.48
Jewish	9.99	11.17	8.21	9.44	8.81	9.18
Mormon	.37	1.23	.54	.76	.68	.60
Eastern Orthodox	.22	.12	.46	.29	1.36	1.11
Nonregular mainline	13.25	16.07	15.18	14.49	14.92	13.86
Regular mainline	7.55	10.92	9.30	5.34	11.64	6.46
Nonregular evangelical	3.26	4.05	3.87	4.10	4.29	3.74
Regular evangelical	2.96	4.05	4.57	2.19	2.49	2.81
Nonregular Catholic	9.33	12.27	15.18	13.35	12.54	16.07
Regular Catholic	13.47	16.81	17.20	14.78	13.22	11.42
(N)	(1,351)	(815)	(1,291)	(1,049)	(885)	(1,176)
Republicans						
Secular	4.61%	4.92%	4.72%	2.85%	4.13%	4.42%
Black Protestant	3.37	.68	.77	1.52	2.48	1.35
Jewish	.89	2.19	2.42	2.09	2.48	2.50
Mormon	1.60	1.50	3.06	4.74	2.27	2.88
Eastern Orthodox	1.06	.68	.51	.95	.62	.58
Nonregular mainline	34.75	35.02	30.10	23.91	24.17	20.58
Regular mainline	22.52	20.66	19.90	18.60	20.04	19.23
Nonregular evangelical	3.90	4.92	4.59	4.36	3.93	4.62
Regular evangelical	6.03	6.02	6.76	9.68	12.81	12.73
Nonregular Catholic	5.67	6.16	7.02	8.16	5.99	7.31
Regular Catholic	9.57	10.26	13.01	15.37	10.32	13.65
(N)	(564)	(731)	(784)	(527)	(484)	(520)

Source: 1972–1992 Convention Delegate Studies.

Percentages do not sum to 100 because the "other Protestant and other religion" category is not included.

participants in a religious "war," as both are centered in the mainstream of American religion. Even by 1992, a clear majority of first-time Republican delegates (60.8 percent) and a near majority of first-time Democrats (47.8 percent) were mainline Protestants or Catholics.

At the same time, the table does provide further evidence of growing religious differences between the parties. The strength of most of the religious traditions in the Democratic party has not changed very much. However, the growth of secularism in the party since 1976 has been accompanied by a change in the type of activists coming from its largest tradition: Catholics. In 1972 and 1976, there were more regularly attending Catholics than less-committed Catholics among first-time Democratic delegates. By 1992, the situation was clearly reversed, so that, as has been consistently the case among mainline Protestants, the majority of Democratic Catholics were nonregular church attenders. The Democratic party now appears to be a party whose core of support comes from secularists, Jews, and the less committed members of the major religious traditions.

The growth of evangelicalism in the GOP has been accompanied by some increase in the percentage of regularly attending Catholic delegates, particularly between 1976 and 1984. More strikingly, there has been a sharp decline in the percentage of less committed mainline Protestants, a group that represented a clear plurality of Republican activists through 1980. Meanwhile, the proportion of regularly attending mainline Protestants changed very little. What is clear is that the Republican party is no longer a party of the nominally religious: upper-status individuals who affiliate with a mainline denomination but do not take an active role within it. It is becoming a party of the traditionally religious and the religiously committed, one whose core of support consists of the highly active members of the evangelical Protestant, mainline Protestant, and Catholic traditions.

Figure 3.2 can help us assess whether the changes in the religious affiliations of Republican and Democratic delegates have been accompanied by a growing religious-versus-secular cleavage between the parties. It shows the percentage of all delegates and first-time delegates in both parties from 1972 to 1992 who attended church almost every week or more and who received a great deal of guidance from their religion.[14] The figure clearly demonstrates a growing difference in the religious participation of the two parties' activists. The proportion of Republican activists who attend church regularly increased steadily after 1976. The Democratic pattern again shows peaks and valleys corresponding to the stands of leading presidential candidates. However, there was a noticeable decline in the presence of regular church attenders at Democratic conventions between 1980 (38.2 percent among first-time delegates) and 1992 (28.9 percent among first-time delegates). The growing partisan

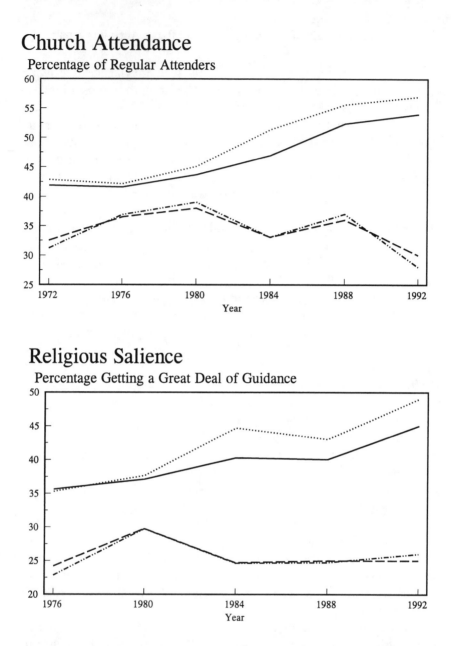

Church Attendance
Percentage of Regular Attenders

Religious Salience
Percentage Getting a Great Deal of Guidance

FIGURE 3.2. Church attendance and levels of religious salience among all and first-time Democratic and Republican convention delegates, 1972–1992

Note: The number of observations ranges from 1,029 to 1,812 for all Democrats, from 839 to 1,091 for all Republicans, from 816 to 1,305 for first-time Democrats, and from 489 to 793 for first-time Republicans.

Source: 1972–1992 Convention Delegate Studies

difference in religious salience is entirely the result of the increasing commitment of Republican activists. The percentage of Democratic delegates who find religion to be highly salient was quite low in 1972 and changed very little over this period. In contrast, the percentage of first-time Republican delegates who received a great deal of guidance from religion increased from 35.2 in 1976 to 49.0 in 1992. It appears that the Republican party is becoming not only more closely associated than the Democratic party with conservative religious traditions, but also just a more religious party than the Democrats.

A casual observer of the 1996 party conventions might conclude that the partisan religious cleavage declined between 1992 and 1996, largely because of the contrast between the Republican party's 1992 and 1996 conventions. As noted in the introduction, the influence of the Christian Right and cultural conservatism on the 1992 convention was made obvious by televised references to a "religious war," a "family values" night, and the highlighting of a "cultural divide" between the GOP and the Clinton Democrats. At their 1996 convention, the Republicans tried to convey a much different image. Pat Buchanan and the leaders of the Christian Right were nowhere to be seen during the prime-time viewing hours, while pro-choice Republicans and racial minorities could not be missed. The presidential nominee, Bob Dole, touted the inclusiveness of the GOP, asserting, "The Republican party is broad and inclusive. It represents many streams of opinion and many points of view. But if there is anyone who has mistakenly attached themselves to our party in the belief that we are not open to citizens of every race and religion, then let me remind you. Tonight this hall belongs to the party of Lincoln and the exits, which are clearly marked, are for you to walk out of as I stand this ground without compromise."

However, despite these differences in the televised picture painted by the GOP in 1992 and 1996, data from the *New York Times*/CBS News surveys of 1996 national convention delegates indicate that the religious polarization of party delegates continued through 1996. Only 13 percent of Democratic delegates considered themselves to be "Evangelical or Born-Again Christians," compared to 31 percent of Republican delegates. Meanwhile, 21 percent of Republican delegates considered themselves to be members of the religious right [a figure up from 8 percent of Republican delegates identifying themselves as religious right members in response to a comparable question in the 1992 Convention Delegate Studies (CDS)], as opposed to a mere 1 percent of Democratic delegates.[15] The percentage of delegates with a favorable opinion of the religious right was 55 among Republican delegates and only 4 among Democratic delegates.

RELIGIOUS POLARIZATION AND THE POLARIZATION OF THE PARTIES ON CULTURAL ISSUES

As noted in the discussion of activist-level change earlier in the chapter, there should be a close association between partisan religious change and partisan change on cultural issues. As the Republican and Democratic parties become increasingly polarized along religious lines, the ideological distance between the two parties on cultural issues should grow. To test this hypothesis, I examine change over time in the aggregate cultural attitudes of Democratic and Republican platforms, and change over time in the types of stands taken by the parties' platforms on cultural matters. Next, I use graphical and statistical techniques to examine the link between religious change in the parties and change in the parties' aggregate positions on cultural issues.

Partisan Differences in Delegates' Cultural Attitudes

Figure 3.3 shows the differences in the orientations of Republican and Democratic convention delegates from 1972 to 1996 toward two of the issues—abortion and the Equal Rights Amendment—and four of the groups—the women's movement, the Moral Majority, gay rights groups, and pro-life groups—associated with the cultural conflict.[16] The scores for each issue and group have been coded to range from the most liberal attitude to the most conservative attitude and were standardized to have a mean of 50 and a standard deviation of 25 for the entire sample in each survey. The partisan-difference measure is the mean Republican position minus the mean Democratic position.

The figure demonstrates that differences in the cultural attitudes of Republican and Democratic activists grew considerably over the time period of this study. Partisan polarization increased with regard to each of these issues and groups, and the growth was especially impressive in attitudes toward abortion. The level of partisan differences on that issue increased from 9 in 1972 to 32 in 1996.

According to the *New York Times*/CBS News polls, the polarization of Republican and Democratic delegates on cultural issues other than abortion also continued through the 1996 conventions. On a question

Partisan Difference Scores

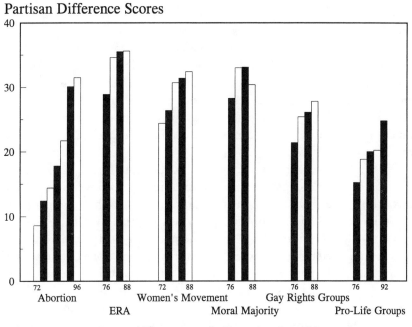

Issue/Group and Convention Year

FIGURE 3.3. Interparty differences in attitude toward cultural issues and groups over time

Note: The partisan difference score for a particular year is the mean position of Republican delegates in that year minus the mean position of Democratic delegates in that year. The number of observations ranges from 326 to 1,098 for Republicans and from 831 to 1,774 for Democrats. Each issue/group is shown only for the years that it was included in the CDS, with the exception of 1976.

Source: 1972–1992 from Convention Delegate Studies; 1996 from delegate polls conducted by CBS and the *New York Times*

about government promotion of traditional values, 56 percent of 1996 Republican delegates and only 27 percent of 1996 Democratic delegates said that the government should do more. On the question of prayer in the public schools, 57 percent of Republicans and only 20 percent of Democrats said that it should be permitted.

The Cultural Stands in the Parties' Platforms

It is important to look not only at the cultural attitudes of the delegates to national conventions, but also at the cultural stands included in the party platforms drafted by the conventions. The platforms are the only official statements of the parties' issue positions. They are read by very few citizens, but they are given considerable attention by the media, particularly with regard to "hot-button" cultural issues such as abortion, and they may send signals to politically attentive potential activists about where the parties stand on certain issues and which groups wield power within the parties. They also place important constraints on the positions that the parties' presidential candidates can take during the general election campaign.

We might expect the content of the parties' platforms to be a close reflection of the ideological composition of national convention delegations. Thus, if religious and cultural traditionalists are becoming a more influential part of the Republican party, while the power of secularists and moral liberals within the Democratic party grows, then there should be increasing differences between the platforms' positions on moral and cultural issues. However, it is entirely possible that the aggregate ideological stands of a party's delegates and the positions taken by the party's platform may diverge. Although the platform ultimately must be approved by the full convention, the full convention plays a very minor role in its construction. The task of writing an initial draft of the platform and revising that draft into the final platform is performed by a platform committee, consisting of party officials and a relatively small and potentially unrepresentative group of delegates, and by smaller subunits of or auxiliaries to that committee (Maisel 1994).

In his examination of how both parties' platforms evolved in 1992, L. Sandy Maisel (1994) argues that the presidential nominee and his campaign operatives have a dominant influence at each stage of the platform-writing process and ultimately over the content of the final document. Since the convention delegation reflects the outcome of the nomination process, the nominee's positions should not fall far from the aggregate views of the delegates. However, the nominee has strong incentives to direct his appeals to the political center for the purposes of a general election campaign (Downs 1957). So in attempting to insert its positions into the party platform, a group with relatively extreme views on controversial matters such as the cultural issues must overcome not only the opposition of its ideological opponents, but perhaps also the resistance of the eventual nominee and his campaign organization. Given the nature of the platform-writing process, the presidential nominee may be a far more formidable opponent.

There are several scenarios under which a group may overcome, and in a number of instances at past conventions have overcome, the tendency of candidates to seek the political center and thrust its controversial positions into the party platform. All of these, however, require considerable numerical strength and political clout within the party. If the faction has enough numerical strength on the platform committee and among delegates in general, then it simply may be able to override the wishes of the nominee. Similarly, if the faction represents a large enough proportion of the parties' delegates, the nominee and his allies simply may insert the faction's views into the platform on their own to avoid a rancorous debate during the televised proceedings of the full convention. The nominee may take similar steps if the faction represents such a large proportion of the pool of potential activists for the general election campaign that antagonizing it may carry greater electoral costs than appeasing it. Finally, the faction may have enough influence within the party and experience in its campaigns that a large number of the important figures in the nominee's campaign, or perhaps the nominee himself, may come from that group. In this case, the faction's ideological goals already may be at the center of the nominee's campaign agenda.

For these reasons, the content of party platforms may provide a more rigorous, though probably less exact, test of the strength of secularists and religious modernists within the Democratic party and of religious traditionalists within the Republican party than does the simple proportion of delegates belonging to these groups. I analyze the platforms from 1972 to 1996,[17] concentrating on not only the content of the parties' cultural statements, but also on the amount of attention the platforms devote to cultural issues. The relative attention that the platforms devote to cultural issues provides some indication of both the importance that the party attaches to these issues for mobilizing support for the presidential campaign and the strength of culturally liberal and culturally conservative groups within the parties. Moreover, a platform that not only takes quite liberal or quite conservative stands on cultural issues but also devotes a good deal of attention to these issues sends a stronger signal about the parties' cultural tendencies to potential activists and voters than does a platform that takes the same cultural stances but devotes less attention to the issues. Figure 3.4 provides a rough measure of this attention: the percentage of all paragraphs in the Democratic and Republican platforms from 1972 to 1996 that make mention of a cultural, religious, or moral issue.

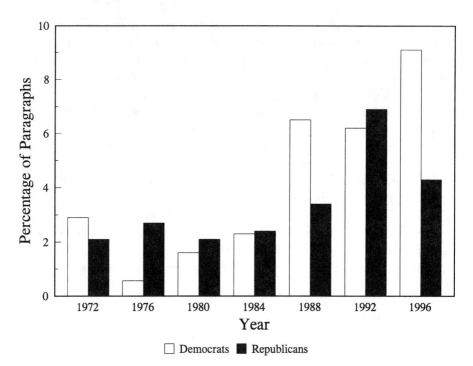

FIGURE 3.4. Percentage of party platform paragraphs devoted to moral and cultural issues, 1972–1996

Note: The total number of paragraphs in the Democratic party's platform was 692 in 1972, 358 in 1976, 858 in 1980, 656 in 1984, 31 in 1988, 97 in 1992, and 165 in 1996. The total number of paragraphs in the Republican party's platform was 746 in 1972, 363 in 1976, 571 in 1980, 497 in 1984, 853 in 1988, 481 in 1992, and 398 in 1996.

1972

The 1972 platform was the first one in which the Democratic party made any specific mention of cultural issues such as women's rights or alternative lifestyles (Johnson 1978). Clearly reflecting the strength of secularists and cultural liberals in the McGovern campaign and at the Democratic convention, the party's first official positions on these cultural matters were staunchly liberal ones. The platform contained full sections on liberal cultural stands such as "The Right To Be Different," "Rights of Women," and "Family Planning." As mentioned in chapter 1, the section on the right to be different provided strong support for alternative lifestyles, arguing that "official policy too often forces people into a mold of artificial homogeneity" and that "Americans should be free to make their own choice of lifestyles and private habits without being subject to discrimination or prosecution." The family planning section held that "family planning services, . . . to permit individuals freely to determine and achieve the number and spacing of their children, should be available to all." In the section on women's rights, the Democrats pledged to make ratification of the Equal Rights Amendment a "priority effort" and provided a detailed list of fourteen other proposals to ensure civil rights and equal opportunity for women. Despite considerable support for such planks in the debates of the full convention,[18] the platform made no specific mention of abortion or homosexuality. However, the party's support for abortion rights and protection of homosexuals from discrimination were implied in the sections on family planning and the right to be different, respectively.

The GOP's platform in 1972 reflected the party's traditional orientations toward cultural issues by devoting little attention to them. There were two exceptions to this, but they did not place the Republicans clearly on the side of cultural conservatism. As it had since 1964, the party took a conservative stand on school prayer, arguing that "voluntary prayer should be freely permitted in public places—particularly, by school children while attending public schools." However, as it had since 1940, the GOP asserted its support for the Equal Rights Amendment. There was some polarization in the platforms' cultural planks in 1972, but that was a result of the Democrats' staunch liberalism rather than of strong cultural traditionalism on the part of the Republican party.

1976

Just as the religious differences between the parties declined between 1972 and 1976, so did the differences in the moral and cultural content of their platforms. As with religious differences, the distinctiveness of the platforms declined largely because of the return of the Carter-led Democratic party to the cultural center. Although they supported the Equal Rights Amendment, the Democrats devoted far less attention to moral and cultural issues than they had in 1972. Despite strong opposition from Reagan forces on the platform committee, the GOP once again lent its support to ratification of the ERA.

Clearly, the most significant development on cultural issues in 1976 was that the parties responded to the Supreme Court's 1973 decision in *Roe v. Wade* by specifically mentioning the abortion issue. Although there were some differences in the parties' initial stands on abortion, they were not large, as both parties took rather vague positions and recognized the legitimacy of both pro-life and pro-choice views.

Despite some opposition from Gerald Ford,[19] the GOP endorsed a constitutional amendment to ban abortion. However, it did so in very cautious terms that acknowledged the diversity of opinion within the party. The abortion plank stated,

> The question of abortion is one of the most difficult and controversial of our time. It is undoubtedly a moral and personal issue but it also involves complex questions relating to medical science and criminal justice. There are those in our Party who favor complete support for the Supreme Court decision. . . . There are others who share sincere convictions that the Supreme Court's decision must be changed by a constitutional amendment prohibiting all abortions. . . . The Republican Party favors a continuance of the public dialogue on abortion and supports the efforts of those who seek enactment of a constitutional amendment to restore protection of the right to life for unborn children.

Although they seemed to be supportive of abortion rights, the Democrats did not take a clear stand on the issue. Instead, they stated, "We fully recognize the religious and ethical nature of the concerns which many Americans have on the subject of abortion. We feel, however, that it is undesirable to attempt to amend the U.S. Constitution to overturn the Supreme Court decision in this area."

1980

With the Republican nomination of Ronald Reagan and the small increase in Democratic secularism from 1976 levels, the parties' platforms in 1980 demonstrated considerably larger distinctions in their positions on moral and cultural matters. The Democrats continued to support the ERA but took that support a considerable step further by criticizing states that had ratified the amendment but then tried to rescind their endorsement of it, by asserting that the Democratic National Committee would not hold meetings in states that had not ratified the amendment, and by promising to withhold financial and technical assistance to Democratic candidates who did not support the ERA. The platform also included full sections on promoting opportunities for women in business and securing economic rights for women. The Democrats included language on protecting homosexuals from discrimination for the first time, asserting that "all groups must be protected from discrimination based on race, color, religion, national origin, language, age, sex, or *sexual orientation*" (emphasis added).

The Republican platform in 1980 devoted slightly less attention than the 1976 platform to cultural matters. Its cultural stands, however, were much more uniformly conservative. For the first time since 1940, the Republican platform did not endorse the ERA; and although it did not specifically oppose the amendment, it did criticize the Carter administration for pressuring states to ratify it. The platform also included an entire section on creating strong families. In its section on education, it took two positions very popular with evangelicals: support for voluntary school prayer and a call for tuition tax credits for parents sending their children to private or parochial schools.

On the abortion issue, both parties continued to recognize diversity of opinion both within the party and across the nation, but both also took clear steps to strengthen their stands. The Republicans moved from supporting those who sought an antiabortion amendment to "affirm[ing] our support of a constitutional amendment to restore protection of the right to life for unborn children." The party also called for restrictions on the use of federal funds for abortion. The Democratic platform held that the party "supports the 1973 Supreme Court decision on abortion rights as the law of the land and opposes any constitutional amendment to restrict or overturn that decision." By 1980, it was clear that the parties had chosen opposite sides on abortion and other issues related to the cultural conflict.

1984

The proportion of committed evangelicals among Republican delegates and that of secularists among Democratic delegates both increased noticeably between 1980 and 1984. Thus, even though the parties' platforms already took rather distinct stands on cultural matters in 1980, one might expect the differences to be even larger in 1984. The 1984 platforms clearly meet these expectations. The Democrats not only continued to take liberal stands on cultural issues such as abortion and the ERA, but also devoted more attention to cultural matters than they had in 1976 and 1980. In a clear response to the Christian Right's influence within the GOP and the Reagan administration's support for expanded religious expression, the platform included a separate section on "Religious Liberty and Church/State Separation." It stated, "The Democratic Platform affirms its support of the principles of religious liberty, religious tolerance, and church/state separation and of the Supreme Court decisions forbidding violations of those principles."

The party also elaborated on its pledge to protect homosexuals from discrimination, asserting, "We will support legislation to prohibit discrimination in the workplace based on sexual orientation. We will assure that sexual orientation *per se* does not serve as a bar to participation in the military. We will support an enhanced effort to learn the cause and cure of AIDS, and to provide treatment for people with AIDS. And we will ensure that foreign citizens are not excluded from this country on the basis of their sexual orientations."

The Republicans continued to support opportunities for religious expression in the public schools and tuition tax credits for parents sending their children to nonpublic schools. The party also added another position in line with the Christian Right's agenda: an antipornography plank arguing, "We and the vast majority of Americans are repulsed by pornography. We will vigorously enforce constitutional laws to control obscene material which degrades everyone, particularly women, and depict the exploitation of children."

Probably the clearest evidence for continued cultural polarization is provided by the parties' even stronger stands on abortion. The Democrats retained much of the language from the 1980 platform, including that recognizing diversity of opinion on the issue. However, for the first time, the platform asserted that reproductive freedom is a "fundamental human right." Responding to the GOP's efforts to restrict federal funds for abortion, the platform held, "We . . . oppose government interference in the reproductive decisions of Americans, especially government interference which denies poor Americans their right to privacy by funding or advocating one or a limited number of reproductive choices only."

The Republicans dropped any mention of dissenting views on abortion and also adopted the language of fundamental rights. The platform stated, "The unborn child has a fundamental individual right to life which cannot be infringed. We therefore reaffirm our support for a human life amendment to the Constitution, and we endorse legislation to make clear that the Fourteenth Amendment's protections apply to unborn children. We oppose the use of public revenues for abortion and will eliminate funding for organizations which advocate or support abortions." The Republicans went on to establish their "litmus test" for the abortion stances of judicial appointments, declaring that "we reaffirm our support for the appointment of judges at all levels of the judiciary who respect traditional family values and the sanctity of innocent human life."

1988–1996

Since 1984, the parties' platforms have continued to take very distinct stands on cultural issues, and in many ways these differences have continued to grow. In 1988, the Democrats adopted a much shorter platform than in previous years and thus had less to say about cultural matters or any other type of policy issues. However, the attention they devoted to cultural issues relative to other issues increased considerably from previous levels. The party found room to reiterate their support for the ERA and for equal rights regardless of sexual orientation. By dropping any reference to dissenting views and shortening the plank on abortion, the Democrats in effect strengthened their position. The platform held that "the fundamental right of reproductive choice should be guaranteed regardless of ability to pay."

The GOP platform in 1988 discussed a wider range of cultural, religious, and moral issues than it ever had before, devoting twenty-eight paragraphs to these matters. The platform reaffirmed the Republicans' traditional support for voluntary school prayer and school choice programs, and the party's abortion plank remained the same as in 1984. In addition, the platform included a full section on adoption, declaring that "Republicans are determined . . . to facilitate the adoption process for those who can offer strong family life based on traditional values." The GOP pledged to work hard in the fight against AIDS, but it also appealed to religious traditionalists by stating that "AIDS education should emphasize that abstinence from drug abuse and sexual activity outside of marriage is the safest way to avoid infection with the AIDS virus." The platform endorsed efforts to "teach teens the traditional values of restraint, respect, and the sanctity of marriage." It also criticized the transmission of liberal moral values in schools, asserting that "values are the core of good education. A free society needs a moral foundation for its learning. We oppose any programs in public schools which provide birth control or abortion services or referrals. Our 'first line of defense' to protect our youth from contracting AIDS and other sexually communicable diseases, from teen pregnancy, and from illegal drug use must be abstinence education."

In line with the large proportions of active evangelicals among Republican delegates and of secularists among Democratic delegates, the parties' platforms in 1992 took the most polarized stands to date on cultural and moral issues. The Democrats reasserted their support for the ERA, their support for *Roe v. Wade,* and their belief in the fundamental "right of every woman to choose." In addition, the party seemed to respond to the Supreme Court's decisions to grant greater latitude for states to restrict abortion by noting its "support for a national law to protect" abortion rights. The 1992 platform was the first in which the Democrats specifically mentioned gays and lesbians. The party promised to "provide civil rights protection for gay men and lesbians and an end to Defense Department discrimination."

Although it was drafted largely by the Bush-Quayle reelection campaign (Maisel 1994), the 1992 Republican platform read like a document written by leaders of the Christian Right. It devoted considerable attention to cultural matters and was arguably the most morally and religiously conservative platform produced by a political party in this century. In the preamble, the party announced, "We believe in traditional family values and in the Judeo-Christian heritage that informs our culture," and the entire platform was imbued with references to traditional religious and moral values. The first substantive section was on family values, emphasizing traditional family structures and asserting the right of families to pass on moral values to their children without intrusion from government. The platform provided the broadest Republican statement yet on the role of religion and moral values in the schools. It declared, "Just as spiritual principles—our moral compass—help guide public policy, learning must have a moral basis. America must remain neutral toward particular religions, but we must not remain neutral toward religion itself or the values religion supports. Mindful of our country's Judeo-Christian heritage and rich religious pluralism, we support the right of students to engage in voluntary prayer in schools and the right of the community to do so at commencements or other occasions."

In a section entitled "Promoting cultural values," the Republican platform lashed out at "elements within the media, the entertainment industry, academia and the Democratic party [who] are waging a guerilla war against American values." This section also asserted the GOP's opposition to any efforts to "include sexual preference as a protected minority receiving preferential status," opposed "any legislation or law that legally recognizes same-sex marriages," called for a "national crusade against pornography," and condemned "the use of public funds to subsidize obscenity and blasphemy masquerading as art." The abortion plank remained the same as it had since 1984.

The unyielding traditionalism of the 1992 Republican platform was all the more remarkable when one considers a number of factors: incumbent presidents seeking reelection generally exercise a controlling influence over party platforms, the Bush-Quayle campaign indeed did play a dominant role in the platform-writing process in 1992, and George Bush was not known for highly conservative stands on cultural issues. Why then did the Bush campaign create a platform that was more culturally conservative than both the nominee and most voters? One possible explanation is that Bush wished to reassure those who had always been suspicious of his conservative credentials, particularly given the challenge from the right launched by Pat Buchanan during the nomination campaign. Another explanation simply may lie in the strength of committed evangelicals and other religious traditionalists on the platform committee and among Republican activists in general. The Bush forces may have realized that more-moderate cultural positions would be defeated and would create considerable acrimony on the floor of the convention. They also may have feared that without highly conservative cultural positions in the platform, Bush would not attract the active support of religious conservatives now required for Republicans to win presidential election campaigns.

Reflecting the attempt by Bill Clinton and his allies to recapture the political center from the Republicans and the very considerable influence of an incumbent president, unopposed for the nomination, over his party's platform, the Democratic platform in 1996 did take some small steps away from the highly liberal cultural stands of 1992. The platform devoted proportionately more attention to moral and cultural matters than did earlier Democratic platforms, but not all of those cultural stands were liberal. The platform still asserted the party's unwavering support for abortion rights, but it also stated that the Democrats "respect the individual conscience of each American on this difficult issue." In stark contrast to the 1984 platform's criticism of Republican efforts to expand opportunities for religious expression in public schools, the 1996 Democratic platform asserted that "Americans have a right to express their love of God in public, and we applaud the President's work to ensure that children are not denied private religious expression in school."

In keeping with the Republican party's effort to downplay cultural and moral conservatism at its 1996 convention, the 1996 Republican platform devoted noticeably less attention to cultural matters than did the 1992 platform, although the percentage of culturally oriented paragraphs was still higher in 1996 than in any year prior to 1992. Similarly, the cultural positions in the 1996 platform were worded in a more inclusive and less religious manner than the stances in the 1992 platform. Ultimately, however, the cultural and moral content of the 1996 platform differed very little from the extremely traditional document produced by the GOP in 1992.

Bob Dole's campaign pressed for the inclusion of a plank in the 1996 Republican platform declaring tolerance for a wide range of views on the abortion issue, but the Republican nominee and his allies could not overcome the resistance of religious conservatives and antiabortion activists to this language.[20] The Republicans' abortion plank remained very similar to the ones that had appeared in GOP platforms since 1984, and it attacked Clinton's vetoes of bills passed by the Republican-controlled Congress that would have banned partial-birth abortion and created an adoption tax credit. The platform extended the party's support for financial assistance for parents not sending their children to public schools to include home schooling. It also reasserted the GOP's support for voluntary school prayer and called for educational initiatives to promote chastity until marriage.

Summary

Trends over time among Democratic and Republican activists show an increasing partisan polarization along religious lines. They do not, however, suggest that the parties have become full participants in a religious and cultural war. The plurality of both parties' delegates remain in the mainstream of American religion. This examination of the party platforms, however, tells a somewhat different story. The party platforms have devoted increasing attention to cultural matters, and it is hard to imagine greater partisan differences on cultural, moral, and religious issues than have appeared in recent party platforms. Republican platforms have been filled with mentions of traditional moral values and the need to return to the nation's Judeo-Christian heritage. They have asserted the fundamental right to life of the unborn; have criticized efforts to extend civil rights protections to homosexuals; have called for an expansion of public religious expression, particularly in the schools; have announced a crusade against pornography; and have endorsed efforts to teach children traditional values in the public schools and to provide financial assistance to parents who wish to educate their children in religious schools. Democratic platforms, in contrast, have asserted the fundamental right of women to choose an abortion, have strongly supported the Equal Rights Amendment, and have called for expanded protection of the rights of homosexuals. Moreover, although there have been clear differences between the parties' stands on cultural matters since 1980, these differences have grown even larger over time. It appears that there has been a marked increase not only in the percentages of secular and religiously liberal Democrats and of traditionally religious Republicans, but also in the influence of these groups within their respective parties.

EXAMINING THE LINK BETWEEN RELIGIOUS CHANGE AND IDEOLOGICAL CHANGE

The fact that this growth in partisan cultural polarization occurred alongside the growth in partisan religious differences, and the fact that religious orientations and cultural attitudes are strongly connected at the individual level certainly suggest that there is a cause-and-effect relationship between the two partisan trends.[21] However, further analysis is necessary to determine how close the aggregate-level association between changes in the religious orientations of party activists and changes in activists' cultural attitudes has been. With so few time points in the delegate data, sophisticated time-series analyses are impossible. However, graphical inspection of the over-time trends in the aggregate religious and cultural orientations of Republican and Democratic activists may provide some indication of the strength of their relationship. Since the abortion issue is the only cultural item included in all of the CDS surveys, the analysis is confined to it.

The first part of figure 3.5 shows the percentage of Republican delegates from 1972 to 1992 who were regularly attending evangelical Protestants, and the percentage of Republican delegates over that period who took the most pro-life position on abortion. The second part of the figure shows the percentage of Democratic delegates who were secularists and the percentage of Democratic delegates who took the most pro-choice position on abortion from 1972 to 1992.[22] Clearly, there is a close relationship between religious change and changing cultural attitudes among Republican party activists. The percentage of pro-life Republicans and the percentage of regularly attending evangelical Republicans demonstrate a nearly one-to-one relationship through 1984. The relationship is not quite as close after 1984, but both series demonstrate a clear increase.

In contrast, there seems to be a strong negative relationship between Democratic secularism and pro-choice sentiments among Democratic delegates between 1972 and 1976. The percentage of secular Democrats fell dramatically over this period, while the percentage of Democrats holding pro-choice views on abortion increased slightly. This may be because

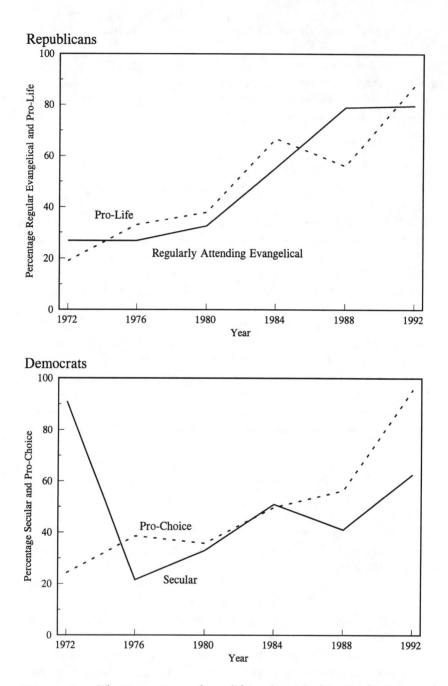

Republicans

Democrats

FIGURE 3.5. The percentage of pro-life and regularly attending evangelical Republican delegates and the percentage of pro-choice and secular
democratic delegates, 1972–1992
Note: All series are standardized (mean = 50, standard deviation = 25).
Source: 1972–1992 Convention Delegate Studies

the Supreme Court's *Roe v. Wade* decision came between these two years, in 1973. In 1972, the abortion issue was not highly politicized and neither party mentioned the issue in its platform. Thus, the link between general religious or cultural orientations and attitudes on abortion may not have been made yet in the minds of many activists and voters. So the staunch secularism and cultural liberalism of the 1972 Democratic delegates led generally to pro-choice sentiments, but not to the overwhelming support that later, and less secular, Democratic conventions would demonstrate. By 1976, the Democratic party already had positioned itself somewhat to the left on the abortion issue, perhaps leading individual Democratic activists to adopt more pro-choice stands. After 1976, however, there is a concomitant growth in secularism and pro-choice sentiments in the Democratic party, and the year-to-year changes in the two series also appear to be closely related.

To provide a better sense of the relationship between partisan polarization on abortion and the overall changes in the religious composition of the parties, figure 3.6 shows the partisan difference on abortion together with the difference between the mean Republican position and the mean Democratic position on the religious orthodoxy scale developed in chapter 2. Again, there is a negative relationship between the religious trend and the trend on abortion between 1972 and 1976. The level of religious polarization declines, because of the sharp decline in Democratic secularism, while the partisan difference on abortion grows. After 1976, however, there is a very close relationship between partisan religious differences and partisan differences on abortion. Both series demonstrate a marked growth, and the year-to-year changes appear to be closely associated.[23] This is a very simple analysis, based on a very small number of time points. However, it does provide some indication that religious trends among the parties' activists have been associated with the polarization of the parties on cultural matters.

SUMMARY

Focusing on the elite group of activists who become delegates to the parties' national conventions, the analysis in this chapter has shown that the division of the Republican and Democratic parties along religious lines is not an entirely new phenomenon. As early as 1972, Democratic activists were considerably more secular than their Republican counterparts, and the Democratic platform took clearly liberal stands on moral

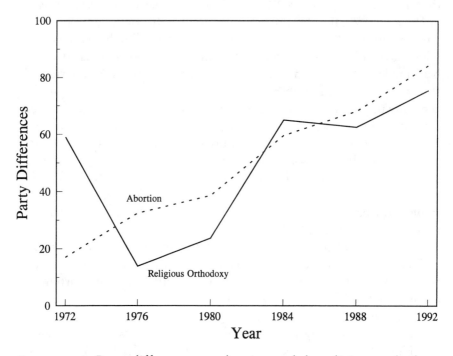

FIGURE 3.6. Party differences on abortion and the religious orthodoxy scale, 1972–1992
Note: Party differences are the mean Republican position minus the mean Democratic position on the religious orthodoxy and abortion scales.
Source: 1972–1992 Convention Delegate Studies

and cultural matters. Over time, however, this religious cleavage has grown. Since 1976 there has been a relatively steady increase in the percentages of regularly attending evangelical Protestants, regular churchgoers, and individuals with high levels of religious salience among Republican activists. The ascendance of religious traditionalism in the GOP does not mean that less religious Republicans have disappeared or given up the fight for party control. Their attempts to change the abortion plank in the party's 1996 platform and their continued battles with conservative Christians for control of the Republican party in several states refutes that notion. However, the ranks of nominally religious Republican activists are clearly thinning. Mainline Protestants with low levels of religious participation were once numerically dominant in the Republican party. Now, they make up a much smaller percentage of party activists, and the GOP is a party of the committed members of the evangelical, main-line Protestant, and Catholic traditions.

The trends have been neither as consistent nor as impressive in the Democratic party. However, since 1976 there has been a clear increase in the percentage of Democratic activists who are secular and who do not attend religious services regularly. This trend has been accompanied by a decline in the proportion of the party's Catholic activists with high levels of religious participation.

Since 1972 there also has been a substantial growth in the differences between the attitudes of Democratic and Republican activists on cultural issues such as abortion and the Equal Rights Amendment and toward culturally liberal and conservative groups. There is a clear empirical link between the cultural and religious trends within the parties. The religious and cultural polarization of the parties' delegates has been reflected clearly in the increasing differences in the stands of the parties' platforms on moral, cultural, and religious concerns.

The growth of religious traditionalism among Republican activists and of religious liberalism and secularism among Democratic activists raises two questions. First, has the partisan ascendance of these groups increased the degree of ideological and political conflict within the parties? Second, is the intraparty conflict resulting from these religious trends greater or less than the level of interparty conflict associated with partisan change along religious lines? These two critical questions are the subject of chapter 4.

NOTES

1. As I discuss later in the chapter, only a small proportion of delegates play a substantial role in the drafting of the party platform. However, since the platform ultimately must be approved by the full convention, the party officials and representatives of the eventual nominee's campaign who do construct the platform are very likely to take the aggregate views of all convention delegates into account.

2. In 1996, according to *New York Times*/CBS News surveys of convention delegates, 58 percent of Democratic delegates and 60 percent of Republican delegates held some type of party office.

3. The Convention Delegate Studies (CDS), the principal longitudinal survey of party activists, did not begin until 1972.

4. Although it surveyed only delegates to the 1972 national conventions, the 1972 CDS, on which Kirkpatrick's book is based, does provide some

indication that 1972 witnessed the emergence of a new set of Democratic activists whose religious and cultural orientations differed considerably from those of earlier groups of Democratic activists. For example, 11 percent of 1972 Democratic delegates who had been delegates to earlier conventions identified themselves as having no religious preference and 34 percent of these delegates said that abortion should always be permitted. Meanwhile, 24 percent of first-time Democratic delegates in 1972 claimed no religious preference and over 43 percent of first-timers took the most pro-choice view on abortion. In contrast to these Democratic differences, there were not noticeable differences in the religious orientations and abortion attitudes of first-time and repeating Republican delegates in 1972.

5. Attitudinal conversion among individual activists plays a significant role in partisan change along ideological lines (Carsey and Layman 1999; Herrera 1995; Rapoport and Stone 1994). However, since individuals' religious orientations should be more stable than their issue attitudes, conversion is less likely to contribute to religious change in the parties. In fact, my analysis of panel data on national convention delegates revealed little change in the religious orientations of the same group of activists over time.

6. Although activists are motivated by factors other than relative policy distances, research shows that a sizeable and growing majority of activists are motivated primarily by policy-related incentives (Aldrich 1995; Layman and Carsey 1998).

7. By potential activists, I, like Aldrich, mean both individuals who are not currently active and current activists. Just as nonactive individuals look to the parties' policy positions to determine whether or not to become active, individuals who are currently active look to the parties' policy positions to determine whether or not to remain active.

8. One possible explanation for the discrepancy in the percentages of regularly attending evangelical Protestants among all Republican delegates and among first-time Republican delegates is that smaller percentages of regularly attending evangelicals than of other religious groups repeat as convention delegates. Analysis using the panel components of the 1980, 1984, and 1988 CDS shows that this is not the case. Regularly attending evangelical delegates are just as likely as other Republican delegates to be delegates to subsequent conventions. Thus, the reason for the discrepancy in the patterns for all delegates and first-time delegates is that regularly attending evangelicals are overrepresented among first-time delegates, and not that regularly attending evangelicals are underrepresented among repeating delegates.

9. It is possible that the analysis underestimates the percentage of seculars in both parties. A fair number of respondents who claim a religious affiliation attend church either "never" or "almost never" and say that religion provides no guidance in their lives. Clearly, these activists are religious in name only and could easily be labeled as secularists. When these respondents

are included in the secular category, the percentage of secular Democrats increases by 5 to 10 percentage points in each year. However, the patterns over time in the percentage of secular Democrats, or in the percentage of any religious group in either party, do not change noticeably from those presented here.

10. Over 81 percent of secular Democrats supported McGovern in 1972. Only 51 percent of other Democratic delegates preferred McGovern for the Democratic nomination.

11. As table 3.1 shows, the percentage of Democratic delegates who were black Protestants was higher in 1988 than in any other year in the analysis. Most of these delegates (74.7 percent) supported Jackson.

12. As table 3.1 shows, the percentage of regularly attending mainline Protestants among Democratic delegates was higher in 1988 than in any other year of the analysis. The clear plurality (45.5 percent) of these delegates supported Gore. Gore's support base also included a smaller percentage (3.5 percent) of seculars than that of any of the serious contenders—those candidates who were the first choice of more than 10 percent of the Democratic delegates—for the Democratic presidential nomination from 1972 to 1992.

13. Brown's support base included a larger percentage (31.6) of seculars than that of any of the other serious contenders for the Democratic nomination from 1972 to 1992. A large percentage (20.9) of Tsongas's support also came from seculars.

14. The patterns on the guidance item are shown only from 1976 to 1992 because it was not included in the 1972 CDS.

15. In a poll of 1996 Republican delegates conducted by ABC News and the *Washington Post*, 21 percent of Republican delegates (the same percentage as in the CBS/*New York Times* poll) identified themselves as members of the religious right.

16. Abortion was the only one of these questions to appear in all of the CDS surveys. The question on the women's movement appeared in the surveys from 1972 through 1988. The question on pro-life groups appeared from 1980 through 1988. The questions on the ERA, the Moral Majority, and gay rights groups appeared from 1980 to 1988. Abortion attitude in 1996 was computed from the polls conducted by CBS News and the *New York Times*.

17. Oldfield (1996) also provides a very thorough analysis of the moral and cultural messages in the parties' platforms from 1972 to 1980 and in the Republican platform in 1992.

18. "The Platform: Few Changes Made in Original Draft." *Congressional Quarterly Weekly Report*, July 15, 1972, pp. 1724–5.

19. "Platform: A Chance for Some Shadow Boxing." *Congressional Quarterly Weekly Report*, August 7, 1976, pp. 2144–5.

20. "GOP's Conservative Camp Makes Its Voice Heard." *Congressional Quarterly Weekly Report*, August 10, 1996, pp. 2267–8.

21. To be clear, I am not making the case for unidirectional causality: that religious changes among party activists caused aggregate changes in cultural attitudes or vice versa. Rather, my argument is one of reciprocal and simultaneous causation. Changes in the religious orientations of a party's activists bring about changes in the party's aggregate cultural attitudes, which in turn lead to further religious change.

22. To ease comparison, all the religious and cultural items have been standardized to a mean of 50 and a standard deviation of 25.

23. This is confirmed by strong and statistically significant correlations between the two series. The correlation between religious polarization and polarization on abortion is .60 ($p < .10$), and when only the years from 1976 to 1992 are considered, the correlation is highly significant, even in a tiny sample, and is very close to 1 (.96). Since there is clearly a temporal trend in both series, I also take the more conservative measure of correlating the first difference of the religious series with the first difference of the abortion series. After 1976, that correlation is strong (.84) and significant ($p < .08$), suggesting that the year-to-year changes in the levels of partisan religious polarization and partisan polarization on abortion are significantly related.

CHAPTER 4

The Internal and External Divides: Religious and Cultural Conflict Within and Between the Parties

THE RELATIVELY SHARP and growing religious polarization of Republican and Democratic activists clearly creates the potential not only for interparty cultural conflict, but also for conflict between activists and elites within the same party. In his prominent account of the partisan change process, James Sundquist (1983) asserts that when a new issue or set of issues emerges in party politics, it is inevitable that intraparty conflict will emerge. Within each of the two major parties, there will be friction between some groups trying to push the party toward one of the ideological poles on the new issues and other groups trying to deemphasize the new issues and keep the party's position on them in the ideological center.

The established leaders of both parties, according to Sundquist, will try to steer their parties toward a centrist position on the new issues. This seems obvious for the leaders of the majority party since their majority coalition is based on the old issues that, to this point, have dominated party politics. If their party takes a clear stand on one side of the new debate, it might increase the political importance of the new issues relative to the old ones, disrupt the harmony of the party's coalition, and thereby threaten its majority status. However, as Riker (1982) and Carmines and Stimson (1989) argue, minority party leaders may have incentives to champion one side of a new issue in order to disrupt the political status quo and potentially divide the majority coalition. Sundquist agrees that minority party leaders may be more likely than their majority party counterparts to advance new issues. However, like Carmines (1991), who contends that minority party activists are more likely than minority party officials to be proponents of new issues, he argues that "the established leadership of a party consists of politicians who are, by definition, the beneficiaries of the party system as it is. . . . The leaders of each party have an abiding interest in keeping [the old] issues alive as a constant source of reinforcement, and by the same token they have a powerful incentive to suppress or avoid any new crosscutting issue that threatens the party's unity" (1983: 306–7).

Within both parties, the establishment's hesitancy to choose sides on the new issues quite likely will be supported by the bulk of the party's traditional corps of activists. These individuals were drawn into the party by its positions on the old issues, and they may disagree with the stands on the new issues of those groups that have infiltrated the party to advance their positions on them. Moreover, these traditional party supporters simply may care much less about the new issues than about the old issues and thus may resist efforts to focus the party's attention on the new concerns.

Standing in opposition to these groups, Sundquist argues, will be groups that champion the new issues and attempt to force their parties' positions on them away from the center. One of these groups is what Sundquist terms the "zealots," new activists within both parties who, like the culturally conservative religious traditionalists who have become active in the GOP and the culturally liberal secularists and religious modernists in the Democratic party, are truly dedicated to their positions on the new issues and become involved in a particular party to promote those positions. The other of these groups is labeled by Sundquist as the "opportunists—out-of-power politicians who may care nothing for the issue but see in it a means to political advancement" (1983: 309). These are the "political losers" discussed in chapter 1. They may be minority party elites who see the issues as a means to improving the electoral status of their party (Riker 1982; Carmines and Stimson 1989). Or, they may be politicians within either party who are not part of the establishment or the dominant wing of their party, and who see the new issues and the constituencies to which they appeal as a means for improving their own chances of winning a party nomination or of gaining a position of power within the party.

In sum, when powerful new issues such as the moral and cultural concerns associated with the contemporary religious cleavage emerge in party politics, they invariably create conflict within both of the major parties. On one side are the traditional party activists and members of the party establishment who want to maintain the focus on the old issues and avoid choosing sides on them. On the other side are the new activists, who become involved in the party to advance their positions on the new issues, and the political leaders who champion their views. Given the centrality of intraparty conflict to any period of partisan change, it is not surprising that scholars and journalists have recently focused a great deal of attention on the intraparty conflicts created by the mobilization of secular and religiously liberal activists into the Democratic party and by the ascendance of religious conservatism in the Republican party.

Particular attention has been paid to religious and cultural divisions within the GOP. Ever since the Christian Right emerged as a force in Republican party politics in the early 1980s, observers have noted the potential for conflict between the newly mobilized evangelical activists (with their religiously motivated cultural conservatism, their hesitancy to engage in pragmatic compromise, and their relatively low levels of socioeconomic status) and the GOP's traditional core of support: upper-status, business-oriented economic conservatives, who (particularly the younger members) tend to hold fairly liberal opinions on cultural issues (Liebman and Wuthnow 1983; Freeman 1986; Green and Guth 1988; Green, Guth, and Fraser 1991; Hertzke 1993; Rozell and Wilcox 1995, 1996, 1997). However, the focus on religion-based tensions within the Republican party seems to have increased in the late 1990s as the Christian Right increased its influence within the party, the GOP lost two consecutive presidential elections, the party's majority in the House narrowed in 1998, culturally conservative Republicans led the highly unpopular impeachment of President Clinton, conservative Christians became increasingly frustrated with the party's inability or unwillingness to enact their legislative agenda, and culturally moderate Republicans called for the party to turn away from that agenda. In fact, of the fifty-two stories in the *New York Times* in 1998 that commented on the Christian Right and the Republican party, thirty-six focused on the divisions between religious and cultural conservatives on the one hand and economic conservatives or "moderate Republicans" on the other, and on the electoral difficulties this split caused for the GOP.

The media's focus on this internal conflict was apparent in a July editorial on "Republican Infighting," which argued that "the party's two historical wings—the corporate pro-business faction and the populist social conservatives—seem inclined to spend eternity canceling out each other's proposals. . . . For a long time, the Republicans have been split into two camps, one obsessing about abortion and family values, the other fixated on the capital-gains tax. But lately they have seemed particularly short on common ground."[1]

There seem to be similar intraparty tensions even in the religiously traditional and culturally conservative South. Commenting on the contest for the Republican gubernatorial nomination in Alabama in 1998, *Times* reporter Kevin Sack noted that "the primary campaign probed the inherent tensions in Southern Republicanism, between the conservative Christians drawn to the party . . . by a deeply felt moral agenda, and business-oriented voters primarily concerned with the state's economic interests."[2]

Despite the focus on the fractious effects of religious conflict in the Republican party, the growth of secularism among Democrats also creates the potential for conflict within that party. As Kirkpatrick (1976) noted in her account of 1972 Democratic activists, the cultural progressivism and disdain for traditional religious values of secular Democratic activists may well clash with the views of many of the party's traditional supporters: African-Americans, Catholics, working-class whites, and southern whites. All of these groups have relatively high levels of religious commitment, hold fairly traditional moral values, and have conservative views on at least some of the issues surrounding the contemporary cultural conflict.

Exacerbating the ideological conflict between secular and nonsecular Democrats and between highly committed evangelical activists and other Republicans may be differences in political style and political goals. Political scientists long have made distinctions between "amateurs" and "professionals," or "purists" and "pragmatists," or activists motivated by "purposive" goals and activists motivated by "material" and "solidary" goals (Wilson 1962; Bowman et al. 1969; Conway and Feigert 1968; Wildavsky 1965; Soule and Clarke 1970; Roback 1975, 1980; Miller and Jennings 1986). Regardless of the labels one uses, the argument is that there is an inherent tension within political parties between individuals who are primarily concerned with electoral victory by the party and are willing to compromise their ideological principles to accomplish that goal and individuals who are primarily concerned with their issue-oriented goals and are unwilling to compromise on their ideological stands so that the party can win elections.

Sundquist contends that a typical characteristic of the groups who become involved in party politics because of their commitment to particular positions on new partisan issues is that they "are more concerned with victory for their position on the new issue than with their party's electoral success" (1983: 308). Scholarly accounts suggest that both secular Democratic activists and religiously conservative Republican activists may fit this bill; they have many of the characteristics of political "amateurs" or "purists." Both Jo Freeman (1986), in her discussion of the political culture of the two parties, and Duane Oldfield (1996), in his account of the ascendance of the Christian Right in the GOP, argue that the hesitancy of traditional Republican activists to accept the newly mobilized evangelical activists as legitimate participants in GOP politics is due not only to differences of opinion on cultural matters, but also to differences in political style. In contrast to the polite, reserved, "country club" style of politics practiced by traditional conservatives, religious conservatives practice a more emotional style of politics and are more overtly passionate about their ideological goals. Even more important, because of the GOP's traditional minority status, Republicans always have placed paramount importance on party unity—as evidenced by Ronald Reagan's "eleventh commandment" that "thou shalt not speak ill of a fellow Republican"—and felt that factional or ideological loyalties should not take precedence over commitment to the party and its electoral success. Committed evangelical activists, on the other hand, typically have made no bones about the fact that their political priority is to advance their conservative positions on issues such as abortion, school prayer, and homosexual rights and not to help Republican candidates get elected.

Similarly, the secular activists who emerged in Democratic party politics in the late 1960s and early 1970s seemed to be the classic political amateurs. They were quite willing to challenge the Democratic party establishment and to back candidates who supported their goals of civil rights, women's rights, tolerance for alternative lifestyles, and the end of the Vietnam War even if those candidates had only slim chances of winning general elections (Kirkpatrick 1976; Miller and Levitin 1976).

It is likely that the mobilization of secular activists into the Democratic party and of highly committed evangelical Protestants into the Republican party has created divisions within the parties. Those divisions may be both ideological and stylistic in nature, and they are probably particularly intense with regard to the cultural issues on which secular Democrats and traditionally religious Republicans hold highly liberal and conservative stances, respectively. However, if the accounts of activist-level partisan change presented by Aldrich (1983a, 1983b, 1995) and in chapter 3 are to be believed, then, over time, the religion-based intraparty divisions on cultural issues should grow smaller relative to the interparty differences on these issues. For instance, although the entry of religiously and culturally conservative activists into the Republican party should decrease the attraction of Republican activity for many secular and nominally religious activists, there may be some secular and religiously liberal individuals who remain active in or become active in the GOP. However, for Republican activity to continue to be attractive to these individuals, they should have, in the aggregate, more conservative cultural attitudes than did previous groups of less religious Republican activists.

In other words, because of the mobilization of religious traditionalists into the party and the associated increase in the conservatism of the GOP's cultural stands, the types of activists within the whole range of religious groups to whom the party appeals should be more culturally conservative than previous sets of Republican activists from the same groups. There should be an aggregate increase in cultural conservatism among Republican activists of all religious stripes. Following this same logic, the growing secularism of the Democratic party and the concomitant growth of cultural liberalism should lead Democratic activists of all religious orientations to adopt, in the aggregate, more liberal stances on cultural issues. In short, the differences between the same religious groups in different parties on cultural issues should grow larger over time and may become more substantial than the divisions between different religious groups in the same parties. Interparty cultural conflict may become more intense than intraparty cultural conflict.

This chapter assesses the role of the religious and cultural divide in fostering conflict within and between the activist bases of the Democratic and Republican parties. I consider these two themes—intraparty and interparty conflict—by examining the relationship between activists' religious characteristics and three political orientations: positions on issues of public policy and general ideological proclivities, preferences for party nominees, and political motivations and priorities. The key components of the chapter are issue and ideological differences. They generally are considered to be at the heart of religion-based intraparty rifts and must be the focus of a comparison of intraparty conflict with interparty conflict. So I save this most important part of the analysis for last and focus first on candidate preferences and political incentives.

RELIGION AND PRESIDENTIAL CANDIDATE PREFERENCES

Regardless of the size of the religion-based ideological splits with a party, those splits may be greatly magnified in the context of a nomination contest. When compared to their counterparts in the other party, almost all

Democratic presidential candidates appear to be fairly liberal on most issues and almost all Republican presidential candidates appear to be fairly conservative. However, in the constrained ideological space of a nomination campaign, the issue positions of "moderate" Democratic politicians such as Bill Clinton or Al Gore and those of "liberal" Democrats such as Jesse Jackson, Tom Harkin, or Jerry Brown may appear to be worlds apart. Similarly, in the context of a Republican nomination campaign, the ideological differences between "moderates" such as George Bush, John McCain, or Bob Dole and "conservatives" such as Pat Buchanan, Pat Robertson, Jack Kemp, or Alan Keyes may appear to be considerable.

That means that religion-based ideological differences may lead to consistently different types of preferences for party nominees. Highly committed evangelical Republicans and other religiously committed and religiously conservative Republican activists may consistently support more-conservative candidates, particularly those with very conservative stands on issues such as abortion and school prayer, while less traditionally religious activists in the GOP may consistently support more-moderate candidates for party nominations. Secular Democrats and other Democratic activists with low levels of religious commitment and modernist religious orientations may be consistent supporters of liberal, particularly culturally liberal, Democratic candidates, while more-religious Democratic activists may be more likely to support moderate candidates. If they indeed are linked to differences in candidate preferences, the religion-based ideological divisions that do exist within a party may be inflamed by emotional loyalties to different political leaders and thus be amplified into impassioned battles over the political direction of the party.

To examine the relationship between religion and preferences for party nominees, I performed binomial and multinomial logit analyses in which the first choice for president of 1988 and 1992 Democratic and Republican convention delegates was the dependent variable,[3] and the primary independent variables were religious commitment,[4] dummy variables for religious traditions—mainline Protestants, Catholics, black Protestants, Jews, and seculars, with evangelical Protestants serving as the comparison category, for Democrats; and mainline Protestants, Catholics, and seculars, with evangelical Protestants serving as the comparison category, for Republicans—and interactions between these variables and commitment.[5] The predicted probabilities from the models for seculars, Jews, and the low-, middle-, and high-commitment groups among Catholics and the three Protestant traditions are shown in figures 4.1 and 4.2.[6]

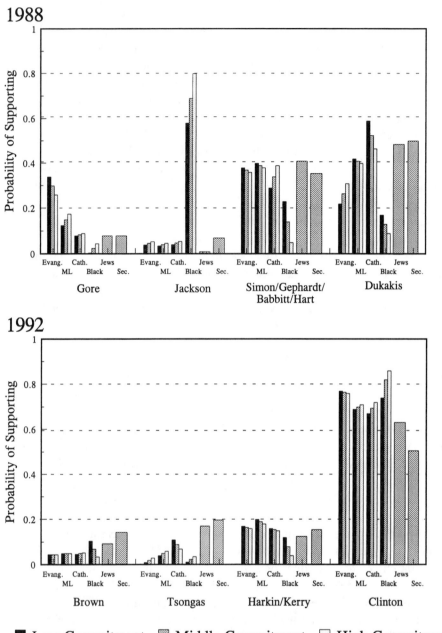

FIGURE 4.1. Candidate preferences of 1988 and 1992 Democratic delegates by religious tradition and religious commitment
Source: Computed by the author from multinomial logit analyses using the 1988 and
1992 Convention Delegate Studies.

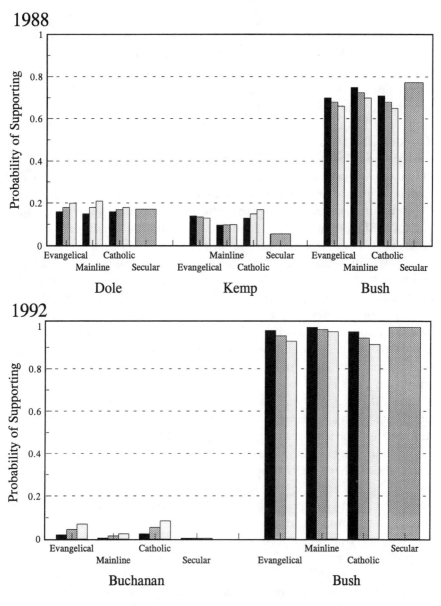

1988

1992

■ Low Commitment   ▦ Middle Commitment   ☐ High Commitment

FIGURE 4.2. Candidate preferences of 1988 and 1992 Republican delegates by religious tradition and religious commitment
Source: Computed by the author from logit and multinomial logit analyses using the 1988 and 1992 Convention Delegate Studies.

Figure 4.1 demonstrates that, in 1988, there were clear differences between the candidate preferences of Democratic activists in different religious groups. Not surprisingly, black Protestants were much more likely than other Democratic delegates to support black religious and political leader Jesse Jackson. Since Jackson used black Protestant churches as the organizational base for his campaign (Hertzke 1993), it is also not surprising that his strongest support came from the most religiously committed black Protestants. In stark contrast, Jackson received almost no support from Jews, reflecting his characterization of New York City as "Hymietown" and his association with black Muslim leader Louis Farrakhan, who has been highly critical of the Jewish faith.

Religion also had a noticeable effect on delegates' support for the party's 1988 nominee, Michael Dukakis, and his closest competitor after Jackson, Al Gore. Dukakis had no formal ties to organized religion, had been governor of Massachusetts, one of the nation's most liberal states, and took highly liberal stands on a whole range of issues, including cultural issues. In contrast, Gore was a devout Southern Baptist, was a U.S. Senator from Tennessee, and, in an attempt to appeal to Democrats in his native South, took fairly moderate positions on most issues. Accordingly, Dukakis received his strongest support from Jews, secularists, and the least-committed Catholics and got much less support from evangelical and black Protestants, while Gore received his strongest support from evangelical Protestants and got very little backing from Jews and secularists. Noteworthy, however, is the fact that Gore received his strongest support from the least-committed evangelical Protestants, while the most-committed evangelicals were actually more supportive of Dukakis. That may indicate that Gore's support among white evangelicals was based more on his ties to the South and the prevalence of evangelical Protestants in the South than on appeals by his campaign to religious traditionalism and cultural conservatism.

Religious tradition and commitment appear to have had less influence on preferences for the 1992 Democratic presidential nomination. The probability of supporting Bill Clinton, the party's nominee, was .5 or greater for every religious tradition and every level of commitment within each tradition. However, the support that Clinton received from black Protestants is interesting. With no black candidate in the 1992 Democratic race, Clinton actively courted African-American voters and followed Jackson's 1988 example by going into to the black churches to mobilize support. This strategy paid off, as Clinton's strongest support came from black Protestant delegates, and that support increased with religious commitment. Also notable is the fact that Clinton, who, like Gore, was a Southern Baptist with strong ties to the centrist Democratic Leadership Council, received his weakest support from secular delegates. In contrast, Jerry Brown and Paul Tsongas, candidates more closely associated with liberal stands on cultural issues, received their strongest support from secularists.

So it does appear that religious differences among Democratic activists translate, to some extent, into support for different types of Democratic candidates, with secular and less religiously committed activists being more likely than more traditionally religious Democrats to support culturally liberal candidates. However, these differences are at the margins. Both secular and highly committed evangelical Democrats gave a plurality of their support to the party's front-runner in 1988 and a majority to the front-runner in 1992.

Figure 4.2 shows that religious tradition and religious commitment seem to have had relatively minor effects on Republican candidate preferences in 1988. The nominee, moderate Republican George Bush, did receive slightly stronger support from seculars and from the least-committed evangelical Protestants, mainline Protestants, and Catholics than from the most-committed activists in those three traditions. Meanwhile, Bush's strongest, and more conservative, challenger, Bob Dole, received slightly more support from the most-committed activists in each tradition than from their less devout counterparts. An even more conservative candidate, Jack Kemp, received his strongest support from the most-committed Catholics. However, none of the religious groups came close to favoring Dole or Kemp over Bush. The probability of backing Bush was greater than .6 for each religious tradition and for every level of commitment within those traditions.

Noticeably absent from the figure is televangelist and Christian Right leader Pat Robertson, a candidate whose campaign was centered in evangelical churches and whose primary appeal to many Republican activists was his moral and cultural conservatism. Surely, religious orientations played a substantial role in shaping support for Robertson. But because some religious traditions in the sample contained no Robertson supporters, it was impossible to include delegates favoring Robertson in the model used to construct the top half of figure 4.2. However, it is clear that Robertson had a very distinct religious appeal. The large majority (84 percent) of his support among 1988 convention delegates came from the evangelical tradition. But as past research has shown (Green and Guth 1988; Wilcox 1992), that support was narrowly focused within

Robertson's own Pentecostal wing of evangelicalism and did not extend to other evangelical denominations.

Robertson's 1988 campaign is widely credited with bringing charismatics and Pentecostals into the Christian Right and the Republican party for the first time (Hertzke 1993; Oldfield 1996). Accordingly, he received very strong support from those delegates who placed themselves in the "Pentecostal/Assemblies of God" category of the CDS's denomination code. Over 78 percent of these delegates identified Robertson as their first choice for president. However, these individuals also comprised less than a quarter of all of the evangelical delegates to the 1988 Republican convention,[7] and Robertson did not fare well among non-Pentecostal evangelicals. Less than 9 percent of the latter delegates claimed Robertson as their leading candidate, while over 63 percent of this group supported Bush. In short, Pat Robertson was unable to reach beyond his Pentecostal base to the whole evangelical constituency, and most of that constituency, just like most mainline Protestants, Catholics, and seculars at the 1988 Republican convention, supported George Bush.

Much like the 1988 nomination campaign, the campaign for the Republican presidential nomination in 1992 would seem to have been tailor-made for religion-based intraparty conflict. Christian Right leaders remained highly suspicious of George Bush's commitment to the culturally conservative agenda and criticized his administration for failing to devote enough time or effort to furthering that agenda (Oldfield 1996). Meanwhile, Bush's only challenger in 1992 was Pat Buchanan, a political operative and commentator who had been very supportive of the pro-life movement and a fervent proponent of cultural conservatism in general. However, Pat Robertson, Ralph Reed, and other leaders of the Christian Right sought to minimize intraparty division and any damage Buchanan's campaign might do to Bush's reelection chances by quickly endorsing the incumbent president (Oldfield 1996). The result appears to be that religion again did not play a very divisive role in the Republican nomination process. The most committed members of the three major traditions were slightly more likely than their less devout counterparts to support Buchanan over Bush. However, Bush received nearly unanimous support from Republican activists of all religious persuasions.

It should be kept in mind that nominee preferences among national convention delegates, particularly Republican national convention delegates, may not provide an entirely accurate representation of candidate support among all party activists. Whereas the national Democratic party requires that candidate preferences among a state's delegates to the national convention be a fair reflection of the preferences of caucus or primary participants in the state, the national GOP has no such rule. Thus, state Republican parties may institute winner-take-all rules, under which all of the delegates from a state may be supporters of the top vote getter in a state's primary or caucuses, or some other procedure that favors the front-runner for the nomination in the composition of national convention delegations. That means that the party's nominee may have more support among national convention delegates than he has among all party activists. Thus, focusing only on the effects of religion on the nominee preferences of convention delegates may underestimate the extent to which it plays a divisive role in the nomination process.

In fact, evidence from both the 1988 and 1992 Republican nomination campaigns suggests just that. Neither Pat Robertson in 1988 nor Pat Buchanan in 1992 had the breadth of support or the financial resources to mount a sustained challenge to George Bush. However, both scored successes in crucial early contests. Robertson parlayed the fervency of Christian Right activists and the ability of evangelical Protestant churches to mobilize them politically into a second-place finish in the 1988 Iowa caucuses, one place ahead of Bush. Bush defeated Buchanan in the 1992 New Hampshire primary, but by a much narrower margin than expected: 60 percent to 40 percent. Neither of these successes came close to costing George Bush his party's nomination in 1988 or 1992. However, they may have prolonged the nomination processes in both years, forced Bush to devote more resources to the nomination campaign than he had planned and to take more conservative positions on cultural issues than he had hoped, and increased the tensions between the traditionally religious faction and the less religious, business-oriented faction of the GOP.

While the data presented in figure 4.2 may provide a less-than-perfect reflection of candidate support among Republican activists in 1988 and 1992, they are telling. They capture the fact that, however disappointing the early Robertson and Buchanan successes may have been to the Bush campaign, Bush ultimately won the primaries and caucuses in a large majority of states, in fact all of the states in 1992, thus gaining the support of a large majority of delegates to the Republican national convention. Moreover, his support was not based principally among mainline Protestants or the less traditionally religious portions of the GOP coalition. Bush received very strong support from Republican delegates in every religious tradition and at every level of religious commitment.[8] Thus, it appears that religion may not play as divisive a role in Republican nomination politics as is often thought.

RELIGION, PARTY SUPPORT, AND POLITICAL PRIORITIES

Although the candidate preferences of traditionally religious Republican activists and the less religious, business-oriented traditional Republicans do not appear to be different enough to greatly strain the relationship between the two Republican factions, their political incentives and goals may be. Committed evangelicals may place less emphasis on the party and its electoral success and more emphasis on ideological goals than do traditional Republicans. Meanwhile, what seems to be a relatively small skirmish between secular Democratic activists and the more religious Democrats over the party's nominees may, in fact, be a large rift if it is coupled with the secularists being less committed to partisan goals and more committed to ideological aims than are their more religious counterparts.

The first step in assessing the relationship between religious orientations and political priorities and motivations is simply to ask whether secular Democrats and committed evangelical Republicans are less attached to their parties than are their fellow activists. The 1992 CDS asked respondents to rank their support for their political party on a seven-point scale ranging from not very strong to very strong. Figure 4.3 shows the mean values on that scale for Democratic and Republican delegates in various religious traditions and with high and low levels of religious commitment.[9] The levels of party support of secular Democrats and of committed evangelical Republicans are lower than those of other Democratic (all nonsecular Democrats) and other Republican (all Republicans who are not highly committed evangelical Protestants) activists, and the differences are statistically significant.[10] However, as the figure makes clear, the differences are quite small. Secular Democrats and committed evangelical Republicans, like all other groups of Democratic and Republican activists, are quite attached to their parties.

Of course, the fact that secular Democrats and committed evangelical Republicans show strong subjective attachments to their respective parties does not mean that they are as committed to achieving the party's electoral goals as are their fellow partisans. When asked to choose between partisan goals and ideological goals, these activists may be more likely than other Democratic and Republican activists to choose the latter. Table 4.1 presents two sets of tests of this notion. The first is based on a series of questions in the 1992 CDS that asked respondents to rate the extent to which their activity in the 1992 presidential campaign was motivated by three different factors: commitment to party, a desire to

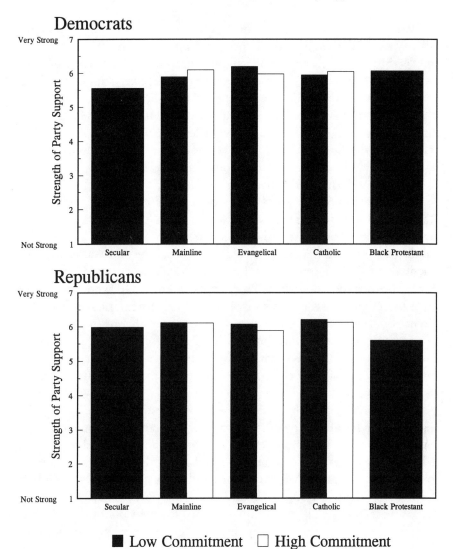

FIGURE 4.3. Mean party support of 1992 Democratic and Republican convention delegates by religious tradition and religious commitment
Source: 1992 Convention Delegate Study

help a particular candidate, and a desire to work for a particular issue. The table shows the percentage of activists in various religious categories indicating that "a lot" of their campaign activity in 1992 was motivated by the particular factor.

Party commitment played a much lesser role in motivating the party activity of secular Democrats than it did for nonsecular Democrats. Not only is this difference statistically significant, but secular Democratic activists were more than 20 percentage points less likely than the whole group of nonsecular Democratic activists to indicate that a lot of their campaign activity was motivated by a commitment to party. Highly committed evangelical Republicans also were less likely than mainline Protestant and Catholic Republicans to be motivated by a commitment to party, and the difference between committed evangelicals and all other Republican activists was statistically significant.[11]

The extent to which secular Democrats and committed evangelical Republicans were motivated by support for particular candidates in 1992 was no different from that of their fellow partisans. Support for particular candidates seems to play a large role in inspiring the party activity of individuals of all religious stripes. However, secularists in the Democratic party and devout evangelical Protestants in the GOP were motivated more than their fellow partisans by support for particular issues. The differences in both parties are statistically significant,[12] but the disparities in the GOP are particularly impressive. Highly committed evangelical Republicans were 22 percent more likely than other Republican activists to say that a lot of their campaign activity was motivated by particular issues.

The second test in the table is based on questions in the 1992 CDS asking delegates about the reasons for their general involvement in politics, rather than just about 1992. The table shows the percentage of delegates in various religious categories indicating that strong attachments to the party, a desire to see particular candidates elected to office, and a desire to get the party and its candidates to support particular issue positions were "extremely important" reasons for their political participation. Secular Democrats were again considerably less likely than other Democratic activists to be motivated by party attachments. Although the differences were not as large as in the Democratic party, committed evangelical Republicans also placed less importance on party attachments in their political involvement than did other Republican activists.[13] Electing particular candidates was again a strong motivation for all types of party activists and the differences between activists with various religious orientations were rather small. The differences in terms of ideological incentives were more noticeable. The political activity of secular Democrats and committed evangelical Republicans was driven more by a desire to persuade the party and its candidates to support particular issue positions

TABLE 4.1

Importance of party, candidates, and issues in motivating 1992 presidential campaign involvement and general political involvement by party, religious tradition, and religious commitment

Party and Religious Tradition/ Religious Commitment	1992 Presidential Campaign Activity[a]			General Political Involvement[b]		
	Commitment to Party	Support for Candidates	Support for Issues	Strongly Attached to Party	Elect Particular Candidates	Get Support for Issue Positions
Democrats						
Secular	45.63%	85.24%	56.78%	25.98%	68.52%	55.12%
Mainline/low	66.82	83.69	47.14	33.07	65.22	41.67
Mainline/high	69.23	83.12	40.56	47.34	64.46	38.69
Evangelical/low	76.83	91.03	43.84	40.23	67.42	37.50
Evangelical/high	77.42	85.29	34.48	50.00	72.22	38.89
Catholic/low	61.73	82.17	47.81	32.37	64.64	44.96
Catholic/high	69.06	86.96	41.28	44.88	65.85	46.80
Black Protestant	80.69	95.59	61.72	42.68	77.91	43.64
Republicans						
Secular	65.22%	81.40%	27.50%	42.86%	60.71%	40.74%
Mainline/low	74.05	75.39	19.74	39.62	62.56	33.80
Mainline/high	77.27	84.26	31.52	43.30	73.99	40.09
Evangelical/low	63.16	81.13	40.43	39.68	68.25	38.71
Evangelical/high	61.36	75.56	56.32	33.66	67.65	56.00
Catholic/low	77.63	77.92	21.74	44.44	62.96	36.59
Catholic/high	71.17	75.00	38.38	42.19	65.35	51.59
Black Protestant	84.62	90.00	33.33	38.46	69.23	30.77

Source: 1992 Convention Delegate Study.

The number of observations ranges from 9 to 361.

Rows in italics are highlighted in the text.

[a] Entries are the percentage of each group indicating that "a lot" of their campaign activity in 1992 was motivated by the particular factor.

[b] Entries are the percentage of each group indicating that the particular factor is an "extremely important" reason for their participation in politics.

than was the activity of any other group of activists in either party. In both parties, these differences were substantial and statistically significant.[14]

It does appear that the growing groups of secular activists in the Democratic party and highly committed evangelical Protestants in the Republican party are more likely than Democratic and Republican activists with other religious characteristics to fit the mold of political "amateurs" or "purists." They are strongly attached to their respective parties, but their political activity is motivated less by a commitment to party and more by a commitment to particular ideological goals than is the participation of their fellow partisans. Although the questions in the CDS surveys do not provide a direct test of this, this evidence suggests that in a choice between compromising ideological goals to enhance the party's chances for electoral success or remaining steadfast in ideological principles even at the expense of partisan electoral defeat, secular Democratic activists and committed evangelical Republican activists are more likely than their fellow partisans to choose the latter.

Whatever the size of the ideological rift between religious groups within the two parties, the issue-oriented motivations of secular Democrats and devout evangelical Republicans may produce tensions between those groups and the more traditional supporters of the two parties who are driven more by partisan goals. The relationship between religiously defined factions within the parties may be particularly strained if the issues that play the biggest role in motivating the political activity of secular Democrats and evangelical Republicans—the issues on which they may be unwilling to compromise to foster party success—are the cultural issues, the very issues that produce the biggest differences between religious groups.

The CDS surveys did not ask delegates to identify the particular issues that motivate their political activity, but a survey of delegates to state party conventions in 1984 did.[15] In this survey, delegates who indicated that their campaign activity was motivated by a particular issue were asked to identify the issue. Table 4.2 shows that secular Democrats and regularly attending evangelical Republicans were markedly more likely than other Democratic and Republican delegates to identify a cultural or moral issue as the primary issue motivating their party activity.[16] In fact, the percentage of regularly attending evangelical Republicans identifying a cultural or moral issue as the principal catalyst for their activity was far higher than the percentage for any other type of issue, while the percentage of secular Democrats mentioning a cultural or moral issue was higher than the percentage for any other type of issue besides foreign policy.

TABLE 4.2
The most important issues in motivating campaign activity for state
convention delegates, by party and religious orientations, 1984

Issue Type	Democrats		Republicans	
	Secular	Nonsecular	Regularly Attending Evangelical Protestants	All Other Religious Orientations[a]
Cultural and moral issues	29.63%	11.81%	48.70%	17.03%
Economic issues	3.70	25.39	29.22	44.38
Social welfare/public services	18.52	25.33	3.90	19.47
Energy and natural resources	11.11	7.08	.97	2.43
Crime and drugs	1.85	.19	.65	.58
Racial issues	1.85	2.97	.65	.35
Defense and foreign policy	31.48	17.75	11.69	8.11
State and local issues	1.85	9.48	4.22	7.64
(N)	(54)	(1,583)	(308)	(863)

Source: 1984 Comparative State Party Activist Survey.
[a]All Republicans who are not regularly attending evangelical Protestants.

So not only do the committed evangelicals in the Republican party and secularists in the Democratic party place a higher priority on ideological goals and a lower priority on partisan goals than do their fellow partisans, but they also are very concerned with those issues that create the most tension between religious groups: the cultural and moral issues. This may make it difficult for them to blend harmoniously into their relatively new partisan environments.

INTRAPARTY AND INTERPARTY IDEOLOGICAL DIVISIONS

Now we come to the heart of the matter: religion-based differences in ideology and attitudes on issues of public policy. Battles over party nominations are based, at least in part, on ideological divisions within a party. Meanwhile, the level of tension caused by the question of whether a party should stand firm on ideological principles or compromise those principles for electoral victory may depend on the size of the ideological schisms within the party. If there is a basic agreement on ideological goals, then there may be just a question of the speed and intensity with which those goals are pursued. But if there is a clear disagreement over policy goals, then the purist-versus-pragmatist debate within a party may be a source of intense conflict. Thus, the central questions of this chapter are, How large is the ideological gap between different religious groups within the same party? and, Are those intraparty splits larger or smaller than the ideological cleavage between the two parties?

To assess the extent to which ideological divisions within the parties take shape along religious lines, I regressed the attitudes on three types of issues—social welfare issues, cultural issues, and defense spending[17]—and the ideological self-identifications of delegates to the 1992 Democratic and Republican national conventions on their levels of religious commitment, dummy variables for religious traditions, interactions between the tradition variables and commitment, several demographic controls, and ideological self-identification (when it was not the dependent variable). The estimates of these regression models are presented in appendix B2. The predicted values from the models for activists in various religious traditions and with various levels of religious commitment are shown in figure 4.4.

Since the effect of religion on attitudes toward social welfare, racial, and defense issues generally pales in comparison to its effect on cultural issue attitudes (Jelen 1991), it is not surprising that there are virtually no differences between the attitudes of different religious groups within the same parties on social welfare issues or on defense spending. On cultural issues, in contrast, there are recognizable differences based on both religious tradition and on commitment. Within both parties and within all of the major religious traditions, the most religiously committed activists have more conservative cultural attitudes than their less devout counterparts. And even after taking into account differences in commitment, evangelical Protestants and Catholics—and, within the Democratic party, black Protestants—are noticeably more conservative than mainline Protestants. Jewish and secular delegates have clearly more liberal cultural attitudes than do their fellow partisans in the Christian traditions. Although not as pronounced as on cultural issues, there are also religion-based differences in ideological self-identification. Within most of the major traditions within both parties, the most committed delegates have more conservative identifications than do the least-committed delegates. Jewish and secular Democrats are more liberal than Christian Democrats.

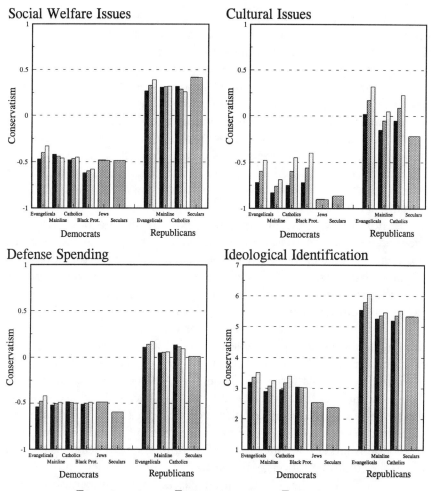

FIGURE 4.4. Ideological orientations of 1992 convention delegates by party, religious tradition, and religious commitment
Source: Computed by the author from regression analyses using the 1992 Convention Delegate Study.

Despite these religion-based intraparty divisions on cultural issues and in general ideological orientations, the principal theme of figure 4.4 is interparty difference. Republican activists are considerably more conservative than Democratic activists in general, and within each religious group, whether defined by religious tradition or commitment levels within traditions, Republicans have markedly more conservative attitudes than Democrats. Even on the cultural issues that are so closely associated with religious orientations, divisions between different religious groups within the same party pale in comparison to splits between Democratic and Republican activists in the same religious groups. It is clear that even though there remain intraparty divisions along religious lines on issues such as abortion, women's rights, and school prayer, these issues, much like social welfare, racial, and defense issues, have become partisan issues: issues characterized by what Aldrich terms "party cleavages," in which the parties are "relatively cohesive internally and relatively distinctive externally" (1983a: 974).

As noted previously, this is not an unexpected finding. It follows from the model of party activism presented in chapter 3 that, as the religious polarization of the parties' activists increases, and as the cultural positions of party leaders and platforms grow more distinct, Democratic activists from the whole range of religious groups should become, in the aggregate, more culturally liberal, while Republican activists of various religious stripes become more culturally conservative. When issues such as abortion, women's rights, and homosexual rights first emerged on the political scene in the late 1960s and early 1970s, the gap between the positions of the two parties' platforms and leaders on the issues was relatively small. Thus, delegates' cultural attitudes should have been defined primarily by their religious orientations and affected rather weakly by their partisanship. Intraparty divisions between religious groups should have been considerably larger than interparty splits within the same religious groups. But as the cultural positions of the parties' platforms, leaders, and activists grew more distinct, the cultural differences between Democratic and Republican activists in the same religious groups should have grown. Interparty splits within religious groups should have increased relative to intraparty rifts between religious groups.

A first test of this hypothesis is provided in figure 4.5, which displays the predicted values for various religious groups in both parties from regressions of the abortion attitudes of delegates to the national conventions from 1972 through 1992 on religious tradition, church attendance, and the interaction between tradition and attendance.[18] To facilitate comparisons between Democratic and Republican delegates, the figure shows predicted values only for evangelical Protestants, mainline Protestants, Catholics, and seculars.

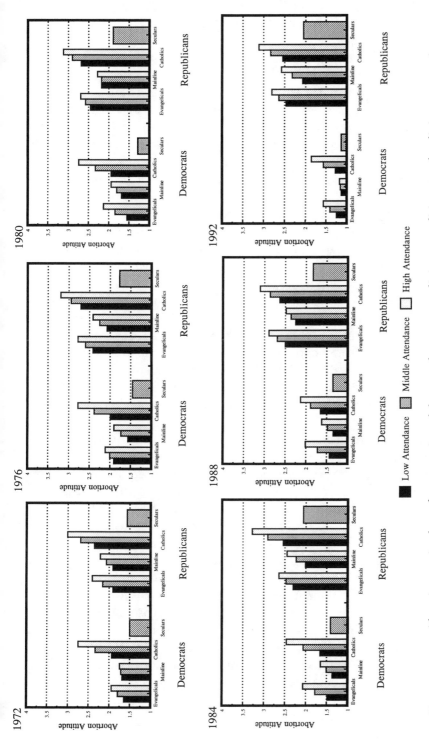

FIGURE 4.5. Abortion attitudes of convention delegates by party, religious tradition, and religious commitment, 1972–1992

Note: Abortion attitudes range from most pro-choice (1) to most pro-life (4).

Source: Computed by the author from regression analyses using the 1972–1992 Convention Delegate Studies.

The evidence clearly supports the hypothesis. In 1972, Republican delegates were slightly more likely than Democratic delegates to have pro-life abortion attitudes. However, the differences between Republican and Democratic delegates in the same religious traditions and with the same levels of religious commitment were fairly small. Much more substantial were the differences between different religious groups within the same parties. In 1972, abortion was clearly a religious issue, drawing very different reactions from party activists in different religious traditions and with varying levels of religious commitment, but it was not yet a partisan issue distinguishing Republican and Democratic activists.

The same description generally holds for abortion attitudes among delegates to the 1976 national conventions. Over time, however, the pattern slowly changed, and by 1992 the pattern shown in figure 4.4 for all cultural issues is apparent. There remain noticeable divisions within the two parties on the abortion issue, with Catholics and evangelical Protestants holding more conservative views than mainline Protestants, Jews, and secularists, and with regular church attenders in the three largest traditions being more opposed to abortion rights than are less frequent attenders. However, the primary division is a partisan one. Intraparty divisions along religious lines pale in comparison to the differences between the attitudes of activists in the same religious group but in different parties.

Figure 4.6 provides a more direct over-time comparison of the abortion attitudes of Republican and Democratic activists within particular religious groups. It shows the predicted abortion attitudes from 1972 to 1992 of Democratic and Republican delegates in seven different religious categories: seculars and regular and nonregular attenders in the mainline Protestant, evangelical Protestant, and Catholic traditions.[19] In each of these groups, the difference in the aggregate abortion attitudes of Democratic and Republican activists increased over time. This growth, similar to the ascendance of Democratic secularism and Republican evangelicalism, was sporadic, and it followed different patterns for different religious categories. In some groups, Republican activists became, in the aggregate, more pro-life and Democratic activists grew more pro-choice. In other groups, the collective attitudes of Republican activists did not change much, while those of Democrats became noticeably more pro-choice. Furthermore, the increase in partisan differences was not enormous in any of the religious groups. However, in every one of these religious categories, the gap between the abortion attitudes of Republican activists

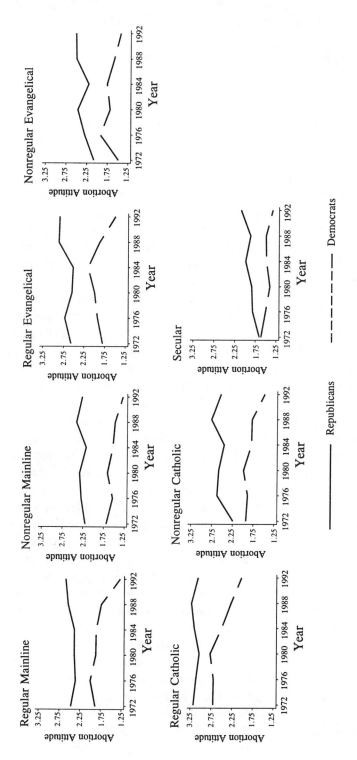

FIGURE 4.6. Predicted positions on abortion, held by Republicans and Democrats in various religious groups, 1972–1992

Note: Abortion attitudes range from most pro-choice (1) to most pro-life (4).

Source: Computed by the author from a regression analysis using the 1972–1992 Convention Delegate Studies (pooled).

and those of Democratic activists was larger in 1992 than it had been in 1972.

EXPLAINING PARTISAN POLARIZATION WITHIN RELIGIOUS GROUPS: REPLACEMENT OR CONVERSION?

This growing partisan polarization within religious groups may be explained, in part, by turnover or replacement among party activists. As the presence of religious traditionalists in the Republican party grows and as Republican candidates become more likely to take conservative stands on cultural issues, Republican activists within any tradition who have liberal cultural views may find activity in the GOP to be less enticing and drop out of the party. Meanwhile, nonactivists in the same traditions who have conservative cultural perspectives may find Republican politics to be more appealing and become active in the GOP. Similarly, the growth of Democratic cultural liberalism may lead culturally conservative Democratic activists within a particular religious group to disengage from party activity and may increase the chances that culturally liberal nonactivists in that group will become involved in Democratic politics.

For example, mainline Protestantism, the traditional religious backbone of the GOP, is a tradition containing a diverse set of cultural viewpoints. Most mainline Protestants tend to have fairly moderate positions on issues such as abortion, but there are also many mainline Protestants with strongly pro-life feelings on abortion, as well as a large number of mainline Protestants who are highly committed to the pro-choice viewpoint (Hunter 1994). As religious traditionalism and cultural conservatism become more closely associated with the GOP, the types of mainline Protestants who become active in and remain active in the party should change. Those mainline Protestants whose views on cultural issues are more liberal should find Republican party activity less appealing, and individuals within this group should become less likely to become active in the GOP or more likely to drop out of Republican activity if they already were active. In contrast, those mainliners who hold more conservative views on cultural issues should find Republican party activity more attractive, and individuals within this group should become more likely to become active or remain active in the Republican party.

Activist turnover may not be the only cause of the growing cultural gap between Democratic and Republican activists in the same religious groups. Individual-level attitudinal conversion also may contribute to this partisan polarization because the cultural stands of party candidates and of other activists may influence those held by individual activists (Layman and Carsey 1998). Increases in the proportion of religiously conservative activists in the Republican party and in the number of candidates for GOP nominations who take conservative positions on cultural issues may lead individuals who are active and remain active in the Republican party to convert to more conservative cultural views. Increases in the presence of secular activists and culturally liberal candidates in the Democratic party may lead individuals who are active and remain active in that party to more liberal cultural attitudes.

As an example, consider the case of a woman who is a mainline Protestant with moderate attitudes on cultural issues and who is active in the Republican party in the late 1970s and remains active in the party through the late 1990s. As the presence of traditionally religious activists in the GOP increases through the 1980s and 1990s, the probability that she will engage in social interaction with people who hold highly conservative views on cultural issues also increases. It increases not just because she is now more likely to be working in the same campaigns or in the same physical space with cultural conservatives, but also because one of the reasons that many people are active in party politics is to make friends and have social contact with other politically interested people (Wilson 1962; Miller and Jennings 1986).[20]

This greater interaction with culturally conservative individuals may affect our mainline activist's own cultural views. A considerable body of literature shows that one's social context and patterns of social interaction have a significant influence on the types of political information one receives and ultimately one's political attitudes (Berelson, Lazarsfeld, and McPhee 1954; Putnam 1966; Huckfeldt and Sprague 1987; Huckfeldt, Plutzer, and Sprague 1993; Wald, Owen, and Hill 1988). So increased interaction with individuals who have culturally conservative views may lead her to convert to more conservative attitudes on cultural issues.

The growth in the religious traditionalism of Republican activists also means that the number of candidates for Republican nominations who take conservative cultural positions should increase, either because candidates reshape their stands on these issues to appeal to a changing activist base or because candidates who already held conservative cultural views find the prospects of winning party nominations more encouraging and become more likely to run. So it is more likely that our mainline

TABLE 4.3
Conversion and replacement effects on abortion among presidential
campaign activists from 1972 to 1980 and from 1980 to 1988

1972–1980

Party and Religious Tradition	Mean Abortion Attitude of Stayers in 1980 (S_{80})[a]	Mean Abortion Attitude of Stayers in 1972 (S_{72})[a]	Conversion $(S_{80} - S_{72})$	Mean Abortion Attitude of Newcomers in 1980 (N_{80})[b]	Mean Abortion Attitude of Dropouts in 1972 (D_{72})[c]	Replacement $(N_{80} - D_{72})$
Democrats						
Secular	1.26	1.38	-.12	1.30	1.23	+.07
Mainline	1.81	1.82	-.01	1.67	2.00	-.33
Evangelical	1.90	2.11	-.21	2.13	2.00	+.13
Black Prot.	1.75	1.50	+.25	1.93	2.00	-.07
Catholic	2.48	2.55	-.07	2.47	2.32	+.15
Republicans						
Mainline	2.16	2.06	+.10	2.23	1.94	+.29
Evangelical	2.42	2.00	+.42	2.61	2.00	+.61
Catholic	2.90	2.73	+.17	2.81	2.67	+.14

1980–1988

	Mean Abortion Attitude of Stayers in 1988 (S_{88})[d]	Mean Abortion Attitude of Stayers in 1980 (S_{80})[d]	Conversion $(S_{88} - S_{80})$	Mean Abortion Attitude of Newcomers in 1988 (N_{88})[e]	Mean Abortion Attitude of Dropouts in 1980 (D_{80})[f]	Replacement $(N_{88} - D_{80})$
Democrats						
Secular	1.15	1.31	-.16	1.21	1.36	-.15
Mainline	1.65	1.67	-.02	1.52	1.76	-.24
Evangelical	1.89	2.12	-.23	1.75	1.63	+.12
Black Prot.	1.96	2.00	-.04	1.66	2.25	-.59
Catholic	2.15	2.48	-.33	1.86	2.53	-.67
Republicans						
Mainline	2.29	2.23	+.06	1.97	2.03	-.06
Evangelical	2.80	2.68	+.12	2.87	2.40	+.47
Catholic	2.98	2.96	+.02	3.00	2.90	+.10

Source: Convention Delegate Studies (1972–1980 and 1980–1988 panels, and 1980 and 1988 cross sections).

Presidential campaign activists are those present and past convention delegates who were active in the presidential campaign of a particular year regardless of whether or not they were delegates in that year. Abortion attitudes range from the most pro-choice position (1) to the most pro-life position (4).

[a]Stayers are those respondents who were active in both 1972 and 1980.

[b]Newcomers are those respondents who were active in 1980 but not in 1972.

[c]Dropouts are those respondents who were active in 1972 but not in 1980.

[d]Stayers are those respondents who were active in 1980 and 1988.

[e]Newcomers are those respondents who were active in 1988 but not in 1980.

[f]Dropouts are those respondents who were active in 1980 but not in 1988.

Protestant activist will be supporting a candidate who espouses cultural conservatism. Since the stands taken by candidates and political leaders often influence the issue-attitudes of their supporters, particularly the most politically attentive ones (Zaller 1992; McCann 1995), this also may lead her to convert to more conservative views on cultural matters.[21]

In table 4.3, I use panel and cross-sectional data on Democratic and Republican activists from 1972 to 1980 and from 1980 to 1988 to consider the notion that attitudinal conversion and activist replacement both have contributed to the growth of partisan cleavages on abortion within religious groups.[22] With a few exceptions, the aggregate conversion and replacement effects are in the expected directions for religious groups in both parties.[23] The conversion effects are particularly consistent. Between 1972 and 1980, Democratic activists within four of the five largest religious traditions who were active in both years became, in the aggregate, more liberal on the abortion issue. Between 1980 and 1988, the abortion attitudes of continuing Democratic activists in all five traditions became more pro-choice. The attitudinal changes among Republican activists are even more uniform. Mainline Protestants, evangelical Protestants, and Catholics who were active in the GOP in both 1972 and 1980 all became, in the aggregate, more conservative on abortion, with evangelicals shifting their abortion attitudes nearly one-half of a scale point in the pro-life direction. Between 1980 and 1988, the abortion attitudes of continuing activists from all three religious traditions also grew more pro-life. Clearly, part of the reason for the growing partisan cleavages on abortion within religious groups is that, on average, members of a religious group who remain active in the Democratic party are converting toward more pro-choice views on abortion, while members of the same religious group who remain active in the Republican party are converting toward the pro-life position.

Activist turnover also appears to have contributed to the growth of partisan cleavages within religious groups, particularly among Republicans. Within the three largest religious traditions, the activists who entered the Republican party between 1972 and 1980 had more pro-life attitudes on abortion, in the aggregate, than did the Republican activists who disengaged from party activity between 1972 and 1980. Among evangelical Protestants, the differences were quite impressive, with the attitudes of newcomers in 1980 being more than one-half of a scale point more conservative than those of 1972 dropouts. Although mainline Protestant activists who were new to Republican activity in 1988 had slightly more liberal abortion attitudes than did mainliners who were active in the

GOP in 1980 but had dropped out by 1988, evangelical and Catholic newcomers in 1988 were more supportive of the pro-life viewpoint on abortion than the evangelical and Catholic dropouts whom they replaced.

Among Democratic activists, the replacement patterns between 1972 and 1980 were very mixed. Mainline Protestants who were new to Democratic activity in 1980 had, collectively, more liberal views on abortion than did the mainline Democrats who disengaged from party activity between 1972 and 1980. However, among secular, evangelical, and Catholic Democrats, newcomers in 1980 were slightly less supportive than 1972 dropouts of the pro-choice stand. It is not entirely surprising that the Democratic party would attract a more culturally conservative group of activists in 1980 than it had in 1972, given the differences in the cultural stands of the party's presidential nominees in the two years.

Between 1980 and 1988, activist turnover clearly pushed four of the five major religious traditions within the Democratic activist base in a pro-choice direction. Among secular, mainline Protestant, black Protestant, and Catholic Democrats, the newcomers to presidential campaign activity in 1988 were more liberal than the 1980 activists whom they replaced.

SUMMARY AND CONCLUSION

This chapter has shown that the ascendance of committed evangelical Protestants and other religious traditionalists within the Republican party, and of secularists and the least committed members of the major religious traditions in the Democratic party, may well have increased the level of conflict within the parties. Although the attitudinal divisions between different religious groups within the parties are quite small on social welfare, racial, and defense issues, particularly when compared to the differences between Democratic and Republican activists, there are clear differences between various religious groups on cultural issues such as abortion, women's rights, and school prayer. The most committed members of the major religious traditions have noticeably more conservative cultural attitudes than do the least committed members of the same traditions, and secular activists have more liberal cultural attitudes than do activists who belong to a religious tradition. Similar divisions within the parties also exist in general liberal–conservative ideological orientations.

The intraparty ideological divisions created by the emergence of cultural issues and the growth of religious traditionalism in the Republican party and of secularism in the Democratic party may well have been exacerbated by differences in candidate preferences and political priorities. Although the cultural split between different religious groups in the Republican party has not resulted in substantial differences in candidate support, religious and cultural divisions among Democrats have been translated into at least modest differences in nominee preferences. Secular activists have been more likely than activists in most other religious groups to support liberal candidates such as Michael Dukakis and Jerry Brown and less likely to support more moderate candidates such as Al Gore and Bill Clinton. Perhaps more important, the ascendant religious groups in the two parties—secularists in the Democratic party and committed evangelical Protestants in the GOP—seem to be more likely than activists in any of the other religious groups in their parties to fit the profile of political "purists." These groups of activists place a higher priority on issue-oriented goals and a lower priority on partisan goals than do their fellow partisans. Perhaps inciting even more intraparty tension is the fact that the issues that secular Democrats and devout evangelical Republicans find to be most important in motivating their party activity are the cultural issues, the very issues on which they differ most from other activists in their parties.

So the religion-based intraparty divisions upon which journalists and political scientists have focused considerable attention are based on real differences in issue attitudes and in political priorities. However, one cannot help but notice that, by the 1990s, the cultural gaps between various religious groups within the same party were clearly smaller than the differences in cultural attitudes between activists in the same religious groups but in different parties. This represents a clear contrast to the situation that existed when abortion and other cultural issues first emerged on the political scene in the early 1970s. At that time, there was a clear division between different religious groups within the parties, but not much difference between Democratic and Republican activists in the same religious groups. Over time, partisan cleavages on cultural issues have emerged within religious groups. They have resulted from both conversion—continuing Republican activists within most religious groups converting, in the aggregate, to more conservative attitudes on cultural issues, and continuing Democratic activists within most religious groups becoming more culturally liberal—and replacement: newcomers to Republican activity in most religious groups being more culturally conservative than the old activists in the same religious groups whom they replaced, and newcomers to Democratic activity in most religious groups being more culturally liberal than the old activists whom they replaced.

These findings suggest that interparty cultural conflict may be becoming more politically important than religion-based intraparty battles over cultural issues. These intraparty battles continue to rage, and they probably are fueled by the differences in political style and priorities between religious groups. However, they seem to be battles that may already have been won, as most groups of Republican activists have moved in a culturally conservative direction and nearly all groups of Democratic activists have taken clear steps toward cultural liberalism.

This should have clear implications for mass politics by providing the electorate with a clear picture of a Republican party with traditionalist views on issues such as abortion, homosexual rights, and school prayer and of a Democratic party with very liberal views on the same issues. As Carmines, Renten, and Stimson (1984) show with regard to racial issues, these changes in mass perceptions should ultimately lead to changes in the parties' coalitions, in this case to the religious and cultural polarization of the Republican and Democratic electoral coalitions. The remainder of this book will assess whether the parties' mass coalitions have become more polarized along religious and cultural lines and whether changes in the mass electorate are linked to religious and cultural changes among partisan activists and elites.

NOTES

1. "Republican Infighting," *New York Times,* July 26, 1998. [Internet, WWW]. *Available:* New York Times on the Web Archives; ADDRESS: http://archives.nytimes.com.

2. Kevin Sack, "Political Memo: Big Victory for the Republican Right," *New York Times,* July 2, 1998. [Internet, WWW]. *Available:* New York Times on the Web Archives; ADDRESS: http://archives.nytimes.com.

3. The media polls of 1996 convention delegates do not contain enough measures of religion or political orientations to examine the individual-level relationship between them. So I use only the 1972 to 1992 CDS surveys for the analyses in this chapter, focusing particularly on 1988 and 1992.

4. The commitment variable combines respondents' frequencies of church attendance and levels of religious salience. See appendix A1 for further details.

5. The estimates of these models are presented in appendix B2. The small numbers of delegates in nontraditional Protestant, Eastern Orthodox, and non-Judeo-Christian religions are excluded from the analyses. Because of the very small number of Jewish and black Protestant Republican delegates, these two traditions are excluded from the analyses for Republicans. These

analyses also included controls for education, income, gender, age, southern residence, and ideological self-identification.

6. The "middle" level of commitment for each tradition is defined as the mean level of religious commitment for each party's delegates within that tradition. The "low" level is one standard deviation below that mean, and the "high" level is one standard deviation above that mean. To compute the predicted values in all the figures in this chapter, all the control variables are held constant at their means for the particular parties' delegates. The models did include interactions between the secular and Jewish variables and commitment. The figures, however, show the predicted values only for the mean level of commitment of these groups.

7. I am referring here to only those delegates who claimed an affiliation with a specific evangelical denomination or religious movement. White delegates who identified themselves as "other Protestants" and also claimed to be fundamentalist Christians are included in the evangelical tradition, but it is impossible to tell whether or not they are Pentecostals or charismatics.

8. Although it does not contain detailed codings of religious affiliations, the ABC News/*Washington Post* poll of delegates to the 1996 Republican national convention shows a similar pattern of support in 1996 for GOP nominee Bob Dole. Delegates who identified themselves as members of the religious right were more likely to support Pat Buchanan (17 percent) than were delegates who did not identify themselves as religious right members (7 percent). However, overwhelming majorities of both religious right members (74 percent) and nonmembers (91 percent) supported Dole for the Republican presidential nomination.

9. To ease the comparisons for this analysis and the analysis in table 4.1, I simply divide the three largest religious traditions into high and low commitment groups. The high commitment group contains those members of the tradition whose levels of religious commitment are above the median value for that tradition. The low commitment group contains those members of the tradition whose levels of religious commitment are at or below the median for that tradition.

10. The t-test of the difference in means between secular and nonsecular Democratic delegates is -4.72 ($p < .001$). The t-test of the difference in means between highly committed evangelical Republicans and all other Republicans is -2.41 ($p < .01$).

11. The t-test of the difference in the mean values of secular and nonsecular Democrats on a variable coded 1 for those individuals indicating that "a lot" of their activity in 1992 was motivated by commitment to party and 0 for those individuals who did not indicate that is -7.94 ($p < .001$). The t-test of the difference in the mean values of highly committed evangelical Republicans and other Republicans is -2.75 ($p < .01$).

12. The t-test of the difference in the mean values of secular and non-

secular Democrats on a variable coded 1 for those individuals indicating that "a lot" of their activity in 1992 was motivated by support for issues and 0 for those individuals who did not indicate that is 3.10 ($p < .001$). The t-test of the difference in the mean values of highly committed evangelical Republicans and other Republicans is 4.76 ($p < .001$).

13. The t-test of the difference in the mean values of secular and non-secular Democrats on a variable coded 1 for those individuals indicating that a strong attachment to party is an "extremely important" reason for their participation in politics and 0 for individuals who did not indicate that is – 7.18 ($p < .001$). The t-test of the difference in the mean values of highly committed evangelical Republicans and other Republicans is –3.65 ($p < .001$).

14. The t-test of the difference in the mean values of secular and non-secular Democrats on a variable coded 1 for those individuals indicating that getting support from the party and its candidates for their issue positions is an "extremely important" reason for their participation in politics and 0 for individuals who did not indicate that is 3.32 ($p < .001$). The t-test of the difference in the mean values of highly committed evangelical Republicans and other Republicans is 3.28 ($p < .001$).

15. The 1984 Comparative State Party Activist Survey was conducted by Tod A. Baker, Charles D. Hadley, Robert P. Steed, and Lawrence W. Moreland. It surveyed 6,272 Democratic delegates and 5,609 Republican delegates to party conventions in 12 states: Arkansas, Connecticut, Indiana, Louisiana, Maine, Mississippi, North Carolina, North Dakota, Oklahoma, South Carolina, Texas, and Utah. I obtained these data directly from Professor Baker.

16. The issues or problems that I included in the category of cultural or moral issues are general state of morality, social breakdown, future of country, religious convictions, need for religion, women's rights issues, Equal Rights Amendment, abortion issues, and other moral issues. The t-test of the difference in the mean values of secular and nonsecular Democratic delegates on a variable coded 1 for those respondents who identified a cultural or moral issue as the most important issue motivating their campaign activity and 0 for respondents who did not identify a cultural or moral issue as the most important issue motivating their campaign activity is 3.92 ($p < .001$). The t-test between the mean values of regularly attending evangelical Republicans and all other Republicans on that variable is 11.57 ($p < .001$).

17. A principal-components factor analysis of the attitudes of each party's delegates on all the issues included in the 1992 CDS yielded these three issue dimensions. The results of that analysis are presented in appendix A2. There were two racial issues—spending on programs for blacks and government responsibility to help blacks—in the 1992 CDS. Both of these issues loaded strongly on the social welfare dimension. Attitudes toward each issue dimension range from –1 to 1.

18. The results of these regression analyses are presented in appendix B3. Abortion attitude is used as the dependent variable in these analyses because abortion is the only cultural issue included in all of the CDS surveys. Church attendance is used rather than religious commitment because attendance is the only measure of commitment included in the 1972 CDS. These analyses also include controls for ideological self-identification, education, income, gender, age, and southern residence.

19. The predictions come from a regression, using data pooled from each convention year from 1972 to 1992, of delegates' abortion attitudes on separate dummy variables for Democrats and Republicans in each of the seven religious categories and in three other religious groups not shown in the figure (black Protestants, Jews, and Mormons), dummy variables for each convention year from 1976 through 1992, and the interactions between each of the dummy variables for partisan and religious groups and each of the dummy variables for convention years. The model also includes controls for ideological self-identification, education, income, gender, age, and southern residence. The estimates of this regression model are presented in appendix B3.

20. Although the proportion of party activists who are motivated by purposive, policy-oriented goals has increased in recent decades (Aldrich 1995), a large number of activists still are motivated by social, "solidary" goals. In the 1992 CDS, 70.1 percent of Democratic and Republican delegates said that the opportunity to make "friendships and social contacts" was an important reason for their involvement in politics.

21. Given the highly emotional nature of abortion and other cultural issues, it generally is assumed that most of the partisan change on them is caused by turnover or replacement rather than changes in individual attitudes (cf. Adams 1997). However, recent research shows that there has been a good deal of conversion on abortion among both Democratic and Republican activists (Layman and Carsey 1998) and that conversion has contributed a great deal to activist-level partisan change on abortion (Carsey and Layman 1999).

22. I use the CDS panels from 1972 to 1980 (and from 1980 to 1988) to measure change in the abortion attitudes of continuing party activists. I also use the panels to identify the activists who dropped out of party activity between 1972 and 1980 (or between 1980 and 1988) and to measure their abortion attitudes in 1972 (or 1980). I use the cross-sectional CDS studies in 1980 and 1988 to gauge the abortion attitudes of the newcomers in those years. This table does not follow Rapoport and Stone's (1994) method of evaluating the contribution of conversion and replacement to overall party change. It simply shows the size and direction of aggregate conversion and the differences between the mean attitudes of newcomers and dropouts.

23. Because the number of individuals who were delegates to both the

1972 and the 1980 conventions or to both the 1980 and the 1988 conventions is very small, this analysis expands the focus beyond convention delegates to all of the CDS respondents (current and former delegates) who were active in the presidential campaigns in particular years. Turnover among presidential campaign activists is much less than it is among convention delegates and, although the number of observations for some groups remains small, focusing on this group allows for a more accurate evaluation of aggregate conversion. Having an adequate number of observations also necessitates focusing only on religious traditions within the parties and not on levels of church attendance within the traditions, as well as eliminating the very small number of secular and black Protestant Republican activists from consideration.

CHAPTER 5

The Changing Religious Face of the Parties' Mass Coalitions

A<small>N</small> EXAMINATION OF whether the partisan religious divisions that have emerged between Democratic and Republican activists also have become apparent between the parties' coalitions in the mass electorate is important for at least two reasons. First, it should provide insight into the mass response to elite behavior. Numerous accounts of partisan change, including, most notably, Carmines and Stimson's (1989) theory of "issue evolution," posit that change in the aggregate issue attitudes and social characteristics of the parties' mass coalitions result from changes in the ideological stands and political statements of partisan elites. If this is true, then change in the partisan behavior of various religious groups and in the religious composition of the parties' coalitions should follow the growing religious and cultural polarization of the parties' elites, activists, and platforms.

Second, changes in the social composition of the parties' mass coalitions have significant implications for the political parties and the behavior of their elites. These changes affect the types of candidates who seek party nominations and are able to win them, the ability of parties to win elections, and the types of policies the parties pursue. As John Petrocik notes, "The party-group alignment will dictate the issue concerns and policy prescriptions of a party. The linkage is completely recursive: groups support a party because of the policies it promotes; the party promotes certain policies because it draws supporters, activists, and candidates from particular groups" (1998: 4).

Of course, changes in the composition of the parties' mass coalitions also affect the characteristics of party activists, not only indirectly through their impact on the policy positions of party candidates and leaders, but also directly, since activists tend to emerge from a party's base of support.

Thus, an increase in the religious and cultural differences between the parties' mass coalitions may not only result from religious and cultural polarization among party activists and elites, but also help to sustain and perhaps increase that polarization.

This chapter assesses whether a traditionalist–modernist religious cleavage has emerged between the Democratic and Republican coalitions in the mass electorate. As suggested in chapter 2, it does so both from the perspective of political differences between religious traditions—for example, whether the more committed members of a relatively orthodox tradition such as evangelical Protestantism have become more Republican while seculars, a group that has abandoned the trappings of traditional religion, have become more Democratic—and from the standpoint of political divisions within traditions between their most committed and doctrinally orthodox members and their least committed and orthodox members.

I first examine changes in the party affiliations and presidential voting behavior of particular religious traditions and of regular and non-regular worship attenders within those traditions. Since the 1960 NES and all the NES surveys since 1964 included measures of religious affiliation and frequency of worship attendance, this analysis is able to trace changes in the religious basis of party politics over a period of nearly four decades. Thus, I can explore not only recent developments in religion and mass politics, but also the response of religious groups to earlier factors such as George McGovern's culturally liberal candidacy in 1972, the formation of the Christian Right in the late 1970s, and the cultural conservatism espoused by Ronald Reagan in his 1980 and 1984 campaigns.

In this part of the analysis, I examine both the change in the political behavior of particular religious groups—seculars, Jews, and regular and nonregular church attenders among Catholics and evangelical, mainline, and black Protestants—and the changing religious composition of the parties' coalitions of identifiers and electoral supporters. The former may provide a better gauge of the mass response to elite change: the extent to which particular religious groups in the mass electorate have responded to changes in the religious and cultural orientations of party activists, candidates, and platforms.

However, the latter has more direct relevance for the types of candidates the parties nominate, the types of stands the parties and their candidates take on cultural issues, and the balance of power between the two parties. As Robert Axelrod (1972) notes, the contribution of a group to a party's electoral coalition is determined not just by the loyalty of the group to the party, but also by the size of the group and the extent to which its members turn out to vote. Changes in the religious composition of the parties' coalitions result not only from changes in the partisan affiliations and voting behavior of particular religious groups, but also from changes in the religious orientations of the mass public and the extent to which various religious groups are mobilized politically. For example, the representation of evangelical Protestants in Republican electoral coalitions could increase over time even if the percentage of evangelicals supporting Republican candidates did not change, because the percentage of Americans affiliating with evangelical denominations has increased over time (Iannaccone 1994) and the organizations of the Christian Right have spurred an increase in the political participation of their evangelical constituents (Oldfield 1996). Examining changes in the religious composition of the parties' mass coalitions should shed light on the combined partisan effects of changes in the political behavior of religious groups, changes in American religious orientations, and changes in the political mobilization of various religious groups.

In the second part of the analysis, I employ the measures of doctrinal orthodoxy and religious commitment that have been available in the NES surveys since 1980 to assess whether traditionalist–modernist political cleavages have emerged within religious traditions. The years from 1980 to the late 1990s represent a fairly short time span but also a particularly important span: one that witnessed the initial involvement and the increasing influence of the Christian Right in Republican campaign politics, the growing presence of committed evangelicals among Republican activists and secularists among Democratic activists, and the growing polarization of the cultural stands taken in Democratic and Republican platforms. If the mass electorate has responded to these elite- and activist-level developments in party politics, then the most orthodox and committed members of the major religious traditions should have grown more Republican relative to their less orthodox and committed counterparts.

THE PARTISANSHIP OF RELIGIOUS TRADITIONS, 1960–1996

Figure 5.1 shows the percentage of members of various religious groups identifying themselves as Democrats, independents, and Republicans from 1960 through 1996.[1] By far the clearest partisan change over this period is among regularly attending evangelical Protestants. Between 1964 and

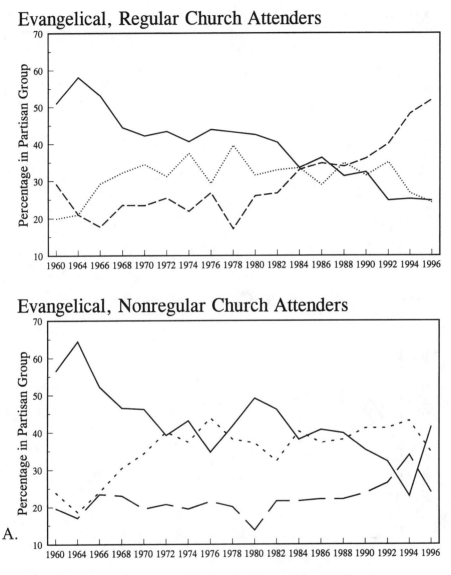

FIGURE 5.1. Party identifications of religious traditions, 1960–1996. A: Evangelical Protestants

Source: 1960–1996 National Election Studies

Mainline, Regular Church Attenders

Mainline, Nonregular Church Attenders

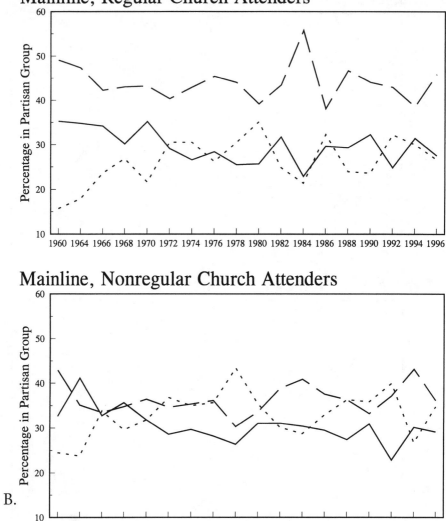

B.

FIGURE 5.1. B: Mainline Protestants

the early to mid-1970s, there was a noticeable decline in the percentage of committed evangelicals identifying with the Democratic party. Those Democratic losses, however, were not accompanied by Republican gains. The percentage of Republicans in this religious group remained quite

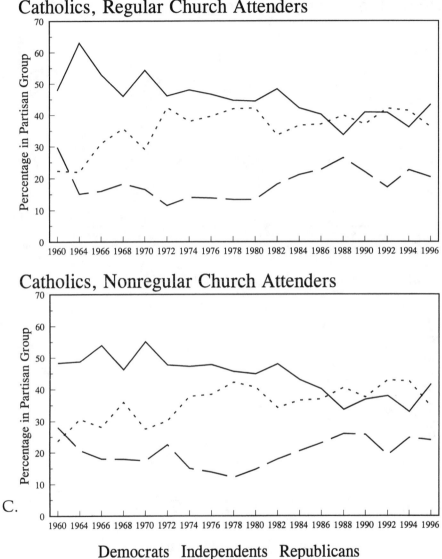

Catholics, Regular Church Attenders

Catholics, Nonregular Church Attenders

C.

Democrats   Independents   Republicans

FIGURE 5.1. C: Catholics

steady and rather small through the 1960s and 1970s, while the percentage of independents rose sharply. Since it began after the 1964 election, when the national parties and their candidates first evinced clearly distinct stands on civil rights for African-Americans, and since evangelical

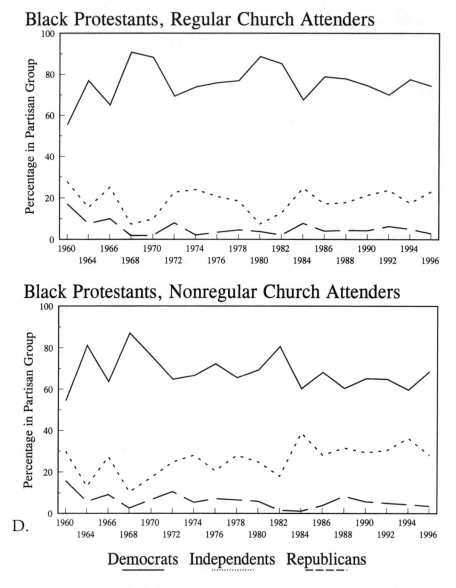

Black Protestants, Regular Church Attenders

Black Protestants, Nonregular Church Attenders

D.

Democrats Independents Republicans

FIGURE 5.1. D: Black Protestants

Protestants were located disproportionately in the South, this dealignment of committed evangelicals was most likely part of the broader movement of southern whites out of the Democratic party in response to Democratic racial liberalism. The partisan trends for southern whites are very

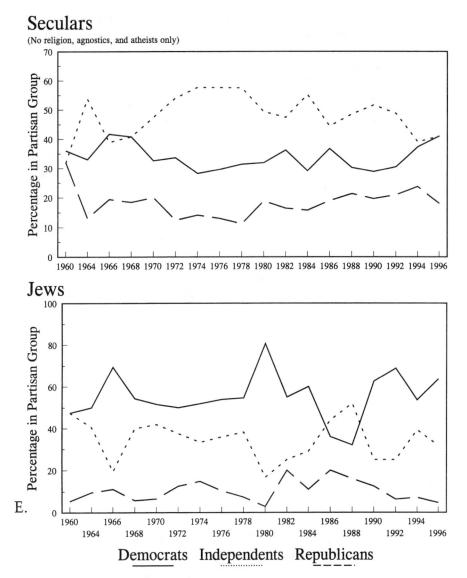

FIGURE 5.1. E: Seculars and Jews

similar to those shown here for evangelicals: Most white southerners did not jump directly from strong Democratic loyalties to Republican identifications but became, in the short run at least, more independent in their partisan ties (cf. Black and Black 1987).

The continued growth of independence among committed evangelicals in the 1970s may have been caused in part by the cultural liberalism of the Democratic party in the late 1960s and early 1970s. With the Republican party not yet presenting a clear culturally conservative alternative, there may have been stronger incentives for religious conservatives to leave the Democratic fold than for them to identify with the GOP. My analysis of the party affiliations of regularly attending evangelicals in the South and outside the South lends some support to the notion that the dealignment of the 1960s was largely based on race and region, while Democratic cultural liberalism perhaps played a role in the continued dealignment of the 1970s.[2]

After 1978, the pattern among regularly attending evangelicals changed from dealignment to realignment. The percentage of Democrats continued to decrease through the 1980s and 1990s. However, rather than being accompanied by increasing independence, this Democratic decline occurred alongside an enormous increase in identification with the Republican party. By the mid-1990s, committed evangelicals were, as a group, very closely tied to the GOP. Clearly, the most devout evangelical Protestants have been attracted by the growing cultural and religious conservatism of the Republican party's candidates, activists, and platforms.

Nonregularly attending evangelicals have not exhibited the same realignment toward the Republican party. There was a substantial decline in their support for the Democrats between 1964 and 1994 (although that support rebounded a good deal in 1996), but that was accompanied largely by a growth in the percentage of independents. Identification with the GOP increased by only a small amount over the 1980s and 1990s. It appears, then, that the growth of evangelicalism in the Republican party has resulted largely from the response of committed evangelical Protestants to the increasingly conservative cultural appeals of the GOP and its candidates.

There has been considerably less change in the partisan ties of other religious groups than in those of devout evangelicals. Regularly attending mainline Protestants were strongly Republican in the 1960s, and they remain strongly Republican in the 1990s. It appears that this relatively upper-status group has remained committed to the GOP's conservative economic program and, not surprisingly, given its religious devotion, has not been repelled by the party's growing moral traditionalism. Less committed mainline Protestants have been fairly evenly divided among the three partisan groups over the past four decades and have displayed little aggregate change in party loyalties.[3]

The level of partisan change among Catholics is a bit more impressive. Several scholars have noted the decline of Catholics' once staunch support for the Democratic party (Lopatto 1985; Petrocik 1987; Green and Guth 1991), and that decline is noticeable among both regular and nonregular church attenders between 1960 and 1988, with Catholic support for the Democrats leveling off in the 1990s. The partisan trends among Catholics in the 1960s and 1970s can best be described as dealigning; the percentage of independents increased noticeably while the percentage of Republican identifiers remained stable. The decade of the 1980s, however, witnessed a noticeable growth in Republicanism among both committed and less committed Catholics, and while Republican support did not increase in the 1990s, it also did not decrease significantly.

To strengthen the argument of this book, it would be nice to say that this growth in Republicanism clearly represents a response by Catholics to the culturally conservative rhetoric of Ronald Reagan and to the parties' increasingly polarized stands on abortion. However, the argument made by others that Catholics have become more Republican because they have, as a group, moved up the socioeconomic ladder and have become disenchanted with government welfare programs can not be ruled out. The fact that the increase in GOP support is as noticeable among less devout Catholics as it is among regular church attenders may support that interpretation over a religious and cultural one.

Not surprisingly, black Protestants became more supportive of the Democratic party in the 1960s and have remained overwhelmingly Democratic since, and Jews have been strongly Democratic, with a temporary foray into independence in the mid 1980s, over the last four decades. It is also not surprising that the same individuals who do not identify with any religious denomination or movement, namely, seculars, also tend to avoid identification with a political party. However, it does appear that the 1990s may represent the start of closer ties between secular citizens and the Democratic party. Perhaps in response to the increase in secularism among Democratic activists and the increasing polarization of the parties on cultural and moral matters, the percentage of secularists identifying with the Democratic party increased from 28 in 1990 to 41 in 1996.

Figure 5.1 sheds considerable light on the nature of partisan religious change over the last four decades. However, as the preceding discussion suggests, it does not demonstrate conclusively that these partisan trends among religious groups actually are based on religion and its connection to politics rather than on some other characteristic of the groups, such as socioeconomic status or region of residence. Mainline Protestant ties to the Republican party and the once strong ties of Catholics and evangelical Protestants to the Democratic party traditionally have been attributed to differences in socioeconomic status and geographical concentration (cf. Parenti 1967), and the considerable sociodemographic differences between these religious groups (Roof and McKinney 1987) lend ample weight to this interpretation.

Socioeconomic explanations of more recent developments in religious politics generally have been discounted in favor of religious and cultural explanations (Wilcox 1989; Hunter 1991; Wald 1997). But there are a fair number of skeptics who argue that these changes are based in status, geography, and other nonreligious variables (see Wald 1997: 191–97 for a review of this argument). And there are empirical reasons to believe them. Catholics have moved up the socioeconomic ladder, and this could be expected to loosen their Democratic attachments. White evangelical Protestants are located disproportionately in the South, a region that has transformed itself from one-party Democratic to the base of the national GOP over the period examined here (Black and Black 1992). In fact, in a recent article in the *American Journal of Sociology*, Jeff Manza and Clem Brooks (1997) find that when variables such as region, age, education, and income are controlled, there is virtually no evidence of a decline in Catholic support for the Democratic party or of a substantial increase in evangelical loyalties to the Republican party.

So to determine if these changes in religious group partisanship are really religious in nature, it is necessary to examine them in the context of a multivariate statistical model that not only controls for various sociodemographic factors, but also accounts for changes in their impact on party identification. I pooled data from all of the NES surveys from 1960 through 1996 and estimated a regression model in which party identification was the dependent variable. The model included dummy variables for seculars, black Protestants, Jews, and regular and nonregular church attenders among evangelical Protestants, mainline Protestants, and Catholics; dummy variables for particular years; and interactions between the religious group dummies and the year dummies.[4] It also included controls for education, income, gender, age, southern residence, and union membership, and, to account for changes in the relationship between sociodemographic factors and party identification, interactions between these variables and the year dummies. The estimates of this model are presented in appendix B4. Figure 5.2 shows the model's predictions for the party identification [ranging from strong Democrat (1) to

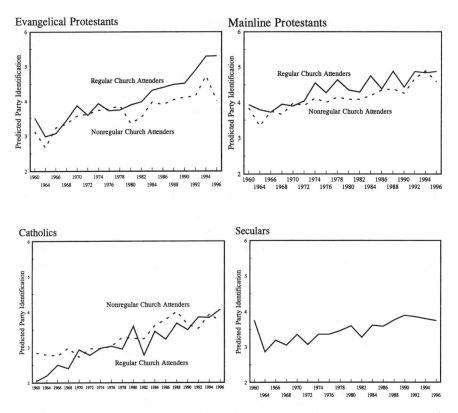

FIGURE 5.2. Predicted party identification by religious tradition and church attendance, 1960–1996
Note: Party identification ranges from strong Democrat (1) to strong Republican (7).
Source: Predicted from a regression analysis using the 1960–1996 National Election Studies (pooled).

strong Republican (7)] of various religious groups, when all of the control variables and their interactions with time are held constant at their means.

Unlike the analysis presented by Manza and Brooks—which does not distinguish between regular and nonregular church attenders and interacts the dummy variable for evangelical Protestants with a linear time variable rather than with year-specific dummy variables—my analysis uncovers a clear increase in the support of evangelical Protestants for the Republican party. The pro-GOP trend over the 1980s and 1990s is more marked among regular church attenders, but it is evident among less devout evangelicals as well. Even when the growing identification of the

South with the Republican party is taken into account, the growing loyalty of white evangelicals to the GOP is evident.

The party identification of mainline Protestants displays little change except for a slight pro-Republican trend over time. The same small shift is evident for seculars, but because most of the variation in secular partisanship is between points 3 (Democratic-leaning independent) and 4 (pure independent), it is more appropriately labeled a dealigning trend. The movement of seculars toward the Democratic party in the 1990s is noticeable as well.

Manza and Brooks find a decline in Catholic identification with the Democratic party between 1960 and 1964, but no evidence of a further drop in Democratic loyalties after 1964. This analysis suggests that that is because their model, by interacting the Catholic variable with only a single dummy variable for all years from 1964 to 1992 rather than with variables for individual years, does not allow for a further decline in Democratic support. When the Catholic variable is interacted with a separate dummy variable for each year, and Catholic partisanship thus is allowed to vary over the full time period, the decline in Catholics' Democratic ties is quite clear. Catholics have not become strongly aligned with the GOP, since their mean identification never reaches point 4 (pure independent) on the scale, but they have become less supportive of the Democrats. This trend is most evident among regular church attenders, but it is noticeable for nonregular attenders as well. Since this analysis has controlled for education, income, union membership, and their interactions with time, it appears that the decline in Democratic support among Catholics may have some roots in the party's growing secularism and cultural liberalism and may not be based entirely on socioeconomic factors.

Before turning to the presidential voting behavior of religious groups, it seems useful to take a closer look at the way in which two demographic variables, region and age, have affected the clearest change in religious group partisanship uncovered here: the Republican realignment of committed evangelical Protestants. As noted previously, evangelicals are located disproportionately in a region—the South—that began a fundamental, pro-Republican shift in its partisan ties more than a decade before the marriage of the Christian Right and the GOP. The growth of southern Republicanism has been particularly strong among young white residents of the ex-Confederate states (Kellstedt 1989). So, although the growing ties of regularly attending evangelicals to the GOP are evident even when I control for region, age, and the changes over time in their relationships with party identification, the changes may be particularly strong among younger evangelical Protestants in the South. On the other hand, in his analysis of partisan trends through 1984, Lyman Kellstedt (1989) suggests that age, more than region, has played the primary role in conditioning the changing partisan ties of committed evangelicals. He shows that the growth in Republicanism between 1980 and 1984 was much larger for young regular attenders of evangelical denominations in both the South and the non-South than it was for young southerners who were not regularly attending evangelicals or for regularly attending older members of evangelical churches in both regions.

To determine if the growth in the Republican loyalties of committed evangelical Protestants has been confined to southerners or to young people (or both),[5] figure 5.3 examines partisan trends among regularly attending evangelicals and all whites who are not regular attenders of evangelical churches by breaking both groups into four smaller units: young nonsoutherners, old nonsoutherners, young southerners, and old southerners. It shows that Kellstedt's findings were not restricted to the period from 1980 through 1984. From the late 1970s through the late 1990s, the growth of Republican loyalties was clearly greater among young regularly attending evangelicals than among their older counterparts in both the South and the non-South. However, the sharpest contrast in partisan trends is not between various groups of committed evangelicals. Older committed evangelicals in the non-South have always had strong ties to the GOP, but they became noticeably more Republican in the late 1980s and 1990s. Older committed evangelicals in the South were slow to give up their long-held Democratic loyalties. However, even they have demonstrated a clear movement toward the Republican party in the 1990s.

Instead, the clearest distinction is between regularly attending evangelicals and all other whites. With the exception of young southerners, there is almost no partisan trend among any group of citizens not in the committed evangelical camp. And even the growing Republicanism of young southern whites who are not committed evangelicals pales in comparison to that of the young committed evangelicals in both regions. In fact, it is, with the exceptions of the 1970s and a sharp upswing in 1994 (which was followed by an equally sharp downturn in 1996), smaller than even the pro-GOP trends among older committed evangelicals outside the South.

Thus, the Republican realignment of committed evangelical Protestants has not been simply part of a broader regional or generational transformation in partisan ties. It has occurred independently of nonreligious

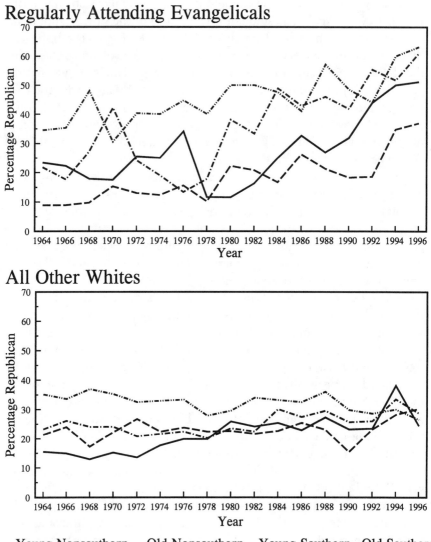

FIGURE 5.3. Republican party identification of regularly attending evangelical Protestants and all other white citizens by age and religion, 1964–1996

Source: 1964–1996 National Election Studies

partisan trends and has clearly overwhelmed them in both speed and magnitude. In fact, the argument that partisan change among evangelicals has been driven by the realignment of the South can, to some extent, be turned on its head. It appears that the partisan transformation of committed evangelicals has played a large role in driving the pro-Republican trends in the former Confederacy.

THE PRESIDENTIAL VOTING BEHAVIOR OF RELIGIOUS TRADITIONS, 1960–1996

The presidential voting behavior of religious groups may provide a less reliable gauge of long-term partisan trends than do the changes in their party identifications. Vote choice is shaped by long-term predispositions, but it is also highly responsive to the idiosyncratic aspects of particular elections, particularly the parties' nominees and their positions on policy issues (Page and Jones 1979; Markus and Converse 1979). Although the candidates' issue-stands are constrained by the positions of their parties' activists and those taken in their parties' platforms, they may diverge from those positions to a greater or lesser extent in particular years. Thus, the voting behavior of religious groups may change considerably from election to election based on the vagaries of the candidates and their issue positions. For example, the highly liberal Democratic campaign of George McGovern in 1972 and the staunch secularism of his supporters may have attracted substantial secular support while making a vote for Richard Nixon, the Republican candidate, more appealing to groups such as committed Catholics and evangelical Protestants that had traditionally identified with the Democratic party. However, the Democratic nomination of a more moderate Southern Baptist in 1976 may have attracted a large number of evangelical voters while producing a drop-off in Democratic voting by secularists.

Nevertheless, an examination of the presidential voting behavior of particular religious groups is important for at least two reasons. First, since party identification is more resistant than voting behavior to new political developments, groups disenchanted with their parties' positions on cultural issues or other matters may change their voting patterns before they change their partisan ties. Voting behavior thus may capture some of the emerging partisan change that party identification does not (Erikson, Lancaster, and Romero 1989). Second, voting behavior may illustrate the types of candidates and policy stances that attract particular groups to a party or that alienate other groups from that party. Thus, voting patterns may serve as a harbinger of the type of coalition a party can expect to attract if it continues to nominate certain kinds of candidates or take certain issue positions.

Figure 5.4 shows the percentage of various religious groups voting Republican in presidential elections from 1960 through 1996.[6] For the most part, the voting behavior of all these groups follows the same general pattern based on the relative success of the two candidates in particular years. However, there are some notable exceptions. The nomination of a Catholic candidate, John F. Kennedy, by the Democratic party in 1960 appears to have created some unique voting patterns. Committed Catholics voted Democratic at a higher rate than they would in any subsequent election, particularly after the 1970s. Regularly attending evangelical Protestants, noted for their commitment to Protestant orthodoxy and their occasional demonstrations of anti-Catholicism, seem to have responded particularly negatively to Kennedy's candidacy. They were slightly more supportive than mainline Protestants of Richard Nixon, the Republican candidate in 1960, despite the fact that they were much less likely than mainliners to identify themselves as Republicans.

The cultural liberalism of George McGovern and the secularism of his Democratic supporters in 1972 seems to have appealed to secular voters to a much greater extent than any other religious group. All the groups voted more Republican in 1972 than in 1968, reflecting the fact that Nixon, facing a weaker Democratic opponent and no third-party alternative to his right, won a much greater percentage of the vote in 1972 than in 1968. The interesting thing, though, is the extent of the change from 1968 to 1972. The largest change in the pro-Republican direction was among regularly attending evangelical Protestants, who were 32 percentage points more supportive of Nixon in 1972 than in 1968, and who, once again, were more supportive of the Republican candidate than mainline Protestants despite their still much weaker identification with the GOP. The smallest increase in support for Nixon came from secularists, who were only 8 percentage points more supportive of the Republican candidate in 1972 than in 1968. In fact, despite the weaknesses of the McGovern campaign, the percentage of secularists voting for the Democratic candidate increased by 7 points between 1968 and 1972.[7] The cultural liberalism of McGovern's campaign and its active supporters seems to have created the type of traditionalist–modernist religious polarization in the electorate that most scholars began to notice only in the 1980s.

White Protestants

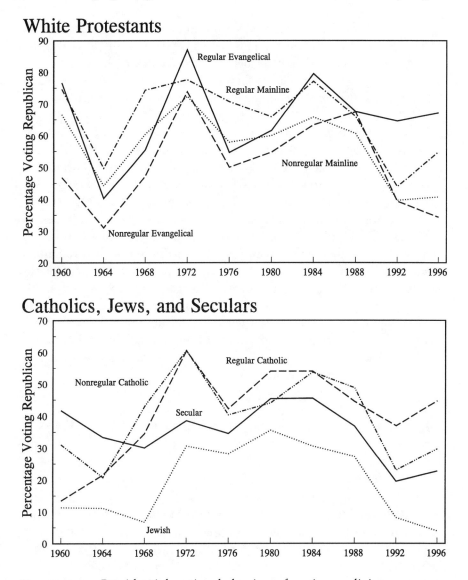

FIGURE 5.4. Presidential voting behavior of various religious groups, 1960–1996
Source: 1960–1996 National Election Studies

Republican voting by almost all of these groups rose in 1980 and either increased or remained at similar levels in 1984, as Republican Ronald Reagan won a landslide victory over Democrat Walter Mondale. Republican support among all religious groups then declined after 1984 as GOP candidate George Bush won by a smaller margin in 1988 than Reagan had in 1984, Bush won less than 38 percent of the vote in 1992, and Republican Bob Dole won only 41 percent of the vote in 1996.

However, as with the increase in Republican voting between 1968 and 1972, it is the extent of Republican losses among religious groups after 1984 that is telling. The Republican percentage of the vote among seculars, Jews, and infrequent attenders in the three largest traditions declined strongly in both 1988 and 1992 and rebounded either slightly or not at all in 1996. The percentage of regularly attending mainline Protestants and regularly attending Catholics voting Republican also dropped off sharply in 1988 and 1992 but then rebounded more strongly (11 percentage points for mainline Protestants, 8 percentage points for Catholics) in 1996. Finally, Republican voting among regularly attending evangelical Protestants dropped off between 1984 and 1988, but it then remained steady in the 1990s despite the weak electoral performances of Republican candidates. The end result of these changes in the 1980s and 1990s is that, as the parties' activists, elites, and platforms have grown more culturally polarized, seculars and Jews (in addition to black Protestants) have become the strongest supporters of Democratic presidential candidates, while committed evangelical Protestants have become by far the strongest backers of Republican candidates.[8]

THE RELIGIOUS COMPOSITION OF THE PARTIES' MASS COALITIONS, 1960–1996

It is clear from the preceding analyses that the contribution that some groups make to the parties' coalitions has changed over time. It is clear because there have been noticeable changes in their party affiliations and presidential voting behavior. For example, the decline in the Democratic ties of Catholics, particularly regularly attending Catholics, suggests that they have become a smaller component of the Democratic coalition. The increase in the loyalties of committed evangelicals to the GOP indicates that they have become a larger part of the Republican coalition, particularly since membership in conservative Protestant churches has grown over the last few decades.

On the other hand, the partisan ties of other groups have not changed much, but the contributions of these groups to the parties' mass coalitions may have changed because of changes in the size of the groups. For example, the increase in the Democratic leanings of seculars has occurred only recently and has not been nearly as impressive as the increased Republicanism of devout evangelicals. However, the increase in the number of secularists in the general population should result in a substantial increase in their representation in the Democratic coalition. Regularly attending mainline Protestants have maintained their strong ties to the GOP. However, the declining membership of mainline churches points to the likelihood that the representation of committed mainliners in the Republican coalition has decreased.

The percentage of Democratic and Republican identifiers represented by particular religious groups from 1960 through 1996 is shown in figure 5.5.[9] Much like the party's activist base, the Democratic coalition of identifiers has become less traditionally religious and more secular over time. There has been a gradual decline in the representation of mainline Protestants, evangelical Protestants, and regularly attending Catholics among Democratic identifiers. In contrast, the percentage of nonregularly attending Catholics in the Democratic coalition increased over the 1960s and early 1970s and has remained relatively stable since.

Most striking is the increase in the percentage of Democratic identifiers with no religious affiliation. The gradual increase in the percentage of Democratic secularists from 1960 to 1988 may well have been caused by the gradual secularization of the American public. In fact, there was a similar trend in Republican secularism through 1988. However, the sharp increase in the percentage of Democrats in the secular category after 1988 cannot be attributed solely to the growth in American secularism.[10] Also contributing to it has been the clear increase in secular ties to the Democratic party over the same time period.

Despite the stability of mainline Protestant identification with the GOP, the dwindling membership of mainline churches seems to have led to a decline in the representation of mainline Protestants in the Republican coalition.[11] Meanwhile, the proportion of regularly attending Catholics has increased slightly. Much more substantial is the increase after 1978 in the proportion of Republican identifiers who are regularly attending evangelical Protestants. Although the growth of conservative Protestantism in the mass public may explain some of this trend, the fact that it accompanies a major rise in the loyalties of committed evangelicals to the GOP suggests that the explanation lies largely in the response of evangelical voters to the growing cultural conservatism of Republican activists, elites, and platforms.[12]

As figure 5.6 shows, similar patterns are evident in the percentage of Democratic and Republican presidential voters represented by particular

Democratic Identifiers

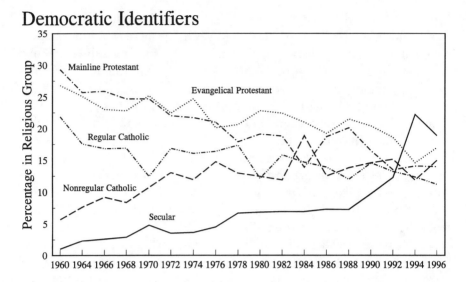

Republican Identifiers

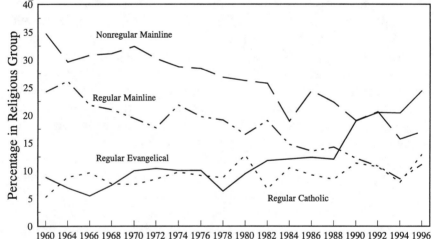

FIGURE 5.5. Changing religious composition of the parties in the electorate
Source: 1960–1996 National Election Studies

religious groups. Just as with its coalition of identifiers, the Democratic party's presidential election coalition has become less traditionally religious and more secular over time. The percentage of mainline Protestants in that coalition declined gradually in the 1960s and 1970s and then exhibited large fluctuations in the 1980s and 1990s. More substantial and consistent is the declining representation of regularly attending Catholics in the Democratic electoral coalition. Not surprisingly, that representation dropped off sharply after Kennedy's 1960 election. However, it continued to decrease throughout the 1960s and 1970s before rebounding slightly in 1984, and then continuing on a steady decline through the late 1980s and 1990s. The same decline has not occurred in the percentage of Democratic voters who are less committed Catholics. In fact, by the 1990s, there were more Democratic voters in this less devout category of Catholics than in the group of regular church attenders.

The greatest increase in religious group representation in the Democratic presidential coalition has been among seculars. Their percentage increased gradually throughout the 1960s and 1970s, most likely because of the growing secularization of the American public. However, the sharpest rise in the secular percentage over those two decades may have a more political explanation: It occurred in 1972, when the party nominated a candidate with very liberal cultural stands and had an unusually high percentage of secularists at its national convention. In the 1980s and 1990s, as the changing support of secularists for Democratic candidates increased noticeably, there was a sharper increase in secular representation in the party's electoral coalition.

The Republican electoral coalition, in contrast, has become more traditionally religious over time. The percentages of both regularly attending and nonregularly attending mainline Protestants in the coalition have declined markedly. Part of the reason for this drop is undoubtedly the shrinking of mainline Protestant membership. But in the 1990s it was also caused by the substantial decline in the Republican voting of mainliners relative to that of Catholics and evangelicals. In fact, by 1996, regularly attending Catholics made up a higher percentage of Republican voters than either group of mainline Protestants. Meanwhile, the percentage of devout evangelical Protestants in the GOP coalition increased markedly after 1980, and the increase was particularly sharp after 1988.

So it is clear that, when gauged by patterns of religious belonging, a traditionalist–modernist religious cleavage has emerged between the Democratic and Republican coalitions in the mass electorate. The Democratic coalition has become increasingly secular, while the presence of white Protestants and committed Catholics in the party has declined. Meanwhile, committed evangelical Protestants clearly have become the religious backbone of the Republican coalition, and the presence of committed Catholics, with their similarly conservative cultural perspectives, also has increased.

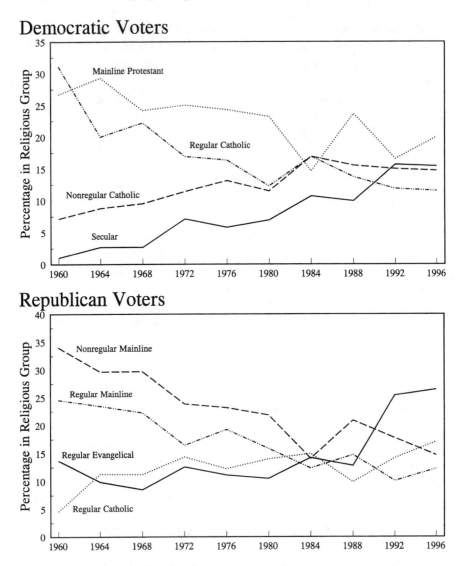

FIGURE 5.6. Changing religious composition of the parties' presidential election coalitions, 1960–1996
Source: 1960–1996 National Election Studies

The development of this cleavage is made clearer in the top half of figure 5.7, which shows the difference in the mean positions of Republican and Democratic identifiers and voters on the religious orthodoxy scale from 1960 through 1996. The traditionalist–modernist polarization

Religious Orthodoxy of Party Identifiers and Presidential Voters

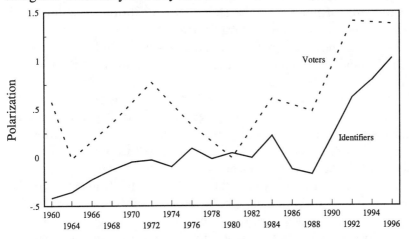

Religious Orthodoxy and Cultural Conservatism Among Party Identifiers*

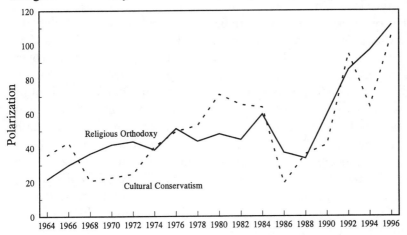

FIGURE 5.7. Religious and cultural polarization of the party coalitions, 1960–1996

Note: Polarization is the Republican mean minus the Democratic mean.
* Both series are standardized (mean = 50, standard deviation = 25).
Source: 1960–1996 National Election Studies

of party identifiers increased over the 1960s, largely because of a decline in the religious orthodoxy of the Democratic coalition, bringing it to approximately the same level of traditionalism as the GOP's coalition. The sharpest change in the series, however, was from 1988 to 1996, and it resulted from both an increase in the religious orthodoxy of Republican identifiers and a decline in the traditionalism of Democratic partisans.

In a pattern similar to those of particular religious groups, the difference in the religious orthodoxy of Democratic and Republican presidential voters rises and falls with particular elections. The defection of evangelical Protestants from the Democratic party's Catholic nominee in 1960 contributed to the Republican coalition's being significantly more traditional than the Democratic coalition in that year. Democratic voters were as religiously orthodox as Republican voters in 1964. However, in 1972, as the Democratic party took strong steps toward cultural liberalism and attracted a highly secular group of activists, Democratic voters grew, in the aggregate, substantially less traditional, and the difference in religious orthodoxy between Republican and Democratic voters grew to a level that it would not reach again until 1992.

The replacement of McGovern by the more religiously and politically conservative Carter as the Democratic standard-bearer in 1976 and 1980 appears to have attracted a more traditionally religious group of voters back to the Democratic fold, at least temporarily. In fact, with the sharp increase in Republican voting by secular voters in 1980, the levels of religious orthodoxy in the two coalitions again became virtually identical. However, as Republican activists and elites became more traditionally religious and the GOP became increasingly associated with cultural conservatism, the degree of religious polarization between the parties' voters increased markedly after 1980. This increase was caused partly by a growth in religious modernism among Democratic voters, but it was mostly the result of a steady and substantial rise in the religious traditionalism of Republican voters.

The bottom half of figure 5.7 shows that the growing polarization of the parties' coalitions along traditionalist–modernist religious lines in the 1980s and 1990s was accompanied by a substantial growth in the polarization of party identifiers on cultural issues, a finding that is not surprising given the strong individual-level relationship between religious traditionalism and cultural conservatism.[13] Both series show some increase in the early 1980s, drop noticeably in the mid-1980s, and then grow substantially in the 1980s and 1990s, with cultural-issue polarization demonstrating more fluctuation. The relationship between partisan religious and cultural polarization is confirmed by some simple statistical tests.[14]

THE POLITICAL IMPACT OF RELIGIOUS BELIEFS AND BEHAVIORS, 1980–1996

There is clearly a growing difference in the religious traditionalism of the Democratic and Republican mass coalitions. An important question is, is this new partisan divide simply an "ethnoreligious" cleavage, with the most committed members of the most morally and culturally conservative religious traditions, namely, Catholicism and particularly evangelical Protestantism, becoming more Republican, and individuals who have abandoned organized religion altogether growing more Democratic? Or, has it also taken shape along "culture wars" lines, with the most traditionalist—the most committed and doctrinally orthodox—members of the major religious traditions moving closer to the GOP and the most modernist—the least committed and doctrinally orthodox—members of those traditions gravitating toward the Democrats? To answer this, I turn to the 1980 through 1996 NES surveys and examine changes over time in the impact of doctrinal conservatism and religious devotion on party identification and presidential voting behavior across and within religious traditions.

The culture wars perspective assumes that similar traditionalist–modernist political divisions will develop across religious traditions, so that political coalitions will be shaped by doctrinal orthodoxy and religious commitment rather than by religious tradition (Hunter 1991). So a first test of this viewpoint is simply to assess whether the impact of orthodoxy and commitment on partisanship and vote choice has grown. To do this, I estimated statistical models that allow the effects of beliefs and behaviors to vary over time, but I assume that those effects and the changes in them are consistent across religious traditions. These models control for the political impact of religious tradition and changes over time in that impact. Thus, whatever changes are uncovered in the effects of doctrinal orthodoxy and religious commitment cannot be attributed to changes in the political behavior of religious traditions (e.g., the growing partisan gap between evangelicals and seculars).[15] Figure 5.8 presents the predicted values of party identification and the predicted probabilities of voting Republican from these models.[16]

Party Identification

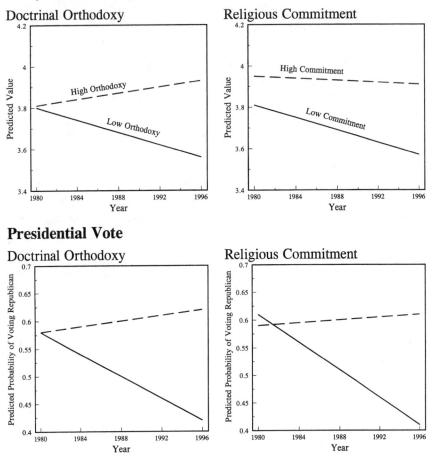

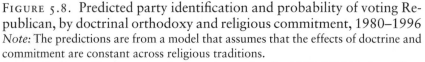

FIGURE 5.8. Predicted party identification and probability of voting Republican, by doctrinal orthodoxy and religious commitment, 1980–1996
Note: The predictions are from a model that assumes that the effects of doctrine and commitment are constant across religious traditions.
Source: Computed by the author from analyses using the 1980–1996 National Election Studies (pooled)

The effect of doctrinal orthodoxy on both party identification and the presidential vote clearly has grown over time, with the most orthodox individuals becoming more likely to identify with the Republican party and vote for its presidential candidates and individuals with low levels of orthodoxy becoming more Democratic in their party affiliations and voting behavior. The political impact of religious commitment also has grown, particularly with regard to presidential voting behavior. Although highly committed individuals have become slightly more likely to vote Republican, the change is largely the result of individuals with low levels of commitment becoming much more supportive of Democratic presidential candidates.

So the growing traditionalist–modernist cleavage between the Democratic and Republican coalitions clearly has been defined by religious beliefs and behaviors, in addition to religious belonging. The impact of beliefs and behaviors has grown independently of the changing effect of religious tradition.

Of course, it is possible, perhaps likely, that changes in the political impact of religious beliefs and behaviors are not constant across religious traditions. For example, one might expect the connection between religious commitment and Republicanism to grow considerably among evangelical Protestants as their clergy have become increasingly politicized (Guth et al. 1997), and the Christian Right has made evangelical churches the bases for its efforts at political mobilization on behalf of culturally conservative Republican candidates (Oldfield 1996). The connection also may be expected to grow among Catholics as the Catholic Church has become increasingly involved in antiabortion efforts and the Republican party has become increasingly opposed to abortion rights. However, Catholicism's liberalism on social welfare and foreign policy issues since Vatican II may have tempered a growing link between Catholic commitment and support for the GOP. There is less reason to expect an increasing association between commitment and Republicanism among mainline Protestants. Their clergy tend to be considerably more liberal on cultural issues than evangelical or Catholic clergy and have become less likely than their evangelical counterparts to address political topics from the pulpit (Guth et al. 1997). Meanwhile, mainline congregants have more varied views on cultural matters than do the members of evangelical and Catholic churches.

To account for the possibility that the changes in the political impact of doctrinal orthodoxy and religious commitment vary across religious traditions, I estimated statistical models in which their effects on party identification and voting behavior vary over time and across religious traditions, and in which the changes over time also vary across religious traditions.[17] Figures 5.9 and 5.10 present the predicted values of party identification and the predicted probabilities of voting Republican from these models. They show three sets of results for each tradition: one for

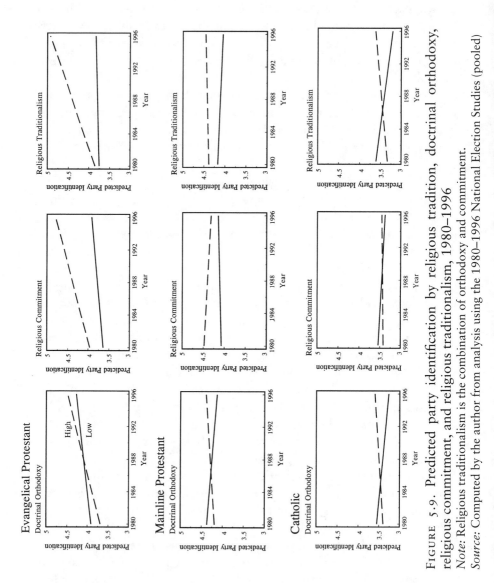

FIGURE 5.9. Predicted party identification by religious tradition, doctrinal orthodoxy, religious commitment, and religious traditionalism, 1980–1996

Note: Religious traditionalism is the combination of orthodoxy and commitment.

Source: Computed by the author from analysis using the 1980–1996 National Election Studies (pooled)

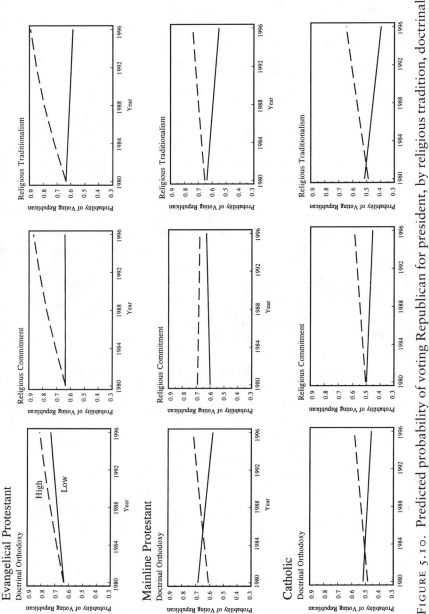

FIGURE 5.10. Predicted probability of voting Republican for president, by religious tradition, doctrinal orthodoxy, religious commitment, and religious traditionalism, 1980–1996.
Note: Religious traditionalism is the combination of orthodoxy and commitment.
Source: Computed by the author from analysis using the 1980–1996 National Election Studies (pooled)

individuals with high and low levels of doctrinal orthodoxy; one for individuals with high and low levels of religious commitment; and one for religious traditionalists, or individuals with high levels of orthodoxy and commitment, and religious modernists, or individuals with low levels of orthodoxy and commitment.[18]

As the culture wars thesis predicts, there has been a growth in traditionalist–modernist political divisions within all three religious traditions. The growth has been largest among evangelical Protestants, but in all three traditions, religious traditionalists have grown more Republican and more likely to support Republican presidential candidates relative to religious modernists. However, more in keeping with the ethnoreligious perspective, the way in which these cleavages have grown varies across religious traditions. Among evangelical Protestants, the major change has been a large increase in the relationship between religious commitment and Republicanism. There has been some increase in the relationship between doctrinal orthodoxy and support for the GOP among evangelicals, but it pales in comparison to the change associated with commitment. The growing politicization of evangelical clergy and the mobilization efforts of the Christian Right appear to have had their desired effect. Those evangelicals with the highest levels of church attendance and who get the most guidance from their faith have become increasingly Republican and increasingly more Republican than their less committed counterparts.

In contrast, the major development among mainline Protestants and Catholics has been an increase in the relationship between doctrinal orthodoxy and support for the Republican party. In both traditions, more orthodox parishioners have become more likely to identify with and vote for the GOP, while less orthodox members have become more likely to identify with and vote for the Democratic party. In fact, it appears that the growing cultural polarization of the parties has been associated with an increase in the relationship between theological conservatism and partisan political behavior in each of the three largest religious traditions.

Among Catholics, greater commitment has become more strongly associated with voting for Republican presidential candidates, but the effect of commitment on party identification changed only slightly. Cultural issues such as abortion and school prayer tend to receive more exposure in presidential elections than in lower-level elections (Shafer 1991). Thus, the combination of Catholic cultural conservatism and cultural-issue salience in presidential elections may have led committed Catholics to be increasingly likely to support Republican presidential candidates.

Meanwhile, the Catholic Church's continued liberalism on other matters of public policy may account for the failure of committed Catholics to move their basic partisan ties much closer to the GOP.

Among mainline Protestants, the relationship between religious commitment and Republican party support actually has decreased. The decline has been small, but the cultural liberalism of mainline clergy, the growing political salience of cultural issues, and the growing cultural conservatism of the Republican party may have combined to reduce the political impact of commitment among mainliners, at least when we control for the growing relationship between mainline doctrinal orthodoxy and Republicanism.

The right-hand columns in figures 5.9 and 5.10 not only provide evidence for the growing political relevance of traditionalist–modernist splits within religious traditions, but also show the continued importance of religious tradition in American politics. Even after two decades of growing political divisions within the major American traditions, there remain clear differences between the traditions, with the most traditionalist evangelical Protestants being more Republican than the most traditionalist mainline Protestants, and with the most orthodox and committed Catholics being noticeably more Democratic than either Protestant group. In fact, among American Protestants, the political impact of religious tradition seems to have grown over time. The most doctrinally orthodox and committed evangelicals have become increasingly more supportive of the GOP than their counterparts in the mainline denominations. Religious beliefs and behaviors are becoming more important politically, but there is no question that belonging still matters.

Summary and Conclusion

This chapter has documented important changes in the political behavior of certain religious groups over the past four decades. The clearest case of party realignment has been among evangelical Protestants who attend church regularly. Strongly Democratic in the 1960s and most of the 1970s, committed evangelicals became steadily more Republican in the 1980s and 1990s and are now the most strongly Republican group in the religious spectrum. Noticeable change also has occurred in the political behavior of Catholics. Once the religious backbone of the Democratic coalition, this group has become steadily less Democratic over time, and regularly attending Catholics have become more loyal to Republican presidential candidates than nonregular church attenders in the mainline and evangelical Protestant traditions. Secular identification with the Democratic party increased conspicuously in the 1990s, and the support of secularists for Republican presidential candidates has declined sharply since 1980.

Perhaps even more important have been the changes in the religious composition of the parties' coalitions in the mass electorate. In the 1960s, a large proportion of the Democratic coalition was made up of white mainline and evangelical Protestants, and the Democratic coalition had a higher overall level of religious orthodoxy than did the Republican coalition. Since then, there has been a substantial increase in the presence of secularists and a substantial decrease in the representation of Protestants and committed Catholics in the Democratic party. Meanwhile, the percentage of Republican identifiers and voters who are mainline Protestants has declined, while the presence of regularly attending evangelical Protestants in the GOP has increased sharply. By the late 1990s, the Republican coalition had become much more religiously orthodox than the Democratic coalition, and the growth in the religious polarization of the parties' mass coalitions was accompanied by a growing party polarization on cultural issues.

There also has been an increase in the political impact of religious beliefs and behaviors within religious traditions. The changing political effects of doctrinal orthodoxy and religious commitment have varied across traditions, but within all the major American religious traditions, there has been a growing relationship between religious traditionalism, or high orthodoxy and commitment, and support for the Republican party. So the traditionalist–modernist religious divide in mass party politics has developed both because of changes in the political behavior of religious traditions—committed evangelical Protestants and Catholics becoming more Republican, secularists becoming more Democratic—and because of changes in the political impact of religious orthodoxy within those traditions.

The fact that this increase in the religious and cultural polarization of the parties' mass coalitions has occurred alongside a growth in the religious and cultural divisions between Democratic and Republican activists and elites suggests that the mass electorate does respond to changes at the elite and activist levels of party politics. Chapter 6 provides a more thorough examination of the links among the cultural stands of party elites, the religious characteristics of party activists, and the religious composition of the parties' mass coalitions.

However, the relationship between the characteristics and issue positions of party elites and activists and those of the parties' mass coalitions is not a one-way street. The makeup of the mass coalitions may respond to changes at the elite and activist levels, but it also structures elite-level and activist-level partisan politics. Activists often come from a party's base of identifiers, party candidates need the support of that base to win elections, and party leaders need to appeal to that base to stay in power. Thus, the fact that the Republican coalition is becoming more traditionally religious while the Democratic coalition becomes less so points to two expectations: (1) that Republican activists should be growing more traditionally religious while religious orthodoxy among Democratic activists declines and (2) that the stands of Republican candidates and platforms on cultural and moral issues should be growing more conservative while those of Democratic candidates and platforms should be growing more liberal. In short, the trends presented in chapters 3 and 4 for party elites, activists, and platforms not only may have stimulated some of the trends shown in this chapter, but also may have occurred in response to them. Moreover, the growth in religious and cultural differences between the parties' mass coalitions may lead to further religious and cultural polarization between Democratic and Republican activists, candidates, and leaders.

NOTES

1. Democrats and Republicans are defined as strong and weak partisans on the NES seven-point party identification scale. The independent category includes pure independents and independent "leaners."

2. The Democratic losses among regularly attending evangelicals between 1964 and 1972 were caused almost entirely by the dealignment of committed evangelicals in the South. In 1964, 73 percent of southerners in this religious group were Democrats and 12 percent were independents. By 1972, only 51 percent of southerners were Democrats and 31 percent were independents, with the percentage of Republicans changing only slightly. In contrast, the percentage of Democrats among committed evangelicals outside the South declined only slightly, from 37 in 1964 to 35 in 1972, and the percentage of independents increased by only 1 point. However, between 1972 and 1978, there was more change among nonsoutherners than among southerners. Among nonsoutherners, the percentage of Democrats decreased from 35 to 28 and the percentage of independents increased from 33 to 46. Among southerners, the percentage of Democrats actually increased from 51

to 54, perhaps in response to the Democratic presidency of southern evangelical Jimmy Carter, and the percentage of independents increased from 31 to 35.

3. This finding seems to run counter to evidence presented by Manza and Brooks (1997) that "liberal" Protestants became significantly and steadily less Republican in their party identifications between 1960 and 1992. Of course, my mainline Protestant category includes both "liberal" Protestants (Episcopalians, Congregationalists/United Church of Christ) and "moderate" Protestants (e.g., Presbyterian Church in the U.S.A., Evangelical Lutheran Church in America). However, even when I examine only the more liberal mainline Protestant denominations, I do not find the sharp and steady decline in Republicanism described by Manza and Brooks. The disparity seems to lie in Manza and Brooks's assumption that there was a linear trend in the partisanship of liberal Protestants from 1960 through 1992. My findings indicate that the trend was far from linear. Liberal Protestant Republicanism declined very sharply immediately after 1960, presumably returning to normal levels following the election of a Catholic Democrat as president. The percentage of Republicans was 69 in 1960, 54 in 1964, and 45 in 1966. Between 1966 and 1996, there was a fair amount of fluctuation in Republican support among liberal Protestants, but no linear trend. In fact, the percentage of Republicans was almost as high in 1988 (53 percent) as it had been in 1964. That percentage declined to 37 percent in 1992, the last year of Manza and Brooks's analysis, but it rebounded to 44 percent in 1994.

4. I interacted the religious variables with dummy variables for year rather than with a linear time variable because the patterns in figure 5.1 do not indicate linear changes in the partisan ties of religious groups from 1960 through 1996. Instead, the change occurs in fits and starts or in certain intervals over the full time period and is thus better modeled with a series of dummy variable interactions.

5. *Young* is defined here as below the median age (44) in the pooled 1960–1996 National Election Studies. The starting point for the figure is 1964 because of the short-term pro-Republican effect of a Catholic Democratic presidential candidate in 1960 on the partisan ties of evangelicals.

6. The one group not shown here that appears in figure 5.1 is black Protestants. They were overwhelmingly supportive of Democratic presidential candidates throughout the whole period.

7. The reason that secular support for both the Republican and Democratic candidates increased between 1968 and 1972 was that there was a strong third candidate, George Wallace, in 1968 who won 15 percent of the secular vote and 13.5 percent of the overall vote. However, secularists were one of only three religious groups to increase their Democratic support over the two elections. The other two were nonregularly attending evangelical Protestants, who increased their Democratic support by 4 percentage points,

and regularly attending mainline Protestants, who increased their Democratic support by 1 percentage point.

8. I estimated a logit model using data pooled from the 1960–1996 NES surveys and including interactions between the dummy variables for particular religious groups and dummy variables for particular election years, as well as interactions between several sociodemographic control variables and the year dummies. The predicted probabilities of voting Republican from that model follow patterns very similar to those shown in figure 5.4.

9. To make the figure readable, I highlight the representation of only some religious groups in the parties' coalitions and, in some cases, combine the regular and nonregular church attenders in particular religious traditions. For the most part, the groups not shown in the figure are groups that constitute a very small percentage of a party's identifiers throughout the whole period (e.g., seculars, Jews, and black Protestants in the GOP) or groups whose contributions to a party's coalition have remained steady over time (e.g., black Protestants and Jews in the Democratic party and nonregularly attending evangelicals and Catholics in the GOP).

10. The percentage of secularists, defined here as only atheists, agnostics, and individuals with no religious affiliation, in the NES sample increased from 8.9 in 1988 to 15 in 1994. In comparison, the percentage of secularists in the Democratic coalition increased from 7.3 in 1988 to 22.2 in 1994. Moreover, the percentage of secularists in the Republican coalition in 1988 (6.6) was comparable to that in the Democratic coalition. However, by 1996, only 8.8 percent of Republicans were secular, as compared to 19.9 percent of Democrats.

11. The percentage of mainline Protestants in the NES sample decreased from 39.3 in 1960 to 19.7 in 1996.

12. The percentage of regularly attending evangelical Protestants in the NES sample increased from 7.8 in 1978 to 13.3 in 1996. In comparison, the percentage of regularly attending evangelical Protestants in the Republican coalition increased from 6.3 in 1978 to 24.4 in 1996.

13. The measurement of cultural issue attitudes in each of the NES surveys from 1964 through 1996 is discussed in appendix A2. Since there were no questions about cultural issues in the 1970 NES, the value for polarization in that year was created through linear interpolation. To facilitate comparisons, both the cultural and religious series have been standardized to have a mean of 50 and a standard deviation of 25.

14. The correlation between the two series is strong (.79) and highly statistically significant ($p = .0002$). Since there is clearly a temporal trend in both series, I also take the more conservative measure of correlating the first difference of the religious series with the first difference of the cultural-issue series. The correlation between first differences is also very strong (.53) and statistically significant ($p = .03$), suggesting that the year-to-year changes in

the levels of partisan religious polarization and partisan polarization on cultural issues are related.

15. These models include doctrinal orthodoxy, religious commitment, dummy variables for religious traditions, and, to assess the change over time in the political impact of these factors, interactions among all of these variables and a linear time variable. The models also include controls for education, income, gender, age, southern residence, and union membership. The estimates are presented in appendix B5.

16. The "high" levels of orthodoxy and commitment in the figure are one standard deviation above the mean for the entire sample. The "low" levels are one standard deviation below the mean. To compute the predictions for doctrinal orthodoxy, I set orthodoxy to its high and low values, let the time variable vary across its range, and held commitment and all the control variables constant at their means. I used the same procedure to compute the predictions for religious commitment, except that I set commitment to its high and low values and held orthodoxy at its mean.

17. These models include dummy variables for religious traditions, indicators of orthodoxy and commitment, and controls for education, income, gender, age, southern residence, and union membership. To account for the possibility that the effects of orthodoxy and commitment may vary across religious traditions and over time, and that changes over time in their effects may vary across traditions, the models include interactions between the dummy variables for religious traditions and the orthodoxy and commitment variables; interactions between the tradition variables and a linear time variable; interactions between orthodoxy or commitment and the linear time variable; and three-way interactions between the tradition variables, orthodoxy or commitment, and the linear time variable. The estimates of these models are presented in appendix B5.

18. High and low levels of orthodoxy and commitment are defined as one standard deviation above and below, respectively, the mean values for the particular tradition. To compute all the predictions, all control variables were held constant at their means. To compute the predictions for doctrinal orthodoxy, orthodoxy is set to its low and high values and commitment is held at its mean for each tradition. To compute the predictions for religious commitment, commitment is set to its low and high values and orthodoxy is held at its mean for each tradition. To compute the predictions for high religious traditionalism, both orthodoxy and commitment are set to their high values for each tradition. To compute the predictions for low traditionalism, both orthodoxy and commitment are set to their low values for each tradition.

CHAPTER 6

Links in the Chain: The Structure and Sequence of Partisan Religious and Cultural Change

THE EVIDENCE PRESENTED thus far suggests that the American political parties are becoming increasingly divided along the lines of a traditionalist–modernist religious and cultural cleavage. The Republican party is becoming the home of committed evangelical Protestants and other highly committed and theologically orthodox Christians. The Democratic party is gaining the loyalties of secularists and the least committed and most theologically liberal members of the major religious traditions. Earlier chapters showed that Republican and Democratic national convention delegates have become increasingly different in their religious orientations and cultural attitudes, and the platforms drafted by those conventions have taken more and more polarized stands on moral and cultural matters. These changes in the parties' religious and cultural bearings have been paralleled by substantial changes in the religious composition of the parties' coalitions in the mass electorate. The change has been most pronounced among committed evangelical Protestants, a previously Democratic group that has now become the religious core of the Republican electoral coalition. But the change among devout evangelicals has been part of a broader religious and cultural polarization of the parties' coalitions.

A remaining question is whether there is a causal connection between religious and cultural change at the elite and activist levels of party politics and religious and cultural change in the parties' mass coalitions. Specifically, did the change among party elites and activists cause the mass change? Did the religious and cultural polarization of the Democratic and Republican mass coalitions occur in response to similar developments among party leaders, candidates, and activists?

In this chapter, I look at the process of partisan religious change from this top-down perspective, examining whether increases in the polarization of Democratic and Republican officeholders on cultural issues led to changes in the religious and cultural characteristics of party activists and ultimately to changes in the religious composition of the parties' coalitions. More generally, I examine the structure and sequence of partisan religious and cultural change, taking up not only the question of what causes what, but also the point at which certain factors fall in the causal process and whether the causal relationship between certain factors is a direct or indirect one.

Of course, a purely top-down model with elites as the starting point and the coalitions in the mass electorate as the end point is an oversimplification of the partisan change process. I did argue in chapter 1 that the ideological and religious makeup of the Democratic and Republican activist bases should respond to changes in the issue positions of party elites, and that the religious composition of the parties' mass coalitions should respond to those elite-level changes and, even more directly, to religious and cultural changes among party activists. So it seems reasonable to test that notion. However, the direction of causality is not one-way. Activist-level change may effect changes in elite issue positions. For example, as Republican activists grow more traditionally religious and culturally conservative, individual politicians who have conservative views on cultural issues should find it easier to win Republican nominations or to gain positions of power within the GOP. Republican politicians who are less culturally conservative and hope to be party nominees or party leaders should have incentives to move their stands on cultural matters in a conservative direction. Furthermore, as I noted in chapter 5, changes in the parties' mass coalitions may lead to further changes in the issue positions of party candidates, leaders, and elected officials as well as in the characteristics of party activists.

I have provided some evidence, anecdotal as it may be, of changes in the cultural positions of the two parties' presidential candidates that have occurred in response to the growing religious and cultural cleavage between the parties' activists and identifiers. However, a more systematic exploration of the reciprocal relationships over time between the cultural stands of Democratic and Republican elites, the religious and cultural characteristics of Democratic and Republican activists, and the religious composition of the Democratic and Republican mass coalitions would require a very complex analysis. The empirical analysis in this chapter is more straightforward. It simply seeks to determine what the causes of the religious polarization of the parties' mass coalitions are, not what the effect of that polarization is. In other words, all I am trying to answer is the questions posed by steps 5 through 8 in figure 1.1: If the positions of Democratic and Republican elites on cultural issues grow more distinct, does that lead to changes in the religious composition of the parties' coalitions? And do changes in the religious and cultural orientations of party activists and in mass perceptions of and feelings about the parties intervene between elite and mass change?

A model that starts with issue polarization between Democratic and Republican elites also begs the question of what caused the elite-level divisions in the first place. That also is not something that the analysis in this chapter can address. However, the model presented in chapter 1 does provide an explanation. In short, strategic politicians within one of the parties see an advantage in championing noncentrist stands on a new set of highly emotional and divisive issues. Within the context of the American parties' participatory nominating process, that leads to an influx into the party of political activists who share those extreme views on the issues, and it increases the chances that activists who have the opposite views will become involved in the other party. The resulting polarization in the positions of Democratic and Republican activists on the issues should lead the parties' leaders, candidates, and platforms also to take more polarized stands on them. That elite-level polarization is the starting point for the analysis that follows.

TRANSLATING ELITE-LEVEL CULTURAL CHANGE INTO MASS-LEVEL RELIGIOUS CHANGE: INTERVENING LINKS

In chapter 1, I argued that party elite polarization on a new set of crosscutting political issues is a necessary but not sufficient condition for the reshaping of the parties' mass coalitions along the lines of those issues and the social cleavages that gave rise to them. Democratic and Republican leaders, candidates, and platforms take divergent stands on a wide array of issues, but the large majority of those issues either go ignored by the electorate or spark only a short-term reaction. Only those issues that capture the sustained attention of the mass public and change its perceptions of and feelings about the parties are capable of creating long-term partisan change. Before citizens will change their partisan ties, or choose a party loyalty for the first time, on the basis of a new set of concerns, they must come to associate the parties with those concerns—the new issues must become relevant to their evaluations of the two parties—and see clear differences between the parties' positions on them. The new issues also must evoke a strong emotional response in voters, particularly those voters who have polarized positions on them. Those polarized views must translate into polarized party affect—individuals who have extreme positions on the issues must come to feel more positively about the party whose stands are closest to theirs and more negatively about the party whose stands are farthest from theirs—before individuals will reshape their partisan ties along these new political and social lines.

Also intervening between party elite change and change in the parties' electoral coalitions is a reshaping of the characteristics of Democratic and Republican activists. Because most citizens pay little attention to elite-level politics, alterations in the positions of party leaders, candidates, and platforms on a set of issues may go largely unnoticed by most of the electorate. Inattentive individuals, however, do garner political information and pick up political cues from the politically active citizens in their families, neighborhoods, churches, and workplaces (Berelson, Lazarsfeld, and McPhee 1954). Thus, if elite-level change on new issues sparks a reaction among politically inclined citizens, leading to a polarization of Democratic and Republican activists along the lines of the issues and their related social cleavage, then the mass public may well come to associate the parties with polarized positions on these matters. As a result, those citizens who hold extreme stands themselves may change their feelings about the parties and ultimately their partisan loyalties.

Figure 6.1 repackages steps 5 through 8 in figure 1.1, showing the proposed indirect relationship between the polarization of Democratic and Republican elites on cultural issues and the polarization of the parties' mass coalitions along traditionalist–modernist religious lines. The elite polarization should spark a reaction among politically active citizens and create a traditionalist–modernist religious cleavage between Democratic and Republican activists. The mass electorate should respond more directly to change among the party activists in their neighborhoods, churches, and workplaces than to the elite-level change. The change at the elite level also should alter the way the mass electorate thinks and feels about the parties. As the cultural stands of Democratic and Republican elites diverge, citizens should come to associate the parties more closely with distinct positions on religious, moral, and cultural matters. There also should be a religious polarization of party affect, with religious traditionalists coming to feel more positively about the Republican party and more negatively about the Democratic party, and religious modernists feeling more

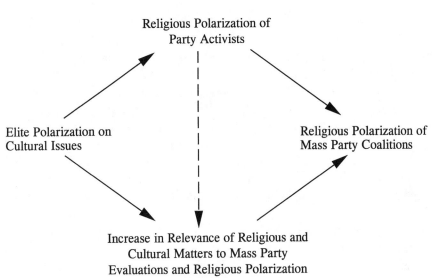

Religious Polarization of
Party Activists

Elite Polarization on
Cultural Issues

Religious Polarization of
Mass Party Coalitions

Increase in Relevance of Religious and
Cultural Matters to Mass Party
Evaluations and Religious Polarization
of Party Affect

FIGURE 6.1. Links between party elite cultural change and the religious polarization of the parties' mass coalitions

positively toward the Democrats and more negatively toward the GOP. Those changes in mass perceptions and affect then should produce a change in the religious composition of the parties' electoral coalitions.

The dotted line in the figure indicates that the effect of elite cultural polarization on mass perceptions of and affect toward the parties also may be indirect, working through its impact on the religious orientations of Democratic and Republican activists. I test this model by focusing on the two most prominent cases of partisan religious change in the mass electorate: the overall polarization of the parties' coalitions along the lines of religious traditionalism and the growing alignment of committed evangelical Protestants with the Republican party.

PARTY POLARIZATION ON THE TRADITIONALIST–MODERNIST RELIGIOUS CLEAVAGE

In the 1980s and 1990s, Democratic and Republican identifiers became increasingly polarized along the lines of the traditionalist–modernist religious cleavage. There was an increase in the political impact of the orthodoxy of religious affiliation and in the effect of doctrinal orthodoxy and religious commitment within religious traditions. The questions here are, Did that polarization occur in response to the polarization of Democratic and Republican elites on cultural issues? And was the effect of the elite cultural alignment on the mass religious alignment direct, or was its effect indirect, working through factors such as the religious alignment of party activists and the mass public's perceptions of and affect for the two parties? To answer those questions, I proceed in two steps. First, I examine the linkages between party elite stands on cultural issues, mass perceptions of and feelings about the parties, and the alignment of Democratic and Republican identifiers along the lines of religious orthodoxy. Next, I analyze whether the religious orientations of grassroots-level party activists play an intervening role between elite cultural change and mass religious change.

Elite Cultural Positions, Mass Perceptions and Feelings, and the Mass Religious Alignment

Thus far, the party activists in this book have been delegates to the parties' national conventions, and there is some relationship over time between the polarization of Democratic and Republican delegates on cultural issues and the religious polarization of the parties' mass coalitions.[1] However, the convention delegate series present two problems for analyzing the links between elite- and mass-level change. First, although most delegates do not hold elective office or play a direct role in making national party policy, a majority of delegates hold or have held official positions in their state or local parties. Moreover, both parties' convention delegations contain a number of national and state elected officials as well as national party officials. Thus, it is difficult to distinguish between party elites and party activists among delegates and, accordingly, to separate elite partisan change from activist-level change. Second, and most important, there are only six time points in the delegate religious series and seven time points in the delegate abortion series, far too few to engage in any sort of time series analysis of elite-mass linkages. Thus, it is necessary to identify different, and separate, indicators of the religious and cultural orientations of party elites and activists.

The Cultural Stands of the Parties in Congress

As Carmines and Stimson (1989) argue, the U.S. Congress is an ideal place to look for changes in the policy positions of party elites. In their roles as both policy initiators and responders to presidential initiatives, a party's members of Congress provide important cues about the party's stands on particular sets of political issues. Most important, the numerous recorded roll-call votes of members of Congress provide a detailed public record of the ebbs and flows of the parties' issue positions. My measure of party elite positions on cultural issues derives from all the roll-call votes pertaining to cultural issues in the House and Senate between 1970 and 1996. That includes any vote on abortion rights, homosexual rights, women's rights, the Equal Rights Amendment, prayer and other religious expression in the public schools and other public places, government's relationship to religious schools, and the funding of "pornographic" or "obscene art" by the National Endowment for the Arts.[2]

Figure 6.2 shows the conservative proportion of all Republican and Democratic cultural roll-call votes cast in both houses over that time period. In the early 1970s, there was a great deal of variation in the conservatism of House and Senate voting patterns. However, the cultural stands of the two parties in both houses were virtually indistinguishable, and the fluctuations resulted largely from the cultural focus of the Congress switching back and forth between women's rights and the Equal Rights Amendment, where both parties in both houses were strongly on the liberal side, and prayer in the public schools, where both parties in both houses were strongly on the conservative side.

Just as Adams (1997) shows for the abortion issue only, the close similarities between the two parties' voting patterns on cultural issues began to disappear in the late 1970s and early 1980s, and the level of polarization between the congressional parties' cultural stands increased steadily after that. House Republicans have been consistently very conservative on cultural matters since 1977, while House Democrats have grown more liberal in their cultural votes. In the Senate, Republicans have become increasingly conservative while Democratic cultural liberalism has clearly grown.

This growing congressional polarization is demonstrated more clearly in figure 6.3, which shows my measure of the congressional party alignment on cultural issues: the average of the difference between the proportion of Republican cultural votes that were conservative and the proportion of Democratic cultural votes that were conservative in the House and that same difference in the Senate. The difference between the cultural stands of the parties in Congress demonstrates a clear growth, a growth that began in the 1970s and continued through the 1980s and early 1990s.

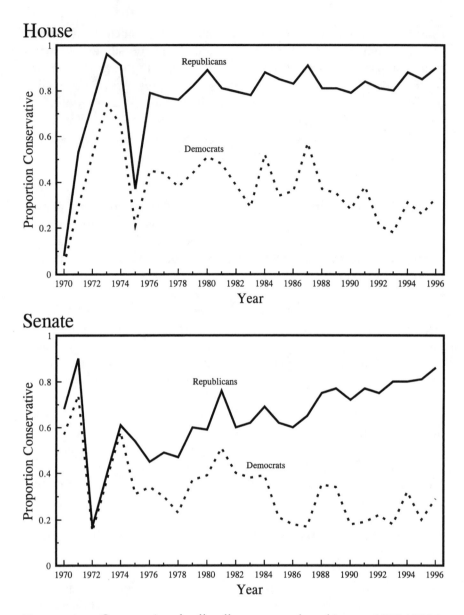

FIGURE 6.2. Congressional roll-call votes on cultural issues, 1970–1996: conservative proportion of Republican and Democratic votes

Source: Computed by the author from roll-call vote reports in *Congressional Quarterly.*

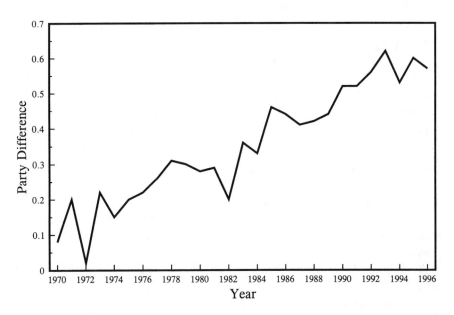

FIGURE 6.3. Difference between proportions of congressional Republicans and Democrats voting conservative on cultural issues, 1970–1996
Source: Computed by the author from roll-call vote reports in *Congressional Quarterly.*

What accounts for the growth of partisan cultural differences in Congress? Part of that growth has resulted from the parties' moving farther apart on issues that have been on the legislative agenda since the early 1970s. The issue of prayer in the public schools and other public settings provides a good example. In October 1970, a large majority of both parties' senators—84 percent of Republicans and 61 percent of Democrats—voted to support the right of persons lawfully assembled in any public building to participate in nondenominational prayer. Even by April 1979, nearly half (48 percent) of Senate Democrats voted to restore the right of voluntary prayer in public schools, while the measure was strongly supported by Republicans (68 percent). However, in January 1992, when Senator Helms introduced a "sense of the Senate" resolution that the Supreme Court should reverse its rulings banning prayer in the public schools, the parties were clearly polarized: Sixty-seven percent of Senate Republicans were for it and 78 percent of Senate Democrats were against it.

Another example is the proposed Equal Rights Amendment to the

Constitution, guaranteeing women equal status under the law with men. When it was proposed in the House in August 1970, 94 percent of Republicans and 97 percent of Democrats voted for it. But after ratification by the states failed and it was proposed again in November 1983, the parties in the House took clearly different stands: Sixty-seven percent of Republicans voted against it and 86 percent of Democrats voted for it. Adams (1997) shows a similar increase in congressional party polarization on issues such as the constitutional protection of abortion rights and federal funding of abortion.

The late 1980s and the 1990s also witnessed the emergence of new cultural issues on the legislative agenda, and the congressional parties have taken highly polarized stands on these matters from the start. For example, much attention in the late 1980s was given to federal funding of work by artists such as Andres Serrano and Robert Mapplethorpe that was considered by many to be obscene and sacrilegious. In response, Republican legislators in both the House and the Senate introduced bills prohibiting the National Endowment for the Arts from funding works that included pornography, obscenity, or the denigration of religion, and these proposals sparked starkly different reactions from Republicans and Democrats. In October 1990, 66 percent of Republicans in the House and 53 percent of Republicans in the Senate voted in favor of such bills, while 76 percent of House Democrats and 89 percent of Senate Democrats voted against them. In his 1992 campaign, Bill Clinton promised to seek an end to the ban on homosexuals in the armed services. When similar bills arose in the House and Senate in September 1993, 61 percent of House Democrats and 55 percent of Senate Democrats supported them while 94 percent of House Republicans and 93 percent of Senate Republicans opposed them. In the 1990s, an old issue, abortion, took a new twist. Pro-life forces focused less on banning all abortions and more on seeking an end to late-term, "partial birth" abortions. When bills that would ban partial birth abortions reached the floor of the House and Senate late in 1995, 93 percent of House Republicans and 85 percent of Senate Republicans supported them, while 63 percent of House Democrats and 80 percent of Senate Democrats voted against them.

Why have Republican and Democratic members of Congress taken increasingly different stands on cultural issues? The answer may well lie in the changes in presidential politics and among party activists documented in chapters 3 and 4. As the platforms drafted by the parties' presidential nominating conventions and the parties' presidential candidates themselves take increasingly extreme stands on cultural matters, members of Congress may face growing pressure from party leaders and/or the presidents of their party to vote in a consistently conservative or liberal way on these issues. The growing religious and cultural polarization of Republican and Democratic activists may require incumbent legislators to adopt more extreme cultural stands to win renomination by their parties and to win reelection.

It also may alter the types of nonincumbent candidates who seek and win House and Senate seats. Those changes may occur because potential candidates alter their cultural positions to fit the changing political reality within their parties. To win the support of their parties' primary voters and activists, Democratic challengers and open-seat candidates may need to take more liberal stands on cultural issues now than they did in the past, while Republican challengers and open-seat candidates may need to take more conservative cultural positions. The changes also may occur because candidates, particularly House candidates, often come from the ranks of party activists. So a change in the religious and cultural orientations of party activists may alter the religious and cultural orientations of the pool of potential candidates for Congress, producing a more culturally liberal pool of potential Democratic candidates and a more culturally conservative group of potential Republican candidates.[3] Whatever the reason for the changing cultural stands of the parties in Congress, it is evident that the parties' elites have become more polarized on cultural matters, sending increasingly clear signals to activists and the electorate of parties divided on these matters.

Mass Perceptions of and Affect Toward the Parties

Before individuals will choose or change their party affiliations on the basis of their religious and cultural orientations, religious, moral, and cultural matters must become relevant to their evaluations of the parties. They must come to associate the political parties with these concerns and see clear differences between the Democratic and Republican stands on them.

To measure the relevance of religious, moral, and cultural matters to party evaluations, I turn to two sets of open-ended questions in the NES surveys. The first set involves respondents' likes and dislikes of the Republican and Democratic parties. In all the NES surveys used here, except for those in 1966, 1970, and 1974, respondents were asked if there was anything they liked about the Republican party, liked about the Democratic party, disliked about the Republican party, and disliked about the Democratic party.[4] Respondents could mention up to five things in response to each of the four questions. These questions give respondents the opportunity to reveal, unprompted by interviewers, the factors that are most relevant to their evaluations of the parties. So if the parties are becoming more closely associated with religious, cultural, and moral matters in the minds of American citizens, then the proportion of individuals who mention these concerns in response to the party likes/dislikes questions should increase.[5]

The second set of open-ended questions asks respondents if they see any differences between the Republican and Democratic parties and what those differences are.[6] Those questions appeared only in the presidential-year NES surveys until 1990, at which time they began to be asked in midterm and presidential-year surveys. If religious and cultural differences between the parties are becoming more apparent to citizens, that should be manifested in an increase in the proportion of individuals who mention religious, cultural, and moral matters in response to the party differences questions.[7]

Figure 6.4 shows that there has been a clear increase over time in the frequency with which individuals have mentioned religious, cultural, and moral matters in response to the party likes/dislikes and party differences questions.[8] These matters were largely irrelevant to citizens' evaluations of the parties until 1980. However, the contemporary cultural conflict has played a much greater role in party politics in the 1980s and 1990s than it did in earlier decades. Ronald Reagan's presidential campaign in 1980 and eight-year presidency were characterized by highly conservative cultural rhetoric. The Christian Right and its constituency of committed evangelical Protestants have gained increasing influence in the Republican party, and secularists, feminists, abortion rights advocates, and homosexuals have become more influential within the Democratic party. The parties in Congress and the parties' platforms have taken increasingly polarized stands on cultural and moral issues.

These developments have not been lost on the American public. Since 1980, religious, cultural, and moral matters have steadily become much more relevant to citizens' evaluations of the Democratic and Republican parties, and the electorate increasingly has come to see these issues as ones on which there are clear party differences.[9] When I examine the links between elite and mass change, the measure of the relevance of religious and cultural matters to citizens' evaluations of the political parties that I use is the mean number of responses to the questions about party likes and dislikes that were religious, cultural, or moral in nature.[10]

Also intervening between elite change and changes in the mass party

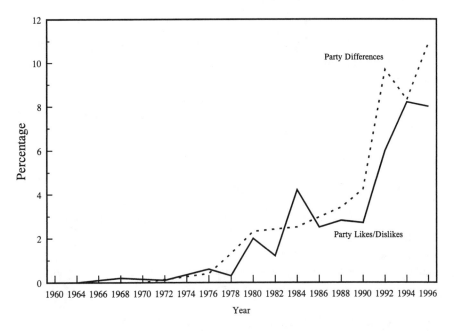

FIGURE 6.4. Percentage of all responses to questions about party likes/
dislikes and party differences about cultural, moral, or religious matters
Note: Means are from six questions about Republican likes and dislikes, six questions
about Democratic likes and dislikes, and three questions about party differences.
Source: 1960–1996 National Election Studies

coalitions is a polarization of party affect along the lines of the new party
cleavage (Carmines and Stimson 1989). Before religious traditionalists
who are Democrats or independents will align or realign themselves with
the Republican party on the basis of religious, moral, and cultural concerns, they should not only come to see a distinction between the parties'
stands on these matters, but also develop more positive feelings toward
the Republican party and more negative feelings toward the Democratic
party. Similarly, religious modernists should come to feel more positively
toward the Democratic party and more negatively toward the GOP before beginning to identify themselves as Democrats. In short, there should
be a polarization of party affect along the lines of religious orthodoxy.

My measure of this polarization is formed in two steps. First, I use
the total numbers of likes and dislikes that respondents expressed toward
the two parties to form a measure of net party affect, in which higher
scores represent greater affect and less disaffect toward the GOP and

greater disaffect and less affect toward the Democratic party.[11] Second, I take the correlation between net party affect and the religious orthodoxy scale. That correlation coefficient captures the degree to which religious traditionalists and religious modernists feel differently about the two parties, and thus it is the measure of the religious polarization of party affect. Religiously polarized affect and partisan cultural relevance are closely related over time.[12]

Estimation Method

The following analysis examines the links between elite- and mass-level factors—specifically, the congressional party alignment on cultural issues, the relevance of cultural and moral matters to citizens' party evaluations, the religious polarization of party affect, and the alignment of party identifiers on the religious orthodoxy scale—using time-series regression models in which the dependent series (e.g., the mass religious alignment) is a function of its own past values and some independent series (e.g., the congressional cultural alignment). Those readers who are uninterested in why I use such a technique and the potential problems raised by the analysis simply should know that such models provide an indication of whether changes in the independent series are associated with changes in the dependent series and should skip to the next section. For those readers who are interested, what follows are the details.

Unfortunately, the limited number of data points in the congressional and mass series—eighteen when only data from the NES are involved, fourteen when the congressional alignment comes into play—places limitations on my ability to establish that these links are causal. Ideally, one would examine these relationships using transfer function models in which one time series is a function of its own past history and another time series (Box and Jenkins 1976), thus allowing tests of "Granger" causality (Freeman 1983).[13] Such techniques, however, require first identifying and estimating the temporal components of each series, something that requires considerably more than fourteen or eighteen observations.

How then to examine the relationships between these various series? One possibility would be to simply regress one series on another and examine the coefficients for possible causal linkages. Such an approach, however, raises the specter of serially correlated regression residuals—a common problem in time series analysis and one that is quite likely to exist here given the clear upward trends in all of these variables—and thus biased regression estimates. Traditionally, analysts have responded to the problem of serial correlation by "fixing" the data: taking the first differences of both the independent and dependent series to remove the trend from the data, or some sort of generalized least squares estimation (cf. Cochrane and Orcutt 1949). More recently, however, scholars have argued that rather than attempt to correct the error term for time dependency, one should model the time dependency within the regression equation (cf. Beck 1985). Moreover, the techniques used for error-term corrections may not always be theoretically appropriate. For instance, regressing first differences on first differences assumes that the year-to-year changes in one variable correspond to the year-to-year changes in another variable. In some cases, I have theoretical and empirical reasons to believe that year-to-year changes in two variables do correspond. In other cases, however, there should be a delayed response of one variable to changes in another, rather than corresponding year-to-year changes.

To take the time dependency in the data into account, but with too few observations to model it explicitly, my approach is to make a simplifying assumption: that the value of the dependent variable at one time point is simply a function of its value at the previous time point and is not dependent on its values in the more distant past. In other words, the serial correlation in the dependent variable follows a first-order autoregressive process. To account for that process, I include the value of the dependent variable in the previous time period (one lag) as an independent variable in each of my models.[14] I then undertake some tests to see if serial correlation remains in the error term and take some simple remedial measures in the few cases in which it does.[15] This procedure does allow me to make some inferences about whether changes in one variable lead to changes in another variable. However, given the necessary simplicity of my models, the reader should take this analysis as providing tentative evidence about the structure and sequence of partisan religious change, rather than a firm documentation of causation.

Examining the Links

Table 6.1 presents the results of regression analyses examining the links between changes in the congressional party alignment on cultural issues, mass perceptions of and affect toward the parties, and the alignment of the parties' mass coalitions along the traditionalist–modernist religious cleavage. Given the political inattentiveness of the mass public and the indirect nature of the link between partisan change at the elite and mass levels, one would expect changes in the mass party alignment to occur as a delayed response to changes in the polarization of the congressional parties' cultural stands. Figure 6.5 suggests that such a delayed

TABLE 6.1

Estimation of the links between elite cultural positions,
mass perceptions of and feelings about the parties,
and the religious alignment of the parties' mass coalitions

(1) The mass religious alignment as a function of the
congressional alignment on cultural issues

	Time Period of Congressional Alignment	
Independent Variables	Lagged 2 Years	Lagged 4 Years
Mass religious alignment	.86**	.74**
(lagged one period)[a]	$(t = 3.24, \beta = .66)$	$(t = 2.84, \beta = .57)$
Congressional alignment	.60	.94*
	$(t = 1.36, \beta = .28)$	$(t = 2.07, \beta = .42)$
(N)	(13)	(12)
Adjusted R^2	.68	.74
Residual mean square	.045	.04
Durbin's h[b]	−.21	.04
Durbin's m[c]	−.15	−.001

(2) The relevance of religious and cultural matters to party evaluations
and the religious polarization of party affect as a function
of the congressional alignment on cultural issues

	Dependent Variable	
Independent Variables	Relevance	Affect
Relevance (lagged one period)	.32	—
	$(t = 1.02, \beta = .27)$	
Affect (lagged one period)	—	.15
		$(t = .45, \beta = .14)$
Congressional alignment	.49**	.21*
(lagged four years)	$(t = 2.40, \beta = .63)$	$(t = 1.97, \beta = .63)$
(N)	(12)	(12)
Adjusted R^2	.67	.43
Durbin's h	—	—
Durbin's m	−1.28	−1.41

(3) The mass religious alignment as a function of the relevance of religious
and cultural matters to party evaluations and the correlation
between net party affect and religious orthodoxy

	Explanatory Variable	
Independent Variables	Relevance	Affect/Orthodoxy Correlation
Religious alignment	.39*	.66**
(lagged one period)[d]	$(t = 2.02, \beta = .33)$	$(t = 2.54, \beta = .54)$

Independent Variables	Explanatory Variable	
	Relevance	Affect/Orthodoxy Correlation
Relevance	1.94** $(t = 4.01, \beta = .65)$	—
Affect/orthodoxy correlation	—	3.38** $(t = 3.11, \beta = .57)$
(N)	(17)	(16)
Adjusted R^2	.88	.81
Durbin's h	.77	—
Durbin's m	.45	.58

(4) The mass religious alignment as a function of the congressional alignment on cultural issues, the relevance of religious and cultural matters to party evaluations, and the correlation between net party affect and religious orthodoxy

Independent Variables	Explanatory Variable (Relevance or Affect)	
	Relevance	Affect/Orthodoxy Correlation
Religious Alignment (lagged one period)[a]	.29 $(t = .99, \beta = .23)$	.48* $(t = 1.91, \beta = .37)$
Relevance	2.06* $(t = 2.20, \beta = .71)$	—
Affect/orthodoxy correlation	—	3.17* $(t = 2.15, \beta = .47)$
Congressional alignment (lagged four years)	.07 $(t = .13, \beta = .03)$	.45 $(t = 1.02, \beta = .20)$
(N)	(12)	(12)
Adjusted R^2	.81	.81
Residual mean square	.028	.029
Durbin's h	—	.14
Durbin's m	.27	.69

Source: The congressional series is from House and Senate roll-call votes. The other series are from the 1960–1996 National Election Studies.

Entries are unstandardized regression coefficients. The t-values (t) and standardized coefficients (β) are in parentheses.

[a]A lag of one period in the mass series is one NES survey or two years.

[b]Durbin's h is distributed normally. It is not presented for some analyses because the product of the first lag of the dependent variable and the number of time points is greater than 1 in those cases. Durbin's h cannot be computed in those circumstances.

[c]Durbin's m is distributed as a t-statistic.

[d]Two lags of the dependent variable were included in the model. Durbin's h and m remained significant when only one lag was included, indicating a first-order autocorrelation process.

*$p < .10$

**$p < .05$

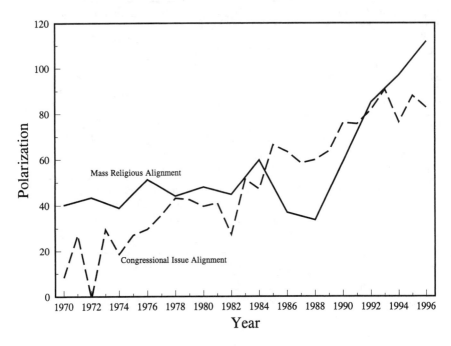

FIGURE 6.5. The alignment of Republican and Democratic identifiers on religious orthodoxy, and the congressional party alignment on cultural issues
Note: Both series are standardized (mean = 50, standard deviation = 25).
Source: Mass data are from 1970–1996 NES; congressional data are from *Congressional Quarterly.*

response in fact did occur. Noticeable increases in congressional cultural polarization began in the mid 1970s, but no increases in mass religious polarization were evident until the early 1980s. In the early to mid 1980s, the cultural differences between the congressional parties began to increase sharply. The largest increases in partisan religious polarization at the mass level did not occur until after 1988.

The regression analyses presented in the first panel of table 6.1 thus model the mass religious alignment as a function of its own value in the previous election year and lagged values of the congressional issue alignment. The results indicate that mass religious change did occur as a delayed response to elite change on cultural issues, and that the response took longer than two years to occur. Whereas the congressional alignment lagged two years does not have a statistically significant effect on the mass alignment, the congressional alignment lagged four years does have a strong and statistically significant effect.[16] The coefficient on the four-year lag of the congressional alignment indicates that an increase of 1 in the difference between the proportion of cultural votes by Republican members of Congress that are conservative and the conservative proportion of cultural votes by Democratic members of Congress leads eventually to an increase of .94 in the difference between Republican and Democratic identifiers on the religious orthodoxy scale.

Of course, changes in elite cultural positions should not have a direct effect on the composition of the parties' mass coalitions. Rather, they should affect the mass alignment indirectly through their influence on mass perceptions of and affect for the political parties. Determining whether changes in mass perceptions and affect do indeed play an intervening role in the mass response to elite cultural change involves asking three questions. First, does the alignment of party elites on cultural issues have a direct effect on the relevance of cultural and moral matters to citizens' evaluations of the parties and on the religious polarization of party affect? The second part of the table shows that the relevance of cultural matters and the relationship between religious orthodoxy and party affect do indeed change as a delayed reaction to changes in the congressional cultural alignment. The congressional alignment lagged four years has a strong and statistically significant effect on both relevance and affect, even when past values of these variables are included in the regression models.

Second, is there a direct relationship between changes in the relevance of cultural matters to mass evaluations of the parties and in the religious polarization of party affect and changes in the mass party–religious alignment? The third part of the table shows that contemporaneous values of cultural relevance and the affect–orthodoxy relationship have very strong and highly significant effects on the mass religious alignment, even when past values of that alignment are controlled. An increase of 1 in the average number of open-ended party evaluations that are cultural or moral in nature is associated with an increase of 1.94 in the difference between Republican and Democratic identifiers on the religious orthodoxy scale. An increase of 1 in the correlation between net party affect and religious orthodoxy is associated with an increase of 3.38 in the religious polarization of the parties' coalitions. In fact, as figure 6.6 demonstrates, relevance, affect, and the mass religious alignment do not just trend together over time; year-to-year changes in each of these variables correspond very closely to each other.[17]

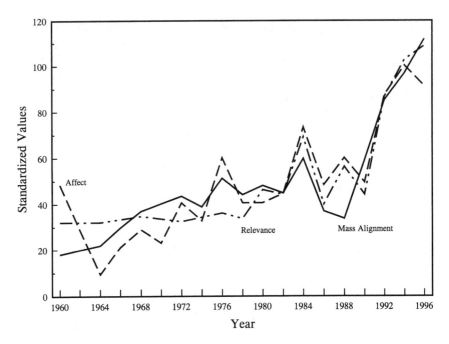

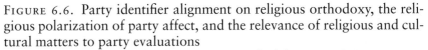

FIGURE 6.6. Party identifier alignment on religious orthodoxy, the religious polarization of party affect, and the relevance of religious and cultural matters to party evaluations

Note: All series are standardized (mean = 50, standard deviation = 25).

Source: 1960–1996 National Election Studies

Third, does the elite cultural alignment have a direct effect on the mass religious alignment when I control for cultural relevance and religiously polarized party affect? The fourth part of table 6.1 shows that, in fact, it does not. Even when controlling for both past values of the mass alignment and the congressional cultural alignment, the relevance of cultural matters to party evaluations and the affect–orthodoxy relationship have strong and statistically significant direct effects on the mass religious alignment. However, with these additional controls included, the effect of the lagged value of the congressional party alignment on the religious composition of the parties' mass coalitions decreases considerably and is not close to statistical significance.[18]

In sum, it appears that changes in the religious characteristics of the Democratic and Republican coalitions have occurred as a delayed response to changes in the cultural stands of party elites. However, that elite–mass linkage has been an indirect one, with changes in the relevance of cultural matters to party evaluations and in the religious polarization of party affect intervening between elite and mass change.

The Role of Party Activists in Connecting Elite and Mass Change

Party activists play an important role in linking change among party elites to changes in the political behavior of a largely inattentive public (Carmines and Stimson 1989). Since the convention delegate series contains a very small number of time points and includes some party elites, I turn to the NES surveys to identify party activists. The NES includes questions regarding six forms of political participation: voting, working for a party or candidate, trying to influence others' votes, going to political meetings or rallies, wearing a campaign button or putting a campaign sticker on one's car or a sign in one's yard, and giving money to a party or candidate. Party activists are defined as those respondents who performed three or more of these acts. This group represented about 15 percent of the NES sample in presidential-election years and 11 percent of the sample in midterm years through the early 1970s. Largely because of the declining activity levels of Republicans, the percentage of activists in NES samples had declined to about 12 percent in presidential years and 8 percent in midterm years by the late 1980s and 1990s.[19] To avoid double counting respondents, I examine the political response of nonactivists—those individuals who engaged in two or fewer of the political activities—to change in the religious alignment of party activists.

Of course, engaging in three of these activities pales in comparison to the types of participation levels exhibited by most convention delegates or the most active members of a party. However, three things should be noted. First, the NES questions ask respondents only whether or not they have performed an activity, not how often or to what extent they have performed it. So included in the group of respondents who have done only three things are people who are very active in politics: for example, people who try to influence the votes of a lot of people, people who attend a lot of political meetings and rallies, and people who give a lot of money to parties and candidates. Second, these activists are much more politically active and much more knowledgeable about politics than are nonactivists.[20] Third, what I am interested in here is not professional politicians or top-level party activists but simply ordinary citizens who are more involved in and know more about politics than their friends, family members, and coworkers, a description that fits the NES respondents who engage in three or more political activities. These citizen activists are the "opinion leaders" in local communities who facilitate the mass response to elite-level changes of which most citizens may be unaware (Carmines and Stimson 1989).

If changes in the religious alignment of citizen activists do indeed play an intervening role between elite cultural change and changes in the partisan religious alignment of ordinary citizens, then three things should be evident. First, changes in the elite alignment should be associated with changes in the religious alignment of party activists. Since they are more politically attentive than less-active citizens, activists should be quicker to respond to elite-level political developments; the lag between elite change and activist change should not be as long as the four-year gap found between elite change and change in the religious alignment of the mass party coalitions. In fact, regressions of the difference between Republican and Democratic activists on the religious orthodoxy scale on its own lagged value and the congressional alignment on cultural issues show that the relationship between elite change and activist change is not concurrent, but the activist alignment does respond more quickly to changes in the congressional alignment than does the religious alignment of the whole mass electorate.[21]

Second, there should be a direct relationship between activist change and change in the religious alignment of nonactivists. The relationship is not likely to be a contemporaneous one, given activists' greater attentiveness and speed in responding to elite change. However, ordinary citizens should respond more quickly to changes in the political behavior of their politically active friends, family members, coworkers, and fellow parishioners than to elite-level political changes. The second and third columns of table 6.2 show that there is a relationship between activist change and nonactivist change—an increase of 1 in the difference between Republican and Democratic activists on the religious orthodoxy scale is associated with an increase of .2 in the difference between Democratic and Republican identifiers on this scale in the next election year—and that the political behavior of nonactivists responds more quickly to changes in the alignment of party activists than to changes among congressional elites. Whereas it is the four-year lag of the congressional cultural alignment that has a statistically significant effect on the nonactivist religious alignment, there is a significant relationship between the activist religious alignment lagged only two years (or one period in NES surveys) and the nonactivist alignment.[22] Moreover, the residual mean square

TABLE 6.2

The religious alignment of nonactivist party identifiers
as a function of the congressional party alignment on cultural issues
and the religious alignment of party activists

| Independent Variables | Explanatory Variables | | |
	Congressional Alignment Only	Activist Alignment Only	Congressional Alignment and Activist Alignment
Nonactivist religious	.67**	.52**	.27
Alignment (lagged one period)[a]	(t = 2.21, β = .50)	(t = 2.53, β = .44)	(t = .95, β = .21)
Congressional alignment	.92*	—	.77*
(lagged four years)	(t = 1.93, β = .44)		(t = 1.99, β = .36)
Activist alignment	—	.20**	.20**
(lagged one period)[a]		(t = 2.91, β = .51)	(t = 2.38, β = .49)
(N)	(12)	(17)	(12)
Adjusted R^2	.69	.69	.80
Residual mean square	.04	.032	.025
Durbin's h	—[a]	1.42	−1.14
Durbin's m	.005	.64	−.35

Source: The congressional series is from House and Senate roll-call votes. The other series are from the 1960–1996 National Election Studies.

Entries are unstandardized regression coefficients. The t-values (t) and standardized coefficients (β) are in parentheses.

[a]A lag of one period in the nonactivist and activist series is one NES survey or two years.

*p < .10

**p < .05

statistics suggest a slightly stronger relationship between the activist and nonactivist alignments than between the elite and nonactivist alignments.

Third, if activist-level change does intervene between elite and mass change, then, when the activist alignment is controlled, the effect of the elite cultural alignment on the nonactivist religious alignment should disappear, or at least be reduced. The fourth column of table 6.2 shows that when the nonactivist alignment is regressed on both the congressional cultural alignment and the activist religious alignment, the effect of the congressional alignment on nonactivist change is still statistically significant. However, its effect is reduced and is both less significant and weaker than that of the two-year lag of the activist alignment. Thus, there

TABLE 6.3
Nonactivist perceptions of and feelings about the parties as a
function of the religious alignment of party activists and
the congressional party alignment on cultural issues

Independent Variables	Dependent Variable	
	Cultural Relevance	Polarized Affect
Nonactivist relevance (lagged one period)[a][b]	.22 ($t = 1.12$, $\beta = .18$)	—
Nonactivist affect (lagged one period)[a]	—	.18 ($t = .68$, $\beta = .18$)
Activist alignment	.07** ($t = 3.64$, $\beta = .54$)	.04** ($t = 2.54$, $\beta = .67$)
Congressional alignment (lagged four years)	.05 ($t = .32$, $\beta = .07$)	.02 ($t = .24$, $\beta = .08$)
(N)	(12)	(12)
Adjusted R^2	.87	.56
Durbin's h	.30	−1.56
Durbin's m	−.11	−1.46

Source: The congressional series is from House and Senate roll-call votes. The other series are from the 1960–1996 National Election Studies.

Entries are unstandardized regression coefficients. The t-values (t) and standardized coefficients (β) are in parentheses.

[a]A lag of one period in the nonactivist and activist series is one NES survey or two years.

[b]Two lags of the dependent variable were included in the model. Durbin's h and m remained significant when only one lag was included, indicating a first-order autocorrelation process.

*$p < .10$

**$p < .05$

is strong evidence that ordinary citizens do respond more quickly and more directly to changes in the political behavior of their friends, associates, and fellow church members than to changes at the elite level of party politics.

Figure 6.1 suggests that the religious polarization of party activists also may intervene between elite polarization on cultural issues and changes in mass perceptions of and feelings about the parties. The analyses in table 6.3 test that by regressing the relevance of religious and cultural matters to the party evaluations of nonactivists and the religious polarization of party affect among nonactivists on the religious alignment of party activists and the congressional alignment on cultural issues (lagged four years). The current value of the activist alignment has a strongly and highly significant effect on both relevance and religiously polarized party affect among nonactivists. As the differences in religious orthodoxy between Republican and Democratic activists grow, the degree to which religious and cultural matters are relevant to the party evaluations of nonactivists and the relationship between religious orthodoxy and party affect among nonactivists also increase. Meanwhile, the effect of the congressional cultural alignment is far from statistically significant in either model.

It appears that religiously oriented changes in mass perceptions of and feelings about the parties have responded more directly to changes in the religious orientations of Democratic and Republican activists than to religious and cultural changes at the more elite levels of party politics. Party activists do provide a link between elite-level and mass-level partisan change.

THE GROWTH OF EVANGELICAL REPUBLICANISM

The clearest change in the relationship between religious orientations and partisan loyalties over the last thirty years has been the realignment of committed evangelical Protestants from being strongly Democratic to becoming the religious core of the Republican coalition. This partisan reorientation of the group that is most clearly committed to traditional Protestant orthodoxy would seem to be clear evidence of the manifestation of the contemporary religious conflict in American party politics.

However, as noted earlier, there are alternative, nonreligious or noncultural explanations for the growth of evangelical Republicanism. Since evangelical Protestants are located disproportionately in the southern states, one possibility is that partisan change among evangelicals is part of a larger Republican realignment in the South based on the region's racial and economic conservatism. Another possibility is that as evangelicals, traditionally the poorest and least well educated of the white religious traditions, have moved up the socioeconomic ladder in recent decades (Oldfield 1996), they have reshaped their partisan ties accordingly.

Of course, evidence presented in earlier chapters points clearly toward the transformation of evangelical partisanship being religiously and culturally based. The fact that the growth in Republican ties is much clearer among committed evangelicals than among their less devout counterparts

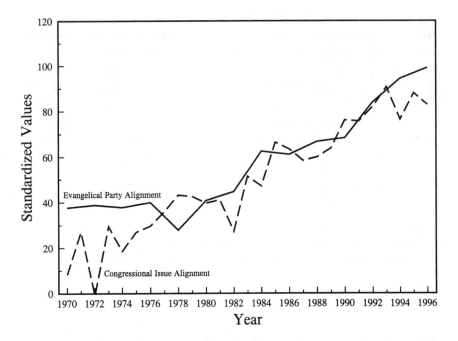

FIGURE 6.7. Party alignment of regularly attending evangelicals, and the congressional party alignment on cultural issues
Note: Both series are standardized (mean = 50, standard deviation = 25).
Source: Mass data are from 1970–1996 NES; congressional data are from *Congressional Quarterly.*

suggests that the change is based in religious orientations. Moreover, the increasing Republicanism of devout evangelicals is evident even when I control for socioeconomic status and southern residence. However, this chapter provides an opportunity for another, perhaps even more conclusive, test. If the Republican realignment of committed evangelical Protestants is based in religious and cultural factors, particularly the growing polarization of the parties and their candidates on cultural issues such as abortion and homosexuality, then there should be a systematic relationship between the alignment of party elites on cultural issues and the party alignment of committed evangelicals, with factors such as the relevance of religious and cultural matters to the party evaluations of these individuals intervening.

Figure 6.7 shows the alignment of the parties in Congress on cultural issues alongside the party alignment of committed evangelical Protestants, measured as the percentage of regular evangelical church attenders who identify themselves as Republicans minus the percentage of regularly attending evangelicals who identify themselves as Democrats. It displays a close parallel between the growing polarization of the congressional parties on cultural issues and the growing loyalties of devout evangelicals to the GOP. However, it also indicates a lag between elite partisan change and the partisan shifts of evangelicals. There is a substantial growth in congressional party differences on cultural issues between 1972 and 1978, but the movement of committed evangelicals toward the Republican party does not begin until after 1978.

The first two panels in table 6.4 provide further evidence that the growth of evangelical Republicanism did occur as a delayed response to the cultural polarization of the parties in Congress. The congressional cultural alignment lagged six years[23] has a very strong and highly statistically significant effect on the party alignment of committed evangelicals.[24] This six-year lag in the congressional alignment also has very strong and statistically significant effects on the relevance of religious and cultural matters to the party evaluations of committed evangelicals and on the net party affect of this religious group. In short, there is clear evidence that the increase in the cultural polarization of the parties in Congress has been associated with an increase in the extent to which committed evangelical Protestants associate the two parties with distinct stands on religious and cultural matters, an increase in the degree of evangelical affect for the Republican party and disaffect for the Democratic party, and finally with a growth in the ties of devout evangelicals to the GOP.

Have changes in religious and cultural relevance and party affect among committed evangelicals played an intervening role between partisan cultural change in Congress and the change in evangelicals' partisan loyalties? The third panel of table 6.4 shows that the relevance of religious and cultural matters to evangelical party evaluations and evangelical party affect both have significant effects on the evangelical party alignment. In fact, figure 6.8 shows that the year-to-year changes in relevance, affect, and the evangelical party alignment correspond very closely to each other, a fact manifested in a highly significant relationship between these changes.[25]

The fourth panel of table 6.4 includes the relevance and affect variables in the same analyses with the congressional cultural alignment. When religious and cultural relevance is brought into the analysis, the impact of the congressional alignment on the evangelical party alignment declines somewhat (from model 1), but it is still highly significant. Relevance also has a statistically significant effect on the evangelical alignment, and its

TABLE 6.4

Estimations of the links between elite cultural positions, the perceptions of and feelings about the parties of regularly attending evangelicals, and the party alignment of regularly attending evangelicals

(1) The evangelical party alignment as a function of the congressional alignment on cultural issues

Independent Variables	Coefficients
Evangelical party alignment (lagged one period)[a][b]	.22 $(t = .99, \beta = .20)$
Congressional alignment (lagged six years)	62.02** $(t = 4.32, \beta = .57)$
(N)	(11)
Adjusted R^2	.95
Residual mean square	13.41
Durbin's h	−1.89
Durbin's m	−2.46

(2) The relevance of religious and cultural matters to the party evaluations of evangelicals and the net party affect of evangelicals as a function of the congressional alignment on cultural issues

Independent Variables	Dependent Variable	
	Relevance	Party Affect
Relevance (lagged one period)[a]	.27 $(t = .83, \beta = .23)$	—
Party affect (lagged one period)[a]	—	.15 $(t = .75, \beta = .15)$
Congressional alignment (lagged six years)	1.24** $(t = 2.47, \beta = .69)$	17.66** $(t = 4.04, \beta = .80)$
(N)	(11)	(11)
Adjusted R^2	.73	.79
Durbin's h	—	.33
Durbin's m	−1.35	−.37

(3) The evangelical party alignment as a function of the relevance of religious and cultural matters to the party evaluations of evangelicals and the net party affect of evangelicals

Independent Variables	Explanatory Variable	
	Relevance	Party Affect
Evangelical party alignment (lagged one period)[a][b]	.65** $(t = 3.99, \beta = .52)$	.54** $(t = 3.85, \beta = .48)$

Independent Variables	Explanatory Variable	
	Relevance	Party Affect
Relevance	33.58**	—
	(t = 3.84, β = .50)	
Party affect	—	2.51**
		(t = 4.23, β = .53)
(N)	(16)	(17)
Adjusted R^2	.89	.92
Durbin's h	−.46	−.18
Durbin's m	.83	−.71

(4) The evangelical party alignment as a function of the congressional alignment on cultural issues, the relevance of religious and cultural matters to the party evaluations of evangelicals, and the net party affect of evangelicals

Independent Variables	Explanatory Variable (Relevance or Affect)	
	Relevance	Party Affect
Evangelical party alignment	.36**	.07
(lagged one period)[a][b]	(t = 2.59, β = .33)	(t = .40, β = .06)
Congressional alignment (lagged six years)	43.17**	29.62
	(t = 2.83, β = .40)	(t = 1.74, β = .27)
Relevance	19.17*	—
	(t = 2.34, β = .32)	
Party affect	—	1.63**
		(t = 2.48, β = .33)
(N)	(11)	(11)
Adjusted R^2	.96	.97
Residual mean square	10.50	7.71
Durbin's h	−.24	−1.39
Durbin's m	−.82	−1.73

Source: The congressional series is from House and Senate roll-call votes. The other series are from the 1960–1996 National Election Studies.

Entries are unstandardized regression coefficients. The t-values (t) and standardized coefficients (β) are in parentheses.

[a]A lag of one period in the mass series is one NES survey or two years.

[b]Two lags of the dependent variable were included in the model. Durbin's h and m remained significant when only one lag was included, indicating a first-order autocorrelation process.

*$p < .10$

**$p < .05$

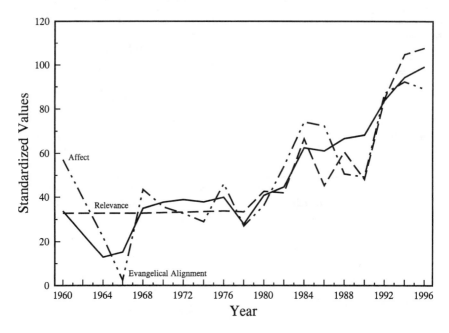

FIGURE 6.8. Regularly attending evangelicals: their party alignment, their net party affect, and the relevance of religious and cultural matters to their party evaluations
Note: All series are standardized (mean = 50, standard deviation = 25).
Source: 1960–1996 National Election Studies

inclusion allows for greater explanatory power than when just the congressional alignment is included. Meanwhile, when evangelical party affect is included as an independent variable, the effect of the congressional cultural alignment is no longer statistically significant. Affect has a strong and statistically significant effect on the evangelical party alignment, and its inclusion provides nearly twice as much explanatory power as the first model. It appears that changes in the partisan relevance of religious and cultural matters to evangelicals and changes in their party affect have intervened between changes in elite-level cultural stands and changes in the evangelical party alignment.

Of course, the party orientations of ordinary evangelical congregants probably respond more directly to changes at the activist level of party politics than to changes in the parties in Congress. That should be true for all citizens, but, as I argued in chapter 1, it may be particularly true for committed evangelicals. The organizations of the Christian Right have long relied on evangelical churches as the basis for mobilizing support for their causes and for culturally conservative Republican candidates. This is not only because evangelicals are highly influenced by the messages delivered from the pulpit (Guth et al. 1997), but also because the church serves as a primary social and friendship group for many evangelical congregants (Ammerman 1987). The hope of the Christian Right organizations has been that if some evangelical parishioners became involved in culturally conservative Republican politics, then their friends and fellow church members might be drawn in as well. Thus, one would expect that changes in the political activity patterns of evangelical churchgoers would have a strong effect on the perceptions of and feelings about the parties of less politically active evangelicals, particularly those who attend church regularly and thus maintain the closest contacts with fellow parishioners.

In fact, figure 6.8 provides some indirect evidence of the response of ordinary evangelicals to activist-level developments. The two largest changes in the party alignment of committed evangelicals coincide with the two most important developments in recent evangelical political activism. The first noticeable movement of devout evangelicals toward the GOP was between 1978 and 1984, a period that witnessed the formation of the Moral Majority and other early Christian Right organizations and their first efforts at mobilizing evangelical activists into Republican politics. The next major growth in evangelical Republicanism is between 1990 and 1996, a period just after the formation of the Christian Coalition, an organization that pursued the political mobilization of evangelical activists with much greater vigor than did its predecessors and directed that mobilization toward gaining control of state and local Republican parties.

Table 6.5 provides more direct evidence by examining the effect of changes in the percentage of regularly attending evangelical Protestants who are Republican party activists on the relevance that committed evangelical nonactivists place on religious and cultural matters in their party evaluations and on the party affect of committed evangelical nonactivists. Republican party activity by committed evangelicals has a very strong and highly significant effect on the extent to which their less politically active fellow parishioners view religious and cultural matters as being germane to their evaluations of the Democratic and Republican parties. It also has a statistically significant effect on the party affect of committed evangelical nonactivists. Thus, it does appear that regular church-goers in the evangelical faith pick up political cues from their fellow parishioners

TABLE 6.5

Perceptions of and feelings about the parties of regularly attending
evangelical nonactivists as a function of the percentage of regularly
attending evangelical Protestants who are Republican activists

| | Dependent Variable | |
Independent Variables	Relevance	Party Affect
Nonactivist relevance (lagged one period)[a][b]	.14	—
	($t = .87$, $\beta = .12$)	
Nonactivist affect (lagged one period)[a]	—	.35
		($t = 1.44$, $\beta = .34$)
Republican activist percentage	.02**	.19*
	($t = .5.09$, $\beta = .58$)	($t = 1.98$, $\beta = .46$)
(N)	(16)	(17)
Adjusted R^2	.92	.45
Durbin's h	.86	.14
Durbin's m	.71	.06

Source: 1960–1996 National Election Studies.

Entries are unstandardized regression coefficients. The t-values (t) and standardized coefficients (β) are in parentheses.

[a]A lag of one period is one NES survey or two years.

[b]Two lags of the dependent variable were included in the model. Durbin's h and m remained significant when only one lag was included, indicating a first-order autocorrelation process.

*$p < .10$

**$p < .05$

who become active in party politics. As more committed evangelicals become active in the GOP, more evangelical nonactivists see religious and cultural differences between the parties and take on more positive feelings toward the Republican party and more negative feelings toward the Democratic party.

In sum, this section provides further evidence that the growth of evangelical Republicanism has not been principally a socioeconomic or racially motivated phenomenon but instead is part of a broader reorientation of party politics along the lines of the contemporary cultural divide. The movement of committed evangelicals into the Republican party has occurred as a systematic response to the polarization of the Democratic and Republican parties on cultural issues, with factors such as the increase in evangelical activity in the GOP and changing evangelical perceptions of and feelings about the parties playing crucial roles in facilitating that response.

SUMMARY

Although data limitations make it less than conclusive, the evidence in this chapter does suggest that the changes in the religious composition of the parties' mass coalitions have occurred as a systematic response to the growing party differences on cultural issues such as abortion, homosexual rights, and school prayer. The change at the level of the electorate has been an inertial reaction to elite-level change, and the electorate seems to have responded more directly to changes in the political activity patterns of their friends, coworkers, and fellow church members than to elite reorientations. Overall, the analyses in this chapter provide support for the notion that changes in the parties' mass coalitions are triggered by changes at the elite and activist levels of party politics.

NOTES

1. The difference between the positions of Democratic and Republican delegates on abortion and the difference between the mean positions of Democratic and Republican identifiers on the religious orthodoxy scale both increased considerably from 1972 to 1996. And most of the year-to-year changes in the two series correspond with each other. Both increase noticeably between 1972 and 1976. Both remain fairly stable between 1976 and 1980. Both increase considerably between 1980 and 1984. There are sharp increases in both between 1988 and 1992 and between 1992 and 1996.

2. Appendix C presents a list of all the roll-call votes included in this analysis. Not included were votes where culturally conservative and culturally liberal positions are unclear, such as on some (but not all) compromise proposals and procedural tactics, particularly those where consistent cultural liberals, such as Senator Kennedy, and consistent cultural conservatives, such as Senator Helms, voted in agreement. I chose 1970 as the starting point because that was the first year in which there was at least one roll-call vote on a cultural issue in both the House and the Senate. The roll-call votes on abortion between 1973 and 1994 were identified by Adams (1997).

3. In his analysis of roll-call votes on abortion, Adams (1997) argues that most of the change in the stands of the congressional parties is the result of a change in the types of Democrats and Republicans who are elected to Congress rather than incumbent legislators changing their voting patterns on the

abortion issue. Of course, that does not preclude vote switching on other cultural issues, and it also does not preclude the possibility that potential and actual candidates change their stands on cultural issues before they run for Congress to better appeal to the cultural proclivities of their parties' core constituencies.

4. In the presidential-year NES surveys, respondents are also asked about their likes and dislikes of the Republican and Democratic presidential candidates. The frequency with which respondents mentioned religious, moral, and cultural matters to these questions and those about the parties themselves follows a very similar pattern over time with one exception: 1960. In 1960, John F. Kennedy's Catholicism prompted a large number of religious responses to the questions about likes and dislikes of him. However, the concerns about or excitement over Kennedy's religion did not translate into party evaluations, as no respondents mentioned a religious, cultural, or moral matter in response to the questions about Democratic and Republican likes and dislikes.

5. There is some variation in the types of responses that I coded as being a religious, cultural, or moral mention. However, to provide an example, the responses that I identified as referring to religious, cultural, or moral matters in the questions about Democratic and Republican likes and dislikes in the 1996 NES were references to the Christian/religious right as in control of the Republican party; a party being religious, moral, God-fearing, too religious, irreligious, or immoral; a party's stand on the separation of church and state/religion and politics, public morality, abortion or birth control, the ERA or women's rights, school prayer, or gay rights; and a party's relationship with women, feminists, women's liberationists, "sexists," gays and lesbians, homosexuals, or the Christian right/religious right.

6. The number of possible mentions of party differences has varied from three to six over the NES surveys. To provide a standard base of measurement over time, I examine only the religious, cultural, and moral mentions in the first three responses in each year.

7. As an example, the responses that I identified as referring to religious, cultural, or moral matters in the questions about party differences in the 1996 NES were references to the parties' stands on control of social behavior, moral standards, family values, school prayer, strong religious beliefs, abortion, women's rights/ERA, and homosexuality/gay rights.

8. To take into account the fact that respondents were allowed a maximum of three mentions about party differences (in some years) but a maximum of twenty mentions about Democratic and Republican likes and dislikes, and the fact that some individuals offer more responses than others, the figure shows the mean percentage of respondents' total mentions that deal with religious, cultural, or moral concerns.

9. A third set of open-ended questions in the NES asks respondents to

identify the things they consider to be the most important problems facing the nation. Since these questions are not directly related to party evaluations, the responses are not shown here. But the percentage of respondents identifying a religious, cultural, or moral matter as one of the most important problems follows a very similar pattern to those for party likes and dislikes and party differences. That indicates that the American public finds these issues to be increasingly salient politically.

10. Since these questions were not asked in 1966, 1970, or 1974, the values for those years were computed through linear interpolation. The party differences questions may provide a more direct measure of the extent to which citizens perceive clear differences between the parties' cultural and moral stands. However, the likes/dislikes questions were asked more consistently than were the party differences questions, and the mean number of religious, cultural, and moral mentions to the likes/dislikes questions and the differences questions are highly correlated, both in actual values ($r = .94, p < .0001$) and in first differences ($r = .46, p < .04$). Moreover, it is unlikely that an individual would consider a religious, cultural, or moral matter to be something that he/she likes or dislikes about a political party unless he/she sees a difference between that party's stand on the issue and that of the other party.

I use the mean number of mentions rather than the percentage of total mentions to avoid eliminating the individuals who do not mention anything in response to the questions about party likes and dislikes. The correlation between the mean and percentage measures is .98 ($p < .0001$) in actual values and .92 ($p < .0001$) in first differences.

11. Specifically, the measure is (number of Republican likes − number of Republican dislikes) − (number of Democratic likes − number of Democratic dislikes).

12. The two time series are highly correlated, both in actual values ($r = .90, p < .0001$) and in year-to-year changes, or first differences ($r = .69, p = .002$).

13. The notion of Granger causality is that one series X_t (Granger) causes another series Y_t if a model in which Y_t is a function of its own past history and X_t provides better predictions of Y_t than does a model in which Y_t is a function of only its own past history.

14. Including one lag of the dependent variable in the model is a common way of modeling time dependency and is often sufficient to account for serial correlation (Beck and Katz 1996).

15. The commonly used test of serial correlation in models including a lagged endogenous variable is the normally distributed Durbin's h statistic, which tests specifically for a first-order autoregressive process in the error term (Durbin 1970). However, there is some question about whether Durbin's h is appropriate in small samples, and this statistic cannot be computed when the product of the variance of the coefficient on the first lag of the dependent

variable and the number of time points in the regression is greater than 1 (Judge et al. 1988). Thus, in addition to Durbin's *h,* I present Durbin's *m,* a test in which the residual from the regression is regressed on its first lag and all of the independent variables in the regression equation. The test is simply a standard *t*-test of the statistical significance of the coefficient of the first lag of the residual. This test is asymptotically equivalent to Durbin's *h* (Durbin 1970) and is thought to be more appropriate in small samples (Gujarati 1995). In only five of the twenty-three regression analyses presented in this chapter did either Durbin's *h* or Durbin's *m* indicate that serially correlated errors remained after one lag of the dependent variable was included in the model. In those cases, the Durbin's *h* and *m* tests indicated that first-order autoregression in the errors was no longer present after a second lag of the dependent variable was included in the model. Only the coefficients on the first lag are shown in the tables.

I also conducted the Ljung-Box (1978) small-sample *Q* test for higher-order autocorrelation for each of the regression models. In twenty-one of the twenty-three final models, *Q* was not statistically significant, indicating no autocorrelation in the errors. In the two cases in which *Q* was significant, the Durbin's *h* and *m* tests indicated that there was no first-order serial correlation in the errors. That suggests that the autocorrelation follows either a moving average or a higher-order autoregressive process. Since there are not enough data points to model the exact nature of the autocorrelation, I do not include additional lags of the dependent variable to account for it. In both cases, however, including additional lags of the dependent variable renders *Q* statistically insignificant and does not affect the substantive results.

16. The residual mean square statistic, presented in the tables, is a measure of unexplained variance in the dependent variable and can be used to compare the explanatory power of models with the same dependent variable (but not models with different dependent variables). Smaller values indicate that the regression model explains a larger proportion of the variance. Thus, the model including a four-year lag of the congressional alignment has slightly greater explanatory power than the model including a two-year lag. A regression model with a six-year lag in the congressional alignment produced nearly identical results—in terms of statistical significance and explanatory power—to the one with a four-year lag. I use the model with a four-year lag because it saves one more observation for analysis.

17. The correlation between the first-order differences (or year-to-year changes) of the mass religious alignment and the relevance of cultural matters to party evaluations is .58 ($p = .01$). The correlation between the first-order differences of the mass religious alignment and the relationship between party affect and religious orthodoxy is .52 ($p = .03$).

18. The residual mean square statistics also indicate that models of the mass religious alignment that include measures of relevance and polarized

affect, in addition to the congressional alignment, have much greater explanatory power than do models that include only the elite cultural alignment.

19. Carmines and Stimson (1989) define activists as those respondents who perform four or more of the six acts of participation. However, because of the decline in overall participation levels over time, using four acts as the threshold resulted in samples of activists that were too small to be reliable in the late 1980s and 1990s. Other recent work also uses three acts as the threshold (Fiorina 1999).

20. The mean number of political activities performed in the 1996 NES was 1.28 for all respondents and 1.01 for nonactivists, and I already have noted that the respondents who engage in three or more activities represent a very small percentage of the sample. Moreover, the mean score on a "political awareness" scale, based on political knowledge questions in the 1996 NES (see Zaller 1992), that ranges from 0 to 25.4 is 18.1 for activists and 12.9 for nonactivists, a statistically significant ($p < .0001$) difference.

21. The regression of the activist alignment on a two-year lag of the congressional cultural alignment produced the following results:

$$\text{Activist}_t = -.20 + .19(\text{activist}_{t-1}) + 2.43(\text{Congress}_{t-2}),$$

with the congressional series having a statistically significant effect ($t = 1.86$). The number of observations for this regression was thirteen, and the adjusted R^2 was .24. Neither Durbin's h nor Durbin's m was statistically significant. A regression of the activist alignment on the current value of the congressional alignment did not uncover a statistically significant effect for the congressional series and had less explanatory power (residual mean square = .66) than this model (residual mean square = .54).

22. The results in table 6.2 represent the best models in terms of statistical significance and explanatory power. The two-year lag of the congressional alignment does not have a statistically significant effect on the nonactivist alignment, and the four-year (or two-period) lag of the activist alignment does not have a significant effect.

23. The model including the six-year lag of the congressional alignment has much greater explanatory power (residual mean square = 13.41) than models including a four-year lag, a two-year lag, and the current value of the congressional alignment (residual mean square = 32.72, 35.03, and 36.48, respectively).

24. The Durbin's h and m statistics are very close to statistical significance in the first model, indicating a strong possibility of first-order autocorrelation in the residuals. I included up to four lags of the dependent variable as independent variables to account for this, but Durbin's h and m remained marginally significant (and the six-year lag of the congressional alignment remained highly significant). This suggests that the model is

probably misspecified, and when the cultural relevance and party affect variables are included in the fourth model in the table, the evidence for first-order autocorrelation disappears.

25. The correlation between the first differences of, or year-to-year changes in, the evangelical party alignment and of the relevance of religious and cultural matters to their party evaluations is .53 ($p = .03$). The correlation between the first differences of the evangelical alignment and of evangelical party affect is .80 ($p = .0001$).

Exploring the Divide: How and When Religion Matters for Contemporary Political Behavior

BY NOW IT SHOULD BE clear that religion, particularly the tradition-alist–modernist religious conflict, matters for American party politics and political behavior, and that its political impact is growing over time. Religious, moral, and cultural concerns are the central motivations for many activists in both parties, and the types of activists attracted to each party have become more and more religiously distinct. The Republican activist base has witnessed a sharp increase in the presence of committed evangelical Protestants and a substantial decrease in the representation of nominally religious mainline Protestants. Democratic activists, as a group, have become less religiously committed and less likely to affiliate with a religious denomination or movement.

Associated with this activist-level religious change has been a grow-ing division of the parties' mass coalitions along traditionalist–modernist lines. Within the Republican coalition, the representation of committed Catholics and particularly committed evangelicals has increased while the presence of more-liberal Protestant groups has declined. The presence of secularists in the Democratic electoral coalition has increased consid-erably. Meanwhile, partisan divisions also have developed within the major religious traditions with the most doctrinally orthodox and reli-giously committed evangelical Protestants, mainline Protestants, and Catholics growing more Republican relative to their less orthodox and committed counterparts.

The focus of this chapter is on the political behavior of individual American citizens. Since we know now that religious traditionalism mat-ters for American political behavior, the logical next question is, how does it matter? Does it have a direct impact on political orientations such as party identification and voting behavior? Or, is its effect on these variables indirect, working through certain political values or positions on particular political issues? Answering these questions should provide insight into not only how religious traditionalism affects the current political behavior of individual citizens, but also why its political impact has grown over time. If the effect of religion is direct, then the growth is most likely the result of an increase in the direct relationship between religious traditionalism on the one hand and partisanship and vote choice on the other. If the effect is indirect through certain attitudes or values, then the growth is most likely the result of an increase in the relationship between those attitudes and values and partisan political behavior.

The impact of religious traditionalism on party loyalties and electoral choice is most likely indirect. Past research shows that the effects of sociodemographic factors such as race, ethnicity, and region on electoral behavior are indirect, working through political predispositions, evaluations of candidate qualities, and attitudes on policy issues (Page and Jones 1979; Miller and Shanks 1996). Studies focused on the political importance of religious factors such as tradition, commitment, and doctrinal orthodoxy find similar indirect effects (cf. Jelen 1991; Kellstedt and Kelly 1998; Miller and Shanks 1996: 233–54).

Furthermore, I argued in chapter 1 that for a "structural" cleavage such as religion, ethnicity, or geography to become a partisan cleavage, it must be associated with a set of genuinely political issues; it has to give rise to questions of the proper course of government action. Thus, an individual's level of religious traditionalism affects his or her party loyalties and electoral decisions because traditionalist–modernist religious orientations produce distinct attitudes on political issues, and those attitudes are directly related to party identification and vote choice. In other words, the parties' officeholders, candidates, and platforms generally do not espouse positions directly on matters of theology or religious practice. But they may take positions on issues of government policy that divide citizens with different religious affiliations, beliefs, and practices. These issue differences then may lead to differences in partisan political behavior.

If religious traditionalism does not have a direct impact on political behavior but is instead linked to partisan orientations and electoral choice by attitudes toward particular political issues, what types of issue attitudes are most likely to provide this link? The answer clearly is the issues associated with the contemporary cultural conflict: those such as abortion, homosexual rights, women's rights, and school prayer. I showed in chapter 2 that there is a very close relationship between cultural issue attitudes and evaluations of the groups related to those issues on the one hand and religious commitment, doctrinal orthodoxy, and religious tradition on the other hand. Religious traditionalism is much more weakly associated with issues not as closely related to questions of personal morality and public moral standards—issues such as economic redistribution, racial equality, and the proper course of foreign policy (Jelen 1991; Layman and Green 1998).

Moreover, in several places in this book, I have demonstrated the close relationship between partisan religious polarization and the growing division between the two parties on cultural issues. Chapter 3 showed that religious changes among party activists have occurred alongside growing cultural differences between Democratic and Republican activists. Chapter 5 showed the same thing in the parties' mass coalitions. Chapter 6 showed that there has been a close connection between the polarization of the parties in government on cultural issues and the division of the parties' mass coalitions along the lines of religious traditionalism. In short, the impact of traditionalist–modernist religious orientations on political behavior should be exerted principally through attitudes toward cultural issues and the groups involved in politicized cultural conflicts.

Another important question that follows from the realization that religious traditionalism matters politically is, When does it matter? Does it matter in all political campaigns and electoral contexts? Does it matter for all citizens? Of course the answer is no. There may never have been a social cleavage or a political issue for which the answer to these questions was an unequivocal yes. The political importance of all socio-demographic factors and issues varies according to the type of office up for election, the issue positions of the candidates and the emphasis that they place on certain factors, and the political priorities of the voters themselves (RePass 1971; Shafer 1991; Carsey 2000).

Of course, during certain extraordinary electoral periods, namely, the major partisan realignments in American history, there have been certain issues that consistently dominated political debate and played a consistently important role in shaping electoral choice. That was true of the slavery issue in the 1860s, currency reform in the 1890s, the role of government/social welfare issues in the 1930s, and perhaps even civil rights issues in 1964. For these issues, in these electoral eras, the answers to the questions "When does it matter?" and "For whom does it matter?" may have been very simple and not terribly interesting: all the time and everyone.

In the 1930s, for example, the issue of government's role in promoting social welfare probably dominated most political campaigns, and the socioeconomic factors that shaped individual attitudes toward this issue probably played an important role in shaping the decisions of almost all voters.

The overwhelming majority of political issues, however, do not meet the criteria of major realigning issues, dominating political debate and pushing all other issues to the political background. For these issues, the question of when they and the social cleavages related to them matter for electoral behavior is much more important. They are likely to have a significant political impact only in certain types of campaigns and electoral contexts and only for certain types of voters.

Religious, moral, and cultural concerns clearly have not reached the level of political dominance achieved by the issues associated with major partisan realignments. They have become more salient to voters, more relevant to their partisan evaluations, and more influential in their electoral decisions. In fact, some observers argue that abortion and other cultural matters have been the key issues in particular elections at both the state and federal levels (Cook, Jelen, and Wilcox 1993, 1994; Howell and Sims 1993; Abramowitz 1995; Rozell and Wilcox 1995, 1997). However, these issues still appear to be less politically important than the bread-and-butter issues of economic health, taxation, and economic redistribution.

In the 1992 presidential election, for instance, the campaign slogan of Democratic challenger Bill Clinton was "It's the Economy, Stupid," highlighting the economic downturn that plagued the administration of incumbent George Bush. As Alan Abramowitz (1995) notes in his "It's Abortion, Stupid," cultural issues did play an important role in the 1992 election. But, despite attempts by Bush and Vice President Dan Quayle to turn the election into a referendum on foreign policy, traditional "family values," and pregnancies by single mothers on prime-time television, Clinton's success seemed to indicate that the most salient concerns of voters were the health of the economy and whose plan to fix it was most viable (Abramson, Aldrich, and Rohde 1995).

In 1994, the Republican minority in the House of Representatives took the unusual step of drafting a national platform on which all Republican House candidates would run. That platform, called "The Contract with America," may have been less politically important than President Clinton's low approval ratings, but it still played a significant role in helping the GOP to regain control of both houses of Congress for the first time in forty years. The "Contract," however, did not include a word about cultural or moral issues, focusing instead on economic and social welfare matters such as tax cuts, reduction of federal spending, and reform of the federal welfare system that the Republicans felt would resonate better with voters. President Clinton's relatively easy reelection victory in 1996 certainly was aided by a booming stock market, impressive rates of economic growth, and very low interest and unemployment rates (Abramson, Aldrich, and Rohde 1999).

Figure 7.1 addresses the relative political salience of economic, social welfare, and cultural and moral concerns by showing the percentage of NES respondents identifying each type of issue as the "single most important problem" facing the country in presidential-election years from 1972 to 1996. The relevance of economic matters clearly varies with the nation's economic health, peaking during the "stagflation" years of the mid-1970s, rising again to a very high level during the economic recession of the early 1990s, and then dropping sharply with the rapid economic growth of the mid-1990s. These variations notwithstanding, the economy and the government's economic policy nearly always have been the issues most often identified as being most important. Social welfare issues, such as government welfare benefits and government provision of medical care, generally have been much less salient than economic concerns. But with recent legislative initiatives to reform the nation's health insurance system as well as federal welfare and Medicare programs, there has been a sharp rise in the percentage of citizens viewing these issues as the most important. Just as moral and cultural issues have become increasingly relevant to the electorate's evaluations of the parties and their candidates, the percentage of individuals viewing religious, cultural, and moral problems as being the single most important issue increased noticeably over the 1980s and 1990s. However, even by 1996, these issues were much less salient in the eyes of the average citizen than economic and social welfare issues.

There were some indications in the fall of 1998 that moral issues might be on the verge of becoming the dominant issues in American politics. With the scandal over Clinton's sexual indiscretions and misleading testimony about them dominating news coverage, public opinion polls showed that citizens found morality and the decline of moral values to be the most pressing national problems.[1] With the president's impeachment trial fresh in people's minds, with youth violence becoming more frequent, and with continued economic growth making financial concerns less pressing, some polls in 1999 continued to show that religious and

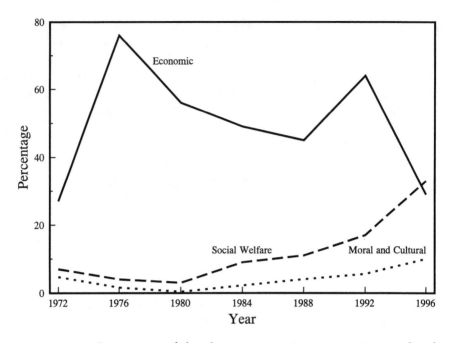

FIGURE 7.1. Percentage of the electorate viewing economic, social welfare, and religious, moral, and cultural issues as the "single most important problem," 1972–1996
Source: 1972–1996 National Election Studies.

moral matters were among the most salient issues to voters and suggested that they may play a pivotal role in the 2000 presidential campaign.[2]

At this point, however, the evidence that the political importance of these concerns is on a par with those of bread-and-butter issues is far from conclusive. For example, voters' stated concern about morality in 1998 did not appear to outweigh the ascendant economy in their political evaluations. Clinton's approval ratings remained very high, and the Democrats achieved an extremely rare feat for the party of the president, actually gaining seats in the House in a midterm-year election. Moreover, a poll conducted in July 1999 by the Pew Research Center for the People and the Press found that national morality ranked only number 10 as the most pressing political concern to voters, with three social welfare issues—health care, Social Security, and Medicare—ranking as the top three.[3]

Early in the 2000 presidential campaign, the abortion issue was a source of heated exchanges in Republican debates, and Bill Bradley and Al Gore both tried to paint themselves as the most pro-choice Democratic candidate. Meanwhile, personal and public morality—as well as abortion—was discussed frequently in the Republican campaign as those candidates tried to distinguish their potential presidencies from the Clinton presidency. However, moral and cultural issues generally took a back-seat to issues such as tax cuts, health care reform, and campaign finance reform in both parties' nomination battles.

In sum, the contemporary religious cleavage and the moral and cultural issues that surround it have not become the overriding factors shaping Americans' political behavior. They do not matter for all voters all of the time. So to understand the circumstances under which political coalitions based on religious traditionalism–modernism will emerge, it is important to find out precisely when they do matter. What types of individuals are most likely to choose their partisan ties and make their voting decisions on the basis of their religious beliefs, behaviors, and affiliations? What religious and political contexts are most conducive to linking religious orientations and political judgements?

The preceding chapters point to clear expectations about the types of individuals for whom religious traditionalism matters politically and the types of circumstances under which religion-based political behavior is most likely to occur. I showed in chapter 6 that the polarization of the parties' elites on cultural issues does not translate directly into similar changes in the parties' mass coalitions. Instead, the connection between elite cultural change and the religious reshaping of the Democratic and Republican coalitions has been facilitated by a growing mass perception of important differences in the positions of the two parties on religious, cultural, and moral matters and the growing relevance of these issues to citizens' affective evaluations of the two parties.

Of course, the political relevance of religious, moral, and cultural matters varies not only over time, but also across individuals. As the literature on issue voting indicates, particular issues are more important to some individuals than to others, and the political impact of issues is greatest for those individuals who find them to be particularly salient (RePass 1971; Brody and Page 1972; Rabinowitz, Prothro, and Jacoby 1982; Krosnick 1991). Moreover, before an issue can affect an individual's voting decisions, the individual must see a difference between the two parties and their candidates on the issue (Campbell et al. 1960; Key 1966; Page and Brody 1972). So religious traditionalism should have a greater effect on the electoral behavior of individuals who find religious, cultural, and moral matters to be politically salient and who see important differences between the parties' orientations on these issues.

In addition to individual-level variance in the salience of moral and cultural issues, it is undoubtedly true that some individuals are better able than others to link their religious and cultural inclinations to support for the party or candidate that best represents those inclinations. One reason simply may be variance in political "awareness": the extent to which an individual pays attention to politics and is able to understand what he or she encounters (Zaller 1992). In *The Nature and Origins of Mass Opinion*, John Zaller (1992) demonstrates that individuals with high levels of political awareness are far more likely than less aware individuals to receive political information, as well as to reject information that runs counter to their political predispositions. Thus, politically aware citizens are much better able than politically unaware citizens to connect their predispositions to the appropriate policy attitudes and to support for the appropriate political candidates.

The same thing should be true for the connection between religious orientations and electoral behavior. Among committed, doctrinally orthodox evangelical Protestants, for example, politically aware individuals should be more likely than less aware individuals to receive information about the stands of the parties and their candidates on cultural and moral issues such as abortion and homosexuality. They should be more likely to know which party and which candidates better represent their own culturally conservative views, and they also should be more likely than their less aware counterparts to reject negative information about the party and candidates that have the most culturally conservative positions. In short, politically aware orthodox evangelicals should be more likely than politically unaware orthodox evangelicals to translate their traditionalist religious orientations into support for the Republican party and its candidates. The impact of religious traditionalism on electoral behavior should increase with political awareness.

Also affecting the ability of individuals to effectively connect their religious and moral values to partisan choice is, of course, the degree to which their religious experiences are politicized: the extent to which they encounter political stimuli in their churches and other religious settings. When individuals hear from their religious leaders or from fellow parishioners that their religious values compel them to support particular political causes, parties, or candidates, the link between those values and their political behavior should grow stronger. The leaders of the Moral

Majority and other early organizations of the Christian Right understood this when they identified evangelical Protestant clergy as key components in their efforts to mobilize evangelical Protestants into culturally conservative Republican politics. Evangelical pastors would be, to some extent, the liaisons to their congregations. If Christian Right leaders could convince them of the necessity of evangelical political action, then the clergy would help to link evangelical religious values and Republican political activity in the minds of their parishioners (Guth 1983; Shupe and Stacey 1984).

The notion that receiving political cues in religious contexts strengthens the link between religious orientations and political behavior is supported by considerable research. A number of studies show that the religious and political values of an individual's pastor and the members of an individual's church congregation exert a significant influence on the individual's political attitudes and behavior, even when the individual's own religious and political orientations are taken into account (Wald, Owen, and Hill 1988, 1990; Jelen 1992; Huckfeldt, Plutzer, and Sprague 1993). In short, the connection between religious traditionalism and political behavior should be greater for those individuals who experience efforts at political mobilization in church or in other religious settings than for individuals who are not exposed to political stimuli in religious settings.

Finally, the political importance of moral and cultural concerns and the degree to which the parties and candidates differ on them also vary across political contexts. Democratic and Republican activists and elites are more sharply divided along religious and cultural lines in some states, cities, and towns than in others. Greater religious polarization among elites and activists should lead to larger cultural divisions between Democratic and Republican candidates and to moral and cultural issues receiving more attention in campaigns. Consequently, the more the party elites and activists in a locale are polarized along religious and cultural lines, the larger the impact of religious traditionalism on political behavior should be.

In the remainder of this chapter, I present empirical tests of these hypotheses about how and when religious traditionalism matters for American political behavior. I first construct a path model of the manner in which religious factors affect party identification and vote choice, and I present its results from the 1996 NES for members of the major American religious traditions. Next, I examine the changing impact of religion by testing a simplified version of the path model with data from 1980 through

252 / Exploring the Divide

1996. Finally, to identify the circumstances under which religious factors matter for political behavior, I test several models that posit that the impact of religious traditionalism on electoral choice is conditioned by various political and religious factors.

How Does Religion Matter? A Path Model of Religious Influence on Political Behavior

The indirect effects of traditionalist–modernist religious orientations on party loyalties and voting decisions should be exerted primarily through attitudes toward cultural issues and evaluations of the groups involved in cultural conflicts: groups such as homosexuals, feminists, pro-life and pro-choice advocates, and members of the political organizations of the Christian Right. However, to gain a precise sense of the direct and indirect impact of religious traditionalism, it is not enough simply to include cultural issue and group attitudes in models of religion and political behavior. Such models would ignore the possibility that some of the influence of religious orientations on electoral choice is channeled through attitudes toward other types of policy issues and other types of politically relevant groups. Failing to account for these attitudes also would overestimate the impact of cultural attitudes on partisanship and vote choice. Thus, to gain a full understanding of the political effects of religious traditionalism, it is necessary to examine these effects in the context of a full-scale model of electoral behavior that includes attitudes toward all the major policy conflicts in American politics as well as general ideological and partisan tendencies.

As figure 7.2 shows, my model of religious influence on political behavior is quite simple. Only two sets of variables—attitudes toward major policy-related conflicts and general ideological and partisan orientations—intervene between the various facets of religious traditionalism—doctrinal orthodoxy, religious commitment, and the orthodoxy of religious affiliations—and comparative evaluations of the two major-party candidates for president.[4] It certainly is simpler than the reality of how voting decisions actually are made (cf. Markus and Converse 1979; Miller and Shanks 1996). There clearly are potentially relevant variables that have been left out of the model. And some of the variables in the model are combinations of other variables that may have unique relationships with religious orientations and with political behavior.[5] However, my purpose here is not to identify the exact path through which religious tradition-

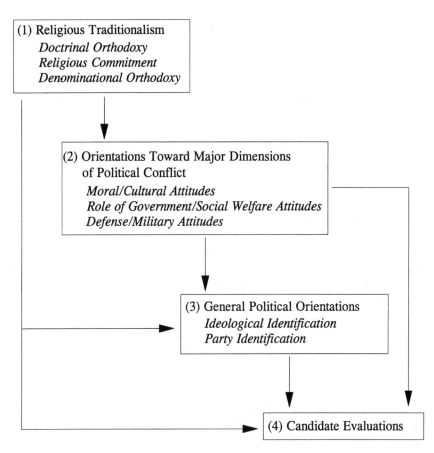

FIGURE 7.2. A path model of religious influence on political behavior

alism affects the vote, a venture that would prove difficult since not all relevant variables are included in the 1996 NES, or any survey for that matter, and since there often are not well-developed theories regarding the causal ordering of particular variables. My purpose is much simpler: finding out whether traditionalism has a direct or an indirect impact on political behavior and assessing whether or not the bulk of its indirect impact is exerted through moral and cultural attitudes. This simple model serves that purpose as well as, and perhaps better than, a more complex and nuanced model.

The model assumes that religious traditionalism—as well as other sociodemographic variables—may have direct effects on general political orientations such as ideological identification, party identification, and, ultimately, comparative candidate evaluations. However, part of—I expect most of—their total effects on these political orientations are indirect, channeled through individuals' orientations toward the major dimensions of American political conflict.

The model includes orientations toward three of the most important conflicts not only in recent American politics, but in American politics over the past fifty years. The first is the contemporary cultural conflict. Again, most of the indirect political impact of religious traditionalism should be funneled through the attitudes and political values associated with this conflict. The second is the conflict over government's role in promoting the social welfare of its citizens, a conflict that emerged in the 1930s with Franklin Roosevelt's activist-government response to the Great Depression and that has intensified in the past two decades with attempts by Ronald Reagan in the 1980s and the Republican Congress in the 1990s to significantly reduce the federal government's welfare responsibilities. The third is the conflict over the proper course of U.S. foreign policy, the role of the military in that foreign policy, and the allocation of resources to the military and national defense.[6] The political centrality of these concerns ebbs and flows with periods of international harmony and disruption, but they always have a place on the national political stage.

There are, of course, political issues that do not fall into one of these conflict dimensions, but most of the major topics of political debate do. Those readers familiar with research on the structure of citizens' policy attitudes may wonder why I have not included a fourth dimension of political conflict: the conflict over government efforts to promote equality for African-Americans and other minorities. Some analyses of the dimensionality of political attitudes have uncovered a distinct racial dimension (Abramowitz 1995; Carmines and Layman 1997). And when the issue of federal efforts to guarantee the civil rights of black citizens first emerged in the 1960s, it clearly was distinct from social welfare issues, as it divided the Democratic party's majority coalition, a coalition based, in part, on social welfare liberalism (Carmines and Stimson 1989). However, the fundamental question surrounding racial issues is basically the same as that involved in social welfare issues: What role should the federal government play in promoting equality? Although the focus of the traditional social welfare issues was on economic equality and the focus of the civil rights issues of the 1960s was on political and social equality, the fundamental question was the same. Accordingly, racial and social welfare issues quickly became linked in the minds of ordinary citizens (Carmines and Stimson 1989). Moreover, the racial policy agenda since the 1960s has moved increasingly beyond questions of political and social equality toward questions of economic equality (Black and Black 1987; Wilson 1987). In fact, a major component of that agenda is government provision of social welfare assistance to poor blacks (Sniderman and Piazza 1993). So, while not all racial issues are social welfare issues, many of them are, and I include those issues in the role of government dimension of conflict.[7]

Included in the orientations toward these three dimensions of political conflict are three variables that Warren E. Miller and J. Merrill Shanks (1996) include separately in their multiple-stage causal model of the voting decision. The first are "policy-related predispositions" or "core values." These long-term predispositions toward ongoing societal conflicts have substantial effects on citizens' attitudes toward current policy issues (McClosky and Zaller 1984; Feldman 1988) and also work to shape current political behavior (Miller and Shanks 1996). One of the core values that plays a key role in shaping attitudes toward the contemporary cultural conflict, and, in fact, one that may lie at the core of that conflict (Hunter 1991), is "moral traditionalism," or one's fundamental views about whether moral values are absolute or should change as society changes and one's tolerance for those whose notions of morality differ from one's own (Conover 1983; Cook, Jelen, and Wilcox 1992; Jelen 1992; Guth et al. 1993).[8] Several scholars show that moral traditionalism intervenes between religious orientations and behaviors and political attitudes and behavior (Tamney, Johnson, and Burton 1992; Emerson 1996; Miller and Shanks 1996).

Two of the policy-related predispositions typically associated with social welfare attitudes are egalitarianism, or a belief in the fundamental value of equality in society, and support for a limited, as opposed to an activist, government (McClosky and Zaller 1984; Feldman 1988; Feldman and Zaller 1992). Core values such as patriotism, anticommunism, and isolationism play an important role in shaping attitudes toward foreign policy and national defense (Miller and Shanks 1996). Unfortunately, there are no indicators of these predispositions included in the 1996 NES survey.

The second set of variables are evaluations of the social groups involved in the various political conflicts. The idea that orientations toward social groups play a key role in structuring individuals' political outlooks is an increasingly popular one in political science. A number of scholars show that group affect has a profound effect on policy preferences and political behavior (Sears et al. 1980; Conover and Gray 1983; Brady and Sniderman 1985; Conover 1988; Huckfeldt and Kohfeld 1989; Miller et al. 1991; Jelen 1993). In fact, studies of political sophistication show that citizens are more likely to think about politics in group-related terms than in ideological or issue-oriented terms (Campbell et al. 1960), and that group affect allows individuals to organize political information and make more sophisticated political judgments (Brady and Sniderman 1985; Sniderman, Brody, and Tetlock 1991).

Within the literature on religion and politics, a number of recent studies show that identification with and affect toward the groups involved in the cultural conflict—groups such as evangelical, charismatic, and fundamentalist Protestants, Christian Right organizations such as the Moral Majority and the Christian Coalition, homosexuals, feminists, and pro-choice and pro-life advocates—exert a strong influence on political attitudes and behavior and play a key role in linking religious variables to those political orientations (Smidt 1988; Smidt and Penning 1991; Jelen 1991, 1992, 1993; Wilcox, Jelen, and Leege 1993; Miller and Shanks 1996; Bolce and De Maio 1998, 1999). The 1996 NES asked respondents to rate four groups involved in the cultural conflict—the women's movement, gays and lesbians, Christian fundamentalists, and the Christian Coalition—on "feeling thermometers" ranging from the most negative to the most positive feelings about the groups. It also included feeling thermometer ratings of the group most closely associated with federal welfare policy, namely, welfare recipients. Particularly relevant to the conflict over the nation's military and defense policies are the thermometer ratings of the military.

The final and most direct indicators of orientations toward particular dimensions of political conflict are attitudes toward the particular policy issues around which the conflicts center. A large body of research shows that attitudes on political issues affect the political behavior, particularly the voting decisions, of many individuals (Key 1966; Brody and Page 1972; Page and Brody 1972; Aldrich, Sullivan, and Borgida 1989). Issue attitudes also play an important role in linking sociodemographic factors such as religion, race, and gender to political behavior (Page and Jones 1979; Miller and Shanks 1996). Relevant to the cultural conflict are questions in the 1996 NES about abortion, women's rights, prayer in the public schools, homosexuals in the armed forces, and laws to protect homosexuals against discrimination. Relevant to the conflict over the welfare role of government are questions about government's responsibility to ensure that its citizens have jobs and a basic standard of living, government's responsibility to provide health insurance, government's responsibility to help African-Americans, and government spending on food stamps, welfare, child care, and programs to help the poor. The principal question about defense and foreign policy issues in the 1996 NES was a question about spending on national defense.

To measure orientations toward each of the three dimensions of political conflict, I combine the policy-related predispositions, group evaluations, and issue attitudes relevant to that particular conflict.[9] The indicator of moral and cultural attitudes combines moral traditionalism, evaluations of the groups such as homosexuals and fundamentalist Christians that are involved in the cultural conflict, and attitudes toward cultural issues such as abortion and school prayer. The index of role of government and social welfare attitudes combines egalitarianism, support for limited government, evaluations of welfare recipients, and attitudes toward several social welfare issues. The measure of military and defense attitudes combines evaluations of the military and attitudes on defense spending.[10]

These policy orientations have direct effects on the general political orientations of ideological identification and party identification, and direct and indirect effects on comparative evaluations of the Democratic and Republican presidential candidates.[11] Ideology and partisanship both have direct effects on candidate evaluations.[12]

The Political Impact of Religious Traditionalism
for All Citizens

I began by estimating two separate versions of the path model for all citizens in 1996. The first includes religious commitment and doctrinal orthodoxy, together with dummy variables for the major religious traditions and seculars. The second provides an examination of the joint effect of all aspects of religious traditionalism by including the "religious traditionalism" index, discussed in chapter 2, which combines doctrinal orthodoxy, religious commitment, and the denominational orthodoxy scale. Table 7.1 shows the direct effects of doctrinal orthodoxy, religious commitment, and overall religious traditionalism on orientations toward the cultural conflict, the conflict over the welfare role of government, and the conflict over military and defense policy. It then shows the direct effects of these religious orientations on ideology, party identification, and candidate evaluations, together with the total indirect effects of the

TABLE 7.1

Direct and indirect effects of religious orientations on the political values, attitudes, and behavior of all citizens, 1996

Dependent Variable	Direct	Indirect	Total
(1) Orientations toward major dimensions of political conflict			
Moral/cultural attitudes			
Doctrinal orthodoxy	.37	—	.37
Religious commitment	.29	—	.29
Religious traditionalism[a]	.58	—	.58
Role of government/social welfare attitudes			
Doctrinal orthodoxy	.12	—	.12
Religious commitment	0	—	0
Religious traditionalism	.13	—	.13
Defense/military attitudes			
Doctrinal orthodoxy	.12	—	.12
Religious commitment	0	—	0
Religious traditionalism	.14	—	.14

		Through Ideology[b]	Through Moral and Cultural Attitudes[c]	Through Social Welfare Attitudes[d]	Through Defense Attitudes[e]	
(2) General political orientations						
Ideological Identification						
Doctrinal orthodoxy	0	—	.13	.04	.02	.19
Religious commitment	.08	—	.11	0	0	.19
Religious traditionalism	.10	—	.20	.05	.02	.37
Party identification						
Doctrinal orthodoxy	0	—	.10	.05	.01	.16
Religious commitment	0	—	.08	0	0	.08
Religious traditionalism	0	—	.15	.05	.01	.21
(3) Candidate evaluations						
Doctrinal orthodoxy	0	0	.14	.04	.01	.19
Religious commitment	0	.01	.11	0	0	.12
Religious traditionalism	0	.01	.22	.04	.01	.28

Source: Entries are standardized path coefficients from regressions using the 1996 NES and including controls for gender, age, education, income, southern residence, and race. For each dependent variable, one regression analysis included doctrinal orthodoxy, religious commitment, and dummy variables for various religious traditions, and a second regression analysis included the religious traditionalism index.

All non-0 paths are significant at $p < .05$. All path coefficients of 0 indicate that the effect is not statistically significant. Positive coefficients indicate that increases in the variable are associated with greater conservatism and Republican support.

[a] Composite index of doctrinal orthodoxy, religious commitment, and denominational orthodoxy.

[b] Indirect effects are based on the direct effect of the religious orientation on ideological identification.

[c] Indirect effects are through orientations toward the cultural conflict.

[d] Indirect effects are through orientations toward the role-of-government/social welfare conflict.

[e] Indirect effects are through orientations toward the defense/military conflict.

religious variables that are exerted through orientations toward the three political conflicts. Because some of the religious orientations exert a direct influence on ideological identification, the table also shows that portion of their indirect effects on candidate evaluations that is channeled directly through ideology.

It is clear that the relationship between religious orientations and moral and cultural attitudes is very strong. Doctrinal orthodoxy and religious commitment both have very substantial effects on orientations toward the cultural conflict, and the impact of overall religious traditionalism is particularly impressive. The effect of religious variables on orientations toward the other political conflicts is considerably weaker. Doctrinal orthodoxy and overall traditionalism both have some effect on social welfare and defense attitudes, but the effects are much smaller than the impact of these variables on moral and cultural orientations. Religious commitment has no impact on the values and attitudes associated with either the role of government conflict or the defense and military conflict.

The impact of traditionalist–modernist religious orientations on political behavior is primarily indirect, but religious commitment and overall religious traditionalism both have modest direct effects on ideological identification, with greater commitment and traditionalism leading to greater conservatism. A noticeable portion of the indirect effects of doctrinal orthodoxy and religious traditionalism on ideology, partisanship, and candidate evaluations are exerted through attitudes toward the social welfare role of government. However, the large majority of the indirect effects of religious traditionalism—in fact, the large majority of its total effects—on these political orientations is channeled though orientations toward the contemporary moral and cultural conflict, and that is true for all three indicators of religious traditionalism. It is clear that the cultural battles that have raged in American party politics over the last three decades constitute far and away the most important reason for the current connection between traditionalist–modernist religious orientations on the one hand and ideological leanings, partisanship, and voting decisions on the other hand.

The Political Impact of Religious Traditionalism Across Religious Traditions

Since the political consequences of doctrinal orthodoxy and religious commitment vary across religious traditions, an important question is whether both the overall political impact of religion and the way in which religion is connected to politics also vary across traditions. To address that question, I estimated path models for the three largest religious traditions: evangelical Protestants, mainline Protestants, and Catholics. Table 7.2 shows the direct and indirect effects of doctrinal orthodoxy and religious commitment on the ideological identifications, party identifications, and comparative candidate evaluations of the members of those traditions. It also shows the portion of the indirect effect of religious orientations that is exerted through orientations toward the three major political conflicts, as well as the portion of the indirect effect on candidate evaluations that is funneled directly through ideological and party identification.

One of the recurring themes in this book is the stronger relationship between religious commitment and political conservatism/Republicanism among evangelical Protestants than among mainline Protestants and Catholics. The organizations of the Christian Right have focused their mobilization efforts on evangelical churches, evangelical clergy have highly conservative attitudes on most political issues and have become increasingly willing to express those conservative political views from the pulpit, and there is a conservative religious, cultural, and political consensus that exists in evangelical congregations (Guth et al. 1997; Wald, Owen, and Hill 1988). Mainline Protestant clergy, in contrast, tend to have views on cultural issues that are more liberal than those of their congregants; their views on other domestic issues tend to have a social justice flavor, pointing toward support for government welfare programs and efforts to promote equality for racial minorities; and they tend to oppose defense buildups and the use of military force in solving international disputes (Guth et al. 1997). The Catholic Church has officially taken conservative stands on abortion, homosexuality, and some matters related to gender equality, but since the Vatican II conference in the 1960s, it also has been supportive of economic and racial justice and nonmilitary solutions to foreign policy problems (Wald 1997). Catholic and mainline Protestant parishioners are much less uniformly conservative in their theological perspectives, cultural and moral values, and political outlooks than are members of evangelical churches. Thus, the experience of attending church and being involved in the religious life of a congregation should be less likely to produce conservative political attitudes and pro-Republican political behavior among mainline Protestants and Catholics than among evangelical Protestants.

Here, these expectations once again are met. The political impact of religious commitment for evangelicals dwarfs its impact for Catholics,

TABLE 7.2

Direct and indirect effects of religious orientations on the political behavior of evangelical Protestants, mainline Protestants, and Catholics, 1996

Religious Tradition and Dependent Variable	Direct Effect	Indirect Effect					Total Effect
		Through Ideology[a]	Through Party Identification[b]	Through Moral and Cultural Attitudes[c]	Through Social Welfare Attitudes[d]	Through Defense Attitudes[e]	
Evangelicals							
Ideological identification							
Doctrinal orthodoxy	0	—	—	.10	.05	0	.15
Religious commitment	.19	—	—	.12	0	0	.31
Party identification							
Doctrinal orthodoxy	0	—	—	.04	.05	0	.09
Religious commitment	.17	—	—	.05	0	0	.22
Candidate evaluations							
Doctrinal orthodoxy	0	0	0	.12	.04	0	.16
Religious commitment	0	.03	.09	.14	0	0	.26
Mainline Protestants							
Ideological identification							
Doctrinal orthodoxy	0	—	—	.14	0	0	.14
Religious commitment	0	—	—	0	0	0	0
Party identification							
Doctrinal orthodoxy	0	—	—	.08	0	0	.08
Religious commitment	0	—	—	0	0	0	0
Candidate evaluations							
Doctrinal orthodoxy	0	0	0	.10	0	0	.10
Religious commitment	0	0	0	0	0	0	0

Catholics

Ideological identification							
Doctrinal orthodoxy	0	0	—	.11	0	.02	.13
Religious commitment	0	0	—	.05	0	0	.05
Party identification							
Doctrinal orthodoxy	0	0	—	.08	0	0	.08
Religious commitment	0	0	—	.04	0	0	.04
Candidate evaluations							
Doctrinal orthodoxy	0	0	0	.11	0	.01	.12
Religious commitment	0	0	0	.05	0	0	.05

Source: Entries are standardized path coefficients from regressions using the 1996 NES and including controls for gender, age, education, income, and southern residence (and, for Catholics, race).

All non-0 paths are significant at *p* < .05. All path coefficients of 0 indicate that the effect is not statistically significant. Positive coefficients indicate that increases in the variable are associated with greater conservatism and Republican support.

[a]Indirect effects are based on the direct effect of the religious orientation on ideological identification.

[b]Indirect effects are based on the direct effect of the religious orientation on party identification.

[c]Indirect effects are through orientations toward the cultural conflict.

[d]Indirect effects are through orientations toward the role-of-government/social welfare conflict.

[e]Indirect effects are through orientations toward the defense/military conflict.

and commitment has no direct or indirect effects on the political orientations and behavior of mainline Protestants.

Among evangelicals, commitment exerts a substantial indirect effect through moral values and cultural attitudes on ideological identification, party identification, and comparative candidate evaluations. It also has a noticeable direct effect on ideological conservatism and Republican party identification. The fact that this direct effect exists even when I control for moral and cultural attitudes and orientations toward other policy conflicts provides convincing evidence for the strong connection between evangelical Protestantism and conservative Republicanism. Being involved in the religious life of an evangelical congregation of course makes one more conservative and Republican by increasing one's moral and cultural traditionalism. But it now seems that there are such close ties between evangelical churches, conservative political causes, and the Republican party that evangelical religious devotionalism creates bonds with conservatism and the GOP over and above its impact on one's moral and cultural outlook.

There is also some variance across traditions in the political impact of doctrinal orthodoxy. Among mainline Protestants, orthodoxy is connected to conservatism and Republicanism solely because of its relationship with moral and cultural traditionalism. A small portion of the effect of orthodoxy on the ideological orientations and candidate evaluations of Catholics is channeled through defense and military attitudes, but the large majority of the effect is exerted through moral and cultural attitudes. Among evangelical Protestants, in contrast, a noticeable share of the total effect of doctrinal orthodoxy on ideology, partisanship, and candidate evaluations is the result of its connection to social welfare conservatism. The reason may be that evangelical Protestant theology is highly individualistic, focusing more on individual salvation and the personal relationship with God than on bettering the society to create a "Kingdom of God on earth," and that theological individualism leads to economic individualism and thus to a rejection of collective, governmental efforts to ensure the welfare of citizens (Barker and Carman 2000). Meanwhile, mainline Protestant and Catholic doctrines place more emphasis on "good works" and applying Christian beliefs to societal betterment, and the clergy of these traditions tend to be committed to collective efforts at achieving economic and social justice.[13]

Despite these differences in the impact of religious commitment and doctrinal orthodoxy across religious traditions, there are also some strong similarities. First, doctrinal orthodoxy has a noticeable impact on conservatism and Republicanism within all three traditions, and the size of that effect is similar for Catholics and both Protestant groups. Second, the large majority of the total effect of orthodoxy on candidate choice is funneled through moral and cultural attitudes in all three traditions. In fact, just as was the case for all citizens, the bulk of the indirect effects of both indicators of religious traditionalism is exerted through orientations toward the contemporary cultural conflict. It seems clear that the transformation of this cultural conflict into a political conflict is the principal reason for the current relationship between the traditionalist–modernist religious divide and political behavior.

The Growing Political Impact of Religious Traditionalism

Evidence provided in earlier chapters certainly supports this idea. In chapters 5 and 6, I showed that there has been a close relationship over time between the religious alignment of the parties' mass coalitions and the polarization of the parties' coalitions on cultural issues, the cultural polarization of the parties in Congress, and the relevance of cultural concerns to mass evaluations of the parties. All of this evidence, however, has been presented at the aggregate level. To be able to say conclusively that the primary reason that the impact of traditionalist–modernist religious orientations on individual electoral behavior has grown is that the political importance of moral and cultural issues has grown, I need individual-level evidence. I need to show that the increase in the total effect of religious traditionalism on political behavior has resulted principally from an increase in its indirect effects through cultural attitudes.

To examine changes over time in the indirect effects of religious traditionalism on political behavior, I turn to the 1980 through 1996 NES surveys and estimate a simplified version of the path model analyzed earlier. Since the measures of policy-related predispositions and group affect included in that model are not present in all of the NES surveys over this period, this model includes only attitudes toward cultural, social welfare, and defense issues, in addition to ideological identification, party identification, candidate evaluations, and several religious and demographic control variables.[14] Table 7.3 shows the indirect effects of religious orientations on comparative evaluations of the Republican and Democratic presidential candidates through attitudes toward the three types of political issues.[15]

For all citizens, the total impact of doctrinal orthodoxy, religious commitment, and overall religious traditionalism on candidate evaluations

TABLE 7.3

The source of the indirect effects of doctrinal orthodoxy, religious commitment, and religious traditionalism on comparative candidate evaluations, 1980–1996

Group, Religious Orientation, and Year	Source of Indirect Effects			
	Through Cultural Attitudes	Through Social Welfare Attitudes	Through Defense Attitudes	Total Effect
All citizens[a]				
Doctrinal orthodoxy				
1980	.01	0	0	.01
1984	.04	.01	.03	.08
1988	.02	.01	.02	.05
1992	.07	0	.02	.09
1996	.06	.04	.02	.12
Religious commitment				
1980	.01	.04	0	.05
1984	.05	0	0	.05
1988	.02	0	0	.02
1992	.06	.02	0	.08
1996	.08	0	0	.08
Religious traditionalism[b]				
1980	.02	.04	.01	.07
1984	.08	.01	.04	.13
1988	.04	.02	.04	.10
1992	.11	.05	.03	.19
1996	.12	.06	.01	.19
Evangelical Protestants				
Doctrinal orthodoxy				
1980	0	0	0	0
1984	.03	0	0	.03
1988	.02	0	0	.02
1992	.06	0	.01	.07
1996	.05	.04	.01	.10
Religious commitment				
1980	0	0	0	0
1984	.07	0	0	.07
1988	.03	0	0	.03
1992	.09	.03	0	.12
1996	.09	.03	0	.12
Mainline Protestants				
Doctrinal orthodoxy				
1980	.05	0	0	.05
1984	.02	−.02	0	0
1988	.02	0	0	.02
1992	.04	0	.04	.08
1996	.06	.06	0	.12

TABLE 7.3 *(continued)*

Source of Indirect Effects

Group, Religious Orientation, and Year	Through Cultural Attitudes	Through Social Welfare Attitudes	Through Defense Attitudes	Total Effect
Religious commitment				
1980	.06	.01	0	.07
1984	.05	.02	0	.07
1988	.01	0	0	.01
1992	0	0	0	0
1996	.04	0	0	.04
Catholics				
Doctrinal orthodoxy				
1980	0	0	0	0
1984	.01	0	0	.01
1988	.01	0	.05	.06
1992	.03	0	0	.03
1996	.05	0	0	.05
Religious commitment				
1980	.01	0	0	.01
1984	.01	0	0	0
1988	.01	.03	0	.04
1992	.06	0	0	.06
1996	.07	0	0	.07

Source: Entries are standardized path coefficients from regression analyses using the 1980–1996 NES and including controls for gender, age, education, income, and southern residence.

All non-0 paths are significant at $p < .05$. All path coefficients of 0 indicate that the effect is not statistically significant. Positive coefficients indicate that increases in the variable are associated with greater conservatism and republican support.

[a]Two separate analyses were conducted for all citizens. One included doctrinal orthodoxy, religious commitment, and dummy variables for religious traditions in the same regression models. The other included only the religious traditionalism index.

[b]Composite index of doctrinal orthodoxy, religious commitment, and denominational orthodoxy.

has grown fairly consistently over time. Corresponding to the increase in the total effect of religion is a noticeable and, again, fairly consistent, growth in the indirect effect of religious orientations through attitudes toward cultural issues. The religious variables do have some indirect effects through attitudes on other types of issues. However, these effects are generally small and inconsistent and show no signs of increasing over time. It is clear that the political impact of religious traditionalism has grown because its indirect effect through cultural attitudes has increased.

The results for particular religious traditions are neither as strong nor as consistent, but they reach the same overall conclusion as the analysis for all citizens. Among evangelical Protestants, the impact of doctrinal orthodoxy and especially religious commitment on positive evaluations of Republican candidates and negative evaluations of Democratic candidates has clearly grown larger over time. Moreover, the bulk of that increase, particularly in the greater impact of commitment, has come through a growth in the indirect effects of these variables through cultural issue attitudes.

As shown in chapter 5, the total effect of religious commitment on the political judgments of mainline Protestants has decreased slightly over time. However, the impact of doctrinal orthodoxy on mainliners' candidate evaluations has increased noticeably. And paralleling that increase has been a steady increase, at least since 1984, in the indirect effect of orthodoxy through attitudes on cultural issues.

For Catholics, there has been a more consistent increase in the total impact of religious commitment on candidate evaluations than in the total impact of doctrinal orthodoxy. However, the impact of both variables was noticeably greater in 1996 than in 1980. Moreover, just as with all citizens and evangelical Protestants, the indirect effects of both orthodoxy and commitment through cultural attitudes have grown steadily. The evidence is clear that, both across and within religious traditions, the growing political impact of traditionalist–modernist religious divisions is primarily a result of the increasing political salience of cultural and moral concerns. The political relevance of these matters and the polarization of the parties on them have played an essential role in creating the religious divide in mass party politics.

WHEN DOES RELIGION MATTER? CONDITIONAL MODELS OF RELIGIOUS INFLUENCE ON POLITICAL BEHAVIOR

The next question to answer is, When does religious traditionalism matter for American political behavior? Does it matter more for certain types of individuals than for others? Does it have a larger impact in certain types of electoral contexts than in others? Here, I examine the role that four factors—the political salience of cultural and moral issues, political awareness, religion-based political mobilization, and the religious polarization of state party elites and activists—play in conditioning the influence of traditionalist–modernist religious orientations on individual electoral decisions.

The Conditional Effect of the Political Salience of Cultural and Moral Issues

Since religious traditionalism is connected to political behavior primarily by moral and cultural attitudes, it should have a greater effect on the electoral behavior of individuals who find cultural and moral matters to be politically salient and who see important differences between the parties' orientations on these issues. As noted in chapter 6, the NES surveys include four sets of "open-ended" questions that provide an indication of the political relevance citizens attach to particular types of concerns: questions about the likes and dislikes of the two parties' presidential candidates, questions about the likes and dislikes of the two parties, questions about important differences between the parties, and questions about the most important problems facing the country.[16] My measure of cultural issue salience is the total number of times an individual mentioned a moral or cultural issue in response to all these open-ended questions.[17]

Figure 7.3 assesses whether cultural issue salience conditions the electoral impact of religious traditionalism by showing the predicted probabilities of voting Republican for religious traditionalists and religious modernists at various levels of cultural and moral salience.[18] The conditional effect of cultural issue salience is smaller for evangelical Protestants than for members of other religious traditions because even those evangelicals who are classified, by evangelical standards, as religious modernists were quite likely to support Bob Dole, the Republican presidential candidate in 1996. However, it is clear that for all citizens and for the members of all three of the major religious traditions, the impact of traditionalist–modernist religious orientations on electoral behavior increases as cultural and moral matters become more politically salient.[19]

As with much else in contemporary religious politics, there is a clear contrast here between evangelical and mainline Protestants. The support of modernist evangelicals for Bob Dole does not decline and, in fact, increases slightly as cultural salience increases, while the likelihood of supporting Dole among modernist mainline Protestants drops off sharply. One reason may be that I employ tradition-specific standards for religious traditionalism and modernism. An individual defined as a modernist in the evangelical tradition may have fairly high levels of religious commitment

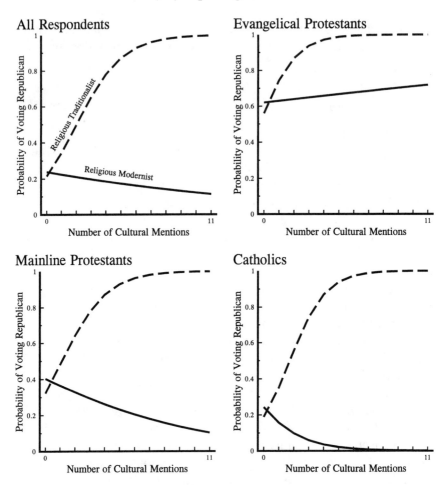

FIGURE 7.3. Impact of religious traditionalism on the predicted probability of voting Republican by the number of religious/cultural mentions to questions about party/candidate likes/dislikes, party differences, and important problems

Note: Religious traditionalists and modernists are defined as one standard deviation above and below, respectively, the mean of religious traditionalism.

Source: Computed by the author from logit analyses using the 1996 NES.

and doctrinal orthodoxy in comparison to members of other traditions, while my definition of a modernist mainliner comes closer to universal standards of religious modernism. So when modernist mainliners are concerned about cultural and moral issues, they are more likely than modernist evangelicals to be motivated by culturally liberal proclivities, and thus they are more likely to translate their religious modernism into support for Democratic candidates.

Another explanation may be the differing religious and political environments faced by evangelical and mainline Protestants. Mainline clergy tend to deliver less theologically and ideologically conservative messages than do evangelical clergy, and mainliners tend to worship in and live in less traditional and homogenous social contexts than do evangelicals. That may mean that mainline Protestants with modernist religious sensibilities and concerns about moral and cultural issues should be more likely than their evangelical counterparts to encounter a social context that is supportive of cultural liberalism and Democratic voting. At the very least, culturally concerned mainline modernists should be less likely than culturally concerned evangelical modernists to face a religious and social environment that is uniformly hostile to cultural liberalism and the cultural stands of Democratic candidates.

The varying patterns for religious modernists notwithstanding, it is clear that the electoral impact of religious traditionalism increases as the salience of cultural and moral issues increases. So when does religion matter for political behavior? This analysis, like the path analysis and the results in chapter 6, indicates that part of the answer is that it matters when the parties and their candidates differ clearly on cultural and moral issues, and when citizens find moral and cultural concerns to be politically important.

The Conditional Effect of Political Awareness

Just as the political impact of ideology and other political predispositions increases with greater political awareness (Zaller 1992), the effect of religious traditionalism on voting behavior should grow as political awareness grows. People who pay attention to politics and understand political information should be better able than less aware individuals to connect their religious orientations and the moral values that derive from them to support for the party and candidates that best represent those perspectives.

Figure 7.4 examines the effect of political awareness on the presidential voting behavior of religious traditionalists and modernists.[20] Among all respondents and in all three of the largest religious traditions, the difference in the voting behavior of religious traditionalists and modernists increases noticeably as political awareness increases. Political attention and understanding clearly enhance the connection between

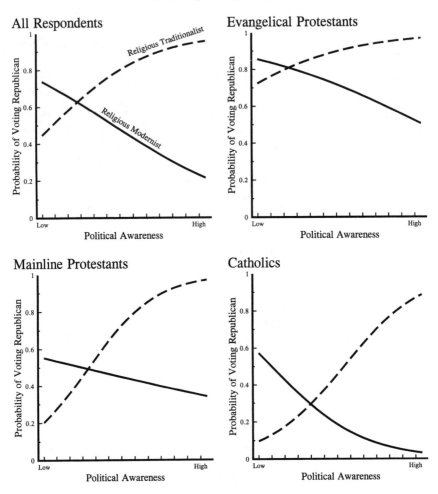

FIGURE 7.4. Impact of religious traditionalism on the predicted probability of voting Republican by level of political awareness

Note: Religious traditionalists and modernists are defined as one standard deviation above and below, respectively, the mean of religious traditionalism.

Source: Computed by the author from logit analyses using the 1996 NES.

religious orientations and political behavior. In other words, among voters who understand the relationship between their religious outlooks and issues of public policy and who recognize and understand the differences in the two parties' ideologies, there is a strong link between religious traditionalism and partisan choice.

The Conditional Effect of Religion-Based Political Mobilization

When individuals encounter political stimuli in their churches and other religious settings, the link between their religious orientations and their political behavior should be strengthened. However, the ability of religion-based efforts at political mobilization to connect religious perspectives to political decisions may be greater in some religious traditions than in others. For example, these efforts are more likely to be successful in evangelical Protestant churches than in mainline Protestant churches for at least three reasons. First, religion is more likely to be central to the lives of evangelicals than to those of mainliners (Guth and Green 1993), the congregation is more likely to be a primary source of friendships and social interaction for evangelicals than for mainliners (Ammerman 1987), and levels of church involvement are higher among evangelicals than among mainliners (Wald, Kellstedt, and Leege 1993). Evangelical Protestants thus should be more likely than mainline Protestants to pick up political cues in religious settings and to put stock in those cues.

Second, mainline Protestant congregations tend to be considerably more diverse—socially, theologically, and politically—than evangelical congregations. When mainliners pick up political cues in church, they are likely to be receiving mixed messages, many of which may run counter to their political and religious predispositions and thus do not strengthen the connection between their religious values and political behavior. Evangelicals are more likely to experience a uniform set of political cues that reenforce their religious values, their political predispositions, and the connection between them (Wald, Owen, and Hill 1990).

Third, political messages delivered from the pulpit are more likely to be viewed as authoritative by evangelicals than by mainline Protestants (Quinley 1974). Not only do mainline Protestants tend to be less religiously committed than evangelicals, but mainliners also are more likely than evangelicals to resist efforts at clerical political suasion (Hadden 1969; Fowler 1989). Moreover, mainline clergy are more likely than evangelical clergy to face congregations that are predisposed to disagree with their political directives. Mainline pastors tend to be considerably more liberal than their congregations, while the generally conservative messages delivered by evangelical clergy are received by congregations also tending toward theological and ideological conservatism (Quinley 1974; Guth et al. 1997).

To examine the conditional effect of religion-based political mobilization on the political impact of traditionalist–modernist religious orientations, I used five questions in the 1996 NES that tapped individuals' levels of exposure to political discussion and efforts at political mobilization in religious settings. The questions asked respondents whether groups concerned with moral or religious issues had tried to encourage them to vote in a particular way, whether information about candidates, parties, or political issues were made available in their churches before the election, whether clergy or other church leaders encouraged them to vote for a particular candidate or party, whether they were part of a church where politics was discussed, and whether they belonged to other groups affiliated with religion in which politics was discussed.[21]

In an analysis of the 1996 presidential vote that included the measure of exposure to religion-based political stimuli, I found that such exposure does not play a significant role in conditioning the effect of traditionalist–modernist religious orientations.[22] In other words, the direct impact of religious traditionalism on the vote does not increase with efforts at religious political mobilization.

There are several possible explanations for this lack of a conditional effect, including the strong possibility of measurement error caused by the unreliability of respondent recall of encountering political mobilization efforts. Another possible explanation is that the conditional effect of exposure to religious political stimuli may be indirect. In other words, it may not influence the direct electoral impact of religious traditionalism, but it may shape the effect of religious traditionalism on other factors that do have a direct impact on the vote, or it may affect factors that themselves condition the direct effect of religious traditionalism on the vote. Two possibilities come to mind.

First, discussions of politics in church and in other religious groups may play less of a role in shaping candidate choice than in shaping attitudes on particular political issues and evaluations of politically relevant groups. In the path analyses of the political influence of religion, I found that religious traditionalism does not, for the most part, have a direct impact on political behavior. It instead works through moral and cultural attitudes and views on other dimensions of political conflict. It would not be surprising if religion-based political mobilization also played a more direct role in shaping issue attitudes, group evaluations, and core values that themselves play a direct role in structuring electoral behavior than in influencing vote choice.

Moreover, religious leaders may be uncomfortable about directly endorsing particular political candidates, but they may see it as within their clerical boundaries to discuss the relationship between their religious faith and certain political values or particular societal and political issues (cf. Guth et al. 1997). In fact, even organizations such as the Christian Coalition or the Interfaith Alliance—groups that are grounded in particular religious perspectives but exist for clearly political purposes—rarely endorse particular candidates. Instead, they engage in "political education," through which they inform parishioners of where the group stands on key issues and where candidates stand relative to the group. A good example is the "scorecards" of candidates' stands on key issues that the Christian Coalition has distributed widely to evangelical churches, and which religiously liberal groups recently have begun distributing to mainline churches. Although they have come under fire for offering tacit endorsements, these scorecards make no explicit recommendations on candidate choice.

So the role of religious political mobilization may be to connect religious orientations to the appropriate attitudes on policy concerns that are related to voting behavior rather than connecting religious orientations directly to vote choice. Of course, most of the indirect effect of religious traditionalism on electoral behavior is exerted through moral and cultural attitudes. So if exposure to religion-based political stimuli does play an indirect role in conditioning the relationship between religious traditionalism and vote choice, its primary effect may be to strengthen the connection between traditionalism and moral and cultural conservatism.

At the same time, the link between religious values and moral and cultural attitudes may be easier to grasp for parishioners than is the link between faith and other types of political attitudes, such as perspectives on the social welfare role of government and military and defense policy. For instance, there may be a connection between the spiritual individualism of evangelical Protestant theology and economic individualism, or support for a limited welfare role for government. However, that link may be less obvious for ordinary evangelical congregants than is the link between evangelical doctrine and opposition to abortion. So political discussions from the pulpit and in other religious settings and "political education" by religion-based political organizations may play a bigger role in linking evangelical religion to social welfare conservatism than in linking evangelical faith to cultural conservatism.

The second possibility is that the political stimuli encountered in religious settings play a part not only in shaping attitudes on issues but also in determining the political importance individuals attach to them. For instance, if an individual regularly attends an evangelical Protestant or Catholic church where the pastor frequently discusses the abortion issue, it is probable that the individual will be more likely not only to have a pro-life view on abortion but also to find abortion to be politically salient. So another effect of religious political mobilization may be to make the issues most closely related to religious values, the moral and cultural issues, more relevant to individuals' political judgements.[23] Then, as I have shown, the salience of moral and cultural matters works to strengthen the direct connection between religious traditionalism and vote choice.

I conducted analyses of whether exposure to religion-based political stimuli helps to solidify the relationship between traditionalist–modernist religious orientations and moral and cultural attitudes, attitudes toward the welfare role of government, and defense and military attitudes.[24] Exposure does not have a significant effect on the connection between religious traditionalism and defense attitudes, but it does condition the relationship between traditionalism and moral and cultural attitudes for all religious traditions and between traditionalism and role-of-government attitudes for some groups.

Figure 7.5 shows the impact of religious traditionalism on moral and cultural attitudes and social welfare attitudes for individuals exposed to religious political stimuli and for individuals not exposed to such stimuli. The conditional effect on attitudes toward the cultural conflict is clear for all respondents and for members of the three largest religious traditions. Cultural conservatism increases with religious traditionalism even among those citizens who do not receive political information and appeals in religious settings, but the positive association between religious and cultural traditionalism is noticeably stronger for those individuals who do receive religion-based political cues.

Religion-based efforts at political mobilization condition the association between religious traditionalism and social welfare attitudes only for all respondents and evangelical Protestants. There is a link between evangelical traditionalism and economic individualism. But it appears that that link must be established by messages delivered from the pulpit or political discussions in other religious settings, as there is no relationship between traditionalism and social welfare conservatism for evangelicals who are not exposed to religious political stimuli. These stimuli do not affect the relationship between religious traditionalism and role-of-government attitudes among either mainline Protestants or Catholics, and there is virtually no relationship in either tradition. Given the social justice orientations of most mainline and Catholic clergy and organizations,

Moral and Cultural Attitudes

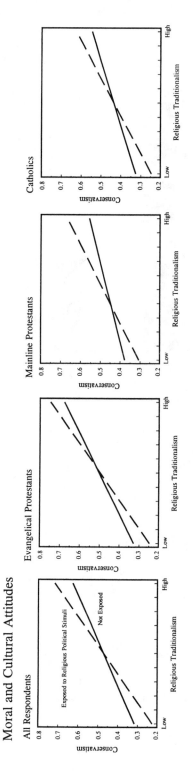

Role of Government/Social Welfare Attitudes

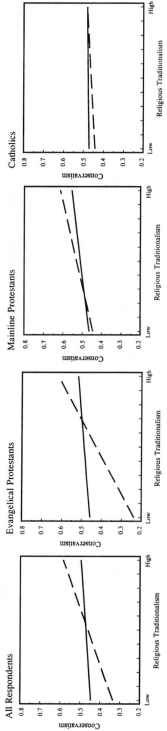

FIGURE 7.5. Impact of religious traditionalism on cultural and social welfare attitudes by exposure to religion-based political stimuli

Note: Cultural and welfare conservatism range from 0 to 1.

Source: Computed by the author from regression analyses using the 1996 NES.

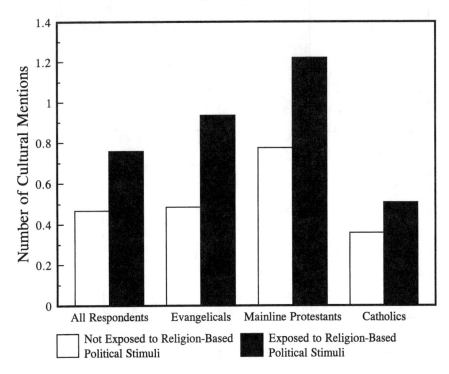

FIGURE 7.6. Impact of exposure to religion-based political stimuli on the salience of moral and cultural issues

Note: Cultural issue salience is the number of answers to open-ended questions concerning cultural, religious, or moral matters.

Source: Computed by the author from regression analyses using the 1996 NES.

most of the religion-based political information that mainline and Catholic parishioners receive on social welfare concerns is likely to have a liberal slant. Thus, it is not that surprising that exposure to religious political stimuli does not push the most committed and orthodox members of these two traditions toward greater opposition to the social welfare role of government.

So we know that religion-based political stimuli conditions the impact of religious traditionalism on attitudes toward moral and cultural matters. The question now is, Does exposure to such stimuli increase the political salience of moral and cultural concerns? In figure 7.6, I examine the direct effect of exposure to religious political stimuli on the number of moral and cultural concerns an individual mentions in response to the four types of open-ended questions in the 1996 NES.[25] It is clear that among all respondents and the two white Protestant traditions, individuals who receive political cues in religious settings are more likely than individuals who do not to find moral and cultural matters to be politically important and relevant to their political judgments. The impact of religious political stimuli is not statistically significant for Catholics.

So it appears that religion-based efforts at political mobilization do strengthen the relationship between individuals' religious orientations and their electoral decisions. They may not bolster the direct connection between religion and the vote. But they strengthen the influence of religious traditionalism on policy-related attitudes that directly affect vote choice, and they increase the political salience of moral and cultural concerns, which themselves fortify the connection between traditionalism and the vote.

The Conditional Effect of the Religious Polarization of State Party Elites and Activists

As I showed in chapter 6, the division of the parties' coalitions along traditionalist–modernist religious lines has followed from the growing religious and cultural polarization of the parties' elites and activists. This elite- and activist-level polarization has led the mass electorate to see increasing differences between the parties on moral and cultural matters and thus made it easier for individuals to choose a partisan home and make voting decisions on the basis of their religious proclivities. Of course, the level of religious and cultural polarization of Democratic and Republican activists and elites is not uniform across the country. The religious, demographic, and political environments in some areas are more conducive to partisan religious polarization than those in others. Since there are few or no data on the religious and cultural orientations of partisan elites and activists in geographic units smaller than states, I focus here on the religious and cultural polarization of state party elites and activists.

Turning to examples at the state level, some states, such as Utah or Mississippi, are more religiously homogeneous than other states, such as California or New York, and thus may have Democratic and Republican elites and activists who are less polarized along religious lines. Also, some state parties have rules and institutional arrangements that are more conducive to infiltration by insurgent groups such as religious conservatives in the Republican party and religious liberals and secularists in the Democratic party (cf. Usher 1997). Finally, for various reasons—the religious characteristics of the state population, party rules, the political and partisan environment within the state—religiously conservative political organizations such as the Christian Coalition have concentrated more resources and made stronger efforts at mobilizing constituents in some states, such as Virginia, than in other states, such as Tennessee (Persinos 1994; Rozell and Wilcox 1995, 1997). Stronger efforts at mobilizing religious conservatives into Republican party politics not only should lead to a larger proportion of religious traditionalists among Republican elites and activists, but also may result in stronger efforts at countermobilization by religiously liberal groups such as the Call for Renewal and the Interfaith Alliance (Green 1997), thus leading to greater religious polarization between Democratic and Republican elites and activists.[26]

In those states where Democratic and Republican leaders and activists are more divided along religious lines, the perception among ordinary voters of religious and cultural differences between the parties should be greater than in those states in which they are less divided. Therefore, the impact of traditionalist–modernist religious orientations on individual partisanship and voting behavior should be greater in states with higher levels of elite religious polarization.

Ideally, one would examine the religious characteristics of state party elites using surveys specifically designed to study the leaders and activists in state-level political parties. A number of surveys of state and local party activists, leaders, convention delegates, and caucus participants have been conducted in the 1980s and 1990s, and they have been usefully employed to examine the religious and cultural orientations of these political actors (cf. Baker and Steed 1992; Rozell and Wilcox 1996). However, these surveys are less useful for exploring interstate variation in party elite religious polarization and particularly for examining the effects of that variation on individual political behavior because they focus on only a small number of states.[27]

An alternative is to use the surveys of national convention delegates employed in chapters 3 and 4. The CDS surveys do present some potential problems: They include only a relatively small number of activists from each state. And since national convention delegates are focused particularly on presidential politics and are often active in the campaigns of particular presidential candidates, they may differ somewhat from the entire set of party elites and activists in a state. However, the surveys did interview delegates from all fifty states and a sizable number of delegates from a number of states. Moreover, the representativeness of their state-level samples is strengthened by the fact that convention delegates come from the ranks of state party elites and activists. Most delegates were active in politics well before the start of the current presidential campaign, and most have held either public office in the state or a position in the state party.[28] My measure of state elite religious polarization is the mean score of Republican delegates in the state on the religious orthodoxy index presented in chapter 2 minus the mean score of the state's Democratic delegates.[29]

To measure the religious orientations and political behavior of individual voters within the states, I used the election-day exit polls conducted in 1988 by CBS News and the *New York Times* and in 1992 by Voter Research and Surveys.[30] Typically, the only religious question asked in exit polls has been classification as Protestant, Catholic, or Jewish. However, beginning in 1984, some, but not all, of the exit polls began asking respondents if they considered themselves to be born-again, fundamentalist, or evangelical Christians.[31] The response to that question is used here as a rough measure of religious traditionalism.

To assess whether the impact of religious traditionalism on individual political behavior is greater in those states in which Democratic and Republican elites and activists are more polarized along religious lines than in states in which they are less religiously divided, I pooled together all the state-level exit polls from 1988 and 1992 (the years corresponding to the two CDS surveys used to create the elite polarization measure) that included the indicator of born-again/fundamentalist/evangelical Christians.[32] I then conducted analyses that assessed whether the impact of religious traditionalism on four indicators of individual partisan loyalties—party identification, presidential vote choice, gubernatorial vote choice,[33] and the vote in U.S. Senate elections—varies with the religious polarization of state party elites and activists.[34]

The religious polarization of state party elites and activists does have a significant influence on the impact of religious traditionalism on each of the four types of political behavior.[35] Figure 7.8 illustrates this by showing the levels of identification with the GOP and probabilities of voting for Republican presidential, gubernatorial, and Senate candidates for born-again/fundamentalist Christians and individuals who are not born-again or fundamentalist Christians at various levels of state party elite religious polarization. It is clear that as the level of elite and activist religious polarization in a state increases, the difference between traditionalist Christians and other individuals grows. This is true not only in statewide voting behavior, but also in party identification and presidential voting.

It appears that increases in religious and cultural conflict at the elite and activist levels of party politics are perceived by ordinary voters and

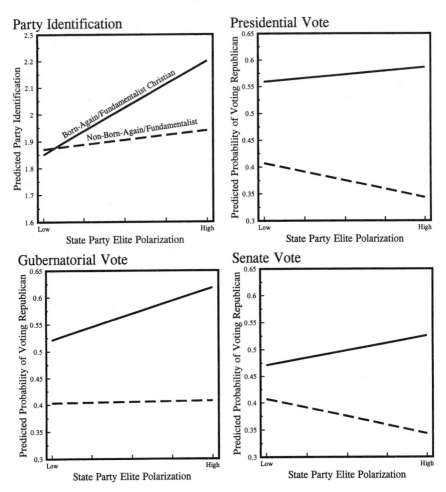

Party Identification

Presidential Vote

Gubernatorial Vote

Senate Vote

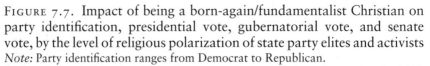

FIGURE 7.7. Impact of being a born-again/fundamentalist Christian on party identification, presidential vote, gubernatorial vote, and senate vote, by the level of religious polarization of state party elites and activists

Note: Party identification ranges from Democrat to Republican.

Source: Computed by the author from regression and logit analyses using the 1988 and 1992 State Election Day Exit Polls (pooled). State elite polarization comes from the 1988 and 1992 Convention Delegate Studies (pooled).

do strengthen the impact of religious traditionalism on their political behavior. This is further evidence that the traditionalist–modernist religious divide in the parties' coalitions in the mass electorate has resulted from the growing religious and cultural differences between Democratic and Republican leaders and activists.

SUMMARY

Since earlier chapters have shown that traditionalist–modernist religious orientations clearly matter for contemporary American political behavior, this chapter has taken up the more subtle questions of how and when religious traditionalism matters politically. I have shown that the impact of traditionalism on political behavior is largely indirect and these indirect effects are exerted primarily through moral values and attitudes toward the issues and groups involved in the contemporary cultural conflict. Meanwhile, the relationship between traditionalist–modernist religious orientations and political behavior is greatest for those individuals who find moral and cultural issues to be politically salient and see differences between the parties on them. That relationship is strengthened further when individuals live in states where the Democratic and Republican elites and activists are clearly divided along religious lines. I also showed that the link between religious and political orientations is, not surprisingly, stronger for individuals who pay attention to politics and understand the political information they receive than for less politically aware individuals. Finally, religion-based efforts at political mobilization have an indirect conditional effect on the political influence of religion, influencing factors such as cultural attitudes, social welfare attitudes, and cultural issue salience that play a more direct role in shaping electoral choice.

These individual-level findings, like the aggregate-level findings in chapter 6, point to clear expectations about the future relationship between religion and political behavior. If cultural issues continue to be politically salient and if the religious and cultural cleavage between Democratic and Republican elites and activists stays wide, the impact of religious factors such as commitment and doctrinal orthodoxy on political behavior will remain strong. However, if the parties and their candidates downplay cultural and moral issues, or if the traditionalist–modernist divide at the elite and activist levels of party politics shrinks, the influence of religion on mass political behavior may decline accordingly.

NOTES

1. Davis S. Broder, "Scandal Underlies Big Voter Shift," *Washington Post,* September 9, 1998, p. A15; CNN *Inside Politics,* September 8, 1998. [Internet, WWW] *Available:* Lexis-Nexis Academic Universe; ADDRESS: *http://web.lexis-nexis.com/universe.*

2. Will Lester, "Poll Shows Morality Is Big Concern," *Des Moines Register,* June 25, 1999, p. 8.

3. B. Drummond Ayres, Jr., "Political Briefing: No Issue Dominates the 2000 Campaign," *New York Times,* National Edition, July 25, 1999. [Internet, WWW]. *Available:* The New York Times on the Web Archives; ADDRESS: http://archives.nytimes.com.

4. Comparative evaluations of the presidential candidates are substituted for the actual presidential vote because they are measured with an interval-level variable and are thus more conducive than the dichotomous vote variable to the path analysis techniques used to compute the direct and indirect effects of religious orientations. Past research shows that comparative candidate evaluations are so closely related to the vote that they can serve as an effective proxy for the voting decision (Page and Jones 1979; Markus and Converse 1979). Candidate evaluations are measured by subtracting the respondent's rating of the Democratic candidate on a feeling thermometer ranging from 0 to 100 from the respondent's rating of the Republican candidate, so that higher scores represent more positive evaluations of the Republican candidate and more negative evaluations of the Democratic candidate. Party identification is the standard seven-point scale, ranging from strong Democrat to strong Republican. Ideological identification is the respondent's self-placement on a seven-point scale ranging from extremely liberal to extremely conservative. To limit the number of missing observations in the analyses, individuals who responded "don't know" or "haven't thought about it" to the ideology question are included with moderates in point four of the seven-point scale.

5. For example, "moral and cultural attitudes" is a variable that combines three variables examined separately in chapter 2: moral traditionalism, evaluations of groups involved in the contemporary cultural conflict, and cultural issue attitudes. Other work posits that religious orientations have more direct effects on moral traditionalism and cultural group evaluations than they do on cultural issue attitudes, while cultural issue attitudes have a more direct impact on vote choice than do the other two variables (Miller and Shanks 1996).

6. The 1996 NES, used here to examine the direct and indirect political effects of religious traditionalism, contained very few questions about defense and foreign policy issues. So the measures employed in the model tap only into attitudes toward defense spending and the military and not into views about the proper course of foreign policy.

7. More recent research on the dimensionality of political attitudes finds evidence that opinions on racial and social welfare issues form a single attitudinal dimension (Layman and Carsey 1999).

8. The measurement of all the policy-related predispositions, group evaluations, and issue attitudes used in this chapter is discussed in appendix A2.

9. In preliminary analyses, I did estimate a path model that included separate indicators of policy predispositions, group evaluations, and current policy preferences. In that model, religious orientations were followed first by policy predispositions and group evaluations, then by current policy preferences, then by ideological and party identifications, and finally by candidate evaluations. The results, in terms of the total effects of religious orientations on political behavior and the extent to which their effects are channeled through moral and cultural attitudes, were very similar to the results presented here.

10. The cultural and social welfare indices were constructed using confirmatory factor analyses. The results of these analyses and the details on constructing the indices are presented in appendix A2. The correlation between military affect and attitude toward defense spending in the 1996 NES is .40.

11. There are strong theoretical and empirical accounts contending that, in a cross-sectional sense, the causal direction of the relationship between party identification and issue attitudes (as well as perhaps group-based attitudes) is from party identification to issue attitudes rather than vice versa (cf. Campbell et al. 1960; Green and Palmquist 1990). Other research argues that the relationship between party identification, candidate evaluations, and policy attitudes is reciprocal (Page and Jones 1979). It should first be noted that the principal purpose of this analysis is not to precisely model the voting decision, but to assess the direct and indirect effects of religious orientations on political behavior. The causal ordering of political variables, it turns out, has little bearing on the overall political impact of religion. Second, it should be restated that the focus of this book is on long-term changes in partisanship. So identifying the role that moral and cultural attitudes have played in linking religious orientations to party identification is a key part of this analysis. Third, there are not enough instrumental variables in the NES surveys to estimate a full, nonrecursive model—a model in which policy attitudes, party identification, ideological identification, and candidate evaluations all exert reciprocal effects on each other—of the impact of religion on the voting decision. However, I have used two- and three-stage least squares to estimate a simpler nonrecursive model including only religious variables, demographic variables, issue attitudes, party identification, and candidate evaluations. The answers reached through that analysis to the question of how religious traditionalism exerts its influence on political behavior are very similar to those presented here.

12. The literature on partisan and ideological identifications has not established a clear causal ordering between these two variables, and the relationship between them is most likely reciprocal. So I simply model partisanship and ideology as intervening between policy attitudes and candidate evaluations and do not examine the relationship between them.

13. See Guth et al. (1997) for evidence of the strong contrast between

the economic individualism of evangelical clergy and the communitarianism of mainline clergy.

14. Also, since most of the analyses for 1996 found that religious orientations had no direct effects on party identification or candidate evaluations, this model allows them to have direct effects only on issue attitudes and ideological identification.

15. All the issue attitudes and religious orientations are measured the same way in each year. See appendices A1 and A2 for the specific measures.

16. In the 1996 NES, respondents were given the opportunity to mention up to five likes and five dislikes of each party and both candidates, up to six party differences, and up to three important problems.

17. I conducted separate logit analyses of the 1996 presidential vote using responses to each of the four open-ended questions. The conditional effects of these responses on the electoral impact of religious traditionalism were very similar to each other and to the effect of the overall measure of cultural salience shown here.

18. These probabilities are predicted from logit models of the vote that are presented in appendix B6. The key independent variables in the models are religious traditionalism, cultural issue salience, and their interaction. The models include controls for party identification, ideological identification, education, income, gender, age, southern residence, and, in the model for all respondents, race. In the model for all respondents, the measure of religious traditionalism is the religious traditionalism index, which is the combination of doctrinal orthodoxy, religious commitment, and denominational orthodoxy. For the particular religious traditions, it is the index of doctrinal–behavioral traditionalism, which is simply the combination of commitment and doctrinal orthodoxy. Religious traditionalists are defined as one standard deviation above the mean of religious traditionalism for all respondents (or the mean of doctrinal–behavioral traditionalism for the particular tradition), and religious modernists are one standard deviation below the mean.

19. In all the religious traditions and among all citizens, this increase in religious traditionalism's electoral importance results more from traditionalists becoming more likely to vote Republican than from modernists growing more likely to vote Democratic. The explanation seems to be largely statistical. For all groups other than evangelicals, religious modernists—and religious traditionalists for that matter—who fail to offer a single culturally oriented response to the open-ended questions are much more likely to vote for Bill Clinton than for Bob Dole. So as cultural salience increases, religious modernists cannot move very far in a pro-Democratic direction, certainly not as far as religious traditionalists can move in a pro-Republican direction.

20. The probabilities in this figure are predicted from logit analyses of the vote in which the independent variables are religious traditionalism, political awareness, and their interaction, in addition to several control variables.

The results of those analyses are presented in appendix B6. To create the political awareness index, I followed Zaller (1992) and used the factual items, party issue placements, and other political knowledge questions in the 1996 NES. See appendix A3 for a list of the questions used to construct the index.

21. The large majority of respondents answered in the negative to all of these questions. Nearly 77 percent of all respondents answered no to each of the five questions, and nearly 92 percent answered yes to one or fewer. The percentage answering yes to one or fewer of the questions increases to 95 among mainline Protestants. So I measure exposure to religion-based political stimuli as a dummy variable coded 1 for respondents who answered yes to at least one of the five questions.

22. The results of all the analyses of the role of religious political stimuli in conditioning the effect of religious traditionalism on the vote are presented in appendix B7.

23. Of course, frequent discussion by clergy or parishioners of nonmoral or cultural issues may make those issues more politically salient as well. I do not examine that possibility here because the salience of other types of issues does not enhance the connection between religious traditionalism and the vote.

24. I regressed the attitudes toward each of the three political conflicts on religious traditionalism, the dummy variable for exposure to religious political stimuli, their interaction, and several demographic control variables.

25. The predictions in the figure are from regressions of cultural issue salience on religious traditionalism; moral traditionalism; the extremity of individuals' cultural attitudes (since individuals with highly liberal or conservative cultural views should be more likely than cultural moderates to attach political importance to cultural and moral issues), measured as the absolute distance from the midpoint of the moral and cultural attitudes scale; the total number of responses individuals offered to all the open-ended questions (since the dependent variable is in raw numbers rather than percentages, so that it is necessary to account for the fact that some individuals simply offer more open-ended responses than others); and several demographic variables.

26. There have been numerous state-level studies that trace the reasons for Christian Right influence in the Republican party in particular states (cf. Rozell and Wilcox 1995, 1997). However, there has been little or no analysis of the factors explaining state-level variation in the religious polarization of party elites and activists. In my own preliminary analyses, I have found that crude measures of state party rules and Christian Right influence in state Republican politics have a significant influence on the level of religious polarization between Democratic and Republican elites (Layman 1996).

27. The one exception is the "Party Elites in the United States" surveys conducted by John S. Jackson III and others. However, these surveys contain

no questions that can be used as indicators of traditionalist–modernist religious orientations.

28. In the 1992 CDS, the mean number of years that respondents had been active in politics was 25. Nearly 65 percent of delegates in 1992 held or had held state public or party office.

29. Since the samples for some states in the CDS surveys are fairly small, I combined the 1988 and 1992 surveys. The religious polarization of each state's delegates is shown in appendix A4. Only thirty-four of the states are used in this analysis because the exit poll data used to measure individual-level religious and political orientations are available for only those states. Of those thirty-four states, twenty-five have samples of at least thirty Republican and thirty Democratic delegates with scores on the religious orthodoxy index, and thirty-one of the states have samples of at least twenty delegates from each party with scores on the index.

30. The biennial NES surveys cannot be used to study state-level variation in political behavior because the state samples are too small and nonrepresentative. The Senate Election Study conducted by NES in 1988, 1990, and 1992 did contain larger and more representative state samples. However, the only religious variable included in that study was religious affiliation.

31. Generally, the question combined two of these categories so that respondents were asked if they considered themselves to be "born-again or fundamentalist Christians" or "evangelical or fundamentalist Christians."

32. It may seem appropriate to include exit polls from 1990 in the analysis since they fall within the time period used to create the elite measure. However, none of the exit polls in 1990 included the born-again/fundamentalist/ evangelical indicator.

33. The results for gubernatorial voting behavior should be viewed as far from conclusive because they are based on only eight elections. Most states hold their governor's elections in non-presidential-election years. So the results here are based on elections in only five states: Indiana, New Hampshire, North Carolina, Missouri, and Washington. Exit polls were conducted in the latter three states in both 1988 and 1992, but only in 1988 in Indiana and in 1992 in New Hampshire. The results for Senate elections should be taken more seriously because they are based on thirty-nine elections in thirty states.

34. The key independent variables in these regression and logit models were the born-again indicator, the religious polarization of the Democratic and Republican activists and elites in the individual's state, and their interaction. All the models included controls for race, gender, southern residence, income, age, and identification as Protestant, Catholic, or Jewish. They also included the measure of state opinion liberalism created by Erikson, Wright, and McIver (1993), but that variable was dropped from the gubernatorial vote model because of multicollinearity. The party identification and presi-

dential vote models included the vote in the last presidential election. The models of voting behavior in governor's and senate elections included the vote in the current presidential election, dummy variables for Republican and Democratic incumbents, and the spending of the Republican and Democratic candidates. The results of these models are presented in appendix B8.

35. There is one caveat to this, which is that the interaction between the born-again indicator and state elite religious polarization was significant in the Senate model only after the 1992 Senate election in North Carolina was removed from the analysis. In that election, incumbent Democrat Terry Sanford, who voted on the liberal side on nearly all the cultural issues considered by the Senate during his term, was defeated by Republican Lauch Faircloth, a highly conservative ally of Senator Jesse Helms, who has voted on the conservative side on nearly all the cultural issues considered by the Senate since his election. Not surprisingly, identification as a born-again or fundamentalist Christian had a highly significant impact on voting behavior in that election. However, that runs counter to the hypothesis that the impact of religious traditionalism increases with state elite religious polarization, because there is virtually no difference in the religious traditionalism of Republican and Democratic activists and elites in North Carolina. So the hypothesis holds true generally, but not for this particular Senate election.

CHAPTER 8

Religious Conflict and American Party Politics: The Nature, Implications, and Future of Their Relationship

IN THE INTRODUCTION to this book, I claimed that to understand the importance of religion—particularly the cleavage between religious traditionalists and religious modernists—for American politics, it is necessary to understand American *party* politics. Comprehending why the Democratic and Republican parties are now divided along traditionalist–modernist religious lines requires more than insight into the contemporary religious cleavage and its relationship to political attitudes and behavior. It requires understanding the nature of the political parties, their institutional structures, the incentives of their members, and how those things relate to the religious divide. By the same token, if we cannot understand recent developments in religion and politics without having a grasp on party politics, then we cannot understand recent party politics without comprehending its relationship with contemporary religious divisions. And exploring that relationship may tell us something more generally about the nature of party politics and the partisan change process.

In this chapter, I assess whether these claims are true. I first ask whether a specific focus on American party politics moves us toward a firmer grasp of the political influence of religion. Next, I examine the implications of the religious change in the political party system for party politics more broadly. Specifically, I focus on what the nature of partisan religious change teaches us about the partisan change process, what the change means for the electoral coalitions of the Democratic and Republican parties and for the long-term electoral success of the two parties, and what this partisan division means for American democracy. I conclude by speculating on the future of the relationship between religion and American party politics.

THE IMPACT OF PARTY POLITICS ON CONTEMPORARY RELIGION AND POLITICS

The roots of today's cultural conflict can be traced to the development of a new cleavage in American religion in the late nineteenth and early twentieth centuries. The emergence of modern, industrial life threatened the dominant role of orthodox beliefs in Protestant, Catholic, and Jewish theology. There arose within the major faith traditions new groups of religious leaders who challenged traditional doctrines and attempted to rationalize religious beliefs with modernization. Those theological modernists were challenged by groups defending traditional religious beliefs and practices—for example, the "Fundamentalist" movement within Protestantism.

This conflict was confined largely to theological seminaries and debates among religious leaders through the 1950s, as most of American society remained firmly on the traditionalist end of the religious and moral spectrum. That changed in the 1960s as the morally liberal and largely secular baby boom generation came into politics in the form of a countercultural "New Left," challenging traditional values and seeking greater freedom for and acceptance of alternative lifestyles. The visibility of the New Left and its influence within many public and private institutions infuriated and threatened religious traditionalists and thus served to translate a division among theologians into a broader cultural conflict.

Given the fundamental differences in the values and beliefs of religious traditionalists on the one hand and religious modernists and secularists on the other, and the possibility that the tensions between these polar forces may be even greater than the old religious and cultural tensions between Protestants, Catholics, and Jews, it is no wonder that this religious cleavage has come to affect American politics. However, intense societal divisions do not necessarily become translated into divisions between the Democratic and Republican parties. The opposing forces in social conflicts have other political options: interest group politics, protest politics, even third-party politics. So, to understand why the conflict between religious traditionalists and modernists has come to affect American two-party politics, we need to understand the American political parties—their nature, their institutional structure, and the strategic incentives of their members—and how the contemporary religious cleavage interacts with these things. Of course, we need to understand the unique features of the religious and cultural cleavage, but we also need a general model of party politics and partisan change.

The Nature of Political Parties

There is, of course, a wide range of ideas about why political parties form and what their objectives are, but a commonly accepted definition of a political party is the one offered by Anthony Downs: "a team of men seeking to control the governing apparatus by gaining office in a duly constituted election" (1957: 24).[1] In other words, the purpose of a political party is to win elections in order to control government. Thus, to affect party politics, a social cleavage must give rise to grievances that people look to the government to redress—to genuine political issues. And those issues must be powerful enough and appeal to enough people to help one or both parties to win elections. Specifically, to reshape the parties' electoral coalitions, a cleavage must be associated with political issues that a large number of people feel strongly about, that are on the political agenda for a relatively long period of time, that provoke resistance (a large number of people are on both sides of the issue), and that cut across existing lines of partisan cleavage.

The traditionalist–modernist religious cleavage is associated with just such a set of political issues: cultural issues such as abortion, homosexual rights, the role of women in society, and prayer in the public schools. These issues have been on the political agenda for several decades, they arouse very strong emotions among large numbers of people in the conservative and liberal camps, and they cut directly across the class cleavage that traditionally has shaped party coalitions.

I have shown that the cultural issues, and the polarized attitudes that religious traditionalists and modernists hold on them, have played a fundamental role in translating the contemporary religious cleavage into a partisan cleavage. The growing presence of committed evangelical Protestants among Republican activists and of secularists among Democratic activists has been associated with greater differences between Democratic and Republican activists on cultural issues and between the cultural stands taken in the parties' platforms. The increasing polarization in the roll-call votes of Democratic and Republican members of Congress on cultural issues has played an important role in triggering religious changes in the parties' mass coalitions. Those mass-level changes have followed even more directly from a growing perception in the electorate that there are important differences between the two parties on cultural matters. The impact of traditionalist–modernist religious orientations on party identification and presidential vote choice is primarily an indirect one and is exerted largely through attitudes on cultural issues. Finally, the effect of religious commitment and doctrinal orthodoxy on voting behavior is much larger for those individuals who find cultural issues to be politically salient than for those individuals who do not. Clearly, a large part of the reason why the contemporary religious cleavage has come to affect party politics is that it is associated with a powerful, highly divisive set of political issues that have become a source of intense partisan conflict.

The Institutional Structure of Parties and the Role of Party Activists in Partisan Change

The intensity of the contemporary religious conflict and the fact that it gives rise to highly emotional and divisive political issues might not be enough for it to become a conflict between the two major parties if the United States had a "closed" party system, a system in which a party's leaders handpick the parties' nominees and set the parties' policy positions with minimal public participation and to the general exclusion of those who disagree with them. In such a system, insurgent groups driven by new political issues should find it very difficult to gain entry into one of the major parties. And major party leaders are unlikely to introduce extreme stands on new issues. Majority party leaders want to emphasize the old issues that made them the majority party in the first place. Even leaders of the minority party have gained their party positions or have won elective office within the context of the current political agenda, and thus they may have little incentive to disrupt that agenda (Carmines 1991). So, the groups motivated by the new issues may find other avenues of political participation—protest activity, interest group politics, or even forming a new political party—to be more fruitful than major-party politics.

The American party system of the nineteenth century approached the characteristics of a closed party system. From the 1830s on, presidential candidates were selected by national party conventions. The delegates to these conventions were handpicked by party leaders, giving party "bosses" control over party nominations and, consequently, over party positions on policy issues. Perhaps as a result, insurgent groups touting new political issues—groups such as the anti-Masons of the 1830s, the nativists of the 1850s, the abolitionists and Free-Soilers of the 1840s and 1850s, and the agrarians and Populists of the 1870s, 1880s, and 1890s—had difficulty gaining influence within the major parties and chose instead the course of forming new political parties.[2]

In the twentieth century, however, the American party system has become increasingly open. The Progressive reforms of the early twentieth century brought with them the direct primary, which gave ordinary party identifiers a role in the selection of party candidates. The McGovern-Fraser reforms of the Democratic party's nomination process in the early 1970s, and the Republican party's subsequent adherence to the same general principles, went a step further and took candidate selection almost entirely out of the hands of party leaders and gave it to the politically active citizens who participate in party primaries and caucuses. This participatory nominating process gives political activists with strong views on new political issues easy access to the two major parties.

So, if insurgent groups such as the young secularists of the New Left in the late 1960s and early 1970s and the committed evangelicals of the Christian Right in the 1980s and 1990s are large enough and politically active enough, they can exercise a great deal of influence over the types of candidates the parties nominate. And that gives them a strong say in the types of issues the parties emphasize and the types of positions that they take on those issues. The fact that these groups have more potential to influence major-party politics in an open party system provides them more incentive to become involved in one of the two major parties, as opposed to choosing an alternative political course. It is probably no coincidence that all the strong "third-party" electoral efforts between World War II and 1996 were simply party labels attached to the campaigns of independent candidates and not really organized political parties existing independently of their standard bearers.[3]

Within an open party system, political activists who are motivated by extreme views on new issues should be able to infiltrate the two major parties, should have a good deal of influence over the parties' positions on the new issues, and should be a crucial element in the process of partisan change along the lines of these new issues. There is substantial evidence that party activists have played a fundamental role in making the traditionalist–modernist religious cleavage into a cleavage between the Democratic and Republican parties. In chapter 3, I showed that there was a substantial influx of secular activists into the Democratic party in 1972 and that inflow was associated with a movement of the party toward highly liberal stands on cultural issues. After a decline with the campaigns of evangelical Christian Jimmy Carter in 1976 and 1980, the representation of secularists among Democratic activists again has increased and been associated with very liberal cultural stands by the party. Meanwhile, the influx of committed evangelical Protestants and other highly committed Christians into the Republican party in the 1980s and 1990s has been associated with an increase in the cultural conservatism of GOP platforms. In chapter 6, I showed that the religious polarization of Democratic and Republican activists has played a key role in linking the polarization of the parties in government on cultural issues to a change in mass perceptions of the parties' stands on these issues and eventually to a reshaping of mass partisanship along traditionalist–modernist religious lines. In chapter 7, I showed that the impact of religious traditionalism on individual political behavior is greater in states where party activists are more polarized along religious lines.

The Strategic Incentives of Party Politicians

The interaction between the nature of the religious conflict and its related issues and the institutional structure of the American political parties creates conditions that are ripe for the development of a partisan religious cleavage. The contemporary religious divide gives rise to groups of political activists advocating extreme positions on powerful new political issues. The open nature of the American two-party system provides an avenue for these activists to infiltrate the parties and push them toward polarized stands on the cultural issues. However, these factors alone do not make traditionalist–modernist religious divisions between the Democratic and Republican parties inevitable. For that to happen, the religious cleavage and its related issues must appeal to the strategic incentives of party politicians.

Before the parties will take distinct stands on a new set of issues, and before the issues and their related social cleavage will effect partisan change, those issues must have the potential to help some set of political actors improve their strategic political positions. The reasons are several: Strategic political leaders play an important role in developing political issues, attention to new issues by political leaders tends to increase their salience among activists and ordinary voters, and, perhaps most important, political leaders serve as a lightning rod for the influx of activists with extreme positions on the new issues into the established political parties. Again, these groups of insurgent activists have other political options besides getting involved in the Democratic or Republican parties.

Unless some political leader within one of the two parties appeals to their political sensibilities, they may choose those options over two-party politics.

It is political losers—either minority party politicians or losers in the struggle for factional control within either the majority or the minority party—who have the strongest incentives to champion noncentrist positions on divisive new political issues. Those issues may disrupt the existing political balance and make the current losers into winners. In chapter 1, I argued that political losers within both parties had incentives to champion extreme stands on the new cultural issues. Factional losers in the Democratic party, such as Eugene McCarthy and especially George McGovern, played a crucial role in attracting the young, culturally liberal secularists of the New Left to Democratic party activity. Factional losers within the losing party, specifically the leaders of the New Right faction of the Republican party, played a major role in the development of the Christian Right and the influx of committed evangelical activists into the GOP.

Beyond these accounts, I did not provide any direct empirical tests of the role of strategic politicians in the process of religious partisan change. However, in chapter 3, I showed that the campaigns of particular politicians have had important effects on the aggregate religious traditionalism or modernism of Republican and Democratic activists. The nomination of the culturally liberal McGovern in 1972 brought with it a very strong presence of secular activists in the Democratic party, while the cultural liberalism of Democratic candidates such as Walter Mondale, Jerry Brown, and even Bill Clinton has helped produce further increases in the secularism and religious liberalism of Democratic activists. Meanwhile, strong campaigns by more culturally moderate candidates such as Jimmy Carter and Al Gore (in 1988) have been associated with decreases in the presence of secular activists in the Democratic party. On the Republican side, the culturally conservative campaigns of candidates such as Ronald Reagan, Pat Robertson, and Pat Buchanan have been accompanied by a strong and growing presence of committed evangelical Protestants and other religious traditionalists among GOP activists.

Summary

This book has shown that the contemporary religious divide has become a cleavage between the Democratic and Republican parties not just because it is deep-seated and incites strong passions, but also because of the way in which it has interacted with the fundamental nature of the political parties, their institutional structures, and the strategic incentives of their members. The traditionalist–modernist divide has given rise to powerful new political issues that have appealed to the strategic incentives of political losers within both parties. These strategic politicians have championed extreme views on the cultural issues and thus have attracted activists who share those views into Democratic and Republican party politics. The open nature of the party system has provided insurgent activists easy entry into the two parties and a clear path to influencing their positions on cultural issues. The resulting ascendance of traditionally religious activists within the GOP and of religiously liberal and secular activists in the Democratic party has pushed the parties and their candidates toward more polarized stands on cultural and moral issues. These polarized stands and the role of grassroots-level activists in communicating them to the mass electorate have led to changes in mass perceptions of and affect toward the two parties, and thus to a restructuring of the parties' mass coalitions along traditionalist–modernist religious lines.

THE RELIGIOUS DIVISION OF THE PARTIES AND THE PARTISAN CHANGE PROCESS

Just as there is something to be learned from viewing the religious polarization of the two parties through a model of the general partisan change process, this particular case of party transformation along religious and cultural lines may tell us something about the general process of partisan electoral change. In particular, it may provide insight into the theoretical model most appropriate for describing partisan change, the types of strategic politicians who are catalysts for partisan change, and the role of party activists in triggering and facilitating partisan transformations.

Modeling Partisan Change: Is Realignment Still Relevant?

One of the preeminent questions in the literature on electoral change is whether partisan shifts are explained best by the realignment model that traditionally has dominated scholarly accounts (cf. Key 1955; Burnham 1970; Clubb, Flanigan, and Zingale 1980; Sundquist 1983) or by newer frameworks such as Carmines and Stimson's (1989) model of "issue evolution," Byron Shafer's (1991) notion of an "electoral order," or Aldrich's (1999) account of "critical eras" in American politics. The meaning of realignment varies widely, perhaps even from scholar to scholar, but it generally is associated with three core concepts: the displacement of one dominant line of partisan cleavage by another, the notion of a "critical election" producing rapid and dramatic change, and a change in the majority party.

The ongoing division of the parties along religious and cultural lines exhibits traces of all of these characteristics, but it does not meet the high standard of a realignment according to any of the criteria. Cultural and moral issues such as abortion, homosexual rights, and school prayer have become more salient relative to older issues such as social welfare and race. They have received more attention in party platforms and are the most important issues to significant numbers of party activists. However, these issues are rarely the centerpiece of candidates' agendas—they were, for example, nowhere to be found in the Contract with America, a document that played a key role in the Republican takeover of Congress in 1994—and, as I showed in chapter 7, they remain far less relevant to the mass public than economic and social welfare concerns. There has not been a clear conflict displacement in the American political agenda.

The evidence presented here does indicate that certain elections have been more important than others in producing traditionalist–modernist divisions in the parties' mass coalitions. The 1980 election was the first in which the Christian Right was involved in Republican presidential politics; it was the first in which the Republican standard-bearer took highly conservative positions on abortion, school prayer, homosexual rights, and the Equal Rights Amendment; and it represented the first step in the shift of committed evangelicals toward the GOP. The 1984 election—coming on the heels of four years of cultural conservatism by the Reagan administration and involving a Democratic nominee, Walter Mondale, with more liberal cultural views than those of his predecessor, Jimmy Carter—witnessed a clear increase in the presence of committed evangelicals among Republican activists and of secularists among Democratic activists, as well as a noticeable growth in the religious differences between the parties' electoral coalitions. The 1992 election—coming after a Republican convention dominated by religious and cultural conservatives and a Republican campaign that paid particular attention to "family values"—saw the largest increases to date in the religious polarization of the parties' mass identifiers.

None of these elections, however, meet the criteria of a critical election. For one thing, I have just mentioned three key elections, and it would be difficult to single out one as the most important. Moreover, in none of these campaigns have moral and cultural concerns been the dominant issues. George Bush and Dan Quayle may have tried to make the 1992 campaign about traditional moral values. But the fact that they won only 38 percent of the popular vote while Ross Perot, whose campaign focused on economic concerns such as the federal budget deficit and the nation's trade imbalance, and Bill Clinton, whose campaign team rallied around the slogan "It's the economy, stupid," won a combined 62 percent shows that Bush and Quayle were less than successful. In none of these elections have moral and cultural matters come close to being the most salient issues for ordinary voters. The polarization of party politics along traditionalist–modernist religious lines is best described as a gradual process, with the rate of change accelerating in certain elections and decelerating in others. It has not been characterized by a rapid shift from a former line of party cleavage to a new line.

Finally, as I shall discuss, partisan change along religious and cultural lines has been associated with some change in the balance of power between the two parties, in my view helping the GOP more than the Democrats. It has not produced, however, a stable Republican majority. And while it may have helped the Republicans in the short run, it has the potential to advantage the Democratic party in the long run.

If realignment, specifically critical-election realignment, does not provide a satisfactory account of partisan religious and cultural change, is there another model of the partisan change process that does explain it? Given the gradual nature of the religious polarization of the parties, a possibility is V. O. Key's concept of "secular realignment" (1959): a very slow, incremental shift in the party loyalties of certain population groups that occurs over an extended time period and for reasons independent of the factors that influence voting decisions in particular elections. Secular realignment is largely a nonpolitical process, resulting from sociodemographic changes such as the movement of a particular group up or down the socioeconomic ladder or changes in immigration or interregional migration patterns.

There are certain aspects of partisan religious change that fit this model. For instance, part of the reason that the Democratic coalition is growing more secular while evangelical Protestants have come to represent a larger portion of the Republican coalition than mainline Protestants is provided by trends in American religion. The number of people who have abandoned organized religion is growing, while evangelical congregations are growing relative to mainline congregations. However, the reasons that the Democratic party appeals to seculars and the Republican party appeals to evangelical Protestants are inherently political: The parties have taken highly polarized stands on cultural political issues, and party activists have helped to communicate those positions to ordinary citizens. So, secular realignment may provide insight into some of the long-term, gradual nature of the process, but it does not explain the fundamental reason why partisan religious change began in the first place or has accelerated in recent years.

An alternative to either critical-election realignment or secular realignment is Carmines and Stimson's (1989) theory of issue evolution. The model, although difficult to summarize briefly, essentially describes a process in which highly emotional, easily understood issues emerge on the political agenda, the two parties' elites take polarized stands on them, and the mass electorate responds to the elite transformation by gradually changing its patterns of partisan support along the lines of the new issues. The issue evolution model may not provide a perfect description of partisan religious change because the cultural issues that have driven it have not achieved the high levels of salience within the mass electorate that characterize issue evolutions. Also, Carmines and Stimson contend that issue evolutions begin with a "critical moment" of fairly dramatic change, then move into a prolonged period of more gradual change. At this point, it is difficult to identify a single critical moment in the process of religious partisan change. However, the idea that electoral change occurs in the form of a gradual mass response to party elite polarization on new issues provides a fairly accurate description of the religious and cultural change in American party politics.

Carmines and Stimson identify four key attributes of issue evolutions (1989: 192–93). Issue evolutions are dynamic; they can be understood only in the context of growth and decay over time. They are complex; they do not have single causes or follow simple patterns. They are subtle; they do not produce sudden, dramatic changes, and their effects are cumulative. And they have extended time horizons. All these characteristics apply to the religious and cultural polarization of the party system. It is something that has occurred over time, to some extent in fits and starts, and it has extended over a long period, nearly three decades now. Partisan religious change is nothing if not complex. It involves certain religious traditions and not others. It involves certain groups within particular traditions (e.g., committed evangelical Protestants), but not other groups within the same traditions (e.g., evangelicals with low levels of religious commitment). And the role of doctrinal orthodoxy and religious commitment in effecting partisan change varies across religious traditions;

commitment has had a greater impact than orthodoxy among evangelicals, while orthodoxy has played a greater role among mainline Protestants and Catholics. Finally, the changes associated with the contemporary religious cleavage have been subtle and not dramatic. They have occurred gradually over time, and they have not produced what the culture wars model ultimately predicts: a Democratic party of religious modernists from all faith traditions and a Republican party of religious conservatives from all faith traditions so that religious tradition is no longer important politically. There have been critical shifts in the religious bases of the party system. But, just as was the case thirty years ago, white Protestants constitute a majority of Republican identifiers, while Catholics, Jews, and black Protestants are much more likely to be Democrats.

So, a model such as the issue evolution framework or the account presented in chapter 1 explains the religious and cultural changes in party politics better than the model of critical-election realignment traditionally employed by political scientists. Does that mean that the realignment perspective is, in the words of Everett Carll Ladd (1991), "useless" for explaining contemporary change in American politics? Or, is there simply something unique about the religious and cultural conflict—for example, the fact that the political issues related to it are highly salient for only a minority of voters, or the fact that those issues are so emotionally charged and divisive that most political candidates do not place them at the forefront of their campaigns—that makes it fit uneasily into the realignment framework?

Well, some scholars contend that the idea of critical realignment is deeply flawed as an account of not just contemporary electoral change, but all partisan transformations (cf. Ladd with Hadley 1975; Carmines and Stimson 1989; Ladd 1991; Shafer 1991). They criticize the association of realignment with a change in the majority party. There is no reason that the party that was on the winning side—the side that appealed to a majority of voters—of the old partisan cleavage cannot be on the winning side of the new line of cleavage. The critics also find the critical election model of partisan change, in which the party system moves from one stable alignment—a steady state with a stable line of cleavage, stable coalitions, and a stable balance of power between the parties—to another over the course of one or two elections, to be overly simplistic. Even the elections typically agreed upon as being critical realigning elections were preceded by gradual shifts in the issue agenda and cleavage structure of party politics and were followed by "aftershocks" that continued to reshape the party system along the new line of cleavage (Sundquist 1983).

Most of all, these scholars take issue with the fact that realignment, as it has come to be defined by scholars and journalists, is a dichotomous notion: An electoral period either is or is not a realignment. That implies that a transformation in party politics that does not live up to the lofty standards of change set by the New Deal era and the other historical realignments is not very important.

While there is certainly some merit to these conceptual criticisms, the notion of stable alignments preceded by and followed by critical realignments has proven to be quite effective in describing and explaining party politics in the nineteenth century and the first half of the twentieth century (cf. Silbey 1991; Burnham 1991). The realignment accounts of the partisan changes in the 1860s, 1890s, and 1930s may have been overly simplified. But the fact is that relatively new issues did emerge during these electoral eras and came to dominate political discussions and political campaigns (Graebner 1961; Durden 1965; Schlesinger 1958). There were relatively rapid and dramatic changes in the parties' coalitions during these periods (cf. Key 1955). And these eras did lead to a fairly prolonged period of stable issue agendas, stable party coalitions, and a stable balance of power between the parties (Sundquist 1983).

The realignment framework, however, has been less effective in explaining recent partisan change. Since the New Deal realignment of the 1930s, there have been fundamental changes in party politics. The religious and cultural changes in the party system documented here were preceded by the polarization of the parties' elites, activists, and identifiers on issues of racial desegregation in the 1960s and the consequent migration of southern whites out of their traditional Democratic party home and eventually into the GOP (Carmines and Stimson 1989; Black and Black 1987). Meanwhile, the class basis of the party system has weakened as lower-status citizens have become much less likely to identify themselves as Democrats and the Republican ties of upper-status citizens have become slightly weaker (Ladd 1991; Carmines and Layman 1997).

Accompanying these changes in the party coalitions has been a clear shift in the balance of power between the parties. The Republicans have not become the majority party, but they are by no means the minority they were from the 1930s through the 1960s. They fashioned a strong presidential majority in the 1970s and 1980s, gained control of Congress during the Democratic presidency of Bill Clinton in the 1990s, are now the party of a majority of the nation's governors, and have control of nearly half the state legislative chambers.

Despite these critical changes, there is no consensus among political scientists, historians, or journalists that there has been a realignment since the 1930s. The realignment model thus appears unable to effectively capture the important shifts in recent party politics. Moreover, this perspective asks a dichotomous question: Has there been or has there not been a realignment? And the fact that the answer seems to be no implies that nothing terribly important has happened. It suggests that the political party system of today is not fundamentally different from the New Deal–era party system, an implication that flies in the face of empirical evidence. So, what Ladd (1991) suggests seems to be true: Not only does realignment not help us to explain recent partisan change, it encourages us to understate and possibly ignore its importance.

Why does realignment theory prove so unsatisfactory for researchers seeking to document recent partisan shifts? One common explanation is that to have a realignment, there has to be an alignment, and the American party system since the 1960s has been in a state of "dealignment." In other words, as the role of political parties in nominating candidates, conducting electoral campaigns, and conveying political information has decreased, the parties have become increasingly irrelevant to the political decisions of voters. With parties so weak and voters so unattached to them, the idea that an electoral period will lead certain groups in the electorate to develop strong and long-term loyalties to one of the parties, a critical feature of realignments, is difficult to fathom (cf. Nie, Verba, and Petrocik 1976; Wattenberg 1986; Silbey 1991; Ladd 1991).[4]

It is true that party leaders have less control over the nomination of candidates than they used to, and that parties are no longer the primary means for conveying campaign messages. However, party organizations in recent years have adapted to the new campaign environment and now play a very large role in recruiting and funding candidates and providing them with new campaign technologies (Beck 1997). Meanwhile, unity within the parties in Congress and polarization between the Democratic and Republican congressional delegations is at very high levels and is still increasing (cf. Rohde 1991). The downward trends in partisan loyalties witnessed in the electorate of the 1960s and 1970s have reversed themselves somewhat, and party identification remains as strong a predictor of the vote as it ever has been (Bartels 2000; Green, Palmquist, and Schickler n.d.). So, the "decline of parties" explanation for why the United States no longer seems to have critical realignments may have provided some insight in the 1970s, but it is not a satisfactory one in the 1990s.

A more convincing explanation for the lack of a critical realignment in contemporary American politics is provided by John Geer (1991). Geer argues that the emergence and increasing influence of public opinion polls in American politics makes it less likely that parties and candidates will take polarized positions on highly salient issues. Since candidates and parties now know where the median, or typical, voter stands on issues, rather than having to guess based on more primitive means of gauging public opinion, they are less likely to take positions that are much different from those of the median, and that tendency makes critical elections much less likely.

There are still theoretical reasons to expect parties to polarize, and there is empirical evidence that they still do. Theoretically, parties and candidates may wish to move to the position of the typical voter and with public opinion polls may be better able to do so. But they are constrained in their ability to do that by party activists. Activists play a preeminent role in party nominations, fund-raising, and general election organizational efforts, and they tend to have more extreme issue positions than the median voter. Thus, candidates who want to win party nominations and obtain enough financial and organizational resources to win general elections cannot take positions that are identical to those of the electoral center. Republicans have to take stands that are more conservative than the median voter, and Democrats have to take stands that are more liberal.

Empirically, the parties do take distinct stands on most issues. I have shown that the positions on cultural issues in the parties' platforms have become increasingly polarized over the last two decades. It is true that these are not the most salient issues to voters, but while these issues have become more salient to voters, the parties' stands on them have become more, not less, polarized. Meanwhile, the positions in the Democratic and Republican platforms on more-salient economic and social welfare issues remain clearly different.

Despite these objections, Geer's argument is telling. Recent examples, such as the poll-tested "Contract with America" that served as the platform for the Republican party's successful House campaign in 1994 and the focus of Bill Clinton on small, uncontroversial issues such as school uniforms and V-chips in televisions in his 1996 presidential campaign, certainly support the argument. Moreover, one must distinguish between the positions of a party and the positions of its candidates. A party convention, composed of ideologically driven party activists, may tout extreme positions on controversial issues such as abortion in its platform, but the candidate, influenced by poll results and cautious handlers, may be much less likely to do so. The candidate may disassociate himself from the platform, as Bob Dole did to some extent in the 1996 presidential campaign. More subtly, he or she simply may not focus much attention on the controversial stands in it, much as many Republican candidates for president, Congress, and governor have said very little about the abortion issue once they secured the party nomination. If the candidates do not focus their attention on these controversial positions, then the election cannot be about those positions. In other words, there cannot be a critical election revolving around the candidates' and parties' polarized stands on controversial issues.

That does not mean there cannot be partisan change. Even if candidates do not publicize the parties' polarized stands on salient political issues, those positions eventually will be communicated to ordinary citizens through the actions of the parties in government, media accounts of the parties, and especially the participation patterns of political activists. However, unlike a critical election in which the campaigns of the two major-party candidates are focused on a divisive new issue and in which the voters choose partisan sides on the basis of that issue, this is a gradual process. Activists and the media gradually communicate the parties' positions on the new issues to voters, voters gradually change their perceptions of the parties' stands on the new issues, and the electorate gradually reshapes its partisan ties along the lines of the new issues. So, a model of partisan change in which citizens progressively respond to the polarization of party elites on new issues appears superior to the critical-election realignment model not only for explaining the religious and cultural shifts in party politics, but also for explaining party change within the context of contemporary campaign politics.

Locating Political Losers: Where Do We Find Strategic Politicians?

A number of scholars argue that strategic politicians play an important role in developing new issues that are capable of creating partisan change, and in attracting activists aroused by those issues into the political parties (Schattschneider 1960; Riker 1982; Carmines and Stimson 1989). They contend that it is political "losers," politicians disadvantaged by the current political status quo, who have strategic incentives to champion extreme positions on divisive new issues and who are most likely to be catalysts for the partisan change process. Typically, members of the minority party are thought of as political losers, with incentives to champion new issues in order to disrupt the political status quo. Majority party members are considered political winners who have incentives to maintain the current status quo. Thus, movement away from the center on a new issue is expected to occur first in the minority party (Carmines 1991).

In my account of the origins of partisan religious change in chapter 1, I argued that strategic politicians did play a key role in championing non-centrist positions on cultural issues and in bringing activists who shared these views into party politics. However, one can find political losers within both the majority and the minority parties. Just as there are losers in the competition between the two parties, there are also losers in the factional struggle for control within both parties. So, the incentive to advance controversial new issues is present not only among minority party politicians, but also among politicians who are in losing factions within the majority party. And with the participatory nominating process that exists in contemporary American politics, majority party losers can exert some influence over the issue agenda and positions of their party by attracting new activists into it. If they attract enough activists with extreme positions on divisive new issues into the party, it may be the majority party, and not the minority party, that makes the initial move away from the center on these issues.

In fact, the evidence presented in chapter 3 shows that it was the majority party that first moved away from the center of the religious and cultural spectrum. Spurred by the liberal cultural stands of presidential nominee George McGovern, large numbers of young, secular activists came into Democratic politics in 1972, and the Democratic party, the majority party at the time, took highly liberal positions on several cultural issues in its 1972 platform. The minority Republican party did not take clear steps toward religious and cultural conservatism until 1980. So, within the context of the highly open American party system, the minority party is not the only breeding ground for new issues that cut across the lines of the existing party cleavage. Those issues also may emerge within the majority party.

Party Activists: The Driving Force Behind the Partisan Change Process

Carmines and Stimson contend that party activists are the "dynamic element in issue evolution" (1989: 90), and activists are the driving force in the model of partisan change in chapter 1 of this book. They not only serve as "opinion leaders" at the grassroots level, communicating changes in the issue positions of party elites to ordinary citizens, they also play a key role in bringing new issues into party politics in the first place and in pushing party elites toward noncentrist positions on those issues.

The evidence presented here confirms the central role of partisan activists in the partisan change process. The influx of secular activists into the Democratic party in the early 1970s established a beachhead for cultural liberalism within that party, and the movement of committed evangelical activists into the Republican party in the 1980s helped push that party away from the moderate cultural stands it espoused in the 1970s. The continued increases in the presence of secular activists in the Democratic party and of devout evangelical activists in the GOP propelled further increases in the polarization of the parties' cultural positions in the 1990s. Moreover, as I showed in chapter 6, changes in the religious characteristics of party activists provided an important link between the cultural polarization of the parties' elites and the reshaping of the religious composition of the parties' mass coalitions.

RELIGIOUS CONFLICT IN THE PARTY SYSTEM: BROADER IMPLICATIONS FOR AMERICAN POLITICS

The manifestation of the contemporary religious conflict in party politics may have implications beyond the religious composition of the parties' coalitions and the parties' stands on cultural issues. It may affect the political importance of other social cleavages and the presence of a variety of social groups in the parties. It may affect the balance of power between the two parties as well as public support for the two-party system more generally. It even may have consequences for the health of American democracy.

The Partisan Religious Divide, Other Partisan Cleavages, and the Partisan Balance

When a new political cleavage such as the contemporary religious divide manifests itself in the party system, it is bound to affect the partisan importance of other political and social cleavages. The past four decades have witnessed changes in the relationship between a number of nonreligious demographic characteristics and the party system. There has been a decline in the partisan class cleavage that was established most firmly during the New Deal era (Ladd with Hadley 1975; Huckfeldt and Kohfeld 1989), and that decline is primarily the result of a reduction in lower-status support for the Democratic party (Carmines and Layman 1997). The regional basis of the party coalitions has changed as southern whites have become much less likely to identify with the Democratic party and much more likely to identify with the GOP (Carmines and Layman 1997). Finally, a political gender gap has emerged recently, with women being clearly more likely than men to support the Democratic party and its candidates (Conway, Steuernagel, and Ahern 1997). The question is have any of these partisan changes been related to the emergence of a partisan religious and cultural divide?

There are certainly reasons to expect a connection. The weakening of the class basis of the party system may be related to the tendency of traditionally Republican upper-status individuals to have lower levels of religious commitment, less orthodox religious affiliations and beliefs, and more liberal views on cultural issues than do traditionally Democratic lower-status individuals. The religious division of the party system should reenforce the pro-Republican trends among southern whites that began in the 1960s since the South is the most traditionally religious and culturally conservative region in the country (Black and Black 1987). Finally, many observers attribute the gender gap in American politics to the influence of the Christian Right in the Republican party and the GOP's resulting lack of support for "women's issues" such as abortion and women's rights. However, the fact that women have higher levels of religious commitment than men (Fowler, Hertzke, and Olson 1999) tempers this expectation.

Table 8.1 takes an empirical look at the relationship between the contemporary religious cleavage and social class (measured by income and education levels), region, sex, and race. It shows that the partisan religious cleavage gives the Republican party some potential to cut into the Democratic stranglehold on the African-American vote. African-Americans are much less likely than whites to be secular, and they have higher levels of doctrinal orthodoxy and religious commitment than whites. This potential, of course, has not yet been realized because of the strong distaste of black voters for the GOP's conservative positions on social welfare and racial issues.

More relevant to the party coalitions is the relationship between socioeconomic status and religious orientations. Higher-income and better-educated citizens are less likely to belong to evangelical Protestant churches and are more likely to be secular than are lower-income and less well educated individuals. Upper-status individuals also have lower levels of doctrinal orthodoxy and religious commitment than do their lower-status

Table 8.1
The religious orientations of demographic groups

Group	Religious Tradition (%)				Other Religious Orientations (Means)[a]		
	Evangelical	Mainline	Catholic	Secular	Doctrinal Orthodoxy	Religious Commitment	Overall Religious Traditionalism[b]
Race							
White	26.71	18.95	25.07	23.93	.39	.51	.48
Black	0.00	0.00	5.73	8.85	.54	.68	.63
Other	35.71	14.29	23.81	16.67	.43	.57	.52
Income							
Low	24.64	13.96	18.07	18.71	.46	.57	.53
Middle	25.59	16.45	23.58	23.58	.40	.53	.49
High	22.06	18.42	26.34	23.77	.34	.50	.45
Education							
No college	28.05	14.23	20.67	20.54	.48	.55	.53
Some college	23.60	16.18	23.37	21.35	.39	.55	.50
BA, advanced	17.18	20.70	25.55	24.89	.31	.50	.44
Region (whites only)							
South	39.04	20.88	17.75	19.00	.47	.57	.54
Non-South	20.32	17.95	28.86	26.49	.35	.49	.44
Sex							
Men	22.19	12.86	24.09	28.55	.37	.48	.45
Women	25.22	19.49	21.81	16.52	.45	.59	.54

Source: 1996 National Election Study.

[a]Doctrinal orthodoxy, religious commitment, and overall religious traditionalism all range from 0 to 1.

[b]Combination of doctrinal orthodoxy, religious commitment, and denominational orthodoxy.

counterparts. So, the contemporary religious cleavage truly does cut across the class-based cleavage that has existed in party politics for most of this century. The religious polarization of the parties may have had some role in weakening the class basis of the party system.

The movement of the Republican party to the religious and cultural right and of the Democratic party to the religious and cultural left clearly reenforces the factors that began pulling southern whites out of the Democratic party and eventually into the GOP in the 1960s. Southern whites are much more likely than nonsouthern whites to belong to evangelical churches and are less likely than nonsouthern whites to be secular. Southern whites also have noticeably more orthodox religious beliefs and higher levels of religious commitment than do white citizens outside the South.

The religious and cultural polarization of the parties does not, at first glance, appear to be an explanation for the growing gender gap in partisan politics. Women may be disaffected from the Republican party for a number of reasons, but the party's increasing religious traditionalism does not seem to be one of them, at least at this highly aggregated level. Women are clearly less likely than men to be secular, and they have higher levels of doctrinal orthodoxy and religious commitment than men.[5]

Of course, what matters most politically is not whether the partisan religious divide affects the nature of the party coalitions, but whether it affects one party's coalition more than the other party's. In other words, has the introduction of the contemporary religious and cultural cleavage into partisan politics helped one party more than the other? Based purely on coincidence, the answer is that it has helped the Republican party at the expense of the Democrats. The religious polarization of the parties began in the 1970s and early 1980s, and since that time the GOP has greatly improved its competitive position. In the late 1970s, the president was a Democrat, the Democrats had firm control of both houses of Congress, the large majority of the nation's governors were Democrats, a clear majority of state legislative bodies were controlled by the Democratic party, and a strong plurality of citizens identified with the Democratic party. Early in 2000, we have a Democratic president, but the Republicans had a stranglehold on the presidency in the 1980s and are favored— according to polls in the summer of 2000—to win the presidency in 2000. At the time of this writing, the Republicans can claim a majority in both houses of Congress, about two-thirds of the nation's governors, and a majority in nearly half of the state legislative bodies. The percentage of citizens identifying themselves as Republicans is also higher than it was in the 1970s.

There are also less coincidental reasons to think that the Republicans have been helped and the Democrats hurt by the partisan religious divide. Focusing for a moment only on religious groups, committed evangelical Protestants have become to the GOP what labor unions and African-Americans long have been to the Democratic party: a solid base of organizational, financial, and electoral support. Committed evangelicals provide the Republicans with a strong foundation not only of votes, but also of activists who are willing to work hard and spend money on behalf of their favored causes. Evangelical religious institutions provide a ready means to mobilize and organize voters, activists, and contributors. As figure 8.1 shows, this base has become increasingly crucial to the Republican party, as its traditional religious base, mainline Protestantism, has declined precipitously while the evangelical tradition actually has grown slightly.

A traditionally religious party also has some numerical and organizational advantages over a secular party in the United States. Numerically, the United States is the most religious nation in the industrialized world (Wald 1997), and a large majority of citizens receive at least some guidance from religion in their lives (78 percent in the 1996 NES), pray at least a few times a week (74 percent), and believe that the Bible is the word of God (85 percent). Moreover, religiously committed individuals make up a disproportionate share of the electorate because of the strong correlation between church attendance and other forms of religious participation on the one hand and political participation on the other hand (Verba, Schlozman, and Brady 1995). Organizationally, churches—particularly evangelical churches but others as well—provide an excellent institutional means of mobilizing activists and electoral support (Hertzke 1993).

In contrast, secular individuals have no such institutions and are less embedded in community organizations in general, a fact that leads to lower levels of political participation than their social status would predict (Green and Guth 1991). Moreover, the growing secularism and cultural liberalism of Democratic activists and elites threaten that party's support among union members and black Protestants. Those groups traditionally have been the party's organizational and electoral base but tend toward moral and cultural conservatism.

Finally, the contemporary religious cleavage has done, or at least has the potential to do, what the minority party always hopes that new

Religious Tradition

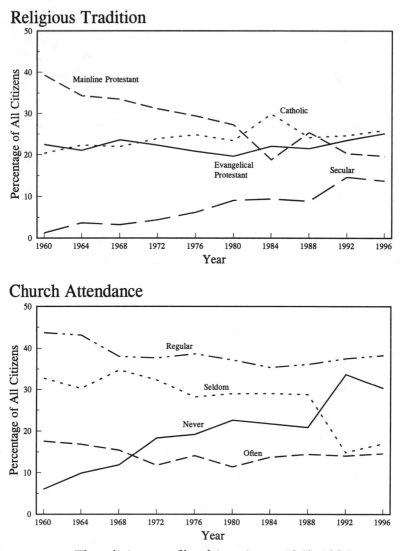

FIGURE 8.1. The religious profile of Americans, 1960–1996
Source: 1960–1996 National Election Studies

partisan cleavages do: It divides the majority party's coalition. The religious and cultural polarization of the parties clearly moves southern whites farther out of the Democratic camp and gives the GOP a chance to appeal to some black voters. Perhaps most important, the religious and cultural divide provides the Republicans an opportunity to break the Democratic party's stranglehold on lower-status white voters. There are certainly nonreligious explanations for the weakening Democratic ties of these citizens. The party's support for affirmative action and other racially liberal policies is one. The increasing working-class disenchantment with the welfare state is another (Edsall with Edsall 1991; Sniderman and Carmines 1997). However, the combination of Democratic cultural liberalism and the relatively orthodox religious orientations of lower-status citizens clearly contributes to the party's losses within its traditional core of support.

There is also some evidence in table 8.1 and figure 8.1 that should be troubling to the Republican party. First, as with any new cross-cutting partisan cleavage, this new religious and cultural cleavage divides not just the electoral coalition of the majority party but those of both parties. Religious and cultural conservatism may open doors for the Republicans among groups such as lower-status and southern whites, but it also has the potential to threaten the GOP's long-standing support among upper-status nonsouthern whites, a group with relatively high levels of secularism and religious modernism.

Second, American religion may have been better able than its counterparts in other Western societies to withstand the secularizing effects of modernization, but it has not been entirely immune. As figure 8.1 shows, this is a country that is growing increasingly secular. The declining numbers of mainline Protestants has coincided with slight increases in the presence of Catholics and evangelical Protestants, but by far the largest gains have come in the secular category. There also has been a sharp increase in the percentage of citizens who never attend worship services.[6] The religious and cultural division of the parties may have benefited the Republicans up to this point, but these secularizing trends may make the religious and cultural liberalism of the Democratic party more profitable in the long run.

To gain a better sense of how the religious divide has affected other partisan cleavages and of whether it has helped one party more than the other, figure 8.2 traces the mean party identification of various demographic groups with various levels of religious traditionalism from 1980 through 1996.[7] It is clear that the religious cleavage has affected the partisan importance of social class, weakening it for the most part. In 1980, there was very little difference in the partisan ties of religious traditionalists and religious modernists within the same income groups. By 1992, religious traditionalism had become clearly more important than income for partisanship. Religious traditionalists from the low-, middle-, and high-income groups all had higher levels of Republican identification

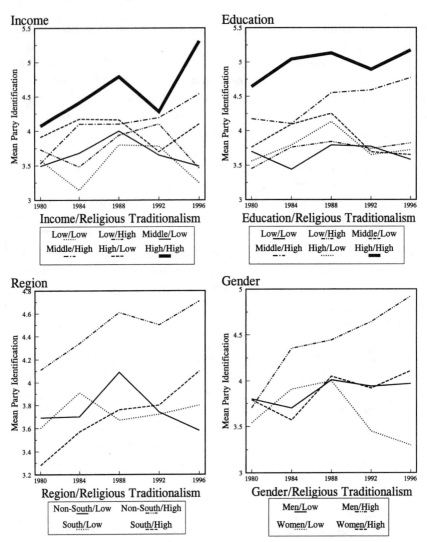

FIGURE 8.2. Mean party identification of demographic and religious groups, 1980–1996 (whites only)
Note: Party identification ranges from strong Democrat (1) to strong Republican (7).
Source: 1980–1996 National Election Studies

than religious modernists from any of the three income groups. In 1996, the GOP placed less emphasis on cultural issues and its conservative stands on them than it had in its 1992 presidential campaign. Perhaps as a consequence, income reasserted some of its partisan influence. Higher-income religious modernists increased their Republican ties, and lower-income religious traditionalists reduced theirs. However, there continued to be large religion-based partisan gaps among middle- and upper-income whites, and middle-income religious traditionalists remained clearly more Republican than upper-income religious modernists.

The clearest growth in traditionalist–modernist partisan divisions within education levels has been in the middle category: individuals who have some college education but do not have a bachelor's degree.[8] Religious traditionalists and modernists within this group had, on average, identical levels of Republican party identification in 1984. Since then, the traditionalists have grown clearly more Republican and the modernists have become noticeably more Democratic. The partisan religious divide does not seem to have affected the Democratic party ties of either modernists or traditionalists with low levels of education. There has been a huge partisan cleavage between religious traditionalists and modernists with high levels of education, since at least 1980. So, Hunter (1991) may be correct in claiming that the political ramifications of the cultural conflict are strongest for well-educated societal elites. But they are growing ever stronger for middle-class citizens as well.

It is difficult to say which party has benefited from these religious effects on the partisan class cleavage. The Republican party clearly has not had much success in splitting the lower-status core of Democratic electoral support. Religious traditionalists with lower incomes and with no college experience have not become much more Republican than religious modernists at the same status level. Also worrisome for the GOP is the fact that higher-status religious modernists, who outnumber higher-status religious traditionalists, have not shown any evidence of strong Republican ties throughout this time period. At the same time, higher-status religious traditionalists have strong and growing loyalties toward the Republican party, and the Republican ties of middle-class religious traditionalists are growing ever stronger. The religious divide has clearly affected the partisan influence of social class, but it is not clear that it has done so to one party's advantage.

The religious divide also has affected the relationship between region and partisanship, seemingly to the advantage of the Republican party. Religious traditionalists in both the South and the non-South have become noticeably more Republican since 1980. The pro-Republican trend has been steeper among southern traditionalists, who outnumber southern modernists, and has made this group clearly more Republican than religious modernists outside the South. Meanwhile, there is no evidence of a Democratic gain among religiously modern southern whites. Non-southern modernists became sharply more Democratic after 1988, but that followed a clear increase in Republican identification between 1984 and 1988.

From the simple perspective of table 8.1, it appeared that the religious and cultural polarization of the parties had nothing to do with the political gender gap. In figure 8.2, however, it is clear that the relationship between the religious divide and the gender gap is more complex and interesting. If there are unique political perspectives that come from gender and from religious traditionalism–modernism, then their effects should be reenforcing for traditionalist men, attracting them into the GOP, and for modernist women, pushing them into the Democratic party. But their effects should counteract each other in the case of modernist men and traditionalist women, restraining these groups from strong loyalties to either party. These expectations are borne out, as traditionalist men have grown increasingly Republican since 1980 and modernist women have become much more Democratic since 1988. Meanwhile, both traditionalist women and modernist men have remained steadily near the midpoint (pure independent) of the party identification scale over this period.

Why exactly are the effects of gender and religious traditionalism reenforcing for traditionalist men and modernist women but offsetting for modernist men and traditionalist women? The answer may lie squarely with the contemporary cultural conflict. Some of the issues surrounding this conflict, particularly abortion rights and equal rights for women, are portrayed by some observers as being "women's issues," which are of particular concern to women and tend to receive more support from women than from men. For whatever reason—perhaps self-interest or socialization—men simply may be predisposed to oppose women's issues and women may be predisposed to support them. Moreover, male opposition is augmented by the culturally conservative inclinations of religious traditionalists, pushing them strongly toward the GOP, but counterbalanced by the culturally liberal values of modernists, limiting their attachment to the Republican party. Female support for women's issues is reenforced by the cultural liberalism of religious modernists, placing them firmly in the Democratic camp, but offset by the cultural conservatism of religious traditionalists, constraining their Democratic loyalties.

Of course, most of the literature on the gender gap finds little difference between men and women on the so-called women's issues. Men are just as pro-choice on abortion as women and are not much less supportive of equal rights for women (cf. Shapiro and Mahajan 1986; Conway, Steuernagel, and Ahern 1997). However, these findings are based on all women and all men, and women, as a group, are more traditionally religious than men. Among religious modernists or among religious traditionalists, women may have more liberal attitudes on cultural issues than do men. A cultural-issue explanation for the gender gap certainly fits the pattern of party identification for religiously modern women. Their sharp move toward the Democratic party began between 1988 and 1992, a period that witnessed the Supreme Court's *Webster* decision giving states more latitude in restricting abortion rights, the growing influence of the Christian Right within state Republican parties, and a Republican national convention dominated by religious and cultural conservatives.

An alternative explanation is that it is noncultural political issues that lead gender and religious traditionalism to reenforce each other for certain groups but to offset each other for other groups. In contrast to the evidence for cultural matters, scholars have found substantial gender differences on economic, racial, and foreign policy issues. Women tend to have less individualistic political outlooks than men and thus to be more likely to support government action to protect the welfare of its citizens. They are, for example, more supportive than men of government programs to help the poor and elderly, to provide for children, to provide medical care for all citizens, and to help racial minorities. Women tend to be more supportive than men of affirmative action programs, perhaps because they are more likely to benefit. They are also less likely than men to favor the use of force to solve international problems and thus are more likely to oppose defense buildups (Shapiro and Mahajan 1986; Wirls 1986; Conover 1988; Fite, Genest, and Wilcox 1990; Conway, Steuernagel, and Ahern 1997).

The evidence in table 8.2 tends to support this explanation more than the women's issues explanation. There is no gender gap in levels of moral traditionalism among religious traditionalists and religious modernists, but there is a big difference in the moral values of traditionalists and modernists within each gender. In contrast, there is a clear gender gap among religious traditionalists and religious modernists in support for limited government. There is also some distinction between traditionalist and modernist men, but there is not a religion-based difference among women.

Turning to specific issues, there are gender differences within the modernist and traditionalist camps on some cultural issues, namely, abortion and homosexual rights. However, these differences pale in comparison

TABLE 8.2
Political predispositions and issue-attitudes by sex and religious
traditionalism, 1996 (whites only)

Predispositions and Issue Attitudes	Sex/Religious Traditionalism			
	Men/Low	Women/Low	Men/High	Women/High
Moral traditionalism[a,b]	.55	.52	.78	.76
Limited government[a,c,d]	.53	.38	.68	.44
Cultural issues				
Abortion[a,b,c,d]	.23	.15	.64	.56
Women's role[a,b]	.15	.12	.34	.31
Homosexual rights[a,b,c,d]	.38	.25	.67	.52
School prayer[a,b]	.33	.33	.51	.48
Social welfare issues				
Government provides jobs[a,b,c,d]	.63	.53	.70	.60
Spending to help the poor[c,d]	.43	.30	.44	.35
Spending to help the homeless[c,d]	.37	.25	.41	.25
Racial issues				
Government help for blacks[c,d]	.69	.61	.72	.64
Affirmative action[c,d]	.56	.49	.59	.50

Source: 1996 National Election Study.

All predispositions and issue-attitudes range from 0 (most liberal) to 1 (most conservative).
The entries are mean values on these variables.

[a]The difference between the means of low traditionalism men and high traditionalism men is significant at $p < .01$.

[b]The difference between the means of low traditionalism women and high traditionalism women is significant at $p < .01$.

[c]The difference between the means of low traditionalism men and low traditionalism women is significant at $p < .01$.

[d]The difference between the means of high traditionalism men and high traditionalism women is significant at $p < .01$.

to the differences within genders based on religious traditionalism, and there is no gender gap within religious categories in support for women's rights or prayer in the public schools. In direct contrast are the results for government spending to help the poor, spending to help the homeless, and racial issues. On these matters, there is a clear gender gap among religious traditionalists and religious modernists, but there are no differences between traditionalists and modernists of the same sex. There are some religion-based differences on the issue of government providing jobs and a good standard of living, but these differences are smaller than the gap between men and women with similar religious orientations.

From this very simple analysis, it appears that the opinion gap between men and women is based primarily on issues concerning government help for the needy, racial equality, and the size and scope of government. Attitudes on cultural issues are defined more by religious traditionalism than by gender. Thus, the tendency toward political independence of traditionalist women and modernist men seems to be a result of their cultural views coming into conflict with their views on noncultural issues. The increasingly strong party ties of traditionalist men and modernist women appear to result from the ideological harmony between their cultural attitudes and their views on noncultural matters.

Regardless of the explanation, it is clear that gender, the contemporary religious divide, and the political parties interact in interesting and important ways. There is a gender gap in American party politics. However, it is a gap not between all men and women, but only between traditionally religious men and religiously modern women.

The Partisan Religious Divide and Public Support for the Two-Party System

It is possible that the religious and cultural polarization of the parties may affect not only the level of electoral support for one party relative to the other, but also the level of public support for the two-party system more generally. The political journalist E. J. Dionne (1991) argues that the partisan cultural conflict is at the heart of the American public's disenchantment with the political process. Most Americans, according to Dionne, have moved past the cultural battles that arose in the 1960s. They have come to a consensus on issues of private and public morality, racial equality, and the role of women in society, and they want to move on—and wish for their political leaders to move on—to more pressing economic and foreign policy concerns.

But the political parties refuse to move, either toward the cultural consensus of the average citizen or on to other issues. They continue to fight a polarized battle over decades-old cultural issues. Dionne contends that "just as the Civil War dominated American political life for decades after it ended, so is the cultural civil war of the 1960s . . . shaping our politics today. We are still trapped in the 1960s" (1991: 11). The result is that citizens find little appeal in the program of either party. They become disenchanted with the party system and thus detached from politics and government. The cure, Dionne argues, is a "new political center" that offers consensus solutions to cultural matters and refocuses American politics on facing the international problems and domestic economic challenges of the twenty-first century.

Other observers have echoed Dionne's contention that the cultural polarization of the parties—in addition to party polarization on racial and social welfare concerns—has contributed to public disenchantment with two-party politics. For example, the editor of *Campaigns and Elections* magazine recently argued, "In effect, both sides danced not to the music of the middle, but jumped, instead, to the cracking whips of their own party's organizational and financial base. . . . The already cynical . . . 40 percent of the electorate in the middle will begin to look for new alternatives. . . . Both major parties need to be careful. Independents and third-party movements will have a chance to strike."[9]

In fact, Dionne's call for a new political center seems prophetic when judged against the recent campaigns of Ross Perot and his Reform party. Perot won nearly 20 percent of the presidential vote in 1992 with a centrist campaign that ignored divisive cultural issues and focused on things such as trade imbalance, campaign and government reform, and the federal budget deficit. As Perot himself put it when asked about cultural issues such as abortion on *Larry King Live,* "That won't determine the success of the country."[10] Perot later transformed his campaign organization into the Reform party and ran as its nominee for president in 1996. He won only 8 percent of the vote that year, but the party achieved its first major electoral success in 1998 with the election of Jesse Ventura as governor of Minnesota.

There is no question that there is a substantial disenchantment with and disengagement from politics within the American public. Public opinion polls show that trust in government and electoral institutions is reaching record lows, and voter turnout has declined steadily since the 1960s, with presidential turnout in 1996 reaching its lowest point since 1924. The rise of political independence in the 1960s and 1970s has leveled out since then. But the fact that Perot—a candidate with no previous experience in elective office and who dropped out of the race in the summer while making seemingly paranoid claims about "dirty tricks" by President Bush and the Republican party, only to reemerge as a candidate in the fall—could win nearly 20 percent of the vote for president speaks to the public's dissatisfaction with the major party alternatives. The question is, however, "Has the parties' polarized debate on cultural issues played a role in creating this dissatisfaction?"

Some of the key components of Dionne's argument about cultural issues are, of course, correct. The Democratic and Republican stands on them are highly polarized and are growing increasingly so. Most Americans do find economic and social welfare issues to be more important than cultural issues. And the majority of Americans are in the middle of the ideological spectrum on cultural matters (Hunter 1994; Williams 1997), as they are on most political issues. Moreover, there is no question that some groups have been alienated from one of the parties by its cultural stands. The ties of many less-devout mainline Protestants to the Republican party have been severed because of that party's cultural conservatism. The Democratic loyalties of many committed Catholics have been dislodged by that party's cultural liberalism.

But there are also reasons to believe that the growing focus and polarization of the parties on cultural issues is not to blame for a growing alienation from two-party politics. First, the salience of cultural issues for ordinary voters is admittedly lower than that of bread-and-butter issues, but it is growing, not declining. Second, religious orientations play a central role in shaping cultural attitudes. And it seems to be the religious middle (namely, mainline Protestantism), not the religious extremes (seculars and evangelicals), that is shrinking. Thus, a move by the parties to the center on cultural issues might please a group whose representation in the electorate is declining, while alienating groups whose electoral presence is growing.

The negative effects of cultural centrism on political engagement might be particularly strong for committed evangelical Protestants, a group that exhibited very low levels of political participation until the cultural conservatism of the Christian Right and Ronald Reagan drew them into Republican politics in the early 1980s (Oldfield 1996). A move by the GOP to more moderate positions on cultural issues might drive this large block of voters back to its apolitical roots.

In fact, as I will discuss further, recent attempts by Republican leaders and candidates to deemphasize the party's conservative cultural stands have brought threats from Christian Right leaders that their constituents would take their reliably Republican votes and go home. Faulting Bob Dole's inattention to cultural matters in his 1996 presidential campaign, Christian Action Network president Martin Mawyer warned that "all we have to do on Election Day is stay home, and that's what an increasing number of pro-family, born-again voters plan to do this November."[11] In the spring of 1998, James Dobson, head of the conservative Christian organization Focus on the Family, threatened to ask his followers to withdraw from party politics unless the Republican party in Congress made conservative positions on cultural issues a higher legislative priority. Said Dobson, "If I go, I will do everything I can to take as many people with me as possible."[12]

Finally, many political scientists have long argued that political parties that offer clear ideological alternatives to the electorate, "responsible" parties, are better for American democracy than are "tweedledee-tweedledum" parties that seek the political center. As the American Political Science Association's (APSA) Committee on Political Parties argued in 1950, "popular government . . . requires political parties which provide the electorate with a proper range of choice between alternatives of action" (American Political Science Association 1950: 1). An editorial in the Cleveland *Plain Dealer* put it even more elegantly and focused more specifically on cultural issues:

> Although I'm as pro-choice as anyone, I'm saddened by the Republican Party's recent decision to distance itself from its long-standing anti-abortion stance and other controversial issues in pursuit of electoral victory. And it's not just a GOP problem. The Democratic Party has been similarly infected. . . . I believe that people often have passionate views, and that they feel betrayed by this pandering to the political center. I also believe that the major parties' "safe" approach explains not only the poor voter turnout in recent years, but also the growth of alternative parties.[13]

In this view, it is not the cultural polarization of the parties that alienates citizens but the parties' attempts to mask their noncentrist cultural positions to win votes.

Dionne's "cultural civil war" extends beyond the cultural issues such as abortion, homosexual rights, women's rights, and school prayer on which I have focused, and an analysis that is far more detailed than I can provide here is needed to test the role of party polarization, cultural and otherwise, in creating American disengagement from politics. However,

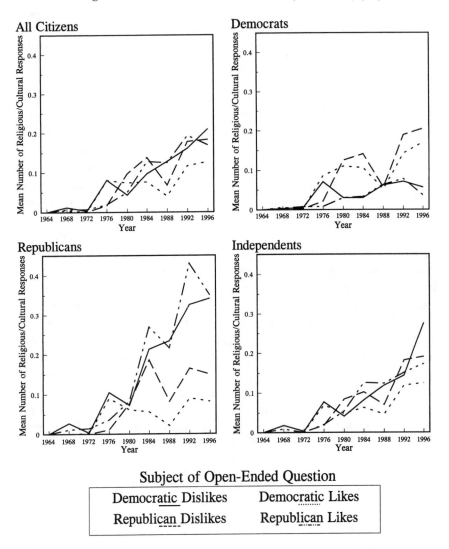

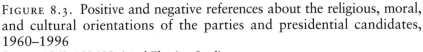

FIGURE 8.3. Positive and negative references about the religious, moral, and cultural orientations of the parties and presidential candidates, 1960–1996

Source: 1960–1996 National Election Studies

I have conducted a couple of simple tests of the notion that the religious and cultural polarization of the major parties has led to disenchantment with the two-party system in general. First, figure 8.3 shows the mean number of responses to questions about the likes and dislikes of both parties that are about religious, moral, and cultural matters. It shows this for all citizens, Democrats, Republicans, and independents. The patterns for Democrats and Republicans are of less interest, because these groups presumably are not alienated from the party system. However, they support the conclusions in earlier chapters by showing that partisans' positive feelings toward their own party and negative evaluations of the other party are based increasingly on cultural and moral matters. From the early 1980s through the late 1990s, Democrats grew increasingly likely to cite cultural concerns as things they liked about the Democratic party and disliked about the Republican party. Republican identifiers became more and more likely to identify moral and cultural issues as things they liked about the GOP and disliked about the Democratic party.

More pertinent are the patterns for independents, a group that presumably is disenchanted with the two major parties, or that is at least more disenchanted than are partisan identifiers. If the parties' noncentrist stands on cultural issues are contributing to a growing disaffection from party politics, then independents should be more likely to mention cultural and moral matters as things they dislike about the parties than as things they like about the parties, and that gap should be growing over time. The evidence, however, does not support that. Independents are becoming more likely to refer to cultural issues not only in the questions about Democratic and Republican dislikes, but also in the questions about party likes. The increase in culturally oriented dislikes of the Democratic party does appear to be sharper than the growth in culturally oriented responses to the other three sets of questions, but the difference is not substantial.

My second test is even more straightforward. If partisan cultural polarization is a reason for dissatisfaction with the party system, then cultural moderates should be more dissatisfied than cultural liberals and cultural conservatives. So, I simply distinguish individuals who are disenchanted with the two major parties from individuals who have more positive feelings about the parties, and I examine whether there are religious and cultural distinctions between the two groups. Again, I use the open-ended questions about party likes and dislikes, focusing only on the total number of likes and dislikes respondents offer for each party. "Disenchanted" individuals are those who mention more things they dislike about each party than things they like about each party. "Pro-party" individuals are those who offer more likes than dislikes for both parties. "Republican partisans" are those respondents who offer more likes than dislikes of the GOP, but more dislikes than likes of the Democratic party,

TABLE 8.3
Feelings about the Democratic and Republican parties
(in percentages), 1972–1996

Feelings Toward the Parties	1972	1976	1980	1984	1988	1992	1996
Disenchanted[a]	7.33	7.65	3.41	2.97	3.53	5.59	6.47
Pro-party[b]	4.74	4.36	7.25	4.16	6.47	2.82	4.92
Republican partisan[c]	19.57	15.26	15.92	21.09	22.94	16.09	20.74
Democratic partisan[d]	25.56	29.98	32.40	28.27	29.02	31.54	28.54
Neutral[e]	29.85	30.69	34.57	35.71	30.25	31.54	28.42
Anti-Republican[f]	6.43	6.18	3.04	4.56	3.97	7.16	6.35
Anti-Democrat[g]	6.52	5.87	3.41	3.23	3.82	5.27	4.56
(N)	(1,119)	(2,248)	(1,614)	(2,257)	(2,040)	(2,486)	(834)

Source: 1972–1996 National Election Studies.

[a]More dislikes than likes for both parties.

[b]More likes than dislikes for both parties.

[c]More likes than dislikes for the Republicans and either more dislikes than likes or an equal number of likes and dislikes for the Democrats.

[d]More likes than dislikes for the Democrats and either more dislikes than likes or an equal number of likes and dislikes for the Republicans.

[e]Either no likes or dislikes of either party or an equal number of likes and dislikes for both parties.

[f]More dislikes than likes for the Republicans and either no likes and dislikes or an equal number of likes and dislikes for the Democrats.

[g]More dislikes than likes for the Democrats and either no likes and dislikes or an equal number of likes and dislikes for the Republicans.

while "Democratic partisans" offer just the opposite pattern of responses.[14] Individuals who either offer no likes or dislikes of either party or provide an equal number of likes and dislikes for each party are coded as "neutral." "Anti-Republicans" are respondents who mention more things they dislike than like about the GOP and either say nothing about the Democratic party or offer an equal number of likes and dislikes about the Democrats. "Anti-Democrats" provide just the opposite pattern of responses.

Table 8.3 shows the percentage of respondents in each of these categories from 1972 to 1996. It raises some questions about the whole notion of growing public disaffection from the two-party system, because none of these categories exhibits any clear trend. Most important, while the disenchanted, anti-Republican, and anti-Democratic categories increased slightly after 1980, they were all slightly smaller in 1996 than they were in 1972.

Perhaps, however, these aggregate results are masking a more complex pattern. Maybe religious and cultural moderates are becoming increasingly disenchanted, but this is being offset by increasingly positive partisan feelings among religious and cultural extremists. Figure 8.4 assesses that possibility by showing the trends in various categories of partisan affect for individuals with low, middle, and high levels of religious traditionalism and cultural conservatism. Not surprisingly, religious and cultural liberals and religious and cultural traditionalists are moving in opposite directions. Religious and cultural conservatives are becoming less likely to be Democratic partisans and more likely to be Republican partisans. Just the opposite is true for religious and cultural liberals.

For religious and cultural centrists, there is no clear trend. The percentage of these individuals who are disenchanted with both parties or are in the anti-Republican or anti-Democrat categories increased only very slightly after 1988, and there is no trend in the Republican partisan and Democratic partisan groups. Again, more, and more sophisticated, investigations into the relationship between partisan cultural polarization and public disaffection from party politics are needed. However, this preliminary analysis suggests that there is no such relationship.

The Partisan Religious Divide and the Health of American Democracy

The implications of the cultural conflict for American democracy may be even more serious than a weakened two-party system and a cynical electorate, according to James Davison Hunter. In his book *Before the Shooting Begins,* Hunter contends that the cultural conflict is inherently antidemocratic. Each side presupposes the illegitimacy of the other; they view each other through a lens of deep distrust and even hatred. So, rather than trying to communicate and understand their cultural differences and reach a consensus solution, each side engages in an "exchange in vilification" (Hunter 1994: 10) and seeks the utter subjugation of the other. This, according to Hunter, is the stuff not of democratic debate, but of war. It thus has the potential to destroy American democratic institutions and lead to a shooting war. Hunter argues that "when cultural impulses this momentous vie against each other to dominate public life, tension, conflict, and perhaps even violence are inevitable" (1994: 4).

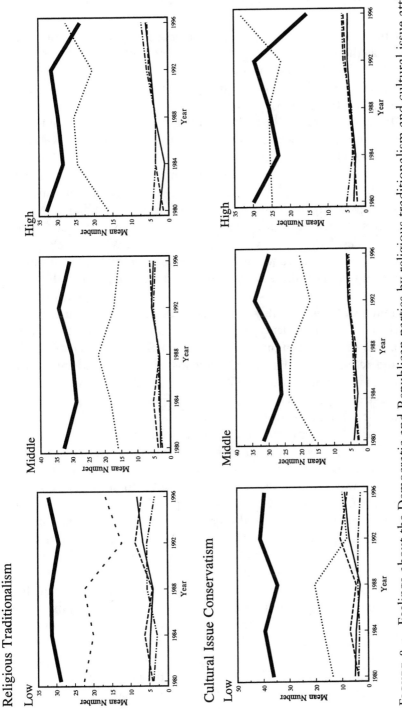

FIGURE 8.4. Feelings about the Democratic and Republican parties by religious traditionalism and cultural issue attitudes, 1980–1996
Source: 1980–1996 National Election Studies

Thus, the question is, "Can democratic practice today mediate differences as deep as these in a manner that is in keeping with the ideals set forth in the founding documents of the American republic? Or will one side, through the tactics of power politics, simply impose its vision on all others?" (Hunter 1994: 5).

Other scholars find Hunter's claim that the culture war could escalate into large-scale violence to be overwrought (Horton 1994; Kellstedt et al. 1994). One of their criticisms is that the type of widespread and deep societal polarization necessary for such an escalation is not present. Most ordinary Americans are rather indifferent toward the cultural conflict and have fairly moderate views on the issues surrounding it. Moreover, levels of societal polarization on these issues have not increased in recent decades (DiMaggio, Evans, and Bryson 1996; Williams 1997). So, not only does the culture war not have the potential to become a shooting war, but perhaps there is really not even a culture war in the mass public.

Hunter's claims probably are overstated. But in his defense, he acknowledges the ambivalence, indifference, and real ignorance of ordinary citizens toward a cultural conflict that takes shape principally at the elite and activist levels. However, unlike his critics, Hunter is not heartened by that. A moderate and vigilant public could act as a strong check on the extremist tendencies of activists and elites. A moderate and oblivious public cannot provide such a check.

My focus here has been not on societal polarization, but on party polarization. Even if the society has not become more culturally divided, the parties surely have. So, I will leave the question of whether or not there is a culture war and whether it is intense enough to become a shooting war in the capable hands of other scholars, and I will address a more relevant question for this book: Is the manifestation of religious and cultural conflict in the political party system good or bad for American democracy? Does it hinder the search for a democratic solution to the cultural conflict, or does it provide a route to such a solution?

Hunter pays little attention to the political parties as either mediators or inciters of the cultural conflict, but he does contend that they have tended to exacerbate, rather than ease, cultural tensions. Not only have they taken highly polarized cultural stands, but they have treated the issues superficially, using the emotional language of fundamental rights— the "fundamental individual right to life" of the unborn or the "fundamental constitutional liberty" of every woman to make her own reproductive decisions—rather than providing reasoned explanations of their positions. They also have failed to acknowledge the diversity of views both throughout the nation and within their own ranks. According to Hunter, "Party involvement has tended to reinforce the artificial character of the controversy. Indeed, despite differences of opinion and position within parties (for example, pro-life Democrats and pro-choice Republicans), such differences tend to be suppressed and publicly unacknowledged; public debate in the parties themselves is hardly tolerated" (1994: 216–17).

There is no question but that the Democrats' and Republicans' stands on cultural matters have grown increasingly polarized over the past three decades. Moreover, the recent struggles over the cultural planks in the party platforms demonstrate the tendency of the two parties to gloss over and attempt to suppress internal differences of opinion. In the spring of 1996, GOP presidential nominee Bob Dole promoted the idea of including a "declaration of tolerance" for those who do not share the party's staunch opposition to abortion within the Republican platform's abortion plank. That was met quickly by harsh reactions and vows to oppose the proposal at the Republican convention from antiabortion and Christian Right leaders. Dole then advanced a compromise plan by which the tolerance language would not be included in the abortion plank. Rather, there would be language in the preamble that acknowledged and welcomed differences of opinion on not only abortion, but also on capital punishment and some other controversial issues. However, even that was viewed as unacceptable by cultural conservatives and was defeated in the party's platform hearings. The result was that there was no specific mention of tolerance for alternative views on abortion, some very vague sentences about diversity were included in the preamble to the platform,[15] and an appendix containing measures rejected by the platform committee, including several advocating abortion rights, was attached at the end of the platform.

The abortion plank in the 1996 Democratic party platform did state that the party respects "the individual conscience of each American on this difficult issue." However, the Democrats have been no less guilty than the GOP of squelching internal debate on cultural issues and prohibiting the presentation of abortion views differing from the party's highly pro-choice stance. In 1992, for instance, Governor Robert Casey of Pennsylvania, a pro-life Democrat, suggested that the party's platform committee add the clause "Democrats do not support abortion on demand and believe the number of abortions should be reduced" to the abortion plank.[16] The proposal was vehemently rejected, and Casey was denied the opportunity to speak at the convention.

Despite the extremity of their cultural stands and their tendency to mask intraparty cultural differences, the political parties may be able to contribute to a democratic solution to the cultural conflict. The degree to which the parties are polarized on cultural issues may make it difficult for them to facilitate compromise. But they may be uniquely positioned to foster a more reasonable, moderately toned debate on cultural matters.

I say this because the overarching purpose of political parties is to win elections. Winning elections within a two-party system means appealing to the ideological center of the electorate and maintaining a diverse electoral coalition. Of course, party candidates are constrained in their ability to move to the electoral center by the extremism of party activists. But the incentive of candidates and the party leaders who are concerned principally with winning elections is to act within those constraints to appeal to, or at least not to alienate, the electoral center, and to maintain the support of party identifiers whose views differ from those of the activists (Chappell and Keech 1986).

Taking the abortion issue as an example, the overwhelmingly pro-life sentiments of Republican activists and pro-choice leanings of Democratic activists mean that the GOP has to be more pro-life than the average voter and the Democrats have to be more pro-choice. However, party leaders and candidates still want to win elections and thus still want to appeal to the cultural center of the electorate. The best way to do that may be to avoid the sort of emotionally charged name-calling that, according to Hunter, passes for discussion among the combatants in the culture war, and instead to engage in a more reasoned discussion of why the party takes a particular position on abortion. Such discourse may at least make centrist voters understand and respect the party's position and may even bring them around to it. It is just this sort of reasoned explication of the pro-life and pro-choice views that Hunter claims is necessary for a democratic solution to the conflict over abortion.

In fact, the inability of the parties to converge at the cultural center and take identical positions on abortion and other cultural issues is probably healthy for American democracy. It not only offers voters a set of true alternatives from which to choose at the voting booth, but also may constrain the polarization, intensity, and potential violence of the cultural conflict. If the Democrats and Republicans did take indistinguishable positions on cultural matters, cultural extremists undoubtedly would pursue political alternatives other than major-party activity—interest groups, new political parties, protests, or even violence—and the cultural debate might be even more polarized and bitter than it is now. As the

APSA's Committee on Political Parties put it, "If the two parties do not develop alternative programs that can be executed, the voter's frustration and the mounting ambiguities of national policy might also set in motion more extreme tendencies to the political left and the political right. . . . Such groups may gravitate beyond the confines of the American system of government and its democratic institutions" (American Political Science Association 1950: 95).

So, given the American electoral system and the institutional structure of the Democratic and Republican parties, it seems reasonable to think that the two parties will be clearly differentiated on moral and cultural matters. But, following their electoral incentives, they may reject emotionally charged harangues on these issues in favor of more reasoned discussions. They may even try to find some compromise and consensus within the cultural debate.

In fact, there is some evidence that being involved in party politics has had a moderating influence on certain elements of the cultural and religious right. Take, for example, the Christian Coalition, the organization that arose out of Pat Robertson's failed 1988 bid for the Republican presidential nomination. It has placed much more emphasis on gaining influence within the Republican party than did the Moral Majority and other earlier incarnations of the Christian Right (Oldfield 1996), and it has been successful in taking over the GOP apparatus in many parts of the country (Persinos 1994). Both as a precursor to and a consequence of hitching its political star to the Republican party's wagon, the Christian Coalition has pursued a more pragmatic course than its Christian Right predecessors (Watson 1999).

Whereas the Moral Majority and its leaders spoke in the language of Jerry Falwell's independent Baptist fundamentalism, the Christian Coalition has schooled its activists in the language of mainstream politics, encouraging them to avoid references to evangelical theology (Rozell and Wilcox 1996). Coalition leaders such as Ralph Reed also have tried to broaden the movement's agenda beyond just moral and cultural issues to include a wide range of issues of concern to Christian families: issues such as tax credits for families, tougher responses to crime, and welfare reform (Reed 1996). There have even been some modest signs of a willingness to compromise on the Christian Right's cultural issue agenda. For instance, Robertson himself has said that it may be time to give up on the pro-life constitutional amendment that the movement has long sought to no avail, and to focus on that which has greater support in the mass public. In November 1993, he said, "I would urge people, as a matter of private choice, not to choose abortion, because I think it is wrong. It's something else though, in the political arena to go out on a quixotic crusade when you know you'll be beaten continuously. So I say let's do what is possible. What is possible is parental consent" (quoted in Rozell and Wilcox 1996: 81).

Of course, a substantial portion of the Christian Coalition's evangelical constituency has balked at its attempts to broaden its agenda and compromise on cultural issues, and other Christian Right organizations have taken a far less pragmatic approach. But this example does suggest that the involvement of the political parties in the cultural conflict has at least some potential to moderate both the tone and content of the cultural debate.

Thus far, however, the parties have not come close to meeting this potential. Recent successful candidates have not engaged in a reasoned, in-depth discussion of the nation's cultural differences. Instead, their approach to dealing with cultural issues has been basically as follows. First, take extreme stands on cultural issues to win party nominations. Second, acquiesce in placing these extreme positions in the party platform so as to sidestep confrontations with the religious and cultural core of the party's activist base. Third, to avoid alienating centrist voters and party identifiers who do not share these views, just ignore the cultural issues during the general election campaign. This has been the course of successful Republican gubernatorial candidates such as George Allen in Virginia and the Bush brothers in Texas and Florida. It was certainly the course followed by the GOP in the 1994 congressional elections when it nominated and elected a large number of candidates with very conservative stands on cultural issues but gave no mention to cultural matters in the Contract with America. And it was clearly the path taken by Bill Clinton and Bob Dole in the 1996 presidential campaign.

What we have, then, are political parties that stake out extreme positions on cultural issues but then fail to provide any detailed explanations for why they took them or engage in any in-depth discussion of those positions during general election campaigns, the only time that most Americans are paying attention to party politics. As Hunter puts it, "The official positions of each party have come to reflect the hard lines of the activist organizations. In itself, this is not a problem. The problem, rather, is that neither party offers anything more than the slogans of solidarity for the already committed. Political parties act as though there are no arguments to be made, only the recapitulation of the symbols of partisan identity" (1994: 218).

Why do party politicians pursue this strategy? Or, better yet, why do they get away with it? The culprit may be the multifaceted issue agenda of contemporary American politics. Cultural issues are not the only salient political issues and, in fact, are much less salient to the average voter than are economic and social welfare concerns. In this situation, candidates can placate the activists who are motivated principally by cultural issues and who have extreme views on them by taking noncentrist cultural positions. But they can avoid alienating centrist voters by ignoring these issues in general-election campaigns and focusing more attention on the bread-and-butter issues that voters care about and on which there may be more leeway to move to the political center. In fact, this is just the course that some political scientists say that rational politicians will pursue in a multidimensional issue space (Geer 1991; Carmines 1994).

In other words, an important reason why the parties are able to avoid a thorough conversation with the electorate about their polarized stands on cultural issues is that most voters do not care much about these matters. So the thing that some scholars point to as evidence that the nation's cultural divisions are not a cause of much concern—the public's general indifference—may be the very reason that the political parties do not contribute toward a more reasoned cultural debate and a consensus solution. If more voters cared about cultural issues, party leaders and candidates might be forced to move to the electoral center on them or at least devote more attention and discussion to them. That discussion might lead to just the kind of reasoned national discourse on cultural issues that Hunter seeks.

THE RELIGIOUS DIVIDE AND PARTY POLITICS: LOOKING TO THE FUTURE

The evidence presented here suggests that the 1990s may have been, in the words of Carmines and Stimson (1989), a "critical moment" in the religious and cultural polarization of the American political parties. Of course, partisan divisions along traditionalist–modernist lines have been evident since at least the early 1980s, and they were even apparent when George McGovern's culturally liberal campaign attracted great numbers of secular activists into the Democratic party in 1972. It also can be argued that the years between 1980 and 1984—a period that witnessed a sharp increase in the presence of committed evangelical Protestants among Republican activists and of secularists among Democratic activists, and in which the division of the parties' mass coalitions along traditionalist–modernist lines began in earnest—was a critical moment. However, the most noticeable developments in the religious and cultural polarization of the parties occurred in the 1990s. The Christian Right became a stronger and much more noticeable influence within the GOP (Oldfield 1996; Watson 1999), and the presence of secularists and religious modernists among Democratic activists returned to the levels witnessed in 1972. The identification of devout evangelicals with the Republican party continued to grow at a rapid pace, and secular identification with and voting for the Democratic party increased much more than it did in the 1970s and 1980s. Finally, mass perceptions of important party differences on moral and cultural matters and the overall religious polarization of the parties' mass coalitions increased considerably more in the 1990s than it had in previous decades. In short, most of the trends presented here suggest that the 1990s represented not a tailing off of partisan polarization along traditionalist–modernist lines, but rather a period of rapid increase in the religious and cultural differences between the parties.

Carmines and Stimson suggest that such a period of rapid growth in partisan division along the lines of a new political cleavage, a critical moment, should be followed by continued, but more subtle, increases in party polarization. There are certainly important differences between the religious and cultural case and Carmines and Stimson's description of racial issue evolution. But if they are right and if the 1990s do represent a critical moment in the polarization of the two parties along religious and cultural lines, then we should expect the traditionalist–modernist differences between the Republicans and the Democrats to grow through at least the first decade of the twenty-first century. The growth, however, should occur at a slower pace.

Beyond the predictions of the issue evolution model, there are other reasons to expect the religious and cultural differences between the two parties to continue to increase in the near future. First, the role of party activists in the partisan change process may mean that the trends in partisan religious and cultural polarization are self-sustaining. The growing cultural conservatism of the roll-call votes of Republican members of Congress and of the stands taken in Republican party platforms, and the growing cultural liberalism of the Democratic party's members of Congress and platforms should attract even more religious traditionalists into Republican party activity and even more secularists into Democratic activity, while driving religious modernists and secularists out of the ranks of GOP activists and religious traditionalists out of the Democratic activist pool. That further increase in activist-level religious polarization should mean not only that Republican candidates and platforms continue to take highly conservative stands on cultural issues while Democratic candidates and platforms keep staking out highly liberal cultural positions, but also that the public's perception of the parties as highly differentiated on cultural matters continues to grow. If that happens, there should be further increases in the religious and cultural polarization of the Democratic and Republican coalitions in the mass electorate.

Second, the cultural conflict remains unsolved, and the two sides remain unwilling to compromise on its key issues; there are still major political battles to fight. For the most part, cultural conservatives continue to pursue a ban on all abortions other than those involving rape, incest, or danger to the life of the mother (of course, not all abortion opponents favor even these exceptions); the return of organized prayer and religious observance to the public schools; and restrictions on the rights and responsibilities of homosexuals. As a result, cultural liberals keep fighting to sustain abortion rights, to prevent religion from having a formal role in public education, and to protect and extend the rights of homosexuals. As long as these battles rage, the two sides, already entrenched within the two major political parties, will keep trying to use the parties as vehicles to carry them to victory. Consequently, party politicians will continue to have strategic incentives to take noncentrist positions on cultural matters.

On the other hand, there are factors that may act as constraints on the continued growth of partisan religious and cultural divisions.[17] One of the most important of those is the fact that contemporary American politics is characterized by multiple dimensions of salient policy issues and multiple cross-cutting partisan cleavages. This means that the ability of the Democratic party to make further gains among religious modernists and secularists and the potential for the GOP to gain greater support from religious traditionalists are hampered by the fact that their positions on cultural issues may appeal to these groups, but their stands on other important issues may not.

The Republican party, for example, has garnered the consistent support of only a portion of the traditionally religious electorate. The GOP has done very well at attracting the loyalties of committed evangelical Protestants and at maintaining the support of committed and doctrinally orthodox mainline Protestants. It has done less well at drawing conservative Catholics, not to mention traditionalist black Protestants and orthodox Jews, into the party fold.

That is not to say that the Republicans and the Christian Right have not tried to become more attractive to religious traditionalists outside of white Protestantism or that they have not made some inroads among these groups. Christian Right and Catholic leaders, together with many GOP leaders, have long been allies in battles against abortion, and committed Catholics slowly but surely have become more Republican in their party ties and voting behavior. There also have been alliances of evangelical and black Protestant leaders on the conservative side of several local- and state-level cultural battles (Greenberg 1994), and surveys have uncovered significant support among African-Americans for Christian Right organizations and for Christian Right leaders such as Pat Robertson (Wilcox 1990a, 1991). Meanwhile, some Republican candidates have won substantial majorities of the vote in urban communities populated largely by orthodox Jews (Sigelman 1991).

The Christian Coalition, in particular, has made special efforts to reach out to nonevangelical religious traditionalists to build a broader and longer-lasting coalition of cultural conservatives. One way it has done that is simply by employing a more ecumenical political language based on the values of all religious and moral traditionalists and tempering leaders' and activists' public references to evangelical theology (Oldfield 1996; Watson 1999). Another way is through specific measures such as creating the Catholic Alliance, a wing of the Christian Coalition headed by Catholics and reserved exclusively for Catholic members,[18] or devoting funds to efforts to deter and prosecute the burning of black churches in the South (Watson 1999).

However, the problem faced by the Christian Right and the GOP is that traditionalist Catholics, black Protestants, and Jews may agree with Republican positions on cultural issues, but they tend not to be enthusiastic about the party's stands on other salient issues. The Catholic Church, for example, has been committed since Vatican II to government efforts to ensure economic and social justice and has been staunchly opposed to nuclear proliferation. In short, it has been officially opposed to Republican positions on most major policy issues outside of the cultural realm. Of course, the African-American church has had a long and very intimate relationship with American liberalism and tends to be quite liberal on racial and social welfare issues. What this means is that the most committed Catholics and black Protestants, the members of those two traditions who are most likely to support the cultural agenda of the Republican party and the Christian Right, may be the least likely to support the Republican agenda on other issues. At the very least, they will not be as supportive as committed evangelical Protestants of that agenda.[19]

The Democratic party faces similar constraints in attracting more secularists and religious modernists into its coalition. The individuals in these groups tend to have relatively high income levels and thus fairly conservative views on economic and social welfare issues. In other words, they tend not to be terribly enthusiastic about the Democratic party's traditional opposition to tax cuts and support for economic redistribution and high levels of federal spending.

In sum, there are reasons to believe that the religious and cultural divisions between the Democratic and Republican parties will continue to increase in the next decade or two. But it is unlikely that further growth in partisan religious polarization will occur with the same speed and magnitude that typified the growth in the 1990s. Partly as a result of the multidimensional American political agenda, it may prove more difficult for the Republicans to broaden their support among religious traditionalists and for the Democrats to extend their support among religious modernists and secularists than it was for the parties to develop these support bases in the first place.

A Possible Depolarization of the Parties?

While the literature and my model of the partisan change process point to a future of sustained religious and cultural differences between the parties, there have been some recent signs that there may be a noticeable decline in partisan religious polarization in the near future. Those signs have come principally from the conservative side of the cultural divide.

After its historic victory in the congressional and statewide elections of 1994, the Republican party suffered disappointing losses in 1996 and 1998. In 1996, Bill Clinton easily won a second term as president. In 1998, the conventional wisdom was that the Republicans would gain a substantial number of seats in Congress. The party of the president generally loses seats in a midterm-year election, particularly in the middle of a president's second term, and this president was embroiled in a sex and perjury scandal that eventually led to his impeachment. But the Republicans gained no seats in the Senate and actually lost seats in the House.

These losses were blamed by many journalists and political observers on the GOP's religious and cultural right wing. That was particularly true of the 1998 setback, which seemingly was fueled by voter dissatisfaction with the zealous pursuit of the impeachment of President Clinton by the

Republican-controlled House. That pursuit, in the face of public opinion polls showing overwhelming public opposition to impeachment, was, according to its critics, evidence of a party more responsive to its moralistic activists and contributors than to the sentiments of ordinary citizens. As James P. Pinkerton of the *Los Angeles Times* put it,

> James Carville was right. It was about sex. It wasn't just Bill Clinton's sex life that was at issue in this election, however, but also the private life of the American people. And their message was clear: Voters rejected the Ken Starr/Henry Hyde inquiry into the president's personal behavior, and they repudiated the hard-shell moralism that the Republican party chose to project nationwide. . . . Put simply, the Ralph Reed–Gary Bauer Republicans were trounced, while the pragmatic George W. Bush–[George] Pataki Republicans, mostly governors, were triumphant.[20]

Meanwhile, GOP moderates argued that for the party to regain the electoral momentum it attained in 1994, it had to distance itself from the Christian Right and cultural conservatives. At an early 1999 meeting of the centrist Republican Leadership Council (RLC), New Jersey Governor Christine Whitman contended,

> We have to get away from the perception that all we care about is whether or not Teletubbies are gay [a reference to an earlier statement by Jerry Falwell about the popular children's television show]. . . . Americans aren't an amoral people. They're not a people that accept the kind of behavior we've seen in the White House. But I think part of what has driven Clinton's positives is their fear of some of the rhetoric that they have heard from some of the more extreme spokespersons for the Republican Party that implied, "Yeah, but it's only my morals that are right and if you don't think exactly the way I think you can't be a good Republican."[21]

RLC cochairman John A. Moran insisted that the Republicans had to start ignoring the Christian Right. He claimed that "we can't negotiate with them. They don't want to win."[22]

The dissatisfaction of some Republicans with the party's ties to the Christian Right seemed to come to a head in the 2000 presidential campaign of Senator John McCain. As Christian Right leaders lined up to endorse his rival, Governor George W. Bush, and Bush won an overwhelming majority of the primary votes of religious conservatives, McCain lashed out at individuals such as Pat Robertson and Jerry Falwell and against their influence in the GOP. Calling these Christian Right leaders "the forces of evil," McCain argued that "these people have led our party out of the mainstream of America. They are exclusive, not inclusive. They practice the politics of division, not addition."[23]

These calls from some Republicans for the GOP to abandon the Christian Right and threats from James Dobson and other evangelical leaders that the Christian Right will desert the GOP have been joined recently by suggestions from Christian Right notables for religious traditionalists to abandon politics altogether. In the spring of 1999, Paul Weyrich, one of the founders of the Moral Majority and the originator of its name, called for religious and cultural conservatives to accept political and cultural defeat and drop out of the political fray. Weyrich said, "I believe that we probably have lost the culture war. . . . I no longer believe that there is a moral majority. [If there were,] Bill Clinton would have been driven out of office months ago."[24] Shortly thereafter, Cal Thomas, a conservative columnist and former spokesman for the Moral Majority, and Ed Dobson, a former aide to Jerry Falwell, released a book called *Blinded by Might* (1999), in which they contend that the Christian Right's political power is on the decline and call for religious conservatives to focus less on politics and more on saving souls and changing individual minds about religious, cultural, and moral matters.

Of course, if the Republican party abandoned the Christian Right or the Christian Right deserted the GOP, the consequences for the religious and cultural polarization of the parties would be considerable. The Republican party would be less attractive to traditionally religious activists and voters and thus less threatening to secular and religiously modern citizens. Accordingly, the Democratic party would hold less appeal for secularists and religious liberals and be more attractive to religious conservatives. The party system would become based less on religious orientations and more on other factors, such as social class and economic attitudes.

However, neither of these scenarios is very likely. The GOP and its candidates cannot turn their backs on religious and cultural traditionalists because these individuals, through their increasing activity in Republican party politics and their growing tendency to identify with the GOP, have become the backbone of the Republican coalition. They represent a disproportionate share of primary voters and caucus participants (Oldfield 1996; Rozell and Wilcox 1995, 1997), so candidates cannot win Republican nominations without their support. Committed evangelical Protestants are also the party's most loyal campaign workers and electoral backers. So, Republican nominees cannot hope to win general elections without their active and enthusiastic support. As *Washington Post* columnist Thomas Edsall put it, "For the Republican Party, a mobilized and energetic conservative wing is crucial to victory."[25] In fact, one could argue that the Republican party's failures in 1996 and 1998 were the result not of being tied too closely to the Christian Right, but of failing to sufficiently stoke the fires of traditionally religious voters. James Dobson argued just that, saying that in 1994 "43 percent of the total vote came from those who identified themselves as born-again Christians and pro-lifers. . . . That is what put the Republicans in power; two years later, those numbers dropped to 29 percent."[26]

For the very same reasons, it is not likely that religious and cultural traditionalists will desert the Republican party in the near future. They are unlikely to pursue other party alternatives because the Democratic party has committed itself firmly to cultural liberalism, because third parties almost inevitably are doomed to failure in the American political system, and, most important, because they have accumulated too much political capital within the Republican party. Religious traditionalists exercise a considerable influence over party nominations, they wield a controlling influence over the cultural planks in Republican platforms, and they have control of the party machinery, and all the resources that entails, in a large number of states and localities. To paraphrase Duane Oldfield (1996), as the Christian Right has developed the means to more effectively exercise its "voice" within the Republican party, "exit" from the party has become a less and less plausible political option.

Moreover, the conventional wisdom that the GOP has not returned the favor of evangelical electoral loyalty by actively pursuing a culturally conservative public policy agenda is somewhat misleading. It is true that the Christian Right has not achieved its ultimate goals of securing constitutional amendments to ban abortion and to allow prayer in the public schools. But it is clear that the ascendance of religious traditionalism within the GOP has had real policy consequences. Republican presidents Reagan and Bush were unable, or maybe did not really try, to persuade Congress to pass an antiabortion amendment to the Constitution. But they did appoint Supreme Court justices who were less committed than their predecessors to the *Roe v. Wade* decision, and those justices have provided the key votes in decisions, such as *Webster v. Reproductive Health Services*, that have given states more leeway in restricting abortion rights.

Also, as I showed in chapter 6, Republicans in Congress have become increasingly likely to vote in favor of proposals to restrict or ban abortions, to encourage prayer and other religious expression in the schools and other public places, to restrict the rights of homosexuals, to reduce access to pornography, and to maintain traditional family structures, while growing more and more likely to vote against culturally liberal proposals. They have been successful in restricting the use of federal funds to pay for abortions and in greatly limiting access to abortions in U.S. military hospitals. In fact, since the Republicans took control in January 1995, Congress has passed a bill that bans federal recognition of same-sex marriages and authorizes states to refuse to recognize same-sex marriages conducted in other states; a bill prohibiting federal health insurance plans from covering abortions except in the cases of rape, incest, or to preserve the life of the mother; and two bills greatly restricting partial birth abortions. Some of those bills were vetoed by the Democratic president. That, however, means that the Christian Right's beef is not with the Republican party for a lack of commitment to cultural conservatism, but with the Democratic party for a thorough rejection of such views—all the more reason to stay active in GOP politics.

It is also hard to fathom that the religious and cultural traditionalists active within the Christian Right and the Republican party would heed the calls of Weyrich, Thomas, and Ed Dobson and simply withdraw from politics to concentrate exclusively on spiritual goals. If their efforts were being met with limited success, that might be understandable. And from the standpoint of public policy, they have had limited success. But from the standpoint of party politics, religious conservatives have enjoyed considerable success. They are one of the most powerful components of one of the two major American political parties, a party that currently controls both houses of Congress and whose candidate for president in 2000 leads (in August 2000) Vice President Al Gore, the Democratic nominee, in public opinion polls. Partisan success does not equate to policy success. But if you have been as successful as the Christian Right has been, within a party that is as competitive as the Republican party currently is, it is not a bad start. Now seems like a strange time to pack your bags and go home.

In short, it is unlikely that the place of the Christian Right and its traditionally religious constituents in the Republican party will go away or rapidly decline in the near future. And if this group remains a strong influence with the GOP, secularists and religious modernists will continue to find the Democratic party an attractive political home. Thus, the religious and cultural polarization of the political parties quite likely will be an outstanding feature of American politics well into the new millennium.

NOTES

1. See also Schattschneider (1942), Epstein (1979), and Aldrich (1995) for similar definitions of political parties.

2. The parties formed by these groups include the Anti-Masonic party, the nativist Know-Nothing party, the antislavery Liberty, Free-Soil, and Republican parties, and the agrarian Greenback and People's (or Populist) parties.

3. The third parties that have won at least one electoral vote since World War II are the States' Rights Democratic (or Dixiecrat) party of 1948, a party organized around the segregationist presidential campaign of Strom Thurmond, and the American Independent party of 1968, which was simply a label attached to the presidential campaign of George Wallace. The Reform party, the vehicle for Ross Perot's independent campaign in 1996, did not win any electoral votes, but it did win nearly 9 percent of the popular vote. The Reform party was an outgrowth of Perot's impressive independent candidacy in 1992.

4. To readers familiar with the scholarly literature on realignment, this discussion may bring to mind the work of Paul Allen Beck (1979) on electoral cycles. In Beck's cyclical theory, realignments produce stable alignments. When the issues of the preceding realignment fade and the generation that experienced the realignment is replaced by younger voters, the stable alignment gives way to "dealignment." The characteristics of a dealignment—weakened party attachments and the reduced salience of old issues—create conditions that are ripe for another realignment to occur. So not only is dealignment consistent with realignment, it is necessary for realignment.

The difference between Beck and those observers who contend that party dealignment is incompatible with realignment lies in the ability of the parties to rebound. In Beck's model, the emergence of a powerful new issue and party polarization on the issue reinvigorates the party system. Voters who were disattached from parties that were divided over old, irrelevant issues become reattached to parties that now compete over new, highly salient issues. In the other view, the party system has deteriorated to the extent that powerful new issues do not lead it to recovery. New issues may invigorate voters, but they do not reattach them to political parties. Because parties have become so much less relevant to campaigning and governing, voters do not look to them for representation of their views on the new issues. Instead, they look to actors such as candidates and interest groups that have become more relevant than parties during the dealigning period.

5. The relationships between these demographic factors and religious orientations in 1980 were nearly identical to those shown for 1996. So, the results do not appear to be time bound.

6. The categories of church attendance in figure 8.1 are taken from the 1960 through 1968 NES surveys. The comparable categories in the 1972

through 1996 surveys are never attend for "never," attend a few times a year or less for "seldom," attend once or twice a month for "often," and attend almost every week or more for "regular."

7. "Low" and "high" religious traditionalism in figure 8.2 refer to the bottom third and the top third, respectively, of the index. Income was divided into equal thirds to form the low, middle, and high categories.

8. In figure 8.2, "low" education refers to individuals who have no college experience, "middle" refers to individuals who have some college education but not a bachelor's degree, and "high" refers to individuals who have a bachelor's or advanced degree.

9. Ron Faucheux, "Party Politics: Both Ends against the Middle," *Campaigns and Elections,* June 1999, p. 7.

10. Quoted in Bennett Roth, "Perot Vows Second Stab at Creating Third Party," *Houston Chronicle,* September 26, 1995, p. A1.

11. Quoted in Dick Polman, "This Year, Voters Are Tuning Out," *Arizona Republic,* October 16, 1998, p. A1.

12. Quoted in Michael J. Gerson, "A Righteous Indignation," *U.S. News & World Report,* May 4, 1998, pp. 20–29.

13. Mark Kmetzko, "Those Wavering Party Lines; Democrats and Republicans Would Rather Stand for Nothing than Risk Votes," *Plain Dealer,* November 27, 1998, p. B10.

14. I also include individuals who offer an equal number of likes and dislikes of the Democratic party but more likes than dislikes of the GOP in the "Republican partisan" category, and individuals who offer an equal number of likes and dislikes of the GOP but more likes than dislikes of the Democratic party in the "Democratic partisan" category. These respondents have party identifications and feeling thermometer ratings of the two parties that are very similar to the other individuals in these two categories.

15. The exact language was, "The diversity of our nation is reflected in this platform. We ask for the support and participation of all who substantially share our agenda. In one way or another, every Republican is a dissenter. At the same time we are not morally indifferent."

16. Quoted in Hunter (1994: 217).

17. One of those constraints, of course, is simple numerical reality. As the cultural polarization of the parties grows, the number of cultural conservatives who are not already Republicans and cultural liberals who are not already Democrats grows smaller, and further increases in polarization become less and less likely. In fact, Thomas Carsey and I show that even if we assume constant rates of replacement (of activists with one view on abortion by activists with a different view) and conversion (of individual activists from one position on abortion to another) among Democratic and Republican activists, the aggregate abortion views of the two parties' activists should reach an equilibrium (stable) level two or three decades from now. At that

equilibrium, about 65 percent of Republican activists are pro-life, and about 80 percent of Democratic activists are pro-choice (Carsey and Layman 1999).

18. The Catholic Alliance was formed in 1995 but has since been defunded because of financial problems within the Christian Coalition (Watson 1999).

19. The same also may be true for committed mainline Protestants, given the liberal views of mainline clergy on social welfare, race, and foreign policy (Guth et al. 1997). In fact, while there is a positive and statistically significant relationship between religious commitment and conservative attitudes on cultural issues in all four of the largest religious traditions (the correlation in the 1996 NES was .42 for evangelicals, .26 for mainline Protestants, .21 for Catholics, and .12 for black Protestants), the relationship between commitment and conservative attitudes on social welfare issues is positive and significant only for evangelicals (the correlation in the 1996 NES was .25 for evangelicals, .06 for mainline Protestants, .01 for Catholics, and −.13 for black Protestants).

20. James P. Pinkerton, "Perspectives on the Election; Pragmatism Yes, Moralism No; The Religious Right Was Defeated," *Los Angeles Times*, November 5, 1998, p. A9.

21. Quoted in Kevin Sack, "G.O.P. Moderates Meet to Frown before an Unflattering Mirror," *New York Times*, National Edition, February 15, 1999. [Internet, WWW]. *Available:* The New York Times on the Web Archives; ADDRESS: *http://archives.nytimes.com*.

22. Ibid.

23. Quoted in Terry M. Neal and Dan Balz, "Bush-McCain Debate on the Party Rages On," *Washington Post*, March 1, 2000, p. A7.

24. Quoted in Ray Waddle, "Religion, Politics Not a Very Good Mix Lately," *Tennessean*, March 28, 1999, p. D2.

25. Thomas B. Edsall, "Conservatively, a Profusion of Paradoxes," *Washington Post*, August 22, 1999, p. B1.

26. Ibid.

Measurement

A1: THE MEASUREMENT OF RELIGION

I. Religious Tradition

Chapter 2 (1996 NES)

The assignment of respondents follows a three-step strategy:

(1) Respondents with unambiguous affiliations are assigned to religious traditions as follows:

Seculars: No religious preference, agnostics, and atheists

Evangelical Protestants: Nonblack respondents affiliating with Seventh-Day Adventist; American Baptist Association; American Baptist Churches, U.S.A.; Baptist Bible Fellowship; Baptist General Conference; Baptist Missionary Association of America; Conservative Baptist Association of America; General Association of Regular Baptist Churches; National Association of Free Will Baptists; Primitive Baptists; Reformed Baptist; Southern Baptist Convention; Church of the Brethren; Mennonite Church; Evangelical Covenant Church; Evangelical Free Church; Brethren in Christ; Mennonite Brethren; Christian and Missionary Alliance; Church of God (Anderson, IN); Church of the Nazarene; Free Methodist Church; Salvation Army; Wesleyan Church; Church of God of Findlay, OH; Plymouth Brethren; Independent Fundamentalist Churches of America; Lutheran Church–Missouri Synod; Wisconsin Evangelical Lutheran Synod; Congregational Methodist; Assemblies of God; Church of God (Cleveland, TN); Church of God (Huntsville, AL); International Church of the Four Square Gospel; Pentecostal Church of God; Pentecostal Holiness

Church; Church of God of the Apostolic Faith; Church of God of Prophecy; Apostolic Pentecostal; Cumberland Presbyterian Church; Presbyterian Church in America; Evangelical Presbyterian; Christian Reformed Church

Mainline Protestants: Nonblack respondents affiliating with Episcopalian, United Church of Christ, Congregational Christian, Quakers (Friends), Evangelical Lutheran Church in America, United Methodist Church, Presbyterian Church in the U.S.A., Reformed Church in America, Christian Church (Disciples of Christ)

Black Protestant: All respondents affiliating with National Baptist Convention in the U.S.A., National Baptist Convention of America, National Primitive Baptist Convention of the U.S.A., Progressive National Baptist Convention, African Methodist Episcopal Church, African Methodist Episcopal Zion Church, Christian Methodist Episcopal Church, and Church of God in Christ, and all black members of evangelical and mainline Protestant denominations

Catholic

Jewish: Orthodox, Conservative, and Reformed Jews

Conservative nontraditional: Christian Scientists, Mormons, Jehovah's Witnesses, Fundamentalist Adventist

Liberal nontraditional: Spiritualists, Unitarian–Universalist, Unity Church

Eastern Orthodox

Other religions: Muslim, Buddhist, Hindu, Bahai, American Indian religions, other non-Christian and non-Jewish

(2) Respondents with ambiguous affiliations are assigned to traditions based on other characteristics. There are four different groups of these ambiguous affiliations:

(a) Respondents who identify themselves as belonging to "other" religions: They are placed in the secular category if they do not display a minimal level of religious commitment. Otherwise, they are placed in the other religion category.

(b) Respondents who identify themselves as simply Protestants or Christians: They are placed in one of four categories:

1. Secular: Those who do not display minimal levels of religious commitment.
2. Evangelical Protestants: Those who do display minimal levels of

religious commitment, are nonblack, and identify themselves as fundamentalist, evangelical, or charismatic in a question about what type of Christian they are.

3. Mainline Protestants: Those who do display minimal levels of religious commitment, are nonblack, and identify themselves as moderate to liberal Christians.
4. Black Protestants: Those who do display minimal levels of religious commitment and are black.

(c) Respondents who identify with Protestant denominational families that include both evangelical and mainline denominations (Lutheran, Methodist, and Presbyterian): They are placed in one of four categories:

1. Secular: Those who do not display minimal levels of religious commitment.
2. Evangelical Protestants: Those who do display minimal levels of religious commitment, are nonblack, and identify themselves as fundamentalist, evangelical, or charismatic in a question about what type of Christian they are.
3. Mainline Protestants: Those who do display minimal levels of religious commitment, are nonblack, and identify themselves as moderate to liberal Christians.
4. Black Protestants: Those who do display minimal levels of religious commitment and are black.

(d) Respondents who identify with denominational families associated with the evangelical Protestant tradition (Adventist, Baptist, Holiness, Church of God, Pentecostal, Independent–Fundamentalist): They are placed in the evangelical Protestant category unless they do not display minimal levels of religious commitment (coded as seculars) or they are black (coded as black Protestants).

(3) Respondents in all religious traditions are recoded as seculars if they do not display a minimal level of religious commitment. To be coded as not displaying minimal commitment, respondents have to pray only once a week or less *and* attend church only a few times a year or less *and* receive no guidance in their lives from religion.

Chapter 3 (1972–1992 CDS)

Respondents are assigned to religious traditions as follows:

Secular: Agnostic, atheist, or no religious preference

Jewish

Catholic

Eastern Orthodox: Eastern Orthodox in 1972, Greek Orthodox in all other years

Mormon

Mainline Protestants: Nonblack respondents affiliating with Episcopalian, Congregationalist, United Church of Christ, Presbyterian, Lutheran, Methodist

Evangelical Protestants: Nonblack respondents affiliating with Southern Baptist, "Other" Baptist, Church of Christ, Pentecostal, Assemblies of God

Black Protestants: Black members of mainline Protestant, evangelical Protestant, or "other" Protestant denominations

Chapter 4 (Analyses Involving the 1988 and 1992 CDS Only)

The measurement of religious tradition is the same as in chapter 3 with two exceptions:

(1) Respondents who identify themselves as members of a religious tradition but receive no guidance from religion and "never" or "almost never" attend church are coded as secular.

(2) Nonblack respondents coded as "other Protestants" in the surveys are classified as evangelical Protestants if they identify themselves as fundamentalist Christians, and as mainline Protestants if they do not identify themselves as fundamentalists.

Chapter 5 (Analyses Involving the 1960–1996 NES)

The NES greatly expanded and improved their coding of religious affiliations prior to the 1990 survey. Thus, the measurement of religious tradition in analyses involving NES surveys prior to 1990 is somewhat different from that used for chapter 2. For analyses involving data collected prior to 1980, the assignment of respondents to traditions is a one-step process. There is not sufficient information in those surveys to assign ambiguous affiliations to traditions or to transfer respondents who are only nominally affiliated with a tradition to the secular category. For the 1990–1996 NES in analyses involving NES data prior to 1980, the first two steps used to create the tradition variables in chapter 2 were used, but the third step—transferring nominally affiliated respondents from the traditions to the secular category—was not used to maintain comparability with the pre-1990 data. The assignment of respondents to religious traditions in the 1960–1988 NES is as follows:

Seculars: No religious preference, agnostics, atheists

Evangelical Protestants: Nonblack respondents affiliated with Evangelical Brethren, Baptist, Mennonite, Church of the Brethren, United Missionary, Protestant Missionary, Church of God, Holiness, Nazarene, Free Methodist, Plymouth Brethren, Pentecostal, Assembly of God, Church of Christ, Salvation Army, Primitive Baptist, Free Will Baptist, Missionary Fundamentalist Baptist, Gospel Baptist, Seventh-Day Adventist, Southern Baptist, Missouri Synod Lutheran, "other fundamentalist."

Mainline Protestants: Nonblack respondents affiliated with Presbyterian, Lutheran (except Missouri Synod), United Church of Christ, Episcopalian, Methodist (except Free Methodist), Disciples of Christ, Quakers, Congregational, Reformed

Black Protestants: All respondents affiliating with African Methodist Episcopal or Church of God in Christ, and all black members of evangelical and mainline Protestant denominations

Catholic

Jewish

Conservative nontraditional: Christian Scientists, Mormons, Jehovah's Witnesses

Liberal nontraditional: Spiritualist, Unitarian, Universalist, Unity

Eastern Orthodox

Other Protestants: Protestant with no denomination given, nondenominational Protestant, community church

Other religion: Muslim, Buddhist, Hindu, Bahai, other non-Judeo-Christian

Chapters 5 and 7 (Analyses Involving the 1980–1996 NES)

The assignment of respondents to traditions was the same as in analyses involving the 1960–1996 NES except that respondents in all traditions who do not display a minimal level of religious commitment are recoded as seculars. To be coded as displaying minimal commitment, respondents had to receive no guidance in their lives from religion *and* never attend church.

II. Denominational Orthodoxy

Some of the analyses in chapters 2, 3, 6, and 7 employ a denominational orthodoxy scale. What follows is the coding of the one used in chapter 2. The scales used in chapters 3, 6, and 7 follow a similar coding scheme.

0 = Seculars

1 = Jews

2 = Liberal Protestants (Episcopalian, United Church of Christ, Congregationalist) and Liberal Nontraditional

3 = Catholics

4 = Moderate Protestants (mainline Protestants not in the liberal Protestant category)

5 = Black Protestants and Conservative Nontraditional

6 = Neoevangelicals [all evangelical Protestants not in the fundamentalist/charismatic category (see below)]

7 = Fundamentalists and Charismatics [Baptist Missionary Association of America, Conservative Baptist Association of America, Primitive Baptist, Church of God (Anderson, IN), Plymouth Brethren, Independent Fundamentalist Churches of America, Congregational Methodist, Assemblies of God, Church of God (Cleveland, TN), Church of God (Huntsville, AL), International Church of the Four Square Gospel, Pentecostal Church of God, Pentecostal Holiness Church, Church of God of the Apostolic Faith, Church of God of Prophecy, Apostolic Pentecostal, Church of Christ, and the following ambiguous affiliations: Independent–Fundamentalist, Pentecostal, Church of God]

III. Doctrinal Orthodoxy

Chapter 2 (1996 NES)

Doctrinal orthodoxy is the sum of the dichotomous born-again Christian indicator and the following expanded view of the Bible measure. The reliability coefficient, alpha, is .65, and the variable ranges from 0 to 1.

1. Respondents who say, "The Bible is a book written by men and is not the Word of God."
2. Respondents who say, "The Bible is the Word of God but not everything in it should be taken literally, word for word."

3. Respondents who say, "The Bible is the actual Word of God and is to be taken literally, word for word," and who read the Bible once a week or less.

4. Respondents who say, "The Bible is the actual Word of God and is to be taken literally, word for word," and who read the Bible a few times a week or more.

Chapters 5 and 7 (Analyses Using the 1980–1996 NES)

Doctrinal orthodoxy is the sum of the dichotomous born-again Christian indicator and the standard view of the Bible measure. The reliability coefficient is .49 in 1980, .53 in 1984, .51 in 1988, .57 in 1992, and .60 in 1996. The variable ranges from 0 to 1.

IV. Religious Commitment

Chapter 2 (1996 NES)

Commitment is the sum of respondents' scores on the following items. The reliability is .81, and the variable ranges from 0 to 1.

A. Church Attendance:
1. Never
2. A few times a year
3. Once or twice a month
4. Almost every week
5. Every week
6. More than once a week

B. Religious Salience (amount of guidance respondent receives from religion):
1. None
2. Some
3. Quite a bit
4. A great deal

C. Frequency of Prayer:
1. Never
2. Once a week or less
3. A few times a week
4. Once a day
5. Several times a day

Chapter 3 (1972–1992 CDS)

Two indicators of commitment are used independently:

A. Church attendance:
1. Don't attend religious services
2. Almost never
3. A few times a year
4. Once or twice a month
5. Almost every week

B. Religious salience (amount of guidance respondent receives from religion, 1980–1992 CDS only):
1. None
2. Only some
3. Quite a bit
4. A great deal

Chapter 4 (1988 and 1992 CDS)

Commitment is the sum of respondents' standardized scores on the church attendance and religious salience variables. The reliability coefficient is .75 for 1988 delegates and .79 for 1992 delegates. The variable ranges from 0 to 1.

Chapters 5 and 7 (Analyses Using the 1980–1996 NES)

Commitment is the sum of church attendance (with categories five and six combined) and religious salience. The reliability is .71 in 1980, .71 in 1984, .74 in 1988, .72 in 1992, and .72 in 1996. The variable ranges from 0 to 1.

Chapter 5 (Defining Regular and Nonregular Church Attenders)

Frequency of church attendance is coded as follows in the NES surveys from 1960 through 1996:

A. 1960–1968
1. Never
2. Seldom
3. Often
4. Regularly

B. 1970
1. Never
2. A few times a year
3. Once or twice a month
4. Almost every week

C. 1972–1986
1. Never
2. A few times a year
3. Once or twice a month
4. Almost every week
5. Every week

D. 1988–1996
1. Never
2. A few times a year
3. Once or twice a month
4. Almost every week
5. Every week
6. More than once a week

From 1960 to 1968, regular attenders are those who attend "regularly," and nonregular attenders are those who attend "never," "seldom," or "often." From 1970 to 1996, regular attenders are those who attend "almost every week" or more, and nonregular attenders are those who attend "once or twice a month" or less.

A2: The Measurement of Issue Attitudes, Policy Predispositions, and Group Evaluations

I. Issue Attitudes

Chapter 2 (Cultural Issue Attitudes)

The measure of attitudes toward cultural issues is the sum of respondents' positions on abortion, women's role in society, laws to protect homosexuals from discrimination, homosexuals in the armed forces, and prayer in the public schools. The scores on each issue were coded to range from −1 (most liberal) to 1 (most conservative), with missing values coded as 0. Respondents who had missing values on all five issues were given a missing value on the scale, which also ranges from −1 to 1. The reliability (coefficient alpha) of the scale is .62.

Chapter 3 (Abortion Attitude)

The coding of the abortion item in the 1972–1988 CDS is as follows:

1. Abortion should never be prohibited.
2. Abortion should never be permitted if, for personal reasons, the woman would have difficulty in caring for the child.
3. Abortion should be permitted only if the life and health of the woman is in danger.
4. Abortion should never be permitted.

The coding of the abortion item in the 1992 CDS is as follows:

1. By law, a woman should always be able to obtain an abortion as a matter of personal choice.
2. The law should permit abortion for reasons other than rape, incest, or danger to the woman's life, but only after the need for the abortion has been clearly established.
3. The law should permit abortion only in cases of rape, incest, or when the woman's life is in danger.
4. By law, abortion should never be permitted.

Chapter 4 (Issue Dimensions in the 1992 CDS)

The measures of attitudes toward the various issue dimensions are based on separate principal-components factor analyses (see table A1) of the attitudes of Democratic and Republican convention delegates on

Results of principal-components factor analysis of the
issue attitudes of 1992 convention delegates, by party

Party and Issue	Factor 1 (Social Welfare)	Factor 2 (Cultural)	Factor 3 (Defense and Foreign Policy)
Democrats			
Spending for the poor	**.799**	−.037	−.007
Spending on programs for blacks	**.745**	.158	−.009
Spending for the unemployed	**.710**	−.033	−.020
Welfare spending	**.690**	.074	.114
Government services and spending	**.647**	.129	.262
Government responsibility to help blacks	**.611**	.360	−.010
Government-sponsored health insurance	**.490**	.094	.212
Women's role in society	.140	**.722**	−.119
Abortion	.008	**.703**	.145
School prayer	.115	**.635**	.277
Use of military force	.061	−.014	**.807**
Defense spending	.112	.212	**.671**
Eigenvalues	3.63	1.53	1.09
Percentage of variance explained	30.2	12.7	9.1
Republicans			
Spending of programs for blacks	**.735**	.043	−.026
Spending for the poor	**.731**	.033	−.251
Government services and spending	**.653**	.101	.209
Spending for the unemployed	**.642**	.074	−.277
Government responsibility to help blacks	**.640**	.104	.147
Welfare spending	**.621**	.052	−.046
Government-sponsored health insurance	**.518**	.198	.170
Abortion	.118	**.748**	−.045
School prayer	.028	**.671**	.164
Women's role	.119	**.574**	−.295
Use of military force	−0.53	−.117	**.722**
Defense spending	.161	.423	**.490**
Eigenvalues	3.27	1.40	1.08
Percentage of variance explained	27.2	11.7	9.0

Source: 1992 Convention Delegate Study.

All issue indicators range from the most liberal position (−1) to the most conservative position (1). The factor loadings in boldface denote the variables used to create the measure of attitudes toward the particular issue dimension.

various issues. The scales for each issue dimension are the sum of all of the variables loading strongly on a particular factor. Each scale ranges from −1 (the most liberal attitude) to 1 (the most conservative attitude). The reliability for Democratic delegates is .81 for social welfare and racial attitudes, .54 for cultural attitudes, and .41 for defense and foreign policy attitudes. The reliability for Republican delegates is .78 for social welfare and racial attitudes, .48 for cultural attitudes, and .16 for defense and foreign policy attitudes. Because of the very low reliabilities of the defense and foreign policy scales, I simply use the defense spending scale to measure these attitudes.

Chapter 5 (Cultural Issue Attitudes from 1964 through 1996)

The cultural-issue scales were constructed by summing respondents' scores on all the cultural-issue questions in each NES survey. Each of the individual variables was standardized before summing. The following are the issues included in the scale in each year and the reliability (α) of that scale:

1964: School prayer

1966: School prayer

1968: School prayer

1972: Abortion, women's role in society, legalization of marijuana ($\alpha = .55$)

1974: Women's role in society

1976: Women's role, legalization of marijuana, and abortion ($\alpha = .60$)

1978: Abortion, women's role, and Equal Rights Amendment (ERA) ($\alpha = .54$)

1980: Abortion, women's role, ERA, and school prayer ($\alpha = .60$)

1982: Abortion, women's role, and evaluation of the defeat of the ERA ($\alpha = .64$)

1984: Abortion, women's role, and school prayer ($\alpha = .52$)

1986: Abortion and school prayer ($\alpha = .31$)

1988: Abortion, school prayer, women's role, and laws to protect homosexuals against discrimination ($\alpha = .52$)

1990: Abortion and women's role ($\alpha = .46$)

1992: Abortion, husband's consent for wife to have an abortion, parental consent for abortion, government funding of abortion, laws to protect homosexuals against discrimination, allowing homosexuals to adopt children, allowing homosexuals to serve in the military, women's role, school prayer (α = .76)

1994: Abortion, women's role, and school prayer (α = .46)

1996: Abortion, women's role, school prayer, laws to protect homosexuals against discrimination, allowing homosexuals to serve in the military (α = .62)

Chapter 7 (Path Analyses Using the 1980–1996 NES)

The measures of issue attitudes are the same for each year and are as follows:

Cultural Issues: The sum of attitudes toward abortion, women's role, and school prayer

Social Welfare Issues: The sum of attitudes toward government provision of jobs, government services and spending, and government help for blacks

Defense Issues: Defense spending

II. Attitudes Toward Cultural Groups (1996 NES)

The measure of these attitudes was constructed through the following steps. The reliability is .70, and the measure ranges from 0 to 100.

1. I formed a measure of each respondent's mean score on all of the feeling thermometers in the 1996 NES.
2. I recoded the missing values on the four cultural feeling thermometers (feelings toward the women's movement, gays and lesbians, Christian fundamentalists, and the Christian Coalition) to 50, the midpoint on the thermometer.
3. I took the differences between respondents' scores on the four cultural thermometers and their mean score on all of the feeling thermometers.
4. I reversed the difference scores for the women's movement and gays and lesbians so that all the cultural-difference scores range from the most pro-liberal/anticonservative attitude to the most pro-conservative/antiliberal attitude.
5. I summed the four cultural-difference scores to form the measure of attitudes toward cultural groups.
6. I gave each respondent who had a missing value on all four cultural thermometers a missing value on the overall measure.

III. Policy-Related Predispositions (1996 NES)

Moral Traditionalism

Traditionalism is based on levels of agreement with four statements. Responses were all coded to range from the least traditional to the most traditional and then summed. The reliability is .64, and the variable ranges from 0 to 1.

1. The world is always changing, and we should adjust our view of moral behavior to those changes.
2. We should be more tolerant of people who choose to live according to their own moral standards even if they are very different from our own.
3. This country would have many fewer problems if there were more emphasis on traditional family ties.
4. The newer lifestyles are contributing to the breakdown of our society.

Egalitarianism

Egalitarianism is based on levels of agreement with six statements. Responses were all coded to range from the most to the least egalitarian and then summed. The reliability is .71.

1. Our society should do whatever is necessary to make sure that everyone has an equal opportunity to succeed.
2. We have gone too far in pushing equal rights in this country.
3. This country would be better off if we worried less about how equal people are.
4. It is not really that big a problem if some people have more of a chance in life than others.
5. If people were treated equally in this country, we would have many fewer problems.
6. One of the big problems in this country is that we don't give everyone an equal chance.

Limited Government

Support for limited government is based on the choices between the following three paired items. The reliability is .75.

1. The less government the better *or* there are more things that government should be doing.
2. We need a strong government to handle today's complex economic

problems *or* the free market can handle these problems without government being involved

3. The main reason government has become bigger over the years is because it has gotten involved in things that people should do for themselves *or* government has become bigger because the problems we face have become bigger.

IV. Orientations Toward the Cultural Conflict and the Role of Government/Social Welfare Conflict (1996 NES)

Moral and Cultural Attitudes

To measure orientations toward the cultural conflict, I conducted a principal-components factor analysis of moral traditionalism, evaluations of the groups involved in the cultural conflict, and attitudes toward cultural issues. The first principal component from that analysis has an eigenvalue of 3.73 and explains 37.3 percent of the total variance in all the items. My measure of moral and cultural attitudes is the factor score based on this first principal component. The factor loadings for each variable are as follows: abortion (.59), women's rights (.54), homosexual discrimination (.61), homosexuals in the armed forces (.61), school prayer (.36), evaluations of fundamentalist Christians (.69), evaluations of the Christian Coalition (.69), evaluations of gays and lesbians (.72), evaluations of the women's movement (.59), and moral traditionalism (.63).

Role of Government/Social Welfare Attitudes

To measure orientations toward this conflict, I conducted a principal-components factor analysis of egalitarianism, support for limited government, evaluations of welfare recipients, and attitudes toward a number of social welfare issues. The first principal component from that analysis has an eigenvalue of 5.01 and explains 35.8 percent of the total variance in all the items. My measure of attitudes toward the welfare role of government is the factor score based on this first principal component. The factor loadings for each variable are as follows: government services and spending (.67), government-sponsored health insurance (.53), government provision of jobs and standard of living (.67), spending on food stamps (.61), spending on welfare (.64), spending to help the homeless (.61), spending on social security (.47), spending on child care (.62), spending to help the poor (.70), government help for blacks (pre-election) (.63), government help for blacks (postelection) (.55), egalitarianism (.64), limited government (.62), evaluations of welfare recipients (.34).

A3: The Measurement of Political Awareness

Following Zaller (1992), I created the political awareness scale used in chapter 7 by giving respondents one point for each correct answer to a political knowledge question (relative placements of the parties and candidates on political issues, naming congressional candidates and their party, naming the office held by a political figure) in the 1996 NES survey. I then added this sum to the mean of the interviewer's pre-election and postelection assessments of the respondent's political information level (ranging from 1 for very low to 5 for very high). The resulting scale ranges from 1 to 26 (for analyses, I recoded the scale to range from 0 to 25). Following Zaller, respondents with missing values on one or more of the scale items were not eliminated from the analysis unless more than two-thirds of their responses were missing (in fact, none of the 1996 NES respondents had missing values on more than two-thirds of the items). Rather, for each of the items on which a respondent had a missing value, I gave the respondent his or her mean score on the remaining items.

The items used to construct the scale were as follows:

The mean of the interviewer's pre-election and postelection assessment of political information level (v960070, v960940)

Eleven comparative placements of the two parties and presidential candidates (Clinton and Dole only) on ideological/issue scales: candidates on liberalism–conservatism (v960369, v960371), parties on liberalism–conservatism (v960379, v960380), candidates on government services and spending (v960453, v960455), parties on government services and spending (v960461, v960462), candidates on defense spending (v960466, v960469), parties on defense spending (v960477, v960478), candidates on government-sponsored health insurance (v960480, v960481), candidates on government provision of jobs and standard of living (v960484, v960485), candidates on government help for blacks (v960490, v960492), candidates on abortion (v960506, v960509), and parties on abortion (v960517, v960518)

Ten knowledge items: majority party in House (v961072), majority party in Senate (v961073), and offices held by Al Gore, William Rehnquist, Boris Yeltsin, and Newt Gingrich (v961189-v961192), and one point each for knowing the name of each House candidate and the party of each House candidate, for a possible total of four points (v960261, v960265)

A4: The Religious Polarization of State Party Activists

The measure of the religious polarization of state party activists was formed by pooling the data on delegates to the 1988 and 1992 national party conventions, computing the mean of Republican and Democratic delegates in each state on the religious orthodoxy index, and then subtracting the mean of Democratic delegates in a state from the mean of Republican delegates in that state. The resulting polarization score for each state is as follows, with the states used in the analysis in chapter 7 in bold:

Alabama	.91
Alaska	5.62
Arizona	2.01
Arkansas	.97
California	1.56
Colorado	.82
Connecticut	.25
Delaware	.55
Florida	.87
Georgia	.33
Hawaii	2.30
Idaho	2.08
Illinois	.74
Indiana	.34
Iowa	1.27
Kansas	−.12
Kentucky	1.45
Louisiana	−.52
Maine	.38
Maryland	.29
Massachusetts	.34
Michigan	1.20
Minnesota	3.01
Mississippi	.67

Missouri	.64
Montana	.94
Nebraska	2.30
Nevada	2.45
New Hampshire	.69
New Jersey	.94
New Mexico	.20
New York	.65
North Carolina	−.03
North Dakota	.40
Ohio	1.12
Oklahoma	.91
Oregon	3.82
Pennsylvania	1.12
Rhode Island	1.12
South Carolina	1.51
South Dakota	−.86
Tennessee	.99
Texas	.79
Utah	2.72
Vermont	1.73
Virginia	1.82
Washington	4.95
West Virginia	1.76
Wisconsin	.87
Wyoming	1.34

Statistical Analyses

B1: THE POLITICAL IMPACT OF RELIGIOUS TRADITION, DOCTRINAL ORTHODOXY, AND RELIGIOUS COMMITMENT

To assess the impact of religious tradition, doctrinal orthodoxy, and religious commitment on moral and cultural values, political attitudes, and political behavior, I estimated the following statistical model:

$$
Y_i = \alpha + \sum_{j=1}^{J} \beta_j T_{ij} + \beta_d D_i + \beta_c C_i + \sum_{m=1}^{M} \beta_m T_{ij} D_i + \\
\sum_{n=1}^{N} \beta_n T_{ij} C_i + \sum_{k=1}^{K} \beta_k X_{ik} + e_i,
\tag{B1}
$$

where Y_i represents one of several dependent variables (moral values, cultural issue-attitudes, attitudes toward cultural groups, political ideology, party identification, and the 1996 two-party presidential vote), T_{ij} represents a set of dummy variables for various religious traditions (mainline Protestant, Catholic, black Protestant, Jewish, and secular, with evangelical Protestants serving as the comparison category),[1] D_i represents religious doctrine, C_i represents religious commitment, $T_{ij}D_i$ and $T_{ij}C_i$ represent multiplicative interactions between the dummy variables for traditions and doctrine and the dummy variables for traditions and commitment, and X_{ik} represents a set of sociodemographic control variables (southern residence, education, income, sex, age, and union membership).[2] The interpretation of the coefficients is as follows: The α coefficient is the intercept term, or the predicted value of the dependent variable for evangelical Protestants when religious commitment, religious doctrine, and all the control variables are equal to 0. The β_j terms are the differences between the intercept for particular traditions and the intercept for evangelicals. The β_d and β_c coefficients are the effects of doctrine and commitment, respectively, for evangelical Protestants. The β_m

TABLE B1

Impact of religious tradition, doctrinal orthodoxy, and religious commitment
on moral and political attitudes and political behavior, 1996

Independent Variables	Moral Traditionalism[a]	Cultural Issues[a]	Cultural Groups[a]	Ideology[a]	Party Identification[a]	Presidential Vote[b]
Mainline Protestant	.009	.12	6.59**	.54**	1.37**	1.44**
Catholic	-.002	.11	3.68	.23	.23	.60
Black Protestant	.07	.12	4.12	.45	.43	1.92
Jewish	.10	-.19	-5.74	1.15	-.81	—c
Secular	-.001	.07	1.74	.37*	.74	.64
Commitment	.25***	.55***	21.91***	1.73***	2.22***	2.81**
Doctrine	.11**	.26***	12.50***	.25	.26	.72
Mainline × commitment	-.13*	-.38***	-19.78***	-1.16**	-2.22**	-2.42**
Catholic × commitment	-.08*	-.32**	-15.43**	-1.16**	-1.56**	-1.93*
Black Prot. × commitment	-.20*	-.36*	-7.23	-1.46**	-3.17**	-8.12
Jewish × commitment	-.65**	-.34	-19.05	-5.11**	-1.94	—c
Secular × commitment	-.11	-.25	-18.17**	-1.45**	-2.08**	-.64
Mainline × doctrine	.05	.02	4.91	.12	.42	-.09
Catholic × doctrine	-.02	.06	7.40	.67*	.49	.43
Black Prot. × doctrine	-.11	-.07	-4.95	-.07	.07	-.34
Jewish × doctrine	.49*	.44	18.24	4.82**	2.93	—c
Secular × doctrine	.11	.37**	20.77***	.79	.99	.20
Southern residence	-.01*	.04**	-.06	-.06	-.19*	-.16
Education	-.003	-.04***	-1.23***	-.04**	.07**	.11**
Income	.005***	-.001	.06	.02***	.05***	.09***
Sex (female)	-.01*	-.16***	-4.91***	-.36***	-.46***	-.60***

Age	.001***	.002***	.01	.004**	-.003	.007
Union household	-.004	-.06**	-.88	-.36***	-.67***	-1.13***
Constant	.35***	-.52***	41.79***	3.22***	1.93***	-3.72***
(N)	(1,243)	(1,400)	(1,251)	(1,400)	(1,392)	(835)
Adjusted or pseudo R^2	.28	.30	.36	.16	.17	.20
Chi-square (degrees of freedom)	—	—	—	—	—	224.2 (20)
Correctly predicted (%)	—	—	—	—	—	70.3

Source: 1996 National Election Study.

Evangelical Protestant is the comparison category of religious tradition. Moral traditionalism ranges from 0 (least traditional) to 1 (most traditional). Cultural issue attitudes range from −1 (most liberal) to 1 (most conservative). Cultural group evaluations range from 0 (most favorable toward liberal groups/least favorable toward conservative groups) to 100 (least favorable toward liberal groups/most favorable toward conservative groups). Ideological identification ranges from 1 (extremely liberal) to 7 (extremely conservative). Party identification ranges from 1 (strong Democrat) to 7 (strong Republican). Presidential vote is coded 1 for Dole and 0 for Clinton.

[a]Entries are unstandardized regression coefficients.

[b]Entries are logit coefficients.

[c]All Jewish respondents voted Democratic, so all Jewish respondents were dropped from the analysis.

*$p < .10$

**$p < .05$

***$p < .001$

terms are the difference between the effect of doctrine for a particular tradition and the effect of doctrine for evangelicals, and the β_n coefficients are the difference between the effect of commitment for a particular tradition and the effect of commitment for evangelicals.[3] The β_k terms are the effects of the sociodemographic variables across all religious traditions.

Table B1 presents the final logit and ordinary least squares (OLS) estimates of equation B1 for the six dependent variables from the 1996 NES (the predicted values and probabilities from these estimates are presented in table 2.1). To illustrate the interpretation of these coefficients, I begin with moral traditionalism. The results indicate that there are not significant differences between the moral values of various traditions when doctrine and commitment are both equal to zero (their lowest levels). Both commitment and doctrine have significant positive effects for evangelical Protestants, indicating that more committed and doctrinally orthodox evangelicals have more traditional moral values. Not surprisingly, the relationship between religious commitment and moral traditionalism appears to be stronger for evangelicals than for other traditions, with the effects being significantly weaker for mainline and black Protestants, and with greater commitment actually leading to less moral traditionalism and greater moral tolerance for Jews. The impact of doctrinal orthodoxy for evangelicals does not differ significantly from its impact for other traditions, with the exception of Jews, for whom the greater impact is marginally significant.

The results for attitudes toward cultural issues and cultural groups are similar. Commitment and doctrine both have statistically significant effects for evangelicals, with the effects of commitment often being significantly weaker for other groups and the effects of doctrine generally being fairly similar for other traditions.

The results for general political orientations and voting behavior show a slightly different pattern. Reflecting their long-term association with the Republican party and political conservatism, mainline Protestants are, for the most part, the most conservative and Republican religious group when commitment and orthodoxy are at their lowest levels. However, as commitment levels increase, evangelical Protestants become much more conservative and supportive of the GOP. The effects of commitment are considerably less strong for mainliners and most other religious groups. The influence of doctrine on political orientations for evangelicals is not nearly as strong as that of commitment. However, doctrine's effect is at least slightly stronger for several other religious traditions than it is for evangelicals.

In short, these results indicate that religious tradition, religious commitment, and doctrinal orthodoxy are all important for contemporary political attitudes and behavior. Commitment and doctrine create cultural and political divisions within religious traditions. However, there remain important differences between religious traditions, and the effects of commitment and doctrine also vary across religious traditions.

B2: The Impact of Religious Tradition and Religious Commitment on the Candidate Preferences of National Convention Delegates

To examine the effect of religious tradition and religious commitment on the preferences of Democratic and Republican delegates for their parties' presidential nominees (see figures 4.1 and 4.2), I used logit and multinomial logit analysis to estimate the following equation:

$$Y_i = \alpha + \sum_{j=1}^{J} \beta_j T_{ij} + \beta_c C_i + \sum_{n=1}^{N} \beta_n T_{ij} C_i + \sum_{k=1}^{K} \beta_k X_{ik} + e_i, \qquad \text{(B2)}$$

where Y_i represents Democratic and Republican candidate preferences in 1988 and 1992, T_{ij} represents a set of dummy variables for various religious traditions (mainline Protestant, Catholic, black Protestant, Jewish, and secular, with evangelical Protestants serving as the comparison category),[4] C_i represents religious commitment, $T_{ij}C_i$ represents the interactions between the dummy variables for tradition and religious commitment, and X_{ik} represents a set of control variables (southern residence, education, income, sex, age, and, when it is not the dependent variable, ideological self-identification). The α coefficient is the intercept term for evangelical Protestants, or the predicted value of the dependent variable for evangelicals when religious commitment is equal to zero, its lowest level. The β_j terms represent the difference between the intercepts for particular traditions and evangelicals. The β_c coefficient is the effect of commitment on the ideological orientations of evangelical delegates, and β_n is the difference in the effect of commitment for a particular tradition and the effect of commitment for evangelicals. The β_k terms represent the effects of the control variables across all religious traditions.

Table B2 presents the multinomial logit estimates for Democratic activists. To ease interpretation, I combined Democratic candidate preferences in both 1988 and 1992 into four categories. The comparison category in both years is the party's nominee: Michael Dukakis in 1988 and Bill Clinton in 1992. The other categories are the nominee's two strongest challengers in terms of delegate support—Al Gore and Jesse Jackson in 1988 and Jerry Brown and Paul Tsongas in 1992—and a catch-all category for the other challengers who received some delegate support: Paul Simon, Richard Gephardt, Bruce Babbitt, and Gary Hart in 1988 and Tom Harkin and Bob Kerry in 1992. The multinomial logit coefficients indicate the effect of each variable on the likelihood of supporting a particular candidate or group of candidates as opposed to the party's nominee.

In both years, few of the religious variables reach statistical significance, but the coefficients do reveal some interesting patterns. At the lowest levels of religious commitment in 1988, evangelical Protestants were more likely than Democratic mainline Protestants, Catholics, and seculars to support Al Gore over Michael Dukakis. However, the negative coefficient on commitment indicates that support for Gore tailed off among the more committed evangelical Democrats, while the positive interactions between commitment and the mainline Protestant, Catholic, and black Protestant variables indicate that support for Gore did not tail off with increases in commitment for these groups. Since the black church served as the organizational base of Jesse Jackson's campaign, it is not surprising that black Protestants were more likely than white evangelicals to support Jackson over Dukakis, and that that support increased with greater religious commitment.

The coefficients for 1992 indicate that, at the lowest levels of religious commitment, black Protestants were more likely than evangelical Democrats to support Jerry Brown over Bill Clinton, but that, as commitment increased, black Protestant support for Brown (or Harkin/Kerry) over Clinton decreased. There is also some indication that evangelical Democrats were less likely than mainline Protestants, Catholics, Jews, and seculars to support Paul Tsongas's fiscally conservative but socially liberal candidacy over Clinton's.

Table B3 shows the results of a multinomial logit analysis of Republican preferences for the top three presidential candidates in 1988 and the results of a logit analysis of Republican preferences for the two candidates in 1992.[5] The coefficients indicate that religion did not play a major role in distinguishing supporters of Bob Dole or supporters of Jack Kemp from those delegates who preferred George Bush as the GOP nominee. Low-commitment seculars (which describes almost all secular delegates) were more likely than low-commitment evangelicals to support Dole over Bush. However, evangelical, mainline Protestant, and Catholic delegates became slightly more likely to support Dole over Bush as commitment levels rose. Catholic delegates became more likely to support Kemp over Bush as religious commitment increased. None of these effects, however, reached statistical significance.

Given Pat Buchanan's staunch cultural conservatism and George Bush's reputation among religious traditionalists for not being conservative enough on cultural issues, it is somewhat surprising that none of the religious variables had a statistically significant effect on Republican candidate preferences in 1992. The strong endorsement Bush received

Table B2

Impact of religious tradition, religious commitment, and their interaction on the candidate preferences of democratic convention delegates, 1988 and 1992

| | Year and Candidate Preference | | | | | |
| | 1988[a] | | | 1992[b] | | |
Independent Variables	Gore	Jackson	Simon/Gephardt/Babbitt/Hart	Brown	Tsongas	Harkin/Kerry
Mainline Protestant	-2.54*	-1.16	-1.06	.35	2.22	.39
Catholic	-3.54*	-1.36	-2.17*	-.18	3.98	.02
Black Protestant	-7.68	1.61	.26	2.97	-.14	1.62
Jewish	-2.54	1.67	-.46	1.80	4.44	-.74
Secular	-2.82*	-.57	-1.61	1.02	4.12	.03
Religious commitment	-1.47	-.23	-.95	-.006	2.13	-.09
Mainline × commitment	2.12	1.01	.98	.004	-1.27	-.33
Catholic × commitment	2.08	1.19	1.95	.92	-3.00	-.21
Black Protestant × commitment	7.06	2.41	-.55	-3.40	1.51	-3.06
Jewish × commitment	.77	-9.15	-.46	-1.84	-2.95	1.10
Secular × commitment	.17	2.82	3.29	3.14	-.41	2.13
Ideological identification[c]	.45**	-.68**	.10	-.43**	.15	-.51**
Education	-.08	.01	.004	-.09	.05	-.21**
Income	.03	-.10*	-.02	-.23**	-.06*	-.03
Sex (female)	-.10	-.50*	-.28*	-.66**	-.26	-.70**
Age	-.01*	-.01	.004	-.02*	-.02***	-.003
Southern residence	1.07**	.08	.08	-2.41**	-.22	-.80**
Constant	.63	2.54	.73	2.92	-3.70	2.08

$N = 1,242$
Pseudo $R^2 = .14$
Chi-square (df = 51) = 440.98
% Correctly predicted = 57.23

$N = 1,189$
Pseudo $R^2 = .15$
Chi-square (df = 51) = 382.90
% Correctly predicted = 71.24

Source: 1988 and 1992 Convention Delegate Studies.

Entries are multinomial logit coefficients.

[a]Dukakis is the comparison category.

[b]Clinton is the comparison category.

[c]Ranges from very liberal (1) to very conservative (7).

df, degrees of freedom.

* $p < .05$

** $p < .001$

TABLE B3
Impact of religious tradition, religious commitment,
and their interaction on the candidate preferences of
Republican convention delegates, 1988 and 1992

Independent Variables	Year and Candidate Preference		
	1988[a]		1992[b]
	Dole	Kemp	Buchanan
Mainline Protestant	−.05	−.53	−1.13
Catholic	.07	−.55	1.14
Secular	1.27	−.27	.28
Religious commitment	.63	−.03	3.16
Mainline × commitment	.10	.19	.67
Catholic × commitment	−.09	.82	−.65
Secular × commitment	−7.90	−6.51	.34
Ideological identification[c]	.06	1.23**	1.54**
Education	.03	.09	.03
Income	−.04	−.10**	−.10
Sex (female)	−.05	.07	−.40
Age	−.006	−.008	−.04**
Southern residence	−.60*	−.21	−.60
Constant	−1.46	−7.17**	−10.76*
	N = 995		N = 584
	Pseudo R^2 = .10		Pseudo R^2 = .30
	Chi-square (df = 26) = 166.44		Chi-square (df = 13) = 100.90
	% Correctly predicted = 69.41		% Correctly predicted = 91.61

Source: 1988 and 1992 Convention Delegate Studies.
[a]Entries are multinomial logit coefficients; Bush is the comparison category.
[b]Entries are binomial logit coefficients; Bush is the comparison category.
[c]Ranges from very liberal (1) to very conservative (7).
df, degrees of freedom.
*$p < .05$
**$p < .001$

from most Christian Right leaders may have diminished Buchanan's ability to garner traditionally religious support. There is some indication that greater religious commitment did increase the likelihood of supporting Buchanan over Bush in 1992, but the effect does not reach statistical significance.

B3: The Impact of Religious Tradition and Religious Commitment on the Issue Attitudes and Ideological Orientations of National Convention Delegates

To examine the impact of religious tradition and religious commitment on the issue attitudes and ideological orientations of national convention delegates in 1992 (figure 4.4), I use OLS regression to estimate equation B2 for four dependent variables: attitudes on social welfare issues, attitudes on cultural issues, attitudes on defense spending, and ideological identification. Table B4 presents the results.

Religious commitment has a positive and statistically significant effect on social welfare and cultural conservatism for evangelical Democrats. The positive effect of commitment on social welfare attitudes is significantly less for mainline Protestants, so that mainline Democrats actually become slightly more liberal as commitment increases. Not surprisingly, the effect of commitment is significantly less for seculars on both social welfare and cultural attitudes and for Jews on cultural issues. Commitment has a marginally significant impact on evangelical Democrats' support for greater defense spending. That effect is generally weaker among other Democratic religious groups, and it is significantly so for Catholics. The impact of commitment on the ideological orientations of evangelical Democrats is not statistically significant, but it is fairly strong and is even more so for mainline Protestant and Catholic delegates. Not surprisingly, the effect of commitment on ideological conservatism for black Protestants is slightly negative.

Among Republican delegates, the social welfare attitudes of mainline Protestants, Catholics, and seculars are all more conservative than those of evangelical Protestants when commitment is at its lowest level. However, evangelical Republicans become significantly more conservative as commitment increases, reflecting perhaps the spiritual individualism of evangelical doctrine or the increasingly strong ties of evangelical churches to the Republican party. The positive effect of commitment on social welfare conservatism is considerably less for other religious groups, and the influence of commitment is slightly negative for Catholic Republicans. Similar patterns hold for general ideological orientations. Greater commitment leads to greater ideological conservatism among individuals, but the effect is weaker for other Republican religious groups and is significantly weaker for mainline Protestants.

In contrast, the relationship between religious commitment and

Impact of religious tradition, religious commitment,
and their interaction on the issue attitudes and ideological
orientations of 1992 national convention delegates

Party and Independent Variables	Dependent Variables			
	Social Welfare/ Racial Issues	Cultural Issues	Defense Spending	Ideological Self-Identification
Democrats				
Mainline Protestant	.21**	.04	.10	−.51
Catholic	.10	−.009	.23	−.38
Black Protestant	−.13	−.19	.10	.20
Jewish	.17	.01	.01	−.55
Secular	.16	.08	.10	−.64
Religious commitment	.29**	.48***	.33*	.57
Mainline × commitment	−.34**	−.24	−.20	.34
Catholic × commitment	−.20	.08	−.37*	.33
Black Protestant × commitment	−.14	.26	−.19	−.71
Jewish × commitment	−.31	−.41*	.08	−.22
Secular × commitment	−.31*	−.33*	−.37	−.007
Ideological identification	.13***	.09***	.08***	—
Education	−.004	−.02***	−.02**	−.02
Income	.005*	−.006**	.002	.02**
Sex (female)	.003	−.06***	−.005	−.17**
Age	−.002***	.001**	−.0002	−.001
Southern residence	.05**	.01	.09***	.20**
Constant	−.89***	−1.08***	−.87***	2.95
(N)	(1,231)	(1,221)	(1,221)	(1,231)
Adjusted R^2	.30	.35	.10	.12
Republicans[a]				
Mainline Protestant	.26*	.03	.09	.62
Catholic	.35**	.04	.23	.42
Secular	.40**	.09	.002	.73
Religious commitment	.33**	.66***	.19	1.60***
Mainline × commitment	−.31*	−.19	−.16	−1.12**
Catholic × commitment	−.46**	−.04	−.30	−.90
Secular × commitment	−.34	−.03	.17	−.60
Ideological identification	.11***	.19***	.09***	—
Education	.0001	−.02**	−.007	−.09***
Income	.0001	−.0002	−.007	−.02**
Sex (female)	.01	−.10***	.06**	−.22**
Age	−.004***	.001	−.004**	−.005*
Southern residence	.04*	.01	−.05*	.15**
Constant	−.35**	−1.43***	−.29	5.44***

TABLE B4 *(continued)*

Party and Independent Variables	Dependent Variables			
	Social Welfare/ Racial Issues	Cultural Issues	Defense Spending	Ideological Self-Identification
(N)	(627)	(623)	(619)	(630)
Adjusted R²	.18	.43	.12	.13

Source: 1992 Convention Delegate Study.

Evangelical Protestant is the comparison category of religious tradition. The dependent variables range from most liberal to most conservative (−1 to 1 for issues, 1 to 7 for ideology).

[a]Because of very small numbers, Jews and black Protestants are excluded from the analysis for Republicans.

*p < .10

**p < .05

***p < .001

cultural conservatism is not specific to evangelical Republicans but is common to Republican activists of all religious stripes. The effect of commitment is strong and very significant for evangelical Republicans and is not significantly weaker for Republican delegates in other religious categories. Religious tradition and commitment do not appear to have a strong effect on the attitudes of Republican delegates toward defense spending.

To compare the divisions between the abortion attitudes of activists in the same party but in different religious traditions and with different levels of religious adherence, to the differences between the abortion attitudes of activists with the same religious orientations, but in different parties, over time (see figure 4.5), I estimated a model very similar to the one in equation B2, with the abortion attitudes of delegates to the conventions from 1972 to 1992 as the dependent variables. The only difference is that religious commitment is replaced by frequency of worship attendance (coded to range from 0 to 1) in this model because church attendance was the only measure of religious devotionalism in the 1972 Convention Delegate Studies (CDS). The regression estimates are presented in table B5.

The table shows that more frequent church attendance was significantly related to greater agreement with the pro-life stance on abortion in most years for evangelical Protestants in both parties. Given the uniformly low levels of attendance among seculars and the tradition of

Table B5

Impact of religious tradition, religious commitment, and their interaction on the abortion attitudes of national convention delegates from 1972 to 1992

Party and Independent Variables	Year					
	1972	1976	1980	1984	1988	1992
Democrats						
Mainline Protestant	.25	-.38	.38	.04	.09	.09
Catholic	-.24	-.42	.21	-.11	.23	-.17
Black Protestant	.41	-.30	.28	.01	.60	-.34
Jewish	.24	-.76**	.26	.16	.52	.09
Secular	.06	-.27	.27	.25	.29	.08
Church attendance	.59	.36	1.07***	.93**	.98***	.53**
Mainline × attendance	-.53	.20	-.67**	-.42	-.51	-.48**
Catholic × attendance	.87*	1.01**	.33	.44	-.18	.48**
Black Prot. × attendance	-.34	.11	-.15	-.12	-1.06**	.25
Jewish × attendance	-.86	.36	-.98**	-1.12**	-1.59**	-.55***
Secular × attendance	-.72	-.65	1.53**	-1.51*	-.84	-.41
Ideological identification	.08**	.13***	.18***	.15***	.19***	.10***
Education	-.002	-.03*	-.02	-.02	-.03**	-.0004
Income	-.06***	-.01	-.02**	-.008	-.003	-.01**
Sex (female)	-.23***	-.25***	-.30***	-.33***	-.24***	-.09**
Age	.005**	.006**	.007***	.002	.0006	.002
Southern residence	.11	.01	-.09	.14**	.01	-.01
Constant	1.34***	1.35***	.68**	.97***	.83**	.77***

(N)	(452)	(643)	(1,015)	(825)	(792)	(1,136)
Adjusted R²	.33	.36	.40	.36	.25	.22
Republicans[a]						
Mainline Protestant	.46	-.20	-.19	-.19	.04	-.15
Catholic	.41	.11	-.05	-.12	.24	.09
Secular	.49	-.13	-.22	.23	-.20	.02
Church attendance	1.10*	.69*	.43	.70*	.78**	.94**
Mainline × attendance	-.54	-.09	-.06	.08	-.37	-.05
Catholic × attendance	.16	.28	.45	.70	.03	.17
Secular × attendance	-4.99*	-2.86**	-3.67**	-5.71*	.02	-.17
Ideological identification	.12**	.24***	.25***	.29***	.27***	.40***
Education	-.05	-.03	.001	-.02	-.002	-.03
Income	-.01	-.03**	-.03***	.002	-.04***	-.007
Sex (female)	-.29**	-.21**	-.24***	-.21**	-.15**	-.09
Age	.01**	-.004	.003	-.006*	-.0008	-.001
Southern residence	.28**	.04	.02	.01	.05	.01
Constant	.50	1.36***	.99**	.77	1.05**	-.12
(N)	(183)	(566)	(671)	(436)	(569)	(532)
Adjusted R²	.34	.30	.25	.28	.29	.35

Source: 1992 Convention Delegate Study.

Evangelical Protestant is the comparison category of religious tradition. Abortion attitudes range from the most pro-choice view (1) to the most pro-life view (4).

[a]Because of very small numbers, Jews and black Protestants are excluded from the analysis for Republicans.

*p < .10

**p < .05

***p < .001

political and cultural liberalism in the Jewish faith, it is not surprising that the effect of attendance is often significantly weaker for Jewish Democrats and for secular delegates in both parties. However, in both parties, the effects of worship attendance on the abortion attitudes of activists in the other religious traditions were generally not different from those of evangelicals.

The one clear exception to this is Catholic activists in the Democratic party. The relationship between attendance and antiabortion attitudes is significantly stronger for Catholics than for evangelical Democrats in three of these six years, and the effect of attendance is always greater for Catholics than for mainline Protestants. This is not surprising given the Catholic hierarchy's staunch opposition to abortion and the general support of committed Catholic parishioners for the pro-life view. It is not entirely clear why the effect of attendance is generally greater for Democratic Catholics than for Republican Catholics. However, it may be that other factors, such as ideological conservatism, account for part of the pro-life leanings of committed Catholics in the GOP, while the generally liberal leanings of Democratic Catholics allow (or force) church attendance to play the largest role in creating antiabortion attitudes.

The growth in the differences between the abortion attitudes of Democratic and Republican activists in the same religious groups from 1972 to 1992, shown in figure 4.5, is not readily apparent in these coefficient estimates. However, two facets of the results do point to a growing partisan cleavage on abortion within religious groups. First, the effect of church attendance on abortion attitudes remains strong and significant for most religious traditions over this period. Meanwhile, the differences in attendance levels—both across all traditions and within particular religious traditions—between Republican and Democratic convention delegates have increased.

Second, the relationship between conservative self-identifications and pro-life attitudes on abortion grew considerably over this period for Republican delegates. The link between ideological liberalism and pro-choice views on abortion remained strong but did not grow for Democratic delegates. However, Republican activists within each religious tradition have clearly more conservative ideological identifications than Democratic activists in the same traditions. Thus, the fact that pro-life abortion attitudes have become more deeply ingrained into conservative ideology within the GOP should have led Republican activists in all traditions to become, in the aggregate, more conservative on abortion than Democrats in the same faith traditions.

To provide a more direct test of the hypothesis that partisan cleavages on abortion within religious groups have developed over time, I pool data on convention delegates in each year from 1972 to 1992 and estimate the following equation:

$$Y_i = \alpha + \sum_{k=1}^{K} \beta_k X_{ik} + \sum_{j=1}^{J} \beta_j D_{ij} + \sum_{l=1}^{L} \beta_l R_{il} + \sum_{t=1}^{T} \beta_t Y_{it} +$$
$$\sum_{m=1}^{M} \beta_m D_{ij} Y_{it} + \sum_{n=1}^{N} \beta_n R_{il} Y_{it} + e_i,$$

(B3)

In this equation, Y_i is the abortion attitude of each delegate in the sample. X_{ik} are the six control variables included in equation B2, in addition to ideological identification. D_{ij} are dummy variables for Democratic delegates in each of ten different religious categories—regularly attending evangelical Protestants, nonregularly attending evangelical Protestants, regularly attending mainline Protestants, nonregularly attending mainline Protestants, regularly attending Catholics, nonregularly attending Catholics, secularists, black Protestants, Jews, and Mormons, with "other religions" serving as the comparison category—and R_{il} are dummy variables for Republican delegates in each of those religious groups.[6] Y_{it} are dummy variables for each convention year from 1976 through 1992. The comparison category is 1972.

There are six sets of parameters to be estimated in this model. The intercept term, α, represents the mean abortion attitude of delegates in "other religions" in 1972—the comparison categories in the model—when all the control variables equal 0. The β_k terms represent the effects of the control variables on the abortion attitudes of delegates in both parties and in all religious groups across all years. The β_j terms represent the difference, controlling for demographic characteristics and ideology, between the mean abortion attitude of a particular Democratic religious group—for example, Democrats who are regularly attending mainline Protestants—and the mean abortion attitude of delegates in "other religions" in 1972. The β_l terms represent the difference, controlling for demographic characteristics and ideology, between the mean abortion attitude of a particular Republican religious group and the mean abortion attitude of delegates in "other religions" in 1972.

The β_t terms represent the difference between the mean abortion attitudes of delegates in "other religions" in a particular year and the mean abortion attitudes of delegates in "other religions" in 1972. The β_m terms are the coefficients on interactions between each of the dummy variables for Democratic religious groups and each of the dummy variables for convention years, and the β_n terms are the coefficients on interactions between each of the dummy variables for Republican religious groups and each of the dummy variables for convention years. The difference between the mean abortion attitude of a particular partisan and religious group in a particular year and the mean attitude of that group in 1972 is given by the sum of the β_t term for the particular year and the β_m or β_n term for the interaction between that year variable and the variable for the particular group. Taken together, the coefficients on all the interactions (both Republican and Democratic) for a particular religious group and the coefficients on all the convention year variables indicate the extent to which the abortion attitudes of Republican and Democratic activists in the same religious group have diverged over the 1972–1992 period.

The regression estimates of equation B3 are presented in table B6. The table shows that only a few of the religious and partisan variables or their interactions with years reach statistical significance, which indicates that the mean value of abortion for a particular religious and partisan group is significantly different from the mean value for "other religions" in a particular year.

The set of coefficients for regularly attending mainline Protestants provides an illustration of how the estimates capture the growing partisan divide on abortion within religious groups. The coefficients on the dummy variables for Republican and Democratic delegates in this religious group indicate that, on average, regularly attending mainline Protestants in both the GOP and the Democratic party had slightly, but not significantly, more conservative attitudes on abortion in 1972 than did members of "other" religions, with Republicans being slightly more opposed to abortion than Democrats. Taken together, the coefficients on the dummy variables for particular convention years and the coefficients on the interactions between those variables and the dummy variables for regularly attending mainline Protestants in the Republican and Democratic parties estimate the year-to-year changes in the aggregate abortion attitudes of Republican and Democratic activists in this religious group. They demonstrate that, between 1972 and 1976, the abortion attitudes of Republicans grew, in the aggregate, more liberal ($-.08 - .07 = -.15$ from the 1972 mean), while those of Democrats became slightly more conservative ($-.08 + .14 = .06$ from the 1972 mean). Between 1976 and 1980, Republican activists became slightly more conservative on abortion ($-.03 - .05 = -.08$ from the 1972 mean, .07 from the 1976 mean), while Democratic activists

TABLE B6
Delegates' abortion attitudes as a function of party, religious tradition, church attendance, and their interactions with year, 1972–1992

	Coefficient
Control variables	
Constant	1.35**
Education	-.02***
Income	-.05***
South	.02
Sex (female)	-.22***
Age	.001*
Ideology (conservative)	.23***
Convention year (reference = 1972)	
1976	-.08
1980	-.03
1984	-.01
1988	.06
1992	-.29**

Coefficients on Religious/Partisan Dummy Variables and Their Interactions with Year

	Regularly Attending Evangelicals	Nonregularly Attending Evangelicals	Regularly Attending Catholics	Nonregularly Attending Catholics	Regularly Attending Mainline
Dummy variables for partisans within a particular religious group (reference = other religion)					
Republican	.28	-.24	.85**	-.09	.14
Democrat	.07	-.31	.90**	.11	.06
Interactions					
Republicans × 1976	.19	.25	-.02	.42	-.07
Republicans × 1980	.02	.42	-.10	.38	-.05
Republicans × 1984	-.02	.13	.001	.23	-.07
Republicans × 1988	.15	.31	-.21	.41	-.04
Republicans × 1992	.43*	.57**	.04	.44	.37*
Democrats × 1976	.13	.45*	.01	-.004	.14
Democrats × 1980	.20	.21	.09	.08	.02
Democrats × 1984	.33	.26	-.19	-.13	-.03
Democrats × 1988	.18	-.02	-.55***	-.26	-.25
Democrats × 1992	-.17	.06	-.53***	-.29*	-.44**

	Nonregularly Attending Mainline	Secular	Black Protestant	Jewish	Mormon
Dummy variables for partisans within a particular religious group (reference = other religion)					
Republican	-.23*	-.66**	.78**	-.20	.23
Democrat	-.07	-.15	.29**	-.18	.46
Interactions					
Republicans × 1976	.08	.19	-1.34**	-.25	.14
Republicans × 1980	.12	.21	-.78	-.48	.37
Republicans × 1984	.001	.33	-1.04**	-.05	.28
Republicans × 1988	.09	.09	-.98**	-.31	.13
Republicans × 1992	.22	.58*	-.28	-.13	.12
Democrats × 1976	-.12	-.08	-.25	-.19	.02
Democrats × 1980	-.01	-.19	.04	-.15	.21
Democrats × 1984	-.15	-.13	-.16	-.23	-.02
Democrats × 1988	-.32**	-.24*	-.52**	-.26	-.10
Democrats × 1992	-.24*	-.14	-.48**	-.12	-.37

Source: 1972–1992 Convention Delegate Studies (pooled).

Abortion attitudes range from 1 (most pro-choice) to 4 (most pro-life).

$N = 9,340$; adjusted $R^2 = .44$

*p < .10

**p < .05

***p < .001

became more liberal (−.03 + .02 = −.01 from the 1972 mean, −.07 from the 1976 mean). Between 1980 and 1984, the attitudes of Republicans remained at the same aggregate level (−.08 from the 1972 mean, 0 from the 1980 mean), while those of Democrats became slightly more liberal (−.04 from the 1972 mean, −.03 from the 1980 mean). Between 1984 and 1988, Republicans became more conservative on abortion (.02 from the 1972 mean, .10 from the 1984 mean) and Democrats grew noticeably more liberal (−.19 from the 1972 mean, −.15 from the 1984 mean). Between 1988 and 1992, the abortion attitudes of Republican delegates grew more conservative (.08 from the 1972 mean, .06 from the 1988 mean) while those of Democratic delegates became much more liberal (−.73 from the 1972 mean, −.54 from the 1988 mean). The marked levels of party polarization among regularly attending mainliners in 1992 is evident in the statistical significance of the positive interaction between the Republican dummy variable and the dummy variable for 1992 and of the negative interaction between the Democratic dummy variable and the 1992 variable. These coefficients indicate that Republican delegates in 1992 were significantly more pro-life than members of other religions, while 1992 Democratic delegates were significantly more pro-choice.

B4: MULTIVARIATE MODELS FOR ANALYZING TRENDS IN THE PARTY IDENTIFICATION OF RELIGIOUS GROUPS

To examine changes over time in the party identification of religious groups (figure 5.2), I pooled data from the NES surveys from 1960 through 1996 and estimated the following regression equation:

$$Y_i = \alpha + \sum_{k=1}^{K} \beta_k X_{ik} + \sum_{j=1}^{J} \beta_j D_{ij} + \sum_{t=1}^{T} \beta_t D_{it} +$$
$$\sum_{m=1}^{M} \beta_m D_{ij} D_{it} + \sum_{n=1}^{N} \beta_n X_{ik} D_{it} + e_i. \tag{B4}$$

In this model, Y_i refers to the party identification or presidential vote of each respondent, X_{ik} refers to six control variables (education, income, sex, age, southern residence, and union membership), D_{ij} refers to the dummy variables for religious groups (seculars, Jews, black Protestants, and regular and nonregular attenders within the evangelical Protestant, mainline Protestant, and Catholic traditions, with "other religions" serving as the comparison category),[7] and D_{it} refers to dummy variables for each federal-election year from 1964 through 1996, with 1960 serving as the comparison category.

There are six sets of parameters to be estimated, and I will explain them in terms of the party identification equation. The intercept term α represents the mean party identification of individuals in "other religions" in 1960—the comparison categories in the model—when all the control variables equal 0. The β_k terms represent the effects of the control variables on party identification in 1960. The β_j terms represent the difference, controlling for demographic characteristics and their interactions with year, between the mean party identification of the particular religious group—for example, regularly attending evangelical Protestants—and the mean party identification of individuals in "other religions" in 1960. The β_t terms represent the difference between the mean party identification of members of "other religions" in a particular year and the mean party identification of those individuals in 1960. The β_m terms are the coefficients on interactions between the dummy variables for religious groups and each of the dummy variables for election years. The difference between the mean party identification of a particular religious group in a particular year and the mean party identification of that group in 1960 is given by the sum of the β_t term for the year and the β_m term for the interaction between the dummy variable for that year and the dummy

402

TABLE B7

Ordinary least squares estimates for analyzing trends in the party identification of religious groups, 1960–1996

Dummy Variables for Year and Religious Groups		Interactions Between Religious Group Variables and Year					
Variable	Coeff.	Variable	Coeff.	Variable	Coeff.	Variable	Coeff.
Year (Reference = 1960)		Regular Evangical		Nonregular Evangelical		Regular Mainline	
1964	-1.16*	1964	-.32	1964	-.17	1964	.02
1966	.09	1966	-.79*	1966	-.21	1966	-.46
1968	-.22	1968	-.41	1968	-.11	1968	-.33
1970	-.63	1970	-.53	1970	-.27	1970	-.73*
1972	-.03	1972	-.45	1972	-.04	1972	-.35
1974	-.90*	1974	-.25	1974	-.004	1974	-.07
1976	-.31	1976	-.47	1976	.01	1976	-.36
1978	-.62	1978	-.73*	1978	-.19	1978	-.23
1980	.79	1980	-.49	1980	-.66*	1980	-.39
1982	-.36	1982	.20	1982	.14	1982	.10
1984	.49	1984	-.30	1984	-.25	1984	-.25*
1986	.82*	1986	-.18	1986	-.30	1986	-.51
1988	1.32**	1988	-.56*	1988	-.59*	1988	-.52
1990	.43	1990	.16	1990	.12	1990	-.26
1992	.74	1992	.54*	1992	.22	1992	.16
1994	.13	1994	.47	1994	.38	1994	-.38
1996	.004	1996	.71*	1996	-.14	1996	-.12
		Nonregular Mainline		Regular Catholic		Nonregular Catholic	
Religious Groups (Reference = other religions)		1964	-.25	1964	.41	1964	.29
Regular evangelical	.39*	1966	-.23	1966	.33	1966	-.19
Nonregular evangelical	-.01	1968	-.48	1968	.03	1968	-.11
Regular mainline	.72**	1970	-.42	1970	.38	1970	-.47
Nonregular mainline	.55**	1972	-.32	1972	.35	1972	-.21
Regular Catholic	-1.22**	1974	-.20	1974	.56*	1974	-.21
Nonregular Catholic	-.46*	1976	-.43	1976	.43	1976	-.32
Black Protestant	-.38	1978	-.44	1978	.24	1978	-.23
Secular	.52	1980	-.49	1980	.80*	1980	-.33
Jewish	-1.03**						

Year	(continued)	(continued)	(continued)
1982	.03	.55	.29
1984	-.61*	.46*	-.13
1986	-.37	.33	.05
1988	-.87**	.24	-.18
1990	-.29	.76*	.12
1992	.06	1.10**	.01
1994	-.09	.67*	-.008
1996	-.21	1.07**	.02

Black Protestant

Year	
1964	-.33
1966	-.60
1968	-1.39**
1970	-1.18*
1972	-.60*
1974	-.82*
1976	-.86*
1978	-.85*
1980	-1.36**
1982	-.88*
1984	-1.00**
1986	-1.31**
1988	-1.59**
1990	-.89*
1992	-.84*
1994	-.99*
1996	-.91*

Secular

Year	
1964	-.60
1966	-.79
1968	-1.10*
1970	-.99*
1972	-1.10*
1974	-.86
1976	-.94*
1978	-1.08*
1980	-.99*
1982	-.65
1984	-1.09*
1986	-1.12*
1988	-1.47*
1990	-.60
1992	-.66
1994	-1.12*
1996	-.94*

Jewish

Year	
1964	-.35
1966	-.68
1968	-.71
1970	-.51
1972	-.51
1974	-.16
1976	-.51
1978	-.56
1980	-.83
1982	.21
1984	-.60
1986	.37
1988	-.48
1990	-.15
1992	-.44
1994	-.48
1996	-.38

Source: 1960–1996 National Election Studies (pooled).

The dependent variable ranges from strong Democrat (1) to strong Republican (7). Controls were included for education, income, sex, age, southern residence, union membership, and their interactions with dummy variables for years.

*p < .05

**p < .001

N = 30,477

Adjusted R^2 = .15

Test of all of the interactions between religious and year dummies = 0: $F = 2.11$** (df = 153, 30,189) variable for that group. The β_n terms are coefficients on the interactions between the control variables and each of the dummy variables for election years. They capture the year-to-year changes in the impact of these variables on party identification.

Table B7 presents the OLS estimates of equation B4 for party identification. The coefficients on the dummy variables for religious groups indicate that regularly attending evangelical Protestants and both groups of mainline Protestants were significantly more Republican than members of "other religions" in 1960, while Jews and both groups of Catholics were significantly more Democratic.

Even when various sociodemographic factors and their interactions with year are controlled, changes in the party identifications of religious groups are evident. The coefficients on the dummy variables for year indicate that regularly attending evangelical Protestants grew clearly more Republican in the 1990s, with the growth in Republicanism being significantly greater in 1992 and 1996 for this group than for "other religions." Regularly attending Catholics also demonstrate a pattern of growing attachment to the GOP as the growth in Republicanism among this group was significantly greater than that of other religions in 1980, 1984, and every election year in the 1990s. Meanwhile, the resistance of black Protestants and seculars to Republican party ties is evident in the highly negative and generally significant interactions between the variables for these groups and the year variables. These coefficients indicate that from one election year to the next, these groups were significantly less likely than members of other religions to increase their ties to the GOP.

B5: The Changing Political Impact of Religious Beliefs and Behaviors from 1980 Through 1996

To examine changes over time in the impact of religious commitment and doctrinal orthodoxy on party identification and presidential voting behavior, I pooled data from the NES surveys from 1980 through 1996 and estimated two sets of equations using OLS regression and logit. I began by estimating an equation that assumes that the political effects of commitment and doctrine are constant across religious traditions, and that the changes over time in the political impact of these variables are constant across traditions (see figure 5.8). The equation is as follows:

$$
Y_i = \alpha + \sum_{j=1}^{J} \beta_j R_{ij} + \beta_c C_i + \beta_d D_i + \beta_t T_i + \sum_{m=1}^{M} \beta_m R_{ij} T_i +
$$
$$
\beta_n C_i T_i + \beta_p D_i T_i + \sum_{k=1}^{K} \beta_k X_{ik} + e_i,
$$
(B5)

where Y_i represents either party identification or the presidential vote, R_{ij} refers to dummy variables for religious traditions (mainline Protestant, Catholic, secular, black Protestant, and Jewish, with evangelical Protestant serving as the comparison category), C_i represents religious commitment, D_i represents doctrinal orthodoxy, and T_i represents a linear time variable,[8] coded 0 for 1980, and increasing by 1 in each election year after 1980,[9] and X_{ik} represents a set of demographic controls.

In terms of party identification, the β_j terms represent the difference between the mean party identification of particular religious traditions and that of evangelicals in 1980, when commitment and doctrine (and the control variables) are held constant. The β_c and β_d terms are the effects of commitment and doctrine, respectively, on party identification in 1980 across all religious traditions. The β_t term is the change over time in the mean party identification of evangelicals when commitment and doctrine are equal to 0 (the midpoint of both variables). The β_m terms represent the change over time in the difference between the mean party identification of a particular religious group and the mean party identification of evangelicals when commitment and doctrine are equal to 0. The β_n and β_p terms are the changes over time in the effects of commitment and doctrine, respectively, on party identification across all religious traditions. The β_k terms represent the effects of the control variables on party identification across all religious traditions and over all years.

The second and third columns of table B8 present the coefficient estimates of equation B5.[10] They indicate that in 1980, mainline Protestants were significantly more likely than evangelical Protestants to identify with the Republican party when doctrine and commitment were at their midpoints (equal to 0), but they were not more likely than evangelicals to vote for Ronald Reagan, the Republican presidential candidate. Over time, the gap in mainline and evangelical attachments to the GOP declined significantly, and the tendency of mainliners to vote Republican declined relative to that of evangelicals. Catholics, black Protestants, and Jews all were significantly more likely than evangelical Protestants to vote for and identify with the Democratic party when doctrine and commitment were at their midpoints in 1980. Over time, evangelicals grew even more strongly Republican in their partisan ties relative to those of Catholics and black Protestants. Seculars were more likely than evangelicals to vote Democratic in 1980, but not to identify themselves as Democrats. Neither religious commitment nor doctrinal orthodoxy had a statistically significant effect on party identification or the presidential vote in 1980. However, the connection between orthodoxy and Republican party identification grew significantly between 1980 and 1996. Meanwhile, the relationship between Republican voting and both orthodoxy and commitment grew.

Of course, the evidence presented in table B1 indicates that the political impact of religious commitment and doctrinal orthodoxy is not constant across religious traditions. It is thus possible, perhaps even likely, that the changes over time in the effects of these variables on party identification and vote changes have not been constant across traditions (see figures 5.9 and 5.10). To account for the possibility of variation across traditions, I added interactions between the dummy variables for religious traditions and both commitment and doctrine as well as three-way interactions between the dummy variables for religious traditions, time, and both commitment and doctrine. That model is as follows:

$$Y_i = \alpha + \sum_{j=1}^{J} \beta_j R_{ij} + \beta_c C_i + \beta_d D_i + \sum_{h=1}^{H} \beta_h R_{ij} C_i + \sum_{l=1}^{L} \beta_l R_{ij} D_i +$$

$$\beta_t T_i + \sum_{m=1}^{M} \beta_m R_{ij} T_i + \beta_n C_i T_i + \beta_p D_i T_i + \sum_{r=1}^{R} \beta_r R_{ij} C_i T_i + \qquad \text{(B6)}$$

$$\sum_{z=1}^{Z} \beta_z R_{ij} D_i T_i + \sum_{k=1}^{K} \beta_k X_{ik} + e_i.$$

In this equation, the interpretation of β_j and β_k is the same as in equation B5. The β_c and β_d terms are the effects of commitment and doctrine, respectively, on the party identifications of evangelical Protestants in 1980. The β_h and β_l terms represent the difference between the effect of commitment and doctrine, respectively, in 1980 for a particular religious tradition and the effect of these variables in 1980 for evangelicals. The β_t term is the change over time in the mean party identification of evangelicals when commitment and doctrine are equal to zero. The β_m terms represent the change over time in the difference between the mean party identification of a particular religious group and the mean party identification of evangelicals when commitment and doctrine are equal to zero. The β_n and β_p terms are the changes over time in the effects of commitment and doctrine, respectively, on the party identifications of evangelicals. The β_r and β_z terms represent the difference between the changes over time in the effects of commitment and doctrine, respectively, on the party identification of a particular religious tradition and the changes over time in the effects of these variables for evangelicals.

The last two columns of table B8 present the coefficient estimates of equation B6. They show that in 1980, mainline Protestants were significantly more attached to the Republican party than were evangelical Protestants when commitment and doctrine were both at their midpoints (zero). Seculars, black Protestants, and Jews were all significantly less likely than evangelicals to identify themselves as Republicans. Catholics, seculars, black Protestants, and Jews were all significantly less likely than evangelicals to vote for Ronald Reagan in 1980, when commitment and doctrine were at their midpoints. Religious commitment had a significant, pro-Republican effect on the partisan ties of evangelicals in 1980, while greater commitment pushed Catholics, black Protestants, and Jews in a significantly more Democratic direction. Neither commitment nor doctrinal orthodoxy had any effect on the presidential voting behavior of evangelicals in 1980.

After 1980, the impact of religious commitment on the party identification and voting behavior of evangelical Protestants increased significantly. The growth in the relationship between commitment and support for the GOP was significantly less for mainline Protestants than for evangelicals. In fact, the coefficients indicate that that relationship actually weakened over time for mainliners. It also appears that the relationship between doctrinal orthodoxy and Republican partisanship and voting behavior grew over time for evangelicals, although that increase is not

Estimating changes in the impact of religious commitment
and doctrinal orthodoxy on party identification and
presidential voting behavior from 1980 to 1996

Independent Variables	Changes Constant Across Traditions		Changes Vary Across Traditions	
	Party Identification	Presidential Vote	Party Identification	Presidential Vote
Mainline Protestant	.53**	.01	.41**	.06
Catholic	−.25**	−.53***	−.36	−.50***
Secular	−.16	−.75***	−.37*	−2.24***
Black Protestant	−1.33***	−2.96***	−1.82**	−2.86***
Jewish	−1.32**	−1.58***	−1.73**	−1.60***
Religious commitment (RC)	.09	.009	.27*	.007
Doctrinal orthodoxy	−.05	−.05	−.35	−.005
Mainline × RC	—	—	.07	.34
Catholic × RC	—	—	−.37*	.01
Secular × RC	—	—	−.10	−2.02***
Black Prot. × RC	—	—	−.52*	.04
Jewish × RC	—	—	−.94**	−.89
Mainline × doctrine	—	—	.10	−.43
Catholic × doctrine	—	—	.19	−.18
Secular × doctrine	—	—	.47	1.18
Black Prot. × doctrine	—	—	.82	−.22
Jewish × doctrine	—	—	.50	1.57
Time	.04	−.17**	−.001	−.20***
Mainline × time	−.06**	−.06*	−.02	−.01
Catholic × time	−.07**	−.04	−.03	−.0002
Secular × time	−.03	.09	−.03	.52**
Black Prot. × time	−.07***	−.09	.04	.12**
Jewish × time	−.008	−.27	.06	−.02
RC × time	.01	.12**	.05*	.27**
Doctrine × time	.04**	.17***	.07	.12
Mainline × RC × time	—	—	−.09**	−.32**
Catholic × RC × time	—	—	−.04	−.16
Secular × RC × time	—	—	−.12**	.33
Black × RC × time	—	—	−.04	−.27
Jewish × RC × time	—	—	−.009	−.24
Mainline × doctrine × time	—	—	−.01	.12
Catholic × doctrine × time	—	—	−.01	.07
Secular × doctrine × time	—	—	−.03	−.22***
Black × doctrine × time	—	—	−.12	−.14
Jewish × doctrine × time	—	—	−.07	.21
Constant	3.59***	.25	3.81***	.22

Table B8 (*continued*)

Independent Variables	Changes Constant Across Traditions		Changes Vary Across Traditions	
	Party Identification	Presidential Vote	Party Identification	Presidential Vote
(N)	(10,230)	(4,413)	(10,230)	(4,413)
Adjusted or pseudo R^2	.14	.16	.14	.17
Chi-square (df)	—	944.65 (23)	—	983.05 (43)
% Correctly predicted	—	68.09	—	67.82

Source: 1980–1996 National Election Studies (pooled).

Controls were included for education, income, gender, age, southern residence, and union membership. Entries for party identification are unstandardized regression coefficients. Entries for the presidential vote are logit coefficients. Party identification ranges from strong Democrat (1) to strong Republican (7). The vote is coded 1 for Republican voters and 0 for Democratic voters.

*$p < .10$

**$p < .05$

***$p < .001$

statistically significant. The increase in the impact of doctrine on Republican vote choice seems to have been even greater for mainline Protestants and Catholics than it was for evangelicals. However, the differences between the increases for those groups and the increases for evangelicals are also not statistically significant.

B6: The Conditional Effects of Cultural-Issue Salience and Political Awareness on the Impact of Religious Traditionalism on the Presidential Vote

To assess whether the impact of religious traditionalism on presidential voting behavior is conditional upon the political salience of cultural and moral issues (figure 7.3), I used the 1996 NES and estimated a logit model in which the vote was the dependent variable and the independent variables were the religious traditionalism index, cultural issue salience (the total number of open-ended responses related to cultural or moral issues), and their interaction, in addition to controls for party identification, ideological identification, education, income, southern residence, sex, and age. The coefficient on the interaction term indicates whether the impact of religious traditionalism on the vote increases as the importance of cultural and moral matters to individuals increases.

Table B9 presents the results of this model for all respondents, using the full religious traditionalism index, and for members of the three largest religious traditions, using an index consisting only of religious salience, church attendance, frequency of prayer, the Bible item, and the born-again indicator. The estimates indicate that religious traditionalism has no effect on presidential voting behavior when cultural issues are not salient at all.[11] However, as cultural-issue salience increases for all respondents and the members of the three largest religious traditions, the impact of traditionalism on vote choice increases significantly.

Table B10 examines whether political awareness also conditions the electoral impact of religious traditionalism (figure 7.4). It presents the results of a logit model of the presidential vote, in which the independent variables are religious traditionalism, political awareness, and their interaction, in addition to several control variables. The fact that the coefficient on religious traditionalism is negative and statistically significant for Catholics means that at the lowest levels of political awareness, religious traditionalism led to greater Catholic support for Bill Clinton, the Democratic presidential candidate in 1996. For all respondents and for both groups of white Protestants, religious traditionalism has no effect on the voting behavior of the least politically aware individuals.

However, the interaction between traditionalism and awareness is positive and statistically significant for all respondents, mainline Protestants, and Catholics. This indicates that as individuals became more

TABLE B9
Presidential vote choice as a function of religious traditionalism,
cultural-issue salience, and their interaction, 1996

Independent Variables	All Respondents	Evangelical Protestants	Mainline Protestants	Catholics
Religious traditionalism	−.02	−.31	−.54	−1.44
Cultural-issue salience	−.16	−.09	−.54	−1.50*
Traditionalism × cultural salience	.97**	1.16*	1.54**	3.55**
Party identification	.92***	.91***	1.09***	.98***
Ideological identification	.62***	1.06***	.72**	.54**
Education	.10	.34	.01	.45**
Income	.05**	−.01	.12**	.01
Southern residence	.34	.27	.14	1.15**
Sex (female)	−.22	−.94	.27	.39
Age	.01**	.02	.01	.05***
Race (white)	.71	—[a]	—[a]	−.51
Constant	−9.84***	−10.45***	−11.22***	−11.10***
(N)	(861)	(212)	(174)	(219)
Pseudo R^2	.61	.67	.61	.58
Chi-square (df)	712.65 (11)	188.63 (10)	146.78 (10)	173.09 (11)
% Correctly predicted	89.66	91.98	91.95	89.50

Source: 1996 National Election Study.

Entries are logit coefficients. The dependent variable is coded 1 for Republican voters and 0 for Democratic voters.

[a]Since there are no black respondents in the evangelical or mainline Protestant groups, race is not included in their equations.

*$p < .10$

**$p < .05$

***$p < .001$

politically aware, the relationship between religious traditionalism and voting for Bob Dole, the Republican candidate in 1996, increased. In other words, politically aware individuals are better able than their less aware counterparts to link their traditionalist–modernist religious orientations to the appropriate voting decisions or support for candidates who share their moral and cultural proclivities.

TABLE B10

Presidential vote choice as a function of religious traditionalism, political awareness, and their interaction, 1996

Independent Variables	All Respondents	Evangelical Protestants	Mainline Protestants	Catholics
Religious traditionalism	.04	−3.62	−6.43	−11.29**
Political awareness	−.007	−.22	−.18	−.39**
Traditionalism × awareness	.71***	.34	.49*	.82**
Party identification	.92***	.91***	1.07***	1.04***
Ideological identification	.63***	1.08***	.62*	.63**
Education	.10	.39*	−.09	.39**
Income	.05**	−.003	.12**	.03
Southern residence	.35	.17	.31	1.27**
Sex	−.27	−1.16*	.50	.23
Age	.01**	.02	.01	.05***
Race	.71	—a	—a	−.51
Constant	−9.91***	−8.24**	−8.18**	−6.81**
(N)	(861)	(212)	(174)	(219)
Pseudo R²	.61	.66	.61	.59
Chi-square (df)	711.77 (11)	184.51 (10)	145.36 (10)	173.17 (11)
% Correctly predicted	89.55	91.51	91.95	88.58

Source: 1996 National Election Study.

Entries are logit coefficients. The dependent variable is coded 1 for Republican voters and 0 for Democratic voters.

aSince there are no black respondents in the evangelical or mainline Protestant groups, race is not included in their equations.

*$p < .10$

**$p < .05$

***$p < .001$

B7: The Direct and "Indirect" Conditional Effect of Exposure to Religion-Based Political Stimuli on the Impact of Religious Traditionalism on the Presidential Vote

To assess whether the impact of religious traditionalism on presidential vote choice is greater for individuals who are exposed to political stimuli in church and other religious settings, I estimated a logit model in which the vote was a function of religious traditionalism, the dummy variable for exposure to religion-based political stimuli, and their interaction, in addition to several control variables. As table B11 shows, the interaction

TABLE B11
Presidential vote choice as a function of religious traditionalism, exposure to religion-based political stimuli, and their interaction, 1996

Independent Variables	All Respondents	Evangelical Protestants	Mainline Protestants	Catholics
Religious traditionalism	.52	−.06	.78	1.02
Religious-political stimuli	−.14	−.21	−.70	.46
Traditionalism × stimuli	.46	.86	.97	−.13
Party identification	.91***	.93***	1.03***	.98***
Ideological identification	.67***	1.13***	.63*	.56**
Education	.10	.35*	−.002	.37**
Income	.05**	−.003	.11**	.04
Sex (female)	−.26	−1.16**	.13	.39
Age	.01*	.02	.004	.05***
Southern residence	.32	.26	.46	1.20**
Race (white)	.87*	—[a]	—[a]	−.28
Constant	−10.20***	−10.80***	−10.28***	−12.60***
(N)	(861)	(212)	(174)	(219)
Pseudo R^2	.60	.65	.59	.56
Chi-square (df)	697.69 (11)	183.02 (10)	141.80 (10)	164.70 (11)
% Correctly predicted	89.43	91.04	89.66	86.76

Source: 1996 National Election Study.

Entries are logit coefficients. The dependent variable is coded 1 for Republican voters and 0 for Democratic voters.

[a]Since there are no black respondents in the evangelical or mainline Protestant groups, race is not included in their equations.

*p < .10

**p < .05

***p < .001

between traditionalism and religious political stimuli does not reach statistical significance for all respondents or for members of the three largest religious traditions. This indicates that exposure to efforts at political mobilization in religious settings, as measured here, does not condition the direct impact of religious traditionalism on the presidential vote.

One possible explanation for this lack of statistical significance is that the conditional effect of exposure to religion-based political stimuli is indirect. It may shape the effect of religious traditionalism on factors that have a direct impact on the vote, or it may affect factors that themselves condition the direct effect of religious traditionalism on the vote. In table B12, I test the possibility that exposure to religious political

TABLE B12

The impact of exposure to religion-based political stimuli on moral and cultural attitudes, role of government/social welfare attitudes, and defense and military attitudes, 1996

Independent Variables	All Respondents	Evangelical Protestants	Mainline Protestants	Catholics
Moral and cultural attitudes				
Religious traditionalism	.31***	.35***	.18**	.22***
Religious-political stimuli	−.09***	−.08	−.07	−.08
Traditionalism × stimuli	.18***	.15**	.18*	.16*
Education	−.02***	−.01	−.02**	−.01
Income	.001	.002	−.003	−.0001
Sex (female)	−.06***	−.05**	−.09***	−.06***
Age	.0006**	.001	.0006	.001**
Southern residence	.01	−.01	.01	.01
Race (white)	.04**	—[a]	—[a]	—[a]
Constant	.35***	.35***	.52**	−.56***
(N)	(1,276)	(321)	(218)	(301)
Adjusted R^2	.41	.37	.29	.20
Role of government/social welfare attitudes				
Religious traditionalism	.05**	.06	.09	.01
Religious-political stimuli	−.11***	−.22**	−.02	−.03
Traditionalism × stimuli	.20***	.32***	.08	.03
Education	.004	.01*	.01	.004
Income	.01***	.01***	.01**	.01**
Sex (female)	−.05***	−.03*	−.04	−.04**
Age	.001**	.001**	.0004	.002**
Southern residence	−.001	−.04**	.03	−.02

Table B12 (*continued*)

Independent Variables	All Respondents	Evangelical Protestants	Mainline Protestants	Catholics
Race (white)	.15***	—a	—a	—a
Constant	.19***	.26***	.32***	.31***
(N)	(1,416)	(354)	(238)	(330)
Adjusted R^2	.22	.24	.06	.08
Defense and military attitudes				
Religious traditionalism	.06**	.01	.08	.03
Religious-political stimuli	−.03	.02	−.08	.05
Traditionalism × stimuli	.05	.005	.14	−.09
Education	−.02***	−.01	−.02**	−.02**
Income	.002**	.0002	.004**	.0002
Sex (female)	−.04***	−.02	−.04*	−.04**
Age	.001***	.002**	.001**	.001**
Southern residence	.03***	.02	.03*	.03
Race (white)	.03**	—a	—a	—a
Constant	.48***	.50***	.45***	.53***
(N)	(1,107)	(280)	(195)	(269)
Adjusted R^2	.12	.03	.12	.08

Source: 1996 National Election Study.

Entries are unstandardized regression coefficients.

[a]Race is not included in the equations for evangelical Protestants, mainline Protestants, and Catholics because of the very small number of nonwhite respondents in these traditions.

*$p < .10$

**$p < .05$

***$p < .001$

stimuli conditions the direct effect of religious traditionalism on moral and cultural attitudes, social welfare attitudes, and defense and military attitudes (figure 7.5) by regressing these attitudes on religious traditionalism, religious political stimuli, and their interaction, in addition to several relevant controls. The statistically significant and positive interaction terms for moral and cultural attitudes indicate that the relationship between religious traditionalism and cultural conservatism is greater for individuals who are exposed to political stimuli in religious settings than for individuals who are not. The interaction term is also statistically significant in the social welfare model for all respondents and evangelical Protestants, indicating that religious political stimuli strengthen the connection between religious traditionalism and social welfare conservatism

TABLE B13
The impact of exposure to religion-based political
stimuli on cultural-issue salience, 1996

Independent Variables	All Respondents	Evangelical Protestants	Mainline Protestants	Catholics
Religious traditionalism	.66***	1.08**	.40	1.22***
Religious-political stimuli	.42***	.72***	.54**	.20
Open-ended responses	.09***	.12***	.10***	.05***
Cultural issue extremity	.25*	.09	−.21	.15
Moral traditionalism	.69***	1.87***	−.42	.47
Education	−.04*	−.10*	−.09*	.01
Income	.003	−.002	.01	.002
Sex (female)	.12*	−.01	.21	.20
Age	−.01***	−.02***	−.01***	−.005
Southern residence	−.01	−.21	−.05	−.14
Race (white)	.42***	—a	—a	—a
Constant	−.81***	−.88*	.42	−1.23**
(N)	(1,266)	(319)	(216)	(296)
Adjusted R²	.31	.41	.34	.19

Source: 1996 National Election Study.

Entries are unstandardized regression coefficients.

aRace in not included in the equations for evangelical Protestants, mainline Protestants, and Catholics because of the very small number of nonwhite respondents in these traditions.

*$p < .10$

**$p < .05$

***$p < .001$

for these groups. Exposure to religious political stimuli does not seem to play such a role for mainline Protestants and Catholics, and it does not affect the relationship between traditionalism and defense attitudes for any of the groups.

The regression models in table B13 test the hypothesis that exposure to religious political stimuli itself has a direct effect on the political salience of cultural and moral matters to individuals (figure 7.6). The results confirm the hypothesis. Even when factors such as cultural issue extremity, moral traditionalism, and a respondent's total number of responses to open-ended questions are controlled, exposure to religious political stimuli has a positive and highly significant effect for all respondents and for evangelical and mainline Protestants.

Since exposure to religion-based political stimuli conditions the direct

TABLE B14

A model for assessing the indirect conditional effect of exposure
to religion-based political stimuli on the relationship between
religious traditionalism and presidential vote choice, 1996

Independent Variables	All Respondents[a]	Evangelical Protestants	Mainline Protestants	Catholics
Religious traditionalism	−1.94**	−3.86**	−2.15	−2.32
Cultural issue salience	−.16	−1.50	−.52	−1.79*
Traditionalism × cultural salience	1.08**	2.80*	1.63	4.06**
Moral/cultural attitudes	7.24***	6.43*	8.70**	5.81**
Social welfare attitudes	2.58**	−.08	2.87	3.87*
Defense/military attitudes	.77	−1.38	−4.62	2.78
Party identification	.88***	1.06***	1.06***	.86***
Ideological identification	.33**	.94**	.32	.30
Education	.18*	.51*	−.09	.49**
Income	.05*	.03	.16**	.01
Sex (female)	.23	−1.08	1.06	.80
Age	.01	.02	.01	.05**
Southern residence	.25	.001	.36	1.63**
Race (white)	.06	—[a]	—[a]	—[a]
Constant	−12.22***	−11.92**	−11.53**	−15.87***
(N)	(769)	(190)	(158)	(202)
Pseudo R^2	.66	.73	.66	.63
Chi-square (df)	687.26 (14)	181.59 (13)	143.39 (13)	170.80 (13)
% Correctly predicted	90.84	93.19	90.51	91.67

Source: 1996 National Election Study.

Entries are logit coefficients. The dependent variable is coded 1 for Republican voters and 0 for Democratic voters.

[a]Race in not included in the equations for evangelical Protestants, mainline Protestants, and Catholics because of the very small number of nonwhite respondents in these traditions.

*p < .10

**p < .05

***p < .001

effect of religious traditionalism on some policy-related attitudes and itself has a direct effect on cultural issue salience, the next step in examining the indirect conditional effect of exposure is to examine the effect
of policy-related attitudes and cultural issue salience on the presidential
vote. Table B14 presents the results of a logit model of the vote that
includes religious traditionalism, cultural-issue salience, their interac-

tion, moral and cultural attitudes, social welfare attitudes, and defense attitudes, in addition to controls for party identification, ideological identification, and several demographic variables. Cultural conservatism has a positive and significant effect on Republican vote choice for all respondents and for members of the three religious traditions. Social welfare conservatism has a positive and significant effect for all respondents and Catholics. The interaction between religious traditionalism and cultural-issue salience reaches statistical significance for all respondents, evangelicals, and Catholics, and it approaches significance for mainline Protestants. This indicates, again, that the impact of religious traditionalism on the vote increases as cultural and moral matters become more politically salient.

B8: The Conditional Effect of the Religious Polarization of State Party Elites and Activists on the Impact of Religious Traditionalism on the Political Behavior

To assess whether the effect of religious traditionalism, as measured by the born-again/fundamentalist Christian indicator, has a greater effect on political behavior in states where Democratic and Republican elites and activists are more polarized along religious lines (figure 7.7), I pooled data from the 1988 and 1992 election-day exit polls. Then, I estimated models of party identification, the presidential vote, the gubernatorial vote, and the Senate vote in which the born-again variable, the level of religious polarization between state party elites, and their interaction were the independent variables. The models also included controls for state opinion liberalism (see Erikson, Wright, and McIver 1993); demographic characteristics; identification as a Catholic, Jew, or Protestant (the exit polls did not distinguish between evangelical, mainline, and black Protestant affiliations); party identification (in the vote models); voting behavior in the last presidential election (in the party identification and presidential vote models) and the current presidential election (in the gubernatorial and senate vote models); the party of the incumbent if one was present in a gubernatorial or Senate race; and the spending of the Republican and Democratic candidates in elections for governor and the U.S. Senate.[12]

Table B15 shows that the interaction between the born-again/fundamentalist Christian variable and the religious polarization of state party elites is positive and statistically significant in the model for each dependent variable. That indicates that larger traditionalist–modernist religious cleavages between Democratic and Republican elites and activists in a state increases the impact of religious traditionalism on individual-level political behavior in the state. In other words, as elite religious polarization grows, born-again/fundamentalist Christians become more supportive of the Republican party and its presidential, gubernatorial, and Senate candidates relative to individuals who are not born-again/fundamentalist Christians.

Notes

1. Members of smaller nontraditional Protestant religions, Eastern Orthodox religions, and non-Judeo-Christian religions were dropped from the analysis.

Conditional effect of the religious polarization of state party elites on the
impact of born-again identification on political behavior, 1988 and 1992

Independent Variables	Party Identification	Presidential Vote	Gubernatorial Vote	Senate Vote
	Dependent Variable			
Party identification	—	1.31**	.77**	.78**
Born-again Christian	.01	.65**	.51**	.30*
Elite religious polarization	.01	−.11*	.002	−.05
Born-again × elite polarization	.04**	.06*	.06*	.08*
Race (white)	.21**	.87**	.77**	.46**
Sex (female)	−.02*	−.15**	.07*	−.09*
Southern residence	−.02	.17	2.20**	−.90**
Income	.06**	.12**	.02	.04
Age	−.03**	−.02	.03	.02
Catholic	−.06**	.33**	.18	.08
Jewish	−.15**	−.53**	−.31	−.32*
Protestant	.09**	.26**	.16	.07
State opinion liberalism	−.19	1.19	—[a]	5.74**
Vote in last presidential election	.98**	2.79**	—	—
Current presidential vote	—	—	2.46**	2.30**
Republican incumbent	—	—	−.68	.20
Democratic incumbent	—	—	−.26	−.59**
Spending by Republican candidate	—	—	.05*	.008*
Spending by Democratic candidate	—	—	−.10**	−.007*
Constant	1.04**	−5.99**	−3.38**	−3.80**
(N)	(46,326)	(41,667)	(7,571)	(35,834)
Adjusted or Pseudo R^2	.39	.51	.42	.39
Chi-square (df)	—	28,976.69 (14)	4,354.79 (17)	18,811.00 (18)
% Correctly predicted	—	85.48	83.70	82.04

Source: The party elite polarization variable is from the 1988 and 1992 Convention Delegate Studies (pooled). State opinion liberalism is from Erikson, Wright, and McIver (1993). All other variables, with the exception of incumbency and spending, are from the 1988 and 1992 election-day exit polls (pooled) conducted by CBS News/*New York Times* in 1988 and by Voter Research and Surveys in 1992.

Entries are logit coefficients for the presidential, gubernatorial, and Senate vote, and unstandardized regression coefficients for party identification. The vote variables are coded 1 for Republican voters and 0 for Democratic voters. Party identification is coded 1 for Democrats, 2 for independents, and 3 for Republicans.

[a]State opinion liberalism was not included in the gubernatorial vote model because of very high levels of collinearity with other independent variables.

*p < .05

**p < .001

2. I do not include a control for race because I include a dummy variable for black Protestants, almost all of whom are black.

3. It may seem somewhat odd to include interaction terms between the dummy variable for seculars and doctrine and commitment. Most seculars have low levels of doctrinal orthodoxy and seculars have, by definition, low levels of religious commitment (in fact, some of the individuals in the secular category were placed there despite their affiliation with a denomination because of their very low commitment levels). However, it is necessary for statistical purposes to include those interaction terms in the model. If they are not included, then it becomes impossible to isolate the effects of doctrine and commitment for evangelical Protestants because the β_d and β_c coefficients would then be the effects of doctrine and commitment for evangelicals and seculars. Moreover, it is unlikely that commitment has much of an effect on political attitudes and behavior for seculars—they are not affiliated with a tradition, and the variance on commitment is very low for seculars—and that should be apparent in interaction terms indicating that the effect of commitment is less for seculars than for evangelicals. However, it is possible that doctrinal orthodoxy may have some impact on the political and cultural orientations of seculars. That one is not affiliated with a religious denomination or movement does not necessarily mean that one cannot believe in key tenets of traditional Christian doctrine. Moreover, Hunter (1991) argues that most seculars are on the progressivist side of the contemporary cultural conflict, but that some seculars with traditional moral worldviews are on the orthodox side.

4. The small numbers of delegates in nontraditional Protestant, Eastern Orthodox, and non-Judeo-Christian religions were excluded from the analyses. Because of the very small number of Jewish and black Protestant Republican delegates, these two traditions are excluded from the analyses for Republicans.

5. Pat Robertson's supporters were excluded from the analysis in 1988 because Robertson received no support from secular Republican delegates and virtually no support from mainline Protestants or Catholics.

6. The "other religions" category includes the small number of respondents in Eastern Orthodox religions and the individuals who placed themselves in the "other Protestant" or "other religious preference" categories of the CDS religious classification. Mormons are typically included in a larger family of conservative nontraditional Protestants (Green et al. 1996), but there are no other nontraditional Protestants, conservative or liberal, in the CDS classification.

7. The "other religions" category includes the small number of respondents in Eastern Orthodox religions, conservative and liberal nontraditional Protestant religions, and non-Judeo-Christian religions, as well as individuals with ambiguous religious affiliations (e.g., "Protestant, no denomination

given" in the NES religion codes from 1960 through 1988) for whom there was not enough information to place in a specific religious tradition.

8. The use of this time variable rather than dummy variables for years assumes that the change in the political impact of religious variables is linear over time. I also estimated models using dummy variables for years and their interactions with religious variables. The results showed that the changes over time in the political impact of religious commitment and doctrinal orthodoxy were approximately linear.

9. The logit models of the presidential vote also included dummy variables for the 1992 and 1996 elections because the Republican candidates in those years won a substantially smaller proportion of the vote than the Republican candidates in the elections of the 1980s.

10. Typically, models using data pooled from cross-sectional surveys include dummy variables for the different years in order to account for the possibility that the intercept varies across the various survey years. Unfortunately, it is impossible to include a set of dummy variables for each year of the analysis in this model because that set of variables would be perfectly collinear with the time variable. Failure to account for variance in the intercept across years creates the possibility of heteroskedasticity across years, which violates the assumptions of OLS regression and logit analysis (Beck and Katz 1995; Beck and Tucker 1996). However, while heteroskedasticity does lead to inaccurate estimates of the standard errors of the coefficients, it does not make the OLS and logit coefficients themselves inconsistent (Beck and Katz 1995; Beck and Tucker 1996). Thus, my coefficient estimates should be accurate. To account for the possibility of inconsistent standard error estimates, I computed standard errors using Huber's (1967) and White's (1980) formula for heteroskedasticity-consistent standard errors.

11. This is the coefficient on religious traditionalism, which is the impact of traditionalism when cultural-issue salience is equal to zero, its lowest level.

12. Models using data pooled from various cross-sectional units, such as states, often include dummy variables for those different units to account for cross-sectional differences in the level of the dependent variable. Of course, an alternative to unit dummies is to include substantively interesting variables that account for cross-sectional variance in the level of the dependent variable. That is what I have done here by including variables like state opinion liberalism and the spending levels of the Democratic and Republican candidates. However, since these variables are state specific, they cannot be included in the same model with state-specific dummy variables. Leaving these dummy variables out of the models may create some problems with the standard errors of the coefficient estimates. To account for the possibility of inconsistent standard error estimates, I computed standard errors using Huber's (1967) and White's (1980) formula for heteroskedasticity-consistent standard errors.

Congressional Votes
on Cultural Issues

THE CONGRESSIONAL PARTY ALIGNMENT on cultural issues is based on the following votes, listed by *Congressional Quarterly* roll-call numbers.

House

1970	H.147, 148, 149.
1971	H.196, 197, 245, 246.
1973	H.183, 184.
1974	H.166.
1975	H.167, 168.
1976	H.196, 336, 340, 480.
1977	H.326, 356, 466, 550, 595, 603, 675, 681, 690, 696, 701.
1978	H.381, 382, 584, 618, 619, 620, 621, 638, 790, 810, 815.
1979	H.188, 270, 288, 312, 487, 550, 629, 630, 633.
1980	H.311, 371, 410, 411, 416, 417, 452.
1981	H.37, 76, 77, 78, 171, 181.
1983	H.168, 170, 325, 334, 396, 469.
1984	H.129, 247, 287, 289.
1985	H.216, 246, 247.
1986	H.210.
1987	H.221, 364.
1988	H.203, 307, 360.
1989	H.47, 105, 205, 277, 278.
1990	H.201, 274, 342, 447, 494, 523.
1991	H.109, 148, 149, 308, 309, 314.

1992 H.115, 163, 420, 458.

1993 H.28, 29, 60, 61, 64, 97, 104, 106, 107, 108, 307, 309, 460, 461, 578, 580, 582.

1994 H.30, 31, 66, 67, 68, 69, 70, 71, 74, 75, 76, 85, 91, 92, 157, 158, 159, 426, 455.

1995 H.125, 349, 350, 382, 433, 529, 530, 574, 619, 620, 641, 642, 753, 754, 755, 756.

1996 H.51, 93, 94, 167, 174, 300, 316, 320, 332, 421, 422.

Senate

1970 S.347, 349.

1971 S.40.

1972 S.101, 102, 103, 104, 105, 106, 108, 109, 110.

1974 S.381.

1975 S.130.

1976 S.152, 342, 343, 520, 521.

1977 S.258, 259, 260, 262, 263, 336, 337, 582, 609, 614, 632, 633, 634.

1978 S.387, 413, 414, 432, 433, 435, 436, 437, 438, 446.

1979 S.36, 37, 39, 41, 42, 43, 44, 187, 188, 189, 223, 303, 304, 313, 351, 384, 404, 405.

1980 S.202, 441, 442, 447.

1981 S.132, 373, 374, 375.

1982 S.340, 342, 343, 344, 345, 346, 347, 348, 349, 350, 450.

1983 S.169, 335, 336, 339, 340, 341.

1984 S.34, 202, 257.

1985 S.172, 255, 274, 290, 291.

1986 S.263, 323.

1987 S.289.

1988 S.8, 9, 117, 118, 232, 233, 234, 235, 236, 266, 267, 269, 280, 326, 327, 348, 359.

1989 S.186, 187, 188, 198, 216.

1990 S.68, 212, 234, 252, 253, 266, 298, 307.

1991 S.130, 131, 151, 177, 185.

1992 S.4, 5, 165, 220, 227.

1993   S.9, 235, 250, 290, 369, 370, 371, 372.
1994   S.22, 112, 191, 214, 236, 244.
1995   S.333, 369, 370, 371, 478, 539, 542, 593, 594, 595, 596.
1996   S.163, 280, 281, 284.

BIBLIOGRAPHY

Abramowitz, Alan I. 1995. It's Abortion, Stupid: Policy Voting in the 1992 Presidential Election. *Journal of Politics* 57:176–86.

Abramowitz, Alan I., John McGlennon, and Ronald B. Rapoport. 1986. An Analysis of State Party Activists. In *The Life of the Parties: Activists in Presidential Nominating Politics.* Ronald B. Rapoport, Alan I. Abramowitz, and John McGlennon, eds. Lexington, KY: University of Kentucky Press.

Abramson, Paul R., John H. Aldrich, and David W. Rohde. 1999. *Change and Continuity in the 1996 and 1998 Elections.* Washington, DC: CQ Press.

Adams, Greg D. 1997. Abortion: Evidence of Issue Evolution. *American Journal of Political Science* 41:718–37.

Aldrich, John H. 1983a. A Downsian Spatial Model with Party Activism. *American Political Science Review* 77:974–90.

———. 1983b. A Spatial Model with Party Activists: Implications for Electoral Dynamics. *Public Choice* 41:63–100.

———. 1995. *Why Parties? The Origin and Transformation of Political Parties in America.* Chicago: University of Chicago Press.

———. 1999. Political Parties in a Critical Era. *American Politics Quarterly* 27:9–32.

Allardt, Eric, and Pertti Pesonen. 1967. Cleavages in Finnish Politics. In *Party Systems and Voter Alignments.* Seymour M. Lipset and Stein Rokkan, eds. New York: Free Press.

American Political Science Association. 1950. *Toward a More Responsible Party System.* New York: Rinehart.

Ammerman, Nancy. 1987. *Bible Believers.* New Brunswick, NJ: Rutgers University Press.

Anson, Robert Sam. 1972. *McGovern: A Biography.* New York: Holt, Rinehart, and Winston.

Axelrod, Robert. 1972. Where the Votes Come From: An Analysis of Electoral Coalitions. *American Political Science Review* 66:11–20.

Baker, Tod A., and Robert P. Steed. 1992. Party Activists, Southern Religion, and Culture Wars: An Analysis of Precinct Party Activists in Eleven Southern States. Presented at the annual meeting of the Southern Political Science Association, Atlanta, November.

Baker, Tod A., Robert P. Steed, and Lawrence W. Moreland. 1991. Preachers and

Politics: Jesse Jackson, Pat Robertson, and the 1988 Presidential Nomination Campaign in South Carolina. In *The Bible and the Ballot Box: Religion and Politics in the 1988 Election*. James L. Guth and John G. Green, eds. Boulder, CO: Westview Press.

Barker, David C., and Christopher Jan Carman. 2000. The Spirit of Capitalism? Religious Doctrine, Values, and Economic Attitude Constructs. *Political Behavior* 22:1–27.

Bartels, Larry M. 2000. Partisanship and Voting Behavior, 1952–1996. *American Journal of Political Science* 44:35–50.

Beatty, Kathleen, and Oliver Walter. 1984. Religious Preferences and Practice: Reevaluating Their Impact on Political Tolerance. *Public Opinion Quarterly* 48:312–24.

———. 1989. A Group Theory of Religion and Politics: The Clergy as Group Leaders. *Western Political Quarterly* 42:29–46.

Beck, Nathaniel. 1985. Estimating Dynamic Models Is Not Merely a Matter of Technique. *Political Methodology* 11:71–90.

Beck, Nathaniel, and Johnathan N. Katz. 1995. What to Do (and Not to Do) with Time-Series-Cross-Section Data in Comparative Politics. *American Political Science Review* 89:634–47.

———. 1996. Nuisance vs. Substance: Specifying and Estimating Time-Series-Cross-Section Models. *Political Analysis* 6:1–36.

Beck, Nathaniel, and Richard Tucker. 1996. Conflict in Space and Time: Time-Series-Cross-Section Analysis with a Binary Dependent Variable. Presented at the annual meeting of the American Political Science Association, San Francisco, September.

Beck, Paul Allen. 1979. The Electoral Cycle and Patterns of American Politics. *British Journal of Political Science* 9:129–56.

———. 1997. *Party Politics in America,* 8th ed. New York: Longman.

Benson, Lee. 1961. *The Concept of Jacksonian Democracy*. Princeton, NJ: Princeton University Press.

Berelson, Bernard R., Paul R. Lazarsfeld, and William N. McPhee. 1954. *Voting: A Study of Opinion Formation in a Presidential Campaign*. Chicago: University of Chicago Press.

Bibby, Reginald W., and Merlin Brinkerhoff. 1983. Circulation of the Saints Revisited: A Longitudinal Look at Conservative Church Growth. *Journal for the Scientific Study of Religion* 22:153–62.

Black, Earl, and Merle Black. 1987. *Politics and Society in the South*. Cambridge, MA: Harvard University Press.

———. 1992. *The Vital South: How Presidents Are Elected*. Cambridge, MA: Harvard University Press.

Bolce, Louis, and Gerald De Maio. 1998. The Impact of the Christian Fundamentalist Symbol on Party Coalitions: A Reference Group Theory Approach.

Presented at the annual meeting of the American Political Science Association, Boston, September.

———. 1999. Religious Outlook, Culture War Politics, and Antipathy toward Christian Fundamentalists. *Public Opinion Quarterly* 63:29–61.

Bowman, Lewis, Dennis Ippolito, and William Donaldson. 1969. Incentives for the Maintenance of Grassroots Political Activism. *Midwest Journal of Political Science* 13:126–39.

Box, George E. P., and Gwilym M. Jenkins. 1976. *Time Series Analysis: Forecasting and Control.* San Francisco: Holden Day.

Brady, Henry E., and Paul M. Sniderman. 1985. Attitude Attribution: A Group Basis for Political Reasoning. *American Political Science Review* 79:1061–78.

Brams, Steven J. 1978. *The Presidential Election Game.* New Haven: Yale University Press.

Budge, Ian, and Richard I. Hofferbert. 1990. Mandates and Policy Outputs: U.S. Party Platforms and Federal Expenditures. *American Political Science Review* 84:111–32.

Burnham, Walter Dean. 1991. Critical Realignment: Dead or Alive? In *The End of Realignment: Interpreting American Electoral Eras.* Byron E. Shafer, ed. Madison, WI: University of Wisconsin Press.

Campbell, Angus, Philip E. Converse, Warren E. Miller, and Donald E. Stokes. 1960. *The American Voter.* Chicago: University of Chicago Press.

Campbell, Angus, and Homer C. Cooper. 1956. *Group Differences in Attitudes and Votes.* Ann Arbor, MI: Survey Research Center, Institute for Social Research, University of Michigan.

Carmines, Edward G. 1991. The Logic of Party Alignments. *Journal of Theoretical Politics* 3:65–80.

———. 1994. Political Issues, Party Alignments, Spatial Models, and the Post–New Deal Party System. In *New Perspectives in American Politics.* Lawrence C. Dodd and Calvin Jillson, eds. Washington, DC: Congressional Quarterly.

Carmines, Edward G., and Geoffrey C. Layman. 1997. Issue Evolution in Postwar American Politics: Old Certainties and Fresh Tensions. In *Present Discontents: American Politics in the Very Late Twentieth Century.* Byron E. Shafer, ed. Chatham, NJ: Chatham House.

Carmines, Edward G., Steven H. Renten, and James A. Stimson. 1984. Events and Alignments: The Party Image Link. In *Controversies in Voting Behavior,* 2nd ed. Richard E. Niemi and Herbert F. Weisberg, eds. Washington, DC: Congressional Quarterly.

Carmines, Edward G., and James A. Stimson. 1980. The Two Faces of Issue Voting. *American Political Science Review* 74:78–91.

———. 1989. *Issue Evolution: Race and the Transformation of American Politics.* Princeton, NJ: Princeton University Press.

Carsey, Thomas M. 2000. *Campaign Dynamics: The Race for Governor.* Ann Arbor, MI: University of Michigan Press.

Carsey, Thomas M., and Geoffrey C. Layman. 1999. A Dynamic Model of Political Change Among Party Activists. *Political Behavior* 21:17–41.

Chandler, Ralph Clark. 1984. The Wicked Shall Not Bear Rule: The Fundamentalist Heritage of the New Christian Right. In *New Christian Politics.* David G. Bromley and Anson Shupe, eds. Macon, GA: Mercer University Press.

Chappell, Henry W., Jr., and William R. Keech. 1986. Policy Motivation and Party Differences in a Dynamic Spatial Model of Party Competition. *American Political Science Review* 80:881–900.

Chaves, Mark. 1994. Secularization as Declining Religious Authority. *Social Forces* 72:749–74.

Clubb, Jerome M., William H. Flanigan, and Nancy H. Zingale. 1980. *Partisan Realignment.* Beverly Hills, CA: Sage.

Conover, Pamela Johnston. 1983. The Mobilization of the New Right: A Test of Various Explanations. *Western Political Quarterly* 36:632–49.

———. 1988. Feminists and the Gender Gap. *Journal of Politics* 50:985–1010.

Conover, Pamela Johnston, and Virginia Gray. 1983. *Feminism and the New Right: Conflict over the American Family.* New York: Praeger.

Converse, Philip E., and Gregory B. Markus. 1979. Plus ça Change . . . : The New CPS Election Study Panel. *American Political Science Review* 73:32–49.

Conway, M. Margaret, and Frank B. Feigert. 1968. Motivation, Incentive Systems, and the Political Party Organization. *American Political Science Review* 62:1159–73.

Cook, Elizabeth, Ted Jelen, and Clyde Wilcox. 1992. *Between Two Absolutes: American Public Opinion and the Politics of Abortion.* Boulder, CO: Greenwood.

———. 1993. Generational Differences in Attitudes Toward Abortion. In *Understanding the New Politics of Abortion.* Malcolm L. Goggin, ed. Newbury Park, CA: Sage.

———. 1994. Issue Voting in Gubernatorial Elections: Abortion and Post-*Webster* Politics. *Journal of Politics* 56:187–99.

Dayton, Donald W., and Robert K. Johnston, eds. 1991. *The Variety of American Evangelicalism.* Knoxville, TN: University of Tennessee Press.

Delli Carpini, Michael X., and Scott Keeter. 1996. *What Americans Know About Politics and Why It Matters.* New Haven: Yale University Press.

DiMaggio, Paul, John Evans, and Bethany Bryson. 1996. Have Americans' Social Attitudes Become More Polarized? *American Journal of Sociology* 102:690–755.

Dionne, E. J., Jr. 1991. *Why Americans Hate Politics.* New York: Touchstone.

Downs, Anthony. 1957. *An Economic Theory of Democracy.* New York: Harper & Row.

Durbin, J. 1970. Testing for Serial Correlation in Least-Squares Regression When Some of the Regressors Are Lagged Dependent Variables. *Econometrica* 38:410–21.

Durden, Robert F. 1965. *The Climax of Populism: The Election of 1896.* Lexington, KY: University of Kentucky Press.

Emerson, Michael. 1996. Through Tinted Glasses: Religion, Worldviews, and Abortion Attitudes. *Journal for the Scientific Study of Religion* 35: 41–55.

Epstein, Leon D. 1979. *Political Parties in Western Democracies.* New Brunswick, NJ: Transaction.

Erikson, Robert S., Thomas D. Lancaster, and David W. Romero. 1989. Group Components of the Presidential Vote. *Journal of Politics* 51:337–46.

Erikson, Robert S., Gerald C. Wright, and John P. McIver. 1993. *Statehouse Democracy.* New York: Cambridge University Press.

Feldman, Stanley, and John Zaller. 1992. The Political Culture of Ambivalence: Ideological Responses to the Welfare State. *American Journal of Political Science* 36:268–307.

Fiorina, Morris P. 1999. Whatever Happened to the Median Voter? Presented at the Massachusetts Institute of Technology Conference on Parties and Congress, October, Cambridge, MA.

Fite, David, Marc Genest, and Clyde Wilcox. 1990. Gender Differences in Foreign Policy Attitudes: A Longitudinal Analysis. *American Politics Quarterly* 18:492–513.

Formisano, Ronald. 1971. *The Birth of Mass Political Parties.* Princeton, NJ: Princeton University Press.

Fowler, Robert Booth. 1989. *Unconventional Partners: Religion and Liberal Culture in the United States.* Grand Rapids, MI: Eerdmans.

Fowler, Robert Booth, Allen D. Hertzke, and Laura R. Olson. 1999. *Religion and Politics in America,* 2nd ed. Boulder, CO: Westview Press.

Freeman, Jo. 1986. The Political Culture of Democrats and Republicans. *Political Science Quarterly* 101:327–44.

Geer, John G. 1991. Critical Realignments and the Public Opinion Poll. *Journal of Politics* 53:434–53.

Glazer, Nathan. 1987. Fundamentalism: A Defensive Offensive. In *Piety and Politics: Evangelicals and Fundamentalists Confront the World.* Richard John Neuhaus and Michael Cromrartie, eds. Washington, DC: Ethics and Public Policy Center.

Grant, J. Tobin, Stephen T. Mockabee, and Quin Monson. 1997. Specifying Religion Variables in Multivariate Models. Presented at the annual meeting of the Southern Political Science Association, Norfolk, VA, November.

Green, Donald Philip, and Bradley Palmquist. 1990. Of Artifacts and Partisan Instability. *American Journal of Political Science* 34:872–902.

Green, Donald, Bradley Palmquist, and Eric Schickler. N.d. Partisan Hearts and

Minds: Political Parties and the Social Identities of Voters. Unpublished manuscript.

Green, John C. 1997. The Christian Right and the 1996 Elections: An Overview. In *God at the Grassroots, 1996.* Mark J. Rozell and Clyde Wilcox, eds. Lanham, MD: Rowman and Littlefield.

Green, John C., and James L. Guth. 1988. The Christian Right in the Republican Party: The Case of Pat Robertson's Supporters. *Journal of Politics* 50: 150–65.

———. 1991. Religion, Representation, and Roll Calls. *Legislative Studies Quarterly* 16:571–84.

Green, John C., James L. Guth, and Cleveland R. Fraser. 1991. Apostles and Apostates? Religion and Politics among Party Activists. In *The Bible and the Ballot Box: Religion and Politics in the 1988 Election.* James L. Guth and John C. Green, eds. Boulder, CO: Westview.

Green, John C., James L. Guth, Corwin E. Smidt, and Lyman A. Kellstedt. 1996. *Religion and the Culture Wars.* Lanham, MD: Rowman and Littlefield.

Greenberg, Anna. 1994. Family Values, the Church and the African-American Community. Presented at the annual meeting of the American Political Science Association, New York, September.

Guth, James L. 1983. The New Christian Right. In *The New Christian Right: Mobilization and Legitimation.* Robert C. Liebman and Robert Wuthnow, eds. New York: Aldine.

Guth, James L., and John C. Green. 1986. Faith and Politics: Religion and Ideology among Political Contributors. *American Politics Quarterly* 14:186–99.

———. 1987. The Moralizing Minority: Christian Right Support among Political Contributors. *Social Science Quarterly* 68:598–610.

———. 1989. God and the GOP: Religion among GOP Activists. In *Religion and Political Behavior in the United States.* Ted G. Jelen, ed. New York: Praeger.

———. 1993. Salience: The Core Concept? In *Rediscovering the Religious Factor in American Politics.* David C. Leege and Lyman A. Kellstedt, eds. Armonk, NY: M. E. Sharpe.

———. 1996. Politics in a New Key: Religiosity and Participation among Political Activists. In *Religion and the Culture Wars.* John C. Green, James L. Guth, Corwin E. Smidt, and Lyman A. Kellstedt, eds. Lanham, MD: Rowman and Littlefield.

Guth, James L., and John C. Green, eds. 1991. *The Bible and the Ballot Box: Religion and Politics in the 1988 Election.* Boulder, CO: Westview.

Guth, James L., John C. Green,, Lyman A. Kellstedt, and Corwin E. Smidt. 1996. The Political Relevance of Religion: The Correlates of Mobilization. In *Religion and the Culture Wars.* John C. Green, James L. Guth, Corwin E. Smidt, and Lyman A. Kellstedt, eds. Lanham, MD: Rowman and Littlefield.

Guth, James L., John C. Green, Corwin E. Smidt, Lyman A. Kellstedt and Margaret M. Poloma. 1997. *The Bully Pulpit: The Politics of Protestant Clergy.* Lawrence, KS: University Press of Kansas.

Guth, James L., Ted G. Jelen, Lyman A. Kellstedt, Corwin E. Smidt, and Kenneth D. Wald. 1988. The Politics of Religion in America: Issues for Investigation. *American Politics Quarterly* 16:357–97.

Guth, James L., Corwin E. Smidt, Lyman A. Kellstedt, and John C. Green. 1993. The Sources of Antiabortion Attitudes: The Case of Religious Political Attitudes. *American Politics Quarterly* 21:65–80.

Hadden, Jeffrey K. 1969. *The Gathering Storm in the Churches.* Garden City, NY: Doubleday.

Hadley, Charles D., and Harold W. Stanley. 1996. The Southern Super Tuesday: Southern Democrats Seeking Relief from Rising Republicanism. In *In Pursuit of the White House: How We Choose Our Presidential Nominees.* William G. Mayer, ed. Chatham, NJ: Chatham House.

Harrison, Michael I., and Bernard Lazerwitz. 1982. Do Denominations Matter? *American Journal of Sociology* 88:356–77.

Heinz, Donald. 1983. The Struggle to Define America. In *The New Christian Right: Mobilization and Legitimation.* Robert C. Liebman and Robert Wuthnow, eds. New York: Aldine.

Herrera, Richard. 1992. The Understanding of Ideological Labels by Political Elites: A Research Note. *Western Political Quarterly* 45:1021–35.

———. 1995. The Crosswinds of Change: Sources of Change in the Democratic and Republican Parties. *Political Research Quarterly* 48:291–312.

Hertzke, Allen D. 1993. *Echoes of Discontent: Jesse Jackson, Pat Robertson, and the Resurgence of Populism.* Washington, DC: CQ Press.

Himmelstein, Jerome L. 1983. The New Right. In *The New Christian Right: Mobilization and Legitimation.* Robert C. Liebman and Robert Wuthnow, eds. New York: Aldine.

Hitchcock, James. 1982. *What Is Secular Humanism? Why Humanism Became Secular and How It Is Changing Our Society.* Ann Arbor, MI: Servant Books.

Horton, Michael. 1994. *Beyond Culture Wars.* Chicago: Moody Press.

Howell, Susan, and Robert Sims. 1993. Abortion Attitudes and the Louisiana Governor's Election. *American Politics Quarterly* 21:54–64.

Huber, Peter J. 1967. The Behavior of Maximum Likelihood Estimates Under Non-Standard Conditions. *Proceedings of the Fifth Berkeley Symposium on Mathematical Statistics and Probability* 1:221–33.

Huckfeldt, Robert, and Carol Weitzel Kohfeld. 1989. *Race and the Decline of Class in American Politics.* Urbana, IL: University of Illinois Press.

Huckfeldt, Robert, Eric Plutzer, and John Sprague. 1989. Alternative Contexts of Political Behavior: Churches, Neighborhoods, and Individuals. *Journal of Politics* 55:365–81.

Huckfeldt, Robert, and John Sprague. 1987. Networks in Context: The Social

Flow of Political Information. *American Political Science Review* 81:1197–216.

Hunter, James Davison. 1983. *American Evangelicalism: Conservative Religion and the Quandary of Modernity.* New Brunswick, NJ: Rutgers University Press.

———. 1991. *Culture Wars: The Struggle to Define America.* New York: Basic Books.

———. 1994. *Before the Shooting Begins: Searching for Democracy in America's Culture War.* New York: Macmillan.

Iannaccone, Laurence R. 1994. Why Strict Churches Are Strong. *Journal of Sociology* 99:1180–211.

Inkeles, Alex. 1983. *Exploring Individual Modernity.* Cambridge, MA: Harvard University Press.

Jelen, Ted. 1991. *The Political Mobilization of Religious Beliefs.* New York: Praeger.

———. 1992. Political Christianity: A Contextual Analysis. *American Journal of Political Science* 36:692–714.

———. 1993. The Political Consequences of Religious Group Attitudes. *Journal of Politics* 55:178–90.

———. 1997. Culture Wars and the Party System: Religion and Realignment, 1972–1993. In *Cultural Wars in American Politics: Critical Reviews of a Popular Myth.* Rhys H. Williams, ed. New York: De Gruyter.

Jelen, Ted G., Corwin E. Smidt, and Clyde Wilcox. 1993. The Political Effects of the Born-Again Phenomenon. In *Rediscovering the Religious Factor in American Politics.* David C. Leege and Lyman A. Kellstedt, eds. Armonk, NY: M. E. Sharpe.

Johnson, Daniel Carson. 1997. Formal Education vs. Religious Belief: Soliciting New Evidence with Multinomial Logit Modeling. *Journal for the Scientific Study of Religion* 36:231–46.

Johnson, Donald B. 1978. *National Party Platforms, 1840–1976.* Urbana, IL: University of Illinois Press.

Judge, George G., R. Carter Hill, William E. Griffiths, Helmut Lutkepohl, and Tsoung-Chao Lee. 1988. *Introduction to the Theory and Practice of Econometrics.* New York: Wiley.

Kaufman, Arnold S. 1970. *The Radical Liberal.* New York: Simon and Schuster.

Kelley, Dean M. 1972. *Why Conservative Churches Are Growing.* New York: Harper.

Kellstedt, Lyman A. 1989. Evangelicals and Political Realignment. In *Contemporary Evangelical Political Involvement: An Analysis and Assessment.* Corwin E. Smidt, ed. Lanham, MD: University Press of America.

Kellstedt, Lyman A., and John C. Green. 1993. Knowing God's Many People: Denominational Preference and Political Behavior. In *Rediscovering the Religious Factor in American Politics.* David C. Leege and Lyman A. Kellstedt, eds. Armonk, NY: M. E. Sharpe.

Kellstedt, Lyman A., John C. Green, James L. Guth, and Corwin E. Smidt. 1994. Religious Voting Blocs in the 1992 Election: The Year of the Evangelical? *Sociology of Religion* 55:307–26.

———. 1996. Grasping the Essentials: The Social Embodiment of Religion and Political Behavior. In *Religion and the Culture Wars*. John C. Green, James L. Guth, Corwin E. Smidt, and Lyman A. Kellstedt, eds. Lanham, MD: Rowman and Littlefield.

———. 1997. Is there a Culture War? Religion and the 1996 Election. Presented at the annual meeting of the American Political Science Association, Washington, DC, September.

Kellstedt, Lyman A., and Nathan J. Kelly. 1998. Seculars and Political Behavior: The Neglected Segment of the U.S. Population. Presented at the annual meeting of the American Political Science Association, Boston, September.

Kellstedt, Lyman A., and Corwin E. Smidt. 1993. Doctrinal Beliefs and Political Behavior: Views of the Bible. In *Rediscovering the Religious Factor in American Politics*. David C. Leege and Lyman A. Kellstedt, eds. Armonk, NY: M. E. Sharpe.

———. 1996. Measuring Fundamentalism: An Analysis of Different Operational Strategies. In *Religion and the Culture Wars*. John C. Green, James L. Guth, Corwin E. Smidt, and Lyman A. Kellstedt, eds. Lanham, MD: Rowman and Littlefield.

Kellstedt, Lyman A., Corwin E. Smidt, and Paul M. Kellstedt. 1991. Religious Tradition, Denomination, and Commitment: White Protestants and the 1988 Election. In *The Bible and the Ballot Box: Religion and Politics in the 1988 Election*. James L. Guth and John C. Green, eds. Boulder, CO: Westview.

Key, V. O. 1955. A Theory of Critical Elections. *Journal of Politics* 17:3–18.

———. 1959. Secular Realignment and the Party System. *Journal of Politics* 21:198–210.

———. 1964. *Politics, Parties, and Pressure Groups*. New York: Crowell.

———. 1966. *The Responsible Electorate*. Cambridge, MA: Harvard University Press.

Kirkpatrick, Jeane. 1976. *The New Presidential Elite: Men and Women in National Politics*. New York: Sage.

Kleppner, Paul. 1970. *The Cross of Culture: A Social Analysis of Midwestern Politics, 1850–1900*. New York: Free Press.

———. 1979. *The Third Electoral System, 1853–1892*. Chapel Hill, NC: University of North Carolina Press.

———. 1987. *Continuity and Change in Electoral Politics, 1893–1928*. New York: Greenwood Press.

Krosnick, Jon A. 1991. The Stability of Political Preferences: Comparisons of Symbolic and Nonsymbolic Attitudes. *American Journal of Political Science* 35:547–76.

Ladd, Everett Carll, Jr. 1991. Like Waiting for Godot: The Uselessness of "Realignment" for Understanding Change in Contemporary American Politics.

In *The End of Realignment? Interpreting American Electoral Eras*. Byron E. Shafer, ed. Madison, WI: University of Wisconsin Press.

Ladd, Everett Carll, Jr., with Charles D. Hadley. 1975. *Transformations of the American Party System*. New York: W. W. Norton.

Lamis, Alexander P. 1988. *The Two-Party South*. New York: Oxford University Press.

Layman, Geoffrey C. 1996. The Culture Wars in the States: Religious Polarization among State Party Elites and State Electorates. Presented at the annual meeting of the Midwest Political Science Association, Chicago, April.

———. 1997. Religion and Political Behavior in the United States: The Impact of Beliefs, Affiliation, and Commitment from 1980 to 1994. *Public Opinion Quarterly* 61:288–316.

———. 1999. Culture Wars in the American Party System: Religious and Cultural Change Among Partisan Activists since 1972. *American Politics Quarterly* 27:89–121.

Layman, Geoffrey C., and Edward G. Carmines. 1997. Cultural Conflict in American Politics: Religious Traditionalism, Postmaterialism, and U.S. Political Behavior. *Journal of Politics* 59:751–77.

Layman, Geoffrey C., and Thomas M. Carsey. 1998. Why Do Party Activists Convert? An Analysis of Individual-Level Change on the Abortion Issue. *Political Research Quarterly* 51:723–50.

———. 1999. Ideological Realignment in Contemporary American Politics: General Ideological Polarization Rather Than Conflict Displacement. Presented at the annual meeting of the American Political Science Association, Atlanta, September.

Layman, Geoffrey C., and John C. Green. 1998. The Changing Religious Voter: The Impact of Belonging, Believing, and Behaving in the 1960s and 1990s. Presented at the annual meeting of the Midwest Political Science Association, Chicago, April.

Lazarsfeld, Paul, Bernard Berelson, and Hazel Gaudet. 1948. *The People's Choice*. New York: Columbia University Press.

Lechner, Frank J. 1991. The Case Against Secularization: A Rebuttal. *Social Forces* 69:1103–19.

Leege, David C., and Lyman A. Kellstedt. 1993a. Religious Worldviews and Political Philosophies: Capturing Theory in a Grand Manner Through Empirical Data. In *Rediscovering the Religious Factor in American Politics*. David C. Leege and Lyman A. Kellstedt, eds. Armonk, NY: M. E. Sharpe.

Leege, David C., and Lyman A. Kellstedt, eds. 1993b. *Rediscovering the Religious Factor in American Politics*. Armonk, NY: M. E. Sharpe.

Leege, David C., Kenneth D. Wald, and Lyman A. Kellstedt. 1993. The Public Dimension of Private Devotionalism. In *Rediscovering the Religious Factor in American Politics*. David C. Leege and Lyman A. Kellstedt, eds. Armonk, NY: M. E. Sharpe.

Lichter, S. Robert, and Stanley Rothman. 1983. What Interests the Public and What Interests the Public Interests. *Public Opinion* 6:44–48.

Liebman, Robert C., and Robert Wuthnow, eds. 1983. *The New Christian Right: Mobilization and Legitimation*. New York: Aldine.

Lincoln, C. Eric, and Lawrence H. Mamiya. 1990. *The Black Church in the African-American Experience*. Durham, NC: Duke University Press.

Lipset, Seymour M. 1964. Religion and Politics in the American Past and Present. In *Religion and Social Conflict*. Robert Lee and Martin Marty, eds. New York: Oxford University Press.

Lipset, Seymour M., and Stein Rokkan. 1967. Cleavage Structures, Party Systems, and Voter Alignments. In *Party Systems and Voter Alignments*. Seymour M. Lipset and Stein Rokkan, eds. New York: Free Press.

Ljung, G. M., and George E. P. Box. 1978. On a Measure of Lack of Fit in Time Series Models. *Biometrika* 66:66–72.

Lopatto, Paul. 1985. *Religion and the Presidential Election*. New York: Praeger.

MacDonald, Stuart Elaine, and George Rabinowitz. 1987. The Dynamics of Structural Realignment. *American Political Science Review* 81:775–96.

Maisel, L. Sandy. 1994. The Platform-Writing Process: Candidate-Centered Platforms in 1992. *Political Science Quarterly* 108:671–99.

Manza, Jeff, and Clem Brooks. 1997. The Religious Factor in U.S. Presidential Elections, 1960–1992. *American Journal of Sociology* 103:38–81.

Markus, Gregory B., and Philip E. Converse. 1979. A Dynamic Simultaneous Equation Model of Electoral Choice. *American Political Science Review* 73: 1055–70.

Marsden, George M. 1980. *Fundamentalism and American Culture: The Shaping of Twentieth-Century Evangelicalism, 1870–1925*. New York: Oxford University Press.

———. 1987. The Evangelical Denomination. In *Piety and Politics: Evangelicals and Fundamentalists Confront the World*. Richard John Neuhaus and Michael Cromrartie, eds. Washington, DC: Ethics and Public Policy Center.

———. 1991. *Understanding Fundamentalism and Evangelicalism*. Grand Rapids, MI: Eerdmans.

Marty, Martin E. 1986. *An Invitation to American Catholic History*. Chicago, IL: Thomas More.

McCann, James A. 1995. Nomination Politics and Ideological Polarization: Assessing the Attitudinal Effects of Campaign Involvement. *Journal of Politics* 57:101–20.

McClosky, Herbert, and John R. Zaller. 1984. *The American Ethos: Public Attitudes Toward Capitalism and Democracy*. Cambridge, MA: Harvard University Press.

McCormick, Richard L. 1986. *Party, Period, and Public Policy*. New York: Oxford University Press.

Miller, Arthur H., and Martin P. Wattenberg. 1984. Politics from the Pulpit: Religiosity and the 1980 Elections. *Public Opinion Quarterly* 48:301–17.

Miller, Arthur H., Christopher Wlezien, and Anne Hildreth. 1991. A Reference Group Theory of Partisan Coalitions. *Journal of Politics* 53:1134–49.

Miller, Warren E., and M. Kent Jennings. 1986. *Parties in Transition: A Longitudinal Study of Party Elites and Party Supporters*. New York: Sage.

Miller, Warren E., and Teresa E. Levitin. 1976. *Leadership and Change*. Cambridge, MA: Winthrop.

Miller, Warren E., and the National Election Studies. 1994. *American National Election Studies Cumulative Data File, 1952–1992*, 6th Release. Ann Arbor, MI: University of Michigan, Center for Political Studies and Inter-University Consortium for Political and Social Research.

Miller, Warren E., and J. Merrill Shanks. 1996. *The New American Voter*. Cambridge, MA: Harvard University Press.

Neuhaus, Richard John. 1987. What the Fundamentalists Want. In *Piety and Politics: Evangelicals and Fundamentalists Confront the World*. Richard John Neuhaus and Michael Cromrartie, eds. Washington, DC: Ethics and Public Policy Center.

Nexon, David. 1971. Asymmetry in the Political System: Occasional Activists in the Republican and Democratic Parties. *American Political Science Review* 65:716–30.

Nie, Norman H., Sidney Verba, and John R. Petrocik. 1976. *The Changing American Voter*. Cambridge, MA: Harvard University Press.

Oldfield, Duane M. 1996. *The Right and the Righteous: The Christian Right Confronts the Republican Party*. Lanham, MD: Rowman and Littlefield.

Page, Benjamin I., and Richard A. Brody. 1972. Policy Voting and the Electoral Process: The Vietnam War Issue. *American Political Science Review* 66: 979–95.

Page, Benjamin I., and Calvin C. Jones. 1979. Reciprocal Effects of Policy Preferences, Party Loyalties, and the Vote. *American Political Science Review* 73: 1071–90.

Parenti, Michael. 1967. Political Values and Religious Cultures: Jews, Catholics, and Protestants. *Journal for the Scientific Study of Religion* 6:259–69.

Perrin, Robin D., Paul Kennedy, and Donald E. Miller. 1997. Examining the Sources of Conservative Church Growth: Where Are the New Evangelical Movements Getting Their Members? *Journal for the Scientific Study of Religion* 36:71–80.

Persinos, John F. 1994. Has the Christian Right Taken Over the Republican Party? *Campaigns and Elections* (September):21–4.

Petersen, Larry R., and Gregory V. Donnenwerth. 1997. Secularization and the Influence of Religion on Beliefs About Premarital Sex. *Social Forces* 75: 1071–89.

Peterson, Steven A. 1990. *Political Behavior: Patterns in Everyday Life*. Newbury Park, CA: Sage.

Petrocik, John R. 1981. *Party Coalitions*. Chicago: University of Chicago Press.

———. 1987. Realignment: New Party Coalitions and the Nationalization of the South. *Journal of Politics* 49:347–75.

———. 1998. Reformulating the Party Coalitions: The "Christian Democratic" Republicans. Presented at the annual meeting of the American Political Science Association, Boston, September.

Phillips, Kevin P. 1969. *The Emerging Republican Majority*. New Rochelle, NY: Arlington House.

Pomper, Gerald M., with Susan S. Lederman. 1980. *Elections in America: Control and Influence in Democratic Politics*. New York: Longman.

Putnam, Robert. 1966. Political Attitudes and the Local Community. *American Political Science Review* 60:640–54.

Quinley, Harold E. 1974. *The Prophetic Clergy: Social Activism Among Protestant Ministers*. New York: Wiley Interscience.

Rabinowitz, George, James W. Prothro, and William Jacoby. 1982. Salience as a Factor in the Impact of Issues on Candidate Evaluations. *Journal of Politics* 44:41–63.

Rae, Nicol C. 1989. *The Decline and Fall of the Liberal Republicans: From 1952 to the Present*. New York: Oxford University Press.

Rapoport, Ronald B., and Walter J. Stone. 1994. A Model for Disaggregating Political Change. *Political Behavior* 16:505–32.

Reed, John Shelton. 1972. *The Enduring South: Subcultural Persistence in Mass Society*. Chapel Hill, NC: University of North Carolina Press.

Reed, Ralph. 1996. *Active Faith: How Christians Are Changing the Soul of American Politics*. New York: Free Press.

Reichley, A. James. 1987. The Evangelical and Fundamentalist Revolt. In *Piety and Politics: Evangelicals and Fundamentalists Confront the World*. Richard John Neuhaus and Michael Cromrartie, eds. Washington, DC: Ethics and Public Policy Center.

RePass, David E. 1971. Issue Salience and Party Choice. *American Political Science Review* 65:389–400.

Riker, William H. 1982. *Liberalism Against Populism*. San Francisco: Freeman.

Roback, Thomas H. 1975. Amateurs and Professionals: Delegates to the 1972 Republican National Convention. *Journal of Politics* 37:436–67.

———. 1980. Motivation for Activism Among Republican National Convention Delegates: Continuity and Change. *Journal of Politics* 42:436–68.

Rohde, David W. 1991. *Parties and Leaders in the Postreform House*. Chicago: University of Chicago Press.

Roof, Clark Wade, and William McKinney. 1987. *American Mainline Religion*. New Brunswick, NJ: Rutgers University Press.

Rosenstone, Steven J., and John Mark Hansen. 1993. *Mobilization, Participation, and Democracy in America*. New York: Macmillan.

Rosenstone, Steven J., Donald R. Kinder, Warren E. Miller, and the National Election Studies. 1997. *American National Election Study, 1996: Pre- and Post-Election Survey*. Ann Arbor, MI: University of Michigan Center for Political Studies and Inter-university Consortium for Political and Social Research.

Rosenstone, Steven J., Warren E. Miller, Donald R. Kinder, and the National Election Studies. 1995. *American National Election Study, 1994: Post-Election Survey*. Ann Arbor, MI: University of Michigan Center for Political Studies and Inter-university Consortium for Political and Social Research.

Rothenberg, Stuart, and Frank Newport. 1984. *The Evangelical Voter: Religion and Politics in America*. Washington, DC: Free Congress Research and Education Foundation.

Rothman, Stanley, and S. Robert Lichter. 1983. How Liberal Are the Bureaucrats? *Regulation* 7:16–22.

Rozell, Mark J., and Clyde Wilcox. 1996. *Second Coming: The Christian Right in Virginia Politics*. Baltimore: Johns Hopkins University Press.

Rozell, Mark J., and Clyde Wilcox, eds. 1995. *God at the Grass Roots: The Christian Right in the 1994 Elections*. Lanham, MD: Rowman and Littlefield.

———. 1997. *God at the Grass Roots 1996*. Lanham, MD: Rowman and Littlefield.

Scammon, Richard M., and Ben J. Wattenberg. 1970. *The Real Majority*. New York: Coward-McCann.

Schattschneider, E. E. 1942. *Party Government*. New York: Rinehart.

———. 1960. *The Semisovereign People: A Realist's View of Democracy in America*. New York: Holt, Rinehart, and Winston.

Schlesinger, Arthur M., Jr. 1958. *The Coming of the New Deal*. New York: Houghton Mifflin.

Sears, David O., Richard R. Lau, Tom R. Tyler, and Harris M. Allen, Jr. 1980. Self-Interest vs. Symbolic Politics in Policy Attitudes and Presidential Voting. *American Political Science Review* 74:670–84.

Shafer, Byron E. 1991. The Notion of an Electoral Order: The Structure of Electoral Politics at the Accession of George Bush. In *The End of Realignment? Interpreting American Electoral Eras*. Byron E. Shafer, ed. Madison, WI: University of Wisconsin Press.

Shapiro, Robert Y., and Harpreet Mahajan. 1986. Gender Differences in Policy Preferences: A Summary of Trends from the 1960s to the 1980s. *Public Opinion Quarterly* 50:47–55.

Sherkat, Darren E. 1991. Leaving the Faith: Testing Theories of Religious Switching Using Survival Models. *Social Science Research* 20:171–87.

———. 1998. Counterculture or Continuity? Competing Influences on Baby Boomers? Religious Orientations and Participation. *Social Forces* 76: 1087–115.

Sherkat, Darren E., and Christopher G. Ellison. 1997. The Cognitive Structure of a Moral Crusade: Conservative Protestantism and Opposition to Pornography. *Social Forces* 75:957–80.

———. 1999. Recent Developments and Current Controversies in the Sociology of Religion. *Annual Review of Sociology* 25:363–94.

Shibley, Mark A. 1996. *Resurgent Evangelicalism in the U.S.* Columbia, SC: University of South Carolina Press.

Shupe, Anson, and William Stacey. 1983. The Moral Majority Constituency. In *The New Christian Right: Mobilization and Legitimation.* Robert C. Liebman and Robert Wuthnow, eds. New York: Aldine.

Sigelman, Lee. 1991. Jews and the 1988 Election: More of the Same? In *The Bible and the Ballot Box: Religion and Politics in the 1988 Election.* James L. Guth and John C. Green, eds. Boulder, CO: Westview.

Silbey, Joel H. 1991. Beyond Realignment and Realignment Theory: American Political Eras, 1789–1989. In *The End of Realignment? Interpreting American Electoral Eras.* Byron E. Shafer, ed. Madison, WI: University of Wisconsin Press.

Sims, Robert T. 1996. Re-evaluating the Influence of Religious Belief on the Vote. Unpublished doctoral dissertation, University of New Orleans.

Smidt, Corwin. 1988. Evangelicals Within Contemporary American Politics: Differentiating Between Fundamentalist and Non-Fundamentalist Evangelicals. *Western Political Quarterly* 41:601–20.

Smidt, Corwin E., John C. Green, Lyman A. Kellstedt, and James L. Guth. 1996. The Spirit-Filled Movements and American Politics. In *Religion and the Culture Wars.* John C. Green, James L. Guth, Corwin E. Smidt, and Lyman A. Kellstedt, eds. Lanham, MD: Rowman and Littlefield.

Smidt, Corwin E., and James M. Penning. 1991. Religious Self-Identifications and Support for Robertson: An Analysis of Delegates to the 1988 Michigan Republican State Convention. *Review of Religious Research* 32:321–36.

Smith, Christian. 1998. *American Evangelicalism: Embattled and Thriving.* Chicago: University of Chicago Press.

Smith, C., D. Sikkink, and J. Bailey. 1998. Devotion in Dixie and Beyond. *Journal for the Scientific Study of Religion* 37:494–506.

Sniderman, Paul M., Richard A. Brody, and Philip E. Tetlock. 1991. *Reasoning and Choice: Explorations in Political Psychology.* New York: Cambridge University Press.

Sniderman, Paul M., and Edward G. Carmines. 1997. *Reaching Beyond Race.* Cambridge, MA: Harvard University Press.

Sniderman, Paul M., and Thomas Piazza. 1993. *The Scar of Race.* Cambridge, MA: Harvard University Press.

Soule, John W., and James W. Clarke. 1970. Amateurs and Professionals: A Study of Delegates to the 1968 Democratic National Convention. *American Political Science Review* 64:888–98.

Stark, Rodney, and William Sims Bainbridge. 1985. *The Future of Religion.* Berkeley: University of California Press.

Stark, Rodney, and Charles Glock. 1968. *American Piety: The Nature of Religious Commitment.* Berkeley: University of California Press.

Stewart, John G. 1974. *One Last Chance.* New York: Praeger.

Sundquist, James L. 1983. *Dynamics of the Party System: Alignment and Realignment of Political Parties in the United States.* Washington, DC: The Brookings Institution.

Swierenga, Robert. 1990. Ethnoreligious Political Behavior in the Mid-Nineteenth Century: Voting, Values, and Culture. In *Religion and American Politics.* Mark Noll, ed. New York: Oxford University Press.

Tamney, Joseph B., Stephen D. Johnson, and Ronald Burton. 1992. The Abortion Controversy: Conflicting Beliefs and Values in American Society. *Journal for the Scientific Study of Religion* 31:32–46.

Thomas, Cal, and Ed Dobson. 1999. *Blinded by Might: Can the Religious Right Save America?* Grand Rapids, MI: Zondervan.

Tschannen, Olivier. 1991. The Secularization Paradigm: A Systematization. *Journal for the Scientific Study of Religion* 30:395–415.

Usher, Douglas. 1997. The Religious Right and Republican National Conventions, 1988–1996: State Party Rules and Levels of Influence. Presented at the annual meeting of the Midwest Political Science Association, Chicago, April.

Verba, Sidney, Kay Lehman Schlozman, and Henry E. Brady. 1995. *Voice and Equality: Civic Voluntarism in American Politics.* Cambridge, MA: Harvard University Press.

Viguerie, Richard. 1980. *The New Right: We're Ready to Lead.* Falls Church, VA: Viguerie.

Wald, Kenneth D. 1997. *Religion and Politics in the United States,* 3rd ed. Washington, DC: CQ Press.

Wald, Kenneth D., Lyman A. Kellstedt, and David C. Leege. 1993. Church Involvement and Political Behavior. In *Rediscovering the Religious Factor in American Politics.* David C. Leege and Lyman A. Kellstedt, eds. Armonk, NY: M. E. Sharpe.

Wald, Kenneth D., Dennis E. Owen, and Samuel S. Hill, Jr. 1988. Churches as Political Communities. *American Political Science Review* 82:531–48.

———. 1990. Political Cohesion in Churches. *Journal of Politics* 52:197–215.

Wallis, Roy, and Steve Bruce. 1992. Secularization: The Orthodox Model. In *Religion and Modernization.* Steve Bruce, ed. Oxford: Oxford University Press.

Watson, Justin. 1999. *The Christian Coalition: Dreams of Restoration, Demands for Recognition.* New York: St. Martin's Griffin.

Wattenberg, Martin P. 1986. *The Decline of American Political Parties, 1952–1984.* Cambridge, MA: Harvard University Press.

———. 1991. *The Rise of Candidate-Centered Politics.* Cambridge, MA: Harvard University Press.

Welch, Michael R., David C. Leege, Kenneth D. Wald, and Lyman A. Kellstedt.

1993. Are the Sheep Hearing the Shepherds? Cue Perceptions, Congregational Responses, and Political Communication Processes. In *Rediscovering the Religious Factor in American Politics*. David C. Leege and Lyman A. Kellstedt, eds. Armonk, NY: M. E. Sharpe.

White, Halbert. 1980. A Heteroskedasticity-Consistent Covariance Matrix and a Direct Test for Heteroskedasticity. *Econometrica* 48:817–38.

White, Theodore H. 1973. *The Making of the President, 1972*. New York: Atheneum.

Wilcox, Clyde. 1990a. Blacks and the New Christian Right: Support for the Moral Majority and Pat Robertson Among Blacks. *Review of Religious Research* 32:43–55.

———. 1990b. Religion and Politics Among White Evangelicals: The Impact of Religious Variables on Political Attitudes. *Review of Religious Research* 32: 27–42.

———. 1991. Religion and Electoral Politics Among Black Americans in 1988. In *The Bible and the Ballot Box: Religion and Politics in the 1988 Election*. James L. Guth and John C. Green, eds. Boulder, CO: Westview.

———. 1992. *God's Warriors: The Christian Right in Twentieth-Century America*. Baltimore: Johns Hopkins Press.

Wilcox, Clyde, Ted G. Jelen, and David C. Leege. 1993. Religious Group Identifications: Toward a Cognitive Theory of Religious Mobilization. In *Rediscovering the Religious Factor in American Politics*. David C. Leege and Lyman A. Kellstedt, eds. Armonk, NY: M. E. Sharpe.

Wildavsky, Aaron. 1965. The Goldwater Phenomenon: Purists, Politicians, and the Two-Party System. *Review of Politics* 27:386–413.

Williams, Rhys H., ed. 1997. *Culture Wars in American Politics: Critical Reviews of a Popular Myth*. New York: De Gruyter.

Wills, Garry. 1990. *Under God: Religion and American Politics*. New York: Simon and Schuster.

Wilson, Bryan. 1966. *Religion in Secular Society*. Baltimore: Penguin.

Wilson, James Q. 1962. *The Amateur Democrat: Club Politics in Three Cities*. Chicago: University of Chicago Press.

Wirls, Daniel. 1986. Reinterpreting the Gender Gap. *Public Opinion Quarterly* 50:316–30.

Wolfe, Alan. 1994. Whose Body Politic? *The American Prospect* (Winter): 99.

Wuthnow, Robert. 1986. Religious Movements and Counter-Movements in North America. In *New Religious Movements and Rapid Social Change*. James A. Beckford, ed. Beverly Hills, CA: Sage.

———. 1988. *The Restructuring of American Religion*. Princeton, NJ: Princeton University Press.

———. 1989. *The Struggle for America's Soul: Evangelicals, Liberals, and Secularism*. Grand Rapids, MI: Eerdmans.

Zaller, John. 1992. *The Nature and Origins of Mass Opinion*. New York: Cambridge University Press.

INDEX

Power, Conflict, and Democracy: American Politics Into the Twenty-first Century